SCIENCE FICTION, SCIENCE FACT, AND YOU

Robert J. Lowenherz, Ph. D.

Lila Lowenherz, Ph. D.

AMSCO

AMSCO SCHOOL PUBLICATIONS, INC.
315 Hudson Street / New York, N.Y. 10013

Cover Photo: WESTLIGHT © Image Tec West

When ordering this book, please specify:
either **R 506 S** or

**SCIENCE FICTION,
SCIENCE FACT,
AND YOU.**

ISBN 1-56765-028-7

NYC Item 56765-028-6

Printed in the United States of America

2 3 4 5 6 7 8 9 10   00 99 98 97 96

PREFACE

"In this world," the American statesman Benjamin Franklin once wrote, "nothing is certain but death and taxes." Today, some two centuries later, he might have added one more certainty—change. Nobody knows just what the future will bring, but you can bet your last dollar that it will bring change. Change and the future—they are the certainties in our modern world. They are also the heart and soul of science fiction.

Science Fiction, Science Fact, and You takes you on a tour of six major themes in science fiction. You will explore Space Travel, Time Travel, Robots, Extraterrestrials, Future People, and Future Worlds. Of the eighteen short stories by American and British authors reprinted in this book, a full two-thirds take place in the future. The remaining stories, although set in the present, often point to dramatic changes to come.

The science-fact articles that end each of the six themes serve as bridges between the fiction of the stories and the realities of your life. Some of the articles consider how even the most exotic ideas of science fiction may someday be transformed into science fact. Others describe how things that once existed only in the imaginations of science-fiction authors have already become familiar features of everyday reality. Many of the articles discuss the science and technology behind the stories. Reading these articles will help you to see how the imaginary worlds of the stories connect with your own real world.

As its title indicates, this book is not only about science fiction and science fact. It's also about *you*. Because you are such a key element, the book has been planned to help you read, understand, and become personally involved in each story or article. Here are some of the features of the book that promote this plan.

1. You will find *introductions* to each of the six themes and shorter introductions to the twenty-four stories and articles. These introductions not only provide useful background information, but also pose questions for you to think about as you read.

2. *Biographical sketches* of many of the authors briefly describe some of their special interests, awards, and best-known writings. A number

of the sketches also tell of people, organizations, or events that are important in the history of science fiction.

3. To help you read, *footnotes* explain difficult or unfamiliar words. You will find even more help in the extensive *glossary* at the back of the book.

4. Following each story or article, brief sets of *exercises and activities* help you to understand, appreciate, and use what you have read. Many of the exercises refer to specific pages and lines. Marginal numbers throughout the text will enable you to pinpoint the word, sentence, or passage referred to in the exercises.

   a. You have to know what's happening in a story or article before you can discuss it in greater depth. To this end, the questions titled "Reviewing the Story" help you to achieve a better understanding of what you have read. These questions also help you to sharpen your critical thinking skills, such as recognizing cause and effect, making inferences, and predicting outcomes.

   b. "Building Your Vocabulary" both expands and refines your stock of useful words. These exercises also challenge you to show how you arrived at the correct meaning of a word. In effect, you are asked to think about your own problem-solving strategies.

   c. Questions titled "Studying the Writer's Craft" zero in on the literary devices and techniques the authors use in their stories or articles. In answering these questions, you'll gain a better appreciation of the various skills that go into professional writing, whether fiction or nonfiction. You'll also gather valuable hints for improving your own writing.

   d. In the "Activities for Listening, Speaking, Writing," you will get a chance to use all your communication skills in a broad range of formats: debates, discussions, dramatic readings, speeches, letters, reports, articles, and stories. In all these activities, you will often be working with your classmates.

Working in the area of science fiction gives the writer an opportunity for unlimited creativity. It allows him or her to create new worlds, address moral dilemmas, and mold the future. It gives the reader an opportunity to experience something completely new. Whether you are already a science-fiction fan or a reader who is new to this type of literature, keep an open mind when you read these imaginative works. Suspend your disbelief and enjoy yourself; that's what reading science fiction is all about.

The Authors

CONTENTS

Theme 1
SPACE TRAVEL 2

Nothing Happens on the Moon — *Paul Ernst* 5

The Cold Equations — *Tom Godwin* 26

Wait It Out — *Larry Niven* 53

Exploring Other Worlds and Protecting This One: The Connection — *Carl Sagan* 65

Theme 2
TIME TRAVEL 76

The Sliced-Crosswise Only-on-Tuesday World — *Philip José Farmer* 79

Of Time and Third Avenue — *Alfred Bester* 98

Absolutely Inflexible — *Robert Silverberg* 111

Is Time Travel Possible? — *Mark Davidson* 127

Theme 3
ROBOTS AND ARTIFICIAL INTELLIGENCE 138

Robbie — *Isaac Asimov* 141

Dial F for Frankenstein — *Arthur C. Clarke* 164

Instinct — *Lester del Rey* 176

Smart Skin — *Shawna Vogel* 193

Theme 4
SPACE ALIENS, OR EXTRATERRESTRIALS 202

The Large Ant — *Howard Fast* 205

A Death in the House — *Clifford D. Simak* 219

Things *Zenna Henderson* 241

The Search for Extraterrestrial Intelligence (SETI): Two Views 253

Pro *John P. Wiley, Jr.* 254

Con *Frank Graham, Jr.* 259

Theme 5
FUTURE PEOPLE 266

Changelings *Lisa Tuttle* 269

Pursuit of Excellence *Rena Yount* 285

SQ *Ursula K. Le Guin* 308

High-Tech Loneliness: How Our Inventions Keep Us Apart *Mitchell Gordon* 322

Theme 6
FUTURE WORLDS 330

There Will Come Soft Rains *Ray Bradbury* 333

Arena *adapted by James Blish* 344

A Pail of Air *Fritz Leiber* 359

How Easy to See the Future *Isaac Asimov* 377

Glossary 387

ACKNOWLEDGMENTS

Grateful acknowledgment is made to the following sources for permission to use copyrighted materials. Every effort has been made to obtain permission to use previously published material; any errors or omissions are unintentional.

Agberg, Ltd.: "Absolutely Inflexible" by Robert Silverberg. Copyright © 1956, 1967, by Agberg, Ltd. Reprinted by permission of the author and Agberg, Ltd.

Isaac Asimov: "Robbie" by Isaac Asimov. Copyright © September, 1940 in *Super Science Stories* under the title "Strange Playfellow." "How Easy to See the Future" by Isaac Asimov, with permission from *Natural History*, April 1975; Copyright the American Museum of Natural History, 1975.

Audubon: "The Search for Extraterrestrial Intelligence (SETI): Two Views," "Con" or "Talk of the Trail" by Frank Graham, Jr. From *Audubon* May/June 1990, Volume 92, Number 3.

Bantam, Doubleday, Dell Publishing Group, Inc.: "Arena" from STAR TREK 2 ADAPTED BY James Blish. Excerpt(s) from STAR TREK 2 ADAPTED BY James Blish, copyright © 1968 by Bantam Books, Inc. Copyright © 1968 by Desilu Productions, Inc. Used by permission of Bantam Books, a division of Bantam, Doubleday, Dell Publishing Group, Inc.

Don Congdon Associates, Inc.: "There Will Come Soft Rains" by Ray Bradbury. Reprinted by permission of Don Congdon Associates, Inc. Copyright © 1950, renewed 1977 by Ray Bradbury.

Richard Curtis Associates, Inc.: "A Pail of Air" by Fritz Leiber. Copyright © 1951 by Galaxy Publishing Corporation. Reprinted by permission of the author and his agent, Richard Curtis Associates, Inc.

Curtis Brown, Ltd.: "Things" by Zenna Henderson. Copyright © 1960 by Mercury Press, Inc., renewed 1988 by the author.

Davis Publications, Inc.: "Nothing Happens on the Moon" by Paul Ernst. Copyright 1939 by Street & Smith Publications. First appeared in *Astounding Science Fiction*. Reprinted by permission of Davis Publications, Inc.

Discover Publications: "Smart Skin" by Shawna Vogel/© 1990 Discover Publications.

Mitchell Gordon: "High-Tech Loneliness: How Our Inventions Keep Us Apart."

Virginia Kidd Literary Agency: "SQ". Copyright © 1978 by Ursula K. Le Guin. First appeared in *Cassandra Rising*. Reprinted by permission of the author and the author's agent, Virginia Kidd.

Sterling Lord Literistic, Inc.: "The Large Ant" by Howard Fast. Reprinted by permission of Sterling Lord Literistic, Inc. Copyright © 1972 by Howard Fast.

Scott Meredith Literary Agency, Inc.: "The Cold Equations" by Tom Godwin, copyright 1954 by Street & Smith Publications, Inc. "Dial F for Frankenstein" by Arthur C. Clarke, from *Machines that Think*, edited by Isaac Asimov, Patricia S. Warrick, Martin H. Greenberg (Holt, Rinehart and Winston, Inc. NY 1983). Copyright 1965 by Arthur C. Clarke. "Instinct" by Lester del Rey. Copyright 1952 by Street & Smith Publications, Inc. From *Astounding Science Fiction*, August, 1952. "The Sliced-Crosswise Only-on-Tuesday World" by Philip José Farmer. The story appeared in *The Classic Philip José Farmer* 1964–1973, Volume 5. Copyright © 1984. Story copyright © 1971 by Robert Silverberg. Reprinted by permission of the author and the author's agents, Scott Meredith Literary Agency, Inc., 845 Third Avenue, New York, New York 10022.

Howard Morhaim Literary Agency: "Changelings" by Lisa Tuttle. From *Best of Science Fiction*, the Ninth Annual, edited by Harry Harrison and Brian W. Aldiss (The Bobbs-Merrill Company, Inc., Indianapolis, Indiana 1976).

The Pimlico Agency, Inc.: "A Death in the House" by Clifford D. Simak. Permission granted by the Estate of Clifford D. Simak and the author's agent, The Pimlico Agency, Inc. "Of Time and Third Avenue" by Alfred Bester. © 1951 by Mercury Press, Inc. Reprinted from *The Magazine of Fantasy and Science Fiction*. © renewed 1979. Permission is granted to reprint by the Estate of Alfred Bester and the agent for the Estate, The Pimlico Agency, Inc.

Random House, Inc./Alfred Knopf, Inc.: "Wait It Out" by Larry Niven. From *Tales of Known Space* by Larry Niven. Copyright © 1975 by Larry Niven. Reprinted by permission of Ballantine Books, a division of Random House.

Carl Sagan: "Exploring Other Worlds and Protecting This One: The Connection," copyright © 1990 by Carl Sagan. Reprinted with permission of the author.

Smithsonian Magazine: "The Search for Extraterrestrial Intelligence (SETI): Two Views," "Pro" or "Phenomena, comment and notes" by John P. Wiley, Jr. From *Smithsonian*, February 1986 by John P. Wiley, Jr..

USA Today: "Is Time Travel Possible?" by Mark Davidson. Reprinted from *USA Today Magazine*, copyright January 1990 by the Society for the Advancement of Education.

Rena Yount: "Pursuit of Excellence" by Rena Yount. Copyright © 1984 by Rena Yount. First published in *The Clarion Awards* (Doubleday). Reprinted by permission of the author.

PHOTO CREDITS

SCIENCE FICTION, SCIENCE FACT, AND YOU

SPACE TRAVEL
Theme 1

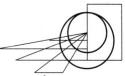

Space travel is one of our oldest dreams. For centuries, people wondered what it would be like to break the bonds of Earth and fly to other worlds. When astronauts landed on the Moon in 1969, the dream became a reality.

Long before the first Moon landing, however, space travel had been a central theme in science fiction. Jules Verne, one of the fathers of science fiction, wrote his novel *From the Earth to the Moon* as long ago as 1865. Another story of space travel, *The First Men in the Moon* by H.G. Wells, appeared in 1901. Later writers created exciting fiction about the wonders, the adventures, and especially the perils of space travel.

Each of the following stories deals with the dangers of space travel in a different way. In "Nothing Happens on the Moon," a watchman stationed on the Moon has a hair-raising encounter with an invisible monster. "The Cold Equations" uses logic and the unbending laws of space travel to tell what happens to a stowaway on a small interstellar Emergency Dispatch Ship. In "Wait It Out," a space traveler is marooned on the planet Pluto, billions of miles from Earth.

Is it worth facing such perils to explore other worlds? Why do we persist in our dreams of space travel? Some say it's because of our natural wanderlust—our itch to travel. Others speak of the great adventure of exploring this last frontier. Perhaps we need to satisfy our curiosity about what's out there. Who knows what strange wealth we might find in outer space? Finally, the more we learn about other worlds, the better able we are to understand and take care of our own. That is the argument for space exploration in the article ending this theme, "Exploring Other Worlds and Protecting This One."

Nothing Happens on the Moon

by Paul Ernst

I wish I'd brought a dog up here, or a cat. I wish there'd be an attempted raid. Anything at all. If only something would happen.

Written exactly thirty years before the first landing on the Moon in 1969, this story is essentially a rousing adventure tale. Don't expect to find important social significance in it. There isn't any. Don't bother reading for profound symbolic meanings. You won't find them. "Nothing Happens on the Moon" is a story to be read just for fun.

Although the words *space travel* conjure up images of brave astronauts steering their rocket ships among the stars, there is another, less romantic side to space travel. In an emergency, the big passenger liners and freighters of outer space need a place to land. Somebody has to be there, waiting.

Meet Clow Hartigan, executive-in-training for Spaceways, a transport company for the solar system and beyond. Month after month, he sits alone in an emergency landing dome on the rocky, lifeless Moon, waiting for something—anything—to happen.

As you read the story, think about the title. Is it true that nothing happens on the Moon? If not, why does Hartigan assure Stacey, at the end of the story, that there is really nothing irregular to report?

Paul Ernst

One of the earlier science-fiction writers, Paul Ernst produced the bulk of his fast-moving fiction in the 1930s. He wrote many short stories for the popular "pulp" magazines of that period. Like other science-fiction authors, he published a good deal of his work under pseudonyms. His stories appeared not only under his real name, but also under the names Kenneth Robeson and Paul F. Stern.

Writing for the "pulp" magazines, which never paid well, was a hard way to make a living. By using pseudonyms, prolific writers like Paul Ernst could publish stories in several magazines at the same time.

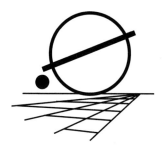

The shining ball of the full Earth floated like a smooth pearl between two vast, angular mountains. The full Earth. Another month had ticked by.

Clow Hartigan turned from the porthole beside the small air lock to the Bliss radio transmitter.

"RC3, RC3, RC3," he droned out.

There was no answer. Stacey, up in New York, always took his time about answering the RC3 signal, confound it! But then, why shouldn't he? There was never anything of importance to listen to from Station RC3. Nothing of any significance ever happened on the Moon. ¹⁰

Hartigan stared unseeingly at the pink cover of a six-month-old *Radio Gazette*, pasted to the wall over the control board.

"RC3, RC3—"

Ah, there Stacey was, the pompous little busybody.

"Hartigan talking. Monthly report."

"Go ahead, Hartigan."

A hurried, fussy voice. Calls of real import waited for Stacey; calls from Venus and Jupiter and Mars. Hurry up, Moon, and report that nothing has happened, as usual.

Hartigan proceeded to do so.

"Lunar conditions the same. No ships have put in, or have reported themselves as being in distress. The hangar is in good shape, with no leaks. Nothing out of the way has occurred."

"Right," said Stacey pompously. "Supplies?"

"No." Hartigan's eyes brooded. "How's everything in Little Old New York?"

Stacey's businesslike voice was a reproof. Also it was a pain in the neck.

"Sorry. Can't gossip. Things pretty busy around here. If you need 10 anything, let me know."

The burr of power went dead. Hartigan cursed with monotony, and got up.

Clow Hartigan was a big young man with sand-red hair and slightly bitter blue eyes. He was representative of the type Spaceways sent to such isolated emergency landing stations as the Moon.

There were half a dozen such emergency landing domes, visited only by supply ships, exporting nothing, but ready in case some passenger liner was crippled by a meteor or by mechanical trouble. The two worst on the Spaceways list were the insulated hell on Mercury, and this great, 20 lonely hangar on the Moon. To them Spaceways sent the pick of their probation executives. Big men. Powerful men. Young men. (Also men who were unlucky enough not to have an old family friend or an uncle on the board of directors who could swing a soft berth for them.) Spaceways did not keep them there long. Men killed themselves, or went mad and began inconsiderately smashing expensive equipment, after too long a dose of such loneliness as that of the Moon.

Hartigan went back to the porthole beside the small air lock. As he went, he talked to himself, as men do when they have been too long away from their own kind.   30

"I wish I'd brought a dog up here, or a cat. I wish there'd be an attempted raid. Anything at all. If only something would *happen*."

Resentfully he stared out at the photographic, black-and-white lunar landscape, lighted coldly by the full Earth. From that his eye went to the deep black of the heavens. Then his heart gave a jump. There was a faint light up there where no light was supposed to be.

He hurried to the telescope and studied it. A space liner, and a big one! Out of its course, no matter where it was bound, or it couldn't have been seen from the Moon with the naked eye. Was it limping in here to the emergency landing for repairs?   40

"I don't wish them any bad luck," muttered Hartigan, "but I hope they've burned out a rocket tube."

Soon his heart sank, however. The liner soared over the landing dome a hundred miles up, and went serenely on its way. In a short time its light faded in distance. Probably it was one of the luxurious around-the-solar-system ships, passing close to the Moon to give the sightseers an intimate glimpse of it, but not stopping because there was absolutely nothing of interest there.

"Nothing *ever* happens in this Godforsaken hole," Hartigan gritted.

Impatiently he took his space suit down from the rack. Impatiently he stepped into the bulky, flexible metal thing and clamped down the headpiece. Nothing else to do. He'd take a walk. The red beam of the 10 radio control board would summon him back to the hangar if for any reason anyone tried to raise RC3.

He let himself out through the double wall of the small air lock and set out with easy, fifteen-foot strides toward a nearby cliff on the brink of which it was sometimes his habit to sit and think nasty thoughts of the men who ran Spaceways and maintained places like RC3.

Between the hangar and the cliff was a wide expanse of gray lava ash, a sort of small lake of the stuff, feathery fine. Hartigan did not know how deep it might be. He did know that a man could probably sink down in it so far that he would never be able to burrow out again.   20

He turned to skirt the lava ash, but paused a moment before proceeding.

Behind him loomed the enormous half globe of the hangar, like a phosphorescent mushroom in the blackness. One section of the half globe was flattened; and here were the gigantic inner and outer portals where a liner's rocket-propelled life shells could enter the dome. The great doors of this, the main air lock, reared halfway to the top of the hangar, and weighed several hundred tons apiece.

Before him was the face of the Moon: sharp angles of rock; jagged, tremendous mountains; sheer, deep craters; all picked out in black and white from the reflected light of Earth.   30

A desolate prospect. . . . Hartigan started on.

The ash beside him suddenly seemed to explode, soundlessly but with great violence. It spouted up like a geyser to a distance of a hundred feet, hung for an instant over him in a spreading cloud, then quickly began to settle.

A meteor! Must have been a fair-sized one to have made such a splash in the volcanic dust.

"Close call," muttered Hartigan, voice sepulchral in his helmet. "A little nearer and they'd be sending a new man to the lunar emergency dome."

But he only grimaced and went on. Meteors were like the lightning 40 back on Earth. Either they hit you or they missed. There was no warning till after they struck; then it was too late to do anything about it.

Hartigan stumbled over something in the cloud of ash that was sifting down around him. Looking down, he saw a smooth, round object, black-hot, about as big as his head.

"The meteor," he observed. "Must have hit a slanting surface at the bottom of the ash heap and ricocheted up and out here. I wonder—"

He stooped clumsily toward it. His right "hand," which was a heavy pincer arrangement terminating the right sleeve of his suit, went out, then his left, and with some difficulty he picked the thing up. Now and then a meteor held splashes of precious metals. Sometimes one was picked up that yielded several hundred dollars' worth of platinum or iridium. A 10 little occasional gravy[1] with which the emergency-landing exiles could buy amusement when they got back home.

Through the annoying shower of ash he could see dimly the light of the hangar. He started back, to get out of his suit and analyze the meteor for possible value.

It was the oddest-looking thing he had ever seen come out of the heavens. In the first place, its shape was remarkable. It was perfectly round, instead of being irregular as were most meteors.

"Like an old-fashioned cannon ball," Hartigan mused, bending over it on a workbench. "Or an egg—"   20

Eyebrows raised whimsically, he played with the idea.

"Jupiter! What an egg it would be! A hundred and twenty pounds if it's an ounce, and it smacked the Moon like a bullet without even cracking! I wouldn't want it poached for breakfast."

The next thing to catch his attention was the projectile's odd color, or, rather, the odd way in which the color seemed to be changing. It had been dull, black-hot, when Hartigan brought it in. It was now a dark green, and was getting lighter swiftly as it cooled!

The big clock struck a mellow note. Time for the dome keeper to make his daily inspection of the main doors.   30

Reluctantly Hartigan left the odd meteor, which was now as green as grass and actually seemed to be growing transparent, and walked toward the big air lock.

He switched on the radio power unit. There was no power plant of any kind in the hangar; all power was broadcast by the Spaceways central station. He reached for the contact switch which poured the invisible Niagara of power into the motors that moved the ponderous doors.

Cr-r-rack!

Like a cannon shot the sound split the air in the huge metal dome, echoing from wall to wall, to die at last in a muffled rumbling.   40

1. **gravy** (slang): extra money.

White-faced, Hartigan was running long before the echoes died away. He ran toward the workbench he had recently quitted. The sound seemed to have come from near there. His thought was that the hangar had been crashed by a meteor larger than its cunningly braced beams, tough metal sheath, and artful angles of deflection would stand.

That would mean death, for the air supply in the dome would race out through a fissure almost before he could don his space suit.

However, his anxious eyes, scanning the vaulting roof, could find no crumpled bracing or ominous downward bulges. And he could hear no thin whine of air surging in the hangar to the almost nonexistent 10 pressure outside.

Then he glanced at the workbench and uttered an exclamation. The meteor he had left there was gone.

"It must have rolled off the bench," he told himself. "But if it's on the floor, why can't I see it?"

He froze into movelessness. Had that been a sound behind him? A sound, here, where no sound could possibly be made save by himself?

He whirled—and saw nothing. Nothing whatever, save the familiar expanse of smooth rock floor lighted with the cold white illumination broadcast on the power band.   20

He turned back to the workbench where the meteor had been, and began feeling over it with his hands, disbelieving the evidence of his eyes.

Another exclamation burst from his lips as his fingers touched something hard and smooth and round. The meteor. Broken into two halves, but still here. Only, *now it was invisible!*

"This," said Hartigan, beginning to sweat a little, "is the craziest thing I ever heard of!"

He picked up one of the two invisible halves and held it close before his eyes. He could not see it at all, though it was solid to the touch. Moreover, he seemed able to see through it, for nothing on the other side 30 was blotted out.

Fear increased within him as his fingers told him that the two halves were empty, hollow. Heavy as the ball had been, it consisted of nothing but a shell about two inches thick. Unless—

"Unless something really did crawl out of it when it split apart."

But that, of course, was ridiculous.

"It's just an ordinary metallic chunk," he told himself, "that split open with a loud bang when it cooled, due to contraction. The only thing unusual about it is its invisibility. That *is* strange."

He groped on the workbench for the other half of the thick, round 40 shell. With a half in each hand, he started toward the stock room, meaning to lock up this odd substance very carefully. He suspected he had something beyond price here. If he could go back to Earth with a substance that could produce invisibility, he could become one of the richest men in the universe.

He presented a curious picture as he walked over the brilliantly lighted floor. His shoulders sloped down with the weight of the two pieces of meteor. His bare arms rippled and knotted with muscular effort. Yet his hands seemed empty. So far as the eye could tell, he was carrying nothing whatever.

"What—"

He dropped the halves of the shell with a ringing clang, and began 10 leaping toward the big doors. That time he *knew* he had heard a sound, a sound like scurrying steps! It had come from near the big doors.

When he got there, however, he could hear nothing. For a time the normal stillness, the ghastly, phenomenal stillness, was preserved. Then, from near the spot he had just vacated, he heard another noise. This time it was a gulping, voracious noise, accompanied by a sound that was like that of a rock crusher or a concrete mixer in action.

On the run, he returned, seeing nothing all this while; nothing but smooth rock floor and plain, metal-ribbed walls, and occasional racks of instruments. 20

He got to the spot where he had dropped the parts of the meteor. The parts were no longer there. This time it was more than a question of invisibility. They had disappeared actually as well as visually.

To make sure, Hartigan got down on hands and knees and searched every inch of a large circle. There was no trace of the thick shell.

"Either something brand-new to the known solar system is going on here," Hartigan declared, "or I'm getting as crazy as they insisted poor Stuyvesant was."

Increased perspiration glinted on his forehead. The fear of madness in the lonelier emergency fields was a very real fear. United Spaceways 30 had been petitioned more than once to send two men instead of one to manage each outlying field; but Spaceways was an efficient corporation with no desire to pay two men where one could handle the job.

Again Hartigan could hear nothing at all. And in swift though unadmitted fear that perhaps the whole business had transpired only in his own brain, he sought refuge in routine. He returned to his task of testing the big doors, which was important even though dreary in its daily repetition.

The radio power unit was on, as he had left it. He closed the circuit.

Smoothly the enormous inner doors swung open on their broad tracks, to reveal the equally enormous outer portals. Hartigan stepped 40 into the big air lock, and closed the inner doors. He shivered a little. It was near freezing out here in spite of the heating units.

There was a small control room in the lock, to save an operator the trouble of always getting into a space suit when the doors were opened. Hartigan entered this and pushed home the switch that moved the outer portals.

Smoothly, perfectly, their tremendous bulk opened outward. They always worked smoothly, perfectly. No doubt they always would. Nevertheless, rules said test them regularly. And it was best to live up to the rules. With characteristic trustfulness, Spaceways had recording dials in the home station that showed by power markings whether or not their planetary employees were doing what they were supposed to do. 10

Hartigan reversed the switch. The doors began to close. They got to the halfway mark; to the three-quarters—

Hartigan felt rather than heard the sharp, grinding jar. He felt rather than heard the high, shrill scream, a rasping shriek, almost above the limit of audibility, that was something to make a man's blood run cold.

Still, without faltering, the doors moved inward and their serrated edges met. Whatever one of them had ground across had not been large enough to shake it.

"Jupiter!" Hartigan breathed, once more inside the huge dome with both doors closed. 20

He sat down to try to think the thing out.

"A smooth, round meteor falls. It looks like an egg, though it seems to be of metallic rock. As it cools, it gets lighter in color, till finally it disappears. With a loud bang, it bursts apart, and afterward I hear a sound like scurrying feet. I drop the pieces of the shell to go toward the sound, and then I hear another sound, as if something were macerating and gulping down the pieces of shell, eating them. I come back and can't find the pieces. I go on with my test of opening and closing the main doors. As the outer door closes, I hear a crunching noise as if a rock were being pulverized, and a high scream like that of an animal in pain. All 30 this would indicate that the meteor *was* a shell, and that some living thing *did* come out of it.

"But that is impossible.

"No form of life could live through the crash with which that thing struck the Moon, even though the lava ash did cushion the fall to some extent. No form of life could stand the heat of the meteor's fall and impact. No form of life could eat the rocky, metallic shell. It's utterly impossible!

"Or—is it impossible?"

He gnawed at his knuckles and thought of Stuyvesant. 40

Stuyvesant had been assigned to the emergency dome on Mercury. There was a place for you! An inferno! By miracles of insulation and supercooling systems, the hangar there had been made livable. But the finest of space suits could not keep a man from frying to death outside. Nothing to do except stay cooped up inside the hangar, and pray for the six-month relief to come.

Stuyvesant had done that. And from Stuyvesant had begun to come queer reports. He thought he had seen something moving on Mercury near his landing field. Something like a rock!

Moving rocks! With the third report of that kind, the corporation had brought him home and turned him over to the board of science for examination. Poor Stuyvesant had barely escaped the lunatic asylum. He 10 had been let out of Spaceways, of course. The corporation scrapped men suspected of being defective as quickly as they scrapped suspect material.

"When a man begins to see rocks moving, it's time to fire him," was the unofficial verdict.

The board of science had coldly said the same thing, though in more dignified language.

"No form of life as we know it could possibly exist in the high temperature and desert condition of Mercury. Therefore, in our judgment, Benjamin Stuyvesant suffered from hallucination when he reported some rocklike entity moving near Emergency Hangar RC10." 20

Hartigan glanced uneasily toward the workbench on which the odd meteor had rested.

"No form of life *as we know it.*"

There was the catch. After all, this interplanetary travel was less than seventy years old. Might there not be many things still unknown to Earth wisdom?

"Not to hear the board of science tell it," muttered Hartigan, thinking of Stuyvesant's blasted career.

He thought of the Forbidden Asteroids.[2] There were over two dozen on the charts on which, even in direst emergency, no ship was supposed 30 to land. That was because ships had landed there, and had vanished without trace. Again and again. With no man able to dream of their fate. Till they simply marked the little globes "Forbidden," and henceforth ignored them.

"No form of life as we know it!"

Suppose something savage, huge, invisible, lived on those grim asteroids? Something that developed from egg form? Something that spread its young through the universe by propelling eggs from one celestial body to another? Something that started growth by devouring its own metallic

2. **asteroids:** very small planets. In our solar system, thousands of asteroids orbit between Mars and Jupiter.

shell, and continued it on a mineral instead of vegetable diet? Something that could live in any atmosphere or temperature?

"I *am* going crazy," Hartigan breathed.

In something like panic he tried to forget the affair in a great stack of books and magazines brought by the last supply ship.

The slow hours of another month ticked by. The full Earth waned, died, grew again. Drearily Hartigan went through the monotony of his routine. Day after day, the term "day" being a strictly figurative one on this drear lunar lump.

He rose at six, New York time, and sponged off carefully in a bit of 10 precious water. He ate breakfast. He read. He stretched his muscles in a stroll. He read. He inspected his equipment. He read. He exercised on a set of homemade flying rings. He read.

"No human being should be called on to live like this," he said once, voice too loud and brittle.

But human beings did have to live like this, if they aspired to one of the big posts on a main planet.

He had almost forgotten the strange meteor that had fallen into lava ash at his feet a month ago. It was to be recalled with terrible abruptness.

He went for a walk in a direction he did not usually take, and came 20 upon a shallow pit half a mile from the dome.

Pits, of course, are myriad on the Moon. The whole surface is made up of craters within craters. But this pit was not typical in conformation. Most are smooth-walled and flat-bottomed. This pit was ragged, as if it had been dug out. Besides, Hartigan had thought he knew every hole for a mile around, and he did not remember ever seeing this one.

He stood on its edge looking down. There was loose rock in its uncraterlike bottom, and the loose rock had the appearance of being freshly dislodged. Even this was not unusual in a place where the vibration of a footstep could sometimes cause tons to crack and fall. 30

Nevertheless, Hartigan could feel the hair rise a bit on the back of his neck as some deep, instinctive fear crawled within him at sight of the small, shallow pit. And then he caught his lips between his teeth and stared with wide, unbelieving eyes.

On the bottom of the pit a rock was moving. It was moving, not as if it had volition of its own, but as if it were being handled by some unseen thing.

A fragment about as big as his body, it rolled over twice, then slid along in impatient jerks as though a big head or hoof nudged at it. Finally it raised up from the ground and hung poised about seven feet in the air!

Breathlessly, Hartigan watched, while all his former, almost superstitious fear flooded through him.

The rock fragment moved up and down in mid-space.

"Jupiter!" Clow Hartigan breathed hoarsely.

A large part of one end suddenly disappeared. A pointed projection from the main mass of rock, it broke off and vanished from sight.

Another large chunk followed, breaking off and disappearing as though by magic.

"Jupiter!"

There was no longer doubt in Hartigan's mind. A live thing had emerged from the egglike meteor twenty-seven days ago. A live thing, that now roamed loose over the face of the Moon.   10

But that section of rock, which was apparently being devoured, was held seven feet off the ground. What manner of creature could come from an egg no larger than his head and grow in one short month into a thing over seven feet tall? He thought of the Forbidden Asteroids, where no ships landed, though no man knew precisely what threat lurked there.

"It must be as big as a mastodon," Hartigan whispered. "What in the universe—"

The rock fragment was suddenly dropped, as if whatever invisible thing had held it had suddenly seen Hartigan at the rim of the pit. Then the rock was dashed to one side as if by a charging body. The next instant 20 loose fragments of shale scattered right and left up one side of the pit as though a big body were climbing up and out.

The commotion in the shale was on the side of the pit nearest Hartigan. With a cry he ran toward the hangar.

With fantastic speed, sixty and seventy feet to a jump, he covered the ragged surface. But fast as he moved, he felt that the thing behind him moved faster. And that there *was* something behind him he did not doubt for an instant, though he could neither see nor hear it.

It was weird, this pygmy human form in its bulky space suit flying soundlessly over the lunar surface under the glowing ball of Earth, racing 30 like mad for apparently no reason at all, running insanely when, so far as the eye could tell, nothing pursued.

But abysmal instinct told Hartigan that he was pursued, all right. And instinct told him that he could never reach the hangar in the lead. With desperate calmness he searched the ground still lying between him and the hangar.

A little ahead was a crack about a hundred feet wide and, as far as he knew, bottomless. With his oversized Earth muscles he could clear that in a gigantic leap. Could the ponderous, invisible thing behind him leap that far?   40

He was in mid-flight long enough to turn his head and look back, as he hurtled the chasm in a prodigious jump. He saw a flurry among the rocks at the edge he had just left as something jumped after him. Then he came down on the far side, lighting in full stride like a hurdler.

He risked slowing his speed by looking back again. A second time he saw a flurry of loose rock, this time on the near side of the deep crack. The thing had not quite cleared the edge, it seemed.

He raced on and came to the small air-lock door. He flung himself inside. He had hardly got the fastener in its groove when something banged against the outside of the door.

The thing pursuing him had hung on the chasm's edge long enough to let him reach safety, but had not fallen into the black depths as he had 10 hoped it might.

"But that's all right," he said, drawing a great sigh of relief as he entered the hangar through the inner door. "I don't care what it does, now that I'm inside and it's out."

He got out of the space suit, planning as he moved.

The thing outside was over seven feet tall and made of some un-. fleshlike substance that must be practically indestructible. At its present rate of growth it would be as big as a small space liner in six months, if it weren't destroyed. But it would have to be destroyed. Either that, or Emergency Station RC3 would have to be abandoned, and his job with 20 it, which concerned him more than the station.

"I'll call Stacey to send a destroyer," he said crisply.

He moved toward the Bliss transmitter, eyes glinting. Things were happening on the Moon, now, all right! And the thing that was happening was going to prove Stuyvesant as sane as any man, much saner than the graybearded goats on the board of science.

He would be confined to the hangar till Stacey could send a destroyer. No more strolls. He shuddered a little as he thought of how many times he must have missed death by an inch in his walks during the past month.   30

Hartigan got halfway to the Bliss transmitter, skirting along the wall near the small air lock.

A dull, hollow, booming sound filled the great hangar, ascending to the vaulted roof and seeming to shower down again like black water.

Hartigan stopped and stared at the wall beside him. It was bulging inward a little. Startled out of all movement, he stared at the ominous, slight bulge. And as he stared, the booming noise was repeated, and the bulge grew a bit larger.

"In the name of Heaven!"

The thing outside had managed to track him along the wall from the 40 air lock, perhaps guided by the slight vibration of his steps. Now it was blindly charging the huge bulk of the hangar like a living, ferocious ram.

A third time the dull, terrible booming sound reverberated in the lofty hangar. The bulge in the tough metal wall spread again; and the two nearest supporting beams gave ever so little at the points of strain.

Hartigan moved back toward the air lock. While he moved, there was silence. The moment he stopped, there was another dull, booming crash and a second bulge appeared in the wall. The thing had followed him precisely, and was trying to get at him.

The color drained from Hartigan's face. This changed the entire scheme of things.

It was useless to radio for help now. Long before a destroyer could get here, the savage, insensate monster outside would have opened a rent in the wall. That would mean Hartigan's death from escaping air in the hangar.

Crash!

Who would have dreamed that there lived anywhere in the universe, on no matter how far or wild a globe, a creature actually able to damage the massive walls of a Spaceways hangar? He could see himself trying to tell about this.

"An animal big enough to crack a hangar wall? And invisible? Well!"

Crash!

The very light globes, so far overhead, seemed to quiver a bit with the impact of this thing of unguessable nature against the vast semisphere of the hangar. The second bulge was deep enough so that the white enamel which coated it began chipping off in little flakes at the bulge's apex.

"What the devil am I going to do?"

The only thing he could think of for the moment was to move along the wall. That unleashed giant outside must not concentrate too long on any one spot.

He walked a dozen steps. As before, the ramming stopped while he was in motion, to start again as he halted. As before, it started at the point nearest to him.

Once more a bulge appeared in the wall, this time bigger than either of the first two. The metal sheets sheathing the hangar varied a little in strength. The invisible terror outside had struck a soft spot.

Hartigan moved hastily to another place.

"The whole base of the hangar will be scalloped like a pie crust at this rate," he gritted. "What can I—"

Crash!

He had inadvertently stopped near a rack filled with spare power bulbs. With its ensuing attack the blind fury had knocked the rack down onto the floor.

Hartigan's jaw set hard. Whatever he did must be done quickly. And it must be done by himself alone. He could not stay at the Bliss transmitter long enough to get New York and tell what was wrong, without giving the gigantic thing outside a fatal number of minutes in which to concentrate on one section of wall.

He moved slowly around the hangar, striving to keep the invisible fury too occupied in following him to get in more than an occasional charge. As he walked, his eyes went from one heap of supplies to another in search of a possible means of defense.

There were ordinary weapons in plenty, in racks along the wall. But none 10 of these, he knew, could do material harm to the attacking fury.

He got to the great inner doors of the main air lock in his slow march around the hangar. And here he stopped, eyes glowing thoughtfully.

The huge doors had threatened in the early days to be the weak points in the Spaceways hangars. So the designers, like good engineers, had made the doors so massive that in the end they were stronger than the walls around them.

Bang!

A bulge near the massive hinges told Hartigan that the thing outside 20 was as relentless as ever in its effort to break through the wall and get at him. But he paid no attention to the new bulge. He was occupied with the doors.

If the invisible giant could be trapped in the main air lock between the outer and inner portals—

"Then what?" Hartigan wondered.

He could not answer his own question. But, anyway, it seemed like a step in the right direction to have the attacking fury penned between the doors rather than to have it loose and able to charge the more vulnerable walls. 30

"If I can coop it in the air lock, I might be able to think of some way to attack it," he went on.

He pushed home the control switch which set the broadcast power to opening the outer doors. And *that* gave him an idea that sent a wild thrill surging through him.

A heavy rumble told him that the motors were swinging open the outer doors.

"Will the thing come in?" he asked himself tensely. "Or has it sense enough to scent a trap?"

Bang! 40

The inner doors trembled a little on their broad tracks. The invisible monster had entered the trap.

"Trap?" Hartigan smiled mirthlessly. "Not much of a trap! Left to itself, it could probably break out in half an hour. But it won't be left to itself."

He reversed the switch to close the outer portals. Then, with the doors closed and the monster penned between, he got to work on the idea that had been born when he pushed the control switch.

Power, oceans of it, flooded from the power unit at the touch of a finger. A docile servant when properly channeled, it could be the deadliest thing on the Moon.

He ran back down the hangar to the stockroom, and got out a drum 10 of spare power cable. As quickly as was humanly possible, he rolled the drum back to the doors, unwinding the cable as he went.

It was with grim solemnity that he made his next move. He had to open the inner doors a few inches to go on with his frail plan of defense. And he had to complete that plan before the thing in the air lock could claw them open still more and charge through. For all their weight the doors rolled in perfect balance; and if the unseen terror could make dents in the solid wall, it certainly was strong enough to move the partly opened doors.

Speed! That was the thing that would make or break him. Speed, 20 and hope that the power unit could stand a terrific overload without blowing a tube.

With a hand that inclined to tremble a bit, Hartigan moved the control switch operating the inner doors, and instantly cut the circuit again.

The big doors opened six inches or so, and stopped.

Hartigan cut off the power unit entirely, and dragged the end of the spare power cable to it. With flying fingers he disconnected the cable leading from the control switch to the motors that moved the portals, and connected the spare cable in its place.

He glanced anxiously at the doors, and saw that the opening be- 30 tween them had widened to more than a foot. The left door moved a little even as he watched.

"I'll never make it!"

But he went ahead.

Grabbing up the loose end of the cable, he threw it in a tangled coil as far as he could through the opening and into the air lock. Then he leaped for the power unit—and watched.

The cable lay unmoving on the air-lock floor. But the left door moved! It jerked, and rolled open another six inches.

Hartigan clenched his hands as he stared at the inert cable. He had 40 counted on the blind ferocity of the invisible terror; had counted on its attacking, or at least touching, the cable immediately. Had it enough intelligence to realize dimly that it would be best to avoid the cable? Was it going to keep on working at those doors till—

The power cable straightened with a jerk. Straightened, and hung still, with the loose end suspended in midair about six feet off the air-lock floor.

Hartigan's hand slammed down. The broadcast power was turned on to the last notch.

With his heart hammering in his throat, Hartigan gazed through the two-foot opening between the doors. Gazed at the cable through which was coursing oceans, Niagaras of power. And out there in the air lock a thing began to build up from thin air into a spectacle that made him cry 10 out in wild horror.

He got a glimpse of a massive block of a head, eyeless and feature-less, that joined with no neck whatever to a barrel of a body. He got a glimpse of five legs, like stone pillars, and of a sixth that was only a stump. ("That's what got caught in the doors a month ago—its leg," he heard himself babbling with insane calmness.) Over ten feet high and twenty feet long, the thing was, a living battering-ram, painted in the air in sputtering, shimmering blue sparks that streamed from its massive bulk in all directions.

Just a glimpse, he got, and then the monster began to scream as it 20 had that first day when the door maimed it. Only now it was with a volume that tore at Hartigan's eardrums till he screamed himself in agony.

As he watched, he saw the huge carcass melt a little, like wax in flame, with the power cable also melting slowly and fusing into the cav-ernous, rocky jaws that had seized it. Then with a rush the whole bulk disintegrated into a heap of loose mineral matter.

Hartigan turned off the power unit and collapsed, with his face in his hands.

The shining ball of the full Earth floated like a smooth diamond between two vast, angular mountains. The full Earth.   30

Hartigan turned from the porthole beside the small air lock and strode to the Bliss radio transmitter.

"RC3, RC3, RC3," he droned out.

There was no answer. As usual, Stacey was taking his time about answering the Moon's signal.

"RC3, RC3—"

There he was.

"Hartigan talking. Monthly report."

"All right, Hartigan."

A hurried, fretful voice. Come on, Moon; report that, as always, 40 nothing has happened.

"Lunar conditions the same," said Hartigan. "No ships have put in, or have reported themselves as being in distress. The hangar is in good shape, with no leaks."

"Right," said Stacey, in the voice of a busy man. "Supplies?"

"I need some new power bulbs."

"I'll send them on the next ship. Nothing irregular to report?"

Hartigan hesitated.

On the floor of the main air lock was a mound of burned, bluish mineral substance giving no indication whatever that it had once possessed outlandish, incredible life. In the walls of the hangar at the base 10 were half a dozen new dents; but ricocheting meteors might have made those. The meteoric shell from which this bizarre animal had come had been devoured, so even that was not left for investigation.

He remembered the report of the board of science on Stuyvesant.

"Therefore, in our judgment, Benjamin Stuyvesant suffered from hallucination—"

He would have liked to help Stuyvesant. But on the other hand Stuyvesant had a job with a secondhand-space-suit store now, and was getting along pretty well in spite of Spaceways' dismissal.

"Nothing irregular to report?" repeated Stacey.   20

"Nothing irregular to report," Hartigan said steadily.

REVIEWING THE STORY _____

(Note: Write all answers on a separate sheet of paper. Do not write in this book.)

THE MAIN IDEA

1. The main conflict, or struggle, in this story is between Clow Hartigan and **(a)** Stacy **(b)** himself **(c)** a dangerous life form **(d)** the Spaceways Company.

DETAILS

2. When the story begins, Hartigan is **(a)** bored **(b)** frightened **(c)** puzzled **(d)** happy.

3. One puzzling characteristic of the strange meteor-like object is that it rapidly becomes **(a)** a plant **(b)** a building **(c)** invisible **(d)** able to talk.

4. The round object that Hartigan finds turns out to be a(an) **(a)** meteor **(b)** spy craft **(c)** cannon ball **(d)** egg.

5. The creature in the story eats **(a)** people **(b)** plants **(c)** rocks **(d)** electricity.

6. Hartigan gets rid of the strange creature by using **(a)** a nuclear weapon **(b)** a cannon ball **(c)** a laser gun **(d)** electricity.

ORDER OF EVENTS

7. Choose the letter that gives the order in which the creature's actions happen.
   (1) It chases Hartigan across the Moon's surface.
   (2) It enters the air lock from outside the emergency landing dome.
   (3) It loses a leg escaping through the outer doors.
   (4) It devours the two halves of the invisible meteor.

       (a) 1-2-3-4 **(b)** 4-3-1-2 **(c)** 3-4-2-1 **(d)** 2-1-3-4

CAUSE AND EFFECT

8. Benjamin Stuyvesant was discharged from Spaceways because he
   (a) deserted his post on Mercury.
   (b) made illegal trips to the Forbidden Asteroids.
   (c) claimed to see rocks moving on Mercury.
   (d) insisted on being transferred to the Moon.

9. Hartigan does not radio Stacey for help in destroying the creature because
   (a) there is not enough time.
   (b) Stacey would never send a destroyer.
   (c) Hartigan would rather defend himself.
   (d) Hartigan felt sorry for the creature.

INFERENCES

10. Hartigan is able to leap sixty or seventy feet at a time because of
    (a) the air in his space suit.
    (b) his strength and athletic ability.
    (c) his great fear.
    (d) the Moon's relatively low gravity.

11. We can infer that Hartigan said nothing to Stacey about the creature because

(a) Hartigan wanted to report directly to Spaceways.
(b) he feared losing his job with Spaceways.
(c) he wanted to help Stuyvesant.
(d) he expected another creature to appear.

PREDICTING OUTCOMES

12. If Hartigan had reported his adventure with the rock-eating creature, which of the following would MOST likely happen?

(a) The Forbidden Asteroids would be blown up.
(b) Scientists would try to capture one of the creatures.
(c) Spaceways would discharge him as unfit because of insanity.
(d) He would be promoted for having saved the emergency landing station.

BUILDING YOUR VOCABULARY

1. Hartigan cursed with *monotony*, and got up.

a. In this sentence, *monotony* (page 7, lines 12–13) means (a) anger (b) great energy (c) sameness of sound (d) shrill wailing notes.

b. The word *monotony* helps to suggest Hartigan's mood of (a) good humor (b) boredom (c) sadness (d) worry.

2. That would mean death, for the air supply in the dome would race out through a *fissure* almost before he could don his space suit.

a. A *fissure* (page 10, lines 6–7) is a(an) (a) porthole (b) air lock (c) break (d) valve.

b. The BEST strategy for choosing the correct meaning of *fissure* is to

(a) scan the story, looking for other uses of the word.
(b) analyze the word's root and suffix.
(c) look for context clues in the sentence around the word.
(d) read only the sentence in which the word appears.

(Note: To answer the type of question in 2b, return to the page indicated in part a *and check the context of the word.)*

3. Still, without faltering, the doors moved inward and their *serrated* edges met.

   Serrated (page 12, lines 16–17) means **(a)** temporary **(b)** toothed **(c)** separate **(d)** soft.

4. As the outer door closes, I hear a crunching noise as if a rock were being *pulverized*, and a high scream like that of an animal in pain.

   The word *pulverized* (page 12, lines 29–30) means **(a)** ground to dust **(b)** cemented together **(c)** spun rapidly **(d)** shot out forcefully.

5. Therefore, in our judgment, Benjamin Stuyvesant suffered from *hallucination* when he reported some rocklike entity moving near Emergency Hangar RC10.

   A person suffering from a *hallucination* (page 13, lines 18–20)

   (a) becomes unconscious.
   (b) collects rocks and minerals.
   (c) is a reliable witness.
   (d) sees things that aren't there.

STUDYING THE WRITER'S CRAFT

1. From the beginning of the story through page 8, line 16, the author creates the opening *tone* or *mood*. He does this chiefly by revealing Hartigan's feelings about his job on the Moon. What are some of the many details that help establish the mood?

2. *Similes* use *like* or *as* to compare something to another more familiar thing. How do each of the following similes help you visualize an object or action more clearly?

   a. "the full Earth floated like a smooth pearl" (page 6, line 1)

   b. "the enormous half globe of the hangar, like a phosphorescent mushroom in the blackness" (pages 8, lines 22–23)

   c. "the ash . . . spouted up like a geyser to a distance of a hundred feet" (page 8, lines 32–34)

3. In *verbal irony*, a speaker or writer means the opposite of the literal meaning of what is said or written.

   a. Identify the three words in the following sentence that are used ironically: "With characteristic trustfulness, Spaceways had recording dials in the home station that showed by power markings whether or not their planetary employees were doing what they were supposed to do." (page 12, lines 8–10)

b. Explain the irony in the story's title.

ACTIVITIES FOR LISTENING, SPEAKING, WRITING

1. In real life, should private companies like Spaceways be allowed to do business in outer space? Should they be allowed to own real estate there? If so, who would have the right to sell the property, and who should be allowed to buy it? Be prepared to discuss these questions with your classmates.

2. After space travel comes the next stage: space colonization. Imagine that you see the following advertisement some years from now:

WANTED: SPACE COLONISTS

NASA project needs M/F volunteers for experiment in living on artificial planetoid in outer space. Singles only. Excel. health: no smoking, alcohol, drugs. Contracts available 1–5 yrs. Hi pay & all benefits. Write with details of education, hobbies, and reasons for volunteering to: Box 77 NASA COLONY, 600 Independence Ave., Washington, DC 20546.

Think about the pros and cons of such a venture. Then write a reply to the advertisement, asking for more information and providing the details requested.

3. *Empathy* is the ability to put yourself in another's place, to think and feel as if you were that other. If the other is like you, it's easy to be empathetic. But what if that other is extremely different? At your teacher's direction, work in small groups or with your entire class to rethink "Nothing Happens on the Moon" from the point of view of the invisible rock monster. Look at things from its perspective. Then prepare a set of notes to retell the story aloud or a draft for a brief rewriting of the story. How much empathy can you evoke in your listeners or readers for this alien creature?

The Cold Equations

by Tom Godwin

It was the law, stated very bluntly and definitely in grim Paragraph L, Section 8, of Interstellar Regulations: "Any stowaway discovered in an EDS shall be jettisoned immediately following discovery."

In Tom Godwin's most famous space-travel story, the pilot of a small emergency spacecraft must make a hard decision. Faced with a stowaway, he must obey the paragraph of Instellar Regulations quoted above. Unlike the milder demands of travel on Earth, space travel leaves no margin for error, no freedom of choice.

Some day, travel in space may be almost as common as travel on Earth. How will humans respond to the relentlessly harsh reality of space travel? If you were the pilot in this story, what would you do?

Tom Godwin

Although Tom Godwin has written several novels and numerous short stories, he is best known for just one story—"The Cold Equations." This landmark short story first appeared in 1954 in *Astounding Science Fiction*, the magazine edited by John W. Campbell. Since then, "The Cold Equations" has been reprinted often. As you read the story, can you see why it is so popular?

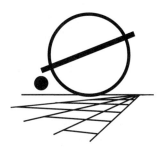

He was not alone.

There was nothing to indicate the fact but the white hand of the tiny gauge on the board before him. The control room was empty but for himself; there was no sound other than the murmur of the drives—but the white hand had moved. It had been on zero when the little ship was launched from the *Stardust*; now, an hour later, it had crept up. There was something in the supplies closet across the room, it was saying, some kind of a body that radiated heat.

It could be but one kind of a body—a living, human body.

He leaned back in the pilot's chair and drew a deep, slow breath, 10 considering what he would have to do. He was an EDS pilot, inured to the sight of death, long since accustomed to it and to viewing the dying of another man with an objective lack of emotion, and he had no choice in what he must do. There could be no alternative—but it required a few moments of conditioning for even an EDS pilot to prepare himself to walk across the room and coldly, deliberately, take the life of a man he had yet to meet.

He would, of course, do it. It was the law, stated very bluntly and definitely in grim Paragraph L, Section 8, of Interstellar Regulations: *"Any stowaway discovered in an EDS shall be jettisoned immediately following dis-* 20 *covery."*

It was the law, and there could be no appeal.

It was a law not of men's choosing, but made imperative by the circumstances of the space frontier. Galactic expansion had followed the development of the hyperspace drive, and as men scattered wide across the frontier, there had come the problem of contact with the isolated first colonies and exploration parties. The huge hyperspace cruisers were the product of the combined genius and effort of Earth and were long and expensive in the building. They were not available in such numbers that small colonies could possess them. The cruisers carried the colonists to their new worlds and made periodic visits, running on tight schedules, but they could not stop and turn aside to visit colonies scheduled to be 10 visited at another time; such a delay would destroy their schedule and produce a confusion and uncertainty that would wreck the complex interdependence between old Earth and the new worlds of the frontier.

Some method of delivering supplies or assistance when an emergency occurred on a world not scheduled for a visit had been needed, and the Emergency Dispatch Ships had been the answer. Small and collapsible, they occupied little room in the hold of the cruiser; made of light metal and plastics, they were driven by a small rocket drive that consumed relatively little fuel. Each cruiser carried four EDS's, and when a call for aid was received, the nearest cruiser would drop into normal 20 space long enough to launch an EDS with the needed supplies or personnel, then vanish again as it continued on its course.

The cruisers, powered by nuclear converters, did not use the liquid rocket fuel, but nuclear converters were far too large and complex to permit their installation in the EDS's. The cruisers were forced by necessity to carry a limited amount of bulky rocket fuel, and the fuel was rationed with care, the cruiser's computers determining the exact amount of fuel each EDS would require for its mission. The computers considered the course coordinates, the mass of the EDS, the mass of pilot and cargo; they were very precise and accurate and omitted nothing from their cal- 30 culations. They could not, however, foresee and allow for the added mass of a stowaway.

The *Stardust* had received the request from one of the exploration parties stationed on Woden, the six men of the party already being stricken with the fever carried by the green kala midges and their own supply of serum destroyed by the tornado that had torn through their camp. The *Stardust* had gone through the usual procedure, dropping into normal space to launch the EDS with the fever serum, then vanishing again in hyperspace. Now, an hour later, the gauge was saying there was something more than the small carton of serum in the supplies closet. 40

He let his eyes rest on the narrow white door of the closet. There, just inside, another man lived and breathed and was beginning to feel assured that discovery of his presence would now be too late for the pilot to alter the situation. It *was* too late; for the man behind the door it was far later than he thought and in a way he would find terrible to believe.

There could be no alternative. Additional fuel would be used during the hours of deceleration to compensate for the added mass of the stowaway; infinitesimal increments of fuel that would not be missed until the ship had almost reached its destination. Then, at some distance above the ground that might be as near as a thousand feet or as far as tens of thousands feet, depending upon the mass of ship and cargo and the preceding period of deceleration, the unmissed increments of fuel would make their absence known; the EDS would expend its last drops of fuel with a sputter and go into whistling free fall. Ship and pilot and stowaway would merge together upon impact as a wreckage of metal and plastic, flesh and blood, driven deep into the soil. The stowaway had signed his own death warrant when he concealed himself on the ship; he could not be permitted to take seven others with him.

He looked again at the telltale white hand, then rose to his feet. What he must do would be unpleasant for both of them; the sooner it was over, the better. He stepped across the control room to stand by the white door.

"Come out!" His command was harsh and abrupt above the murmur of the drive.

It seemed he could hear the whisper of a furtive movement inside the closet, then nothing. He visualized the stowaway cowering closer into one corner, suddenly worried by the possible consequences of his act, his self-assurance evaporating.

"I said *out!*"

He heard the stowaway move to obey, and he waited with his eyes alert on the door and his hand near the blaster at his side.

The door opened and the stowaway stepped through it, smiling. "All right—I give up. Now what?"

It was a girl.

He stared without speaking, his hand dropping away from the blaster and acceptance of what he saw coming like a heavy and unexpected physical blow. The stowaway was not a man—she was a girl in her teens, standing before him in little white gypsy sandals, with the top of her brown, curly head hardly higher than his shoulder, with a faint, sweet scent of perfume coming from her, and her smiling face tilted up so her eyes could look unknowing and unafraid into his as she waited for his answer.

Now what? Had it been asked in the deep, defiant voice of a man he would have answered it with action, quick and efficient. He would have taken the stowaway's identification disk and ordered him into the air lock. Had the stowaway refused to obey, he would have used the blaster. It would not have taken long; within a minute the body would have been ejected into space—had the stowaway been a man.

He returned to the pilot's chair and motioned her to seat herself on the boxlike bulk of the drive-control units that were set against the wall beside him. She obeyed, his silence making the smile fade into the meek and guilty expression of a pup that has been caught in mischief and knows it must be punished.

"You still haven't told me," she said. "I'm guilty, so what happens 10 to me now? Do I pay a fine, or what?"

"What are you doing here?" he asked. "Why did you stow away on this EDS?"

"I wanted to see my brother. He's with the government survey crew on Woden and I haven't seen him for ten years, not since he left Earth to go into government survey work."

"What was your destination on the *Stardust?*"

"Mimir. I have a position waiting for me there. My brother has been sending money home all the time to us—my father and mother and me— and he paid for a special course in linguistics I was taking. I graduated 20 sooner than expected and I was offered this job on Mimir. I knew it would be almost a year before Gerry's job was done on Woden so he could come on to Mimir, and that's why I hid in the closet there. There was plenty of room for me and I was willing to pay the fine. There were only the two of us kids—Gerry and I—and I haven't seen him for so long, and I didn't want to wait another year when I could see him now, even though I knew I would be breaking some kind of a regulation when I did it."

I knew I would be breaking some kind of a regulation. In a way, she could not be blamed for her ignorance of the law; she was of Earth and had not realized that the laws of the space frontier must, of necessity, be as 30 hard and relentless as the environment that gave them birth. Yet, to protect such as her from the results of their own ignorance of the frontier, there had been a sign over the door that led to the section of the *Stardust* that housed the EDS's, a sign that was plain for all to see and heed: UNAUTHORIZED PERSONNEL KEEP OUT!

"Does your brother know that you took passage on the *Stardust* for Mimir?"

"Oh, yes. I sent him a spacegram telling him about my graduation and about going to Mimir on the *Stardust* a month before I left Earth. I already knew Mimir was where he would be stationed in a little over a 40 year. He gets a promotion then, and he'll be based on Mimir and not have to stay out a year at a time on field trips, like he does now."

There were two different survey groups on Woden, and he asked, "What is his name?"

"Cross—Gerry Cross. He's in Group Two—that was the way his address read. Do you know him?"

Group One had requested the serum; Group Two was eight thousand miles away, across the Western Sea.

"No, I've never met him," he said, then turned to the control board and cut the deceleration to a fraction of a gravity, knowing as he did so that it could not avert the ultimate end, yet doing the only thing he could do to prolong that ultimate end. The sensation was like that of the ship 10 suddenly dropping, and the girl's involuntary movement of surprise half lifted her from the seat.

"We're going faster now, aren't we?" she asked. "Why are we doing that?"

He told her the truth. "To save fuel for a little while."

"You mean we don't have very much?"

He delayed the answer he must give her so soon to ask, "How did you manage to stow away?"

"I just sort of walked in when no one was looking my way," she said. "I was practicing my Gelanese on the native girl who does the 20 cleaning in the Ship's Supply office when someone came in with an order for supplies for the survey crew on Woden. I slipped into the closet there after the ship was ready to go just before you came in. It was an impulse of the moment to stow away, so I could get to see Gerry—and from the way you keep looking at me so grim, I'm not sure it was a very wise impulse. But I'll be a model criminal—or do I mean prisoner?" She smiled at him again. "I intended to pay for my keep on top of paying the fine. I can cook and I can patch clothes for everyone and I know how to do all kinds of useful things, even a little bit about nursing."

There was one more question to ask: 30

"Did you know what the supplies were that the survey crew ordered?"

"Why, no. Equipment they needed in their work, I supposed."

Why couldn't she have been a man with some ulterior motive? A fugitive from justice hoping to lose himself on a raw new world; an opportunist seeking transportation to the new colonies where he might find golden fleece[1] for the taking; a crackpot with a mission. Perhaps once in his lifetime an EDS pilot would find such a stowaway on his ship—

---

1. **golden fleece:** something of great value. According to an ancient Greek myth, Jason and the Argonauts went on a long and dangerous quest for the magical fleece of a golden ram.

warped men, mean and selfish men, brutal and dangerous men—but never before a smiling, blue-eyed girl who was willing to pay her fine and work for her keep that she might see her brother.

He turned to the board and turned the switch that would signal the *Stardust*. The call would be futile, but he could not, until he had exhausted that one vain hope, seize her and thrust her into the air lock as he would an animal—or a man. The delay, in the meantime, would not be dangerous with the EDS decelerating at fractional gravity.

A voice spoke from the communicator. "*Stardust*. Identify yourself and proceed."   10

"Barton, EDS 34GII. Emergency. Give me Commander Delhart."

There was a faint confusion of noises as the request went through the proper channels. The girl was watching him, no longer smiling.

"Are you going to order them to come back after me?" she asked.

The communicator clicked and there was the sound of a distant voice saying, "Commander, the EDS requests . . ."

"Are they coming back after me?" she asked again. "Won't I get to see my brother after all?"

"Barton?" The blunt, gruff voice of Commander Delhart came from the communicator. "What's this about an emergency?"   20

"A stowaway," he answered.

"A stowaway?" There was a slight surprise to the question. "That's rather unusual—but why the 'emergency' call? You discovered him in time, so there should be no appreciable danger, and I presume you've informed Ship's Records so his nearest relatives can be notified."

"That's why I had to call you, first. The stowaway is still aboard and the circumstances are so different—"

"Different?" the commander interrupted, impatience in his voice. "How can they be different? You know you have a limited supply of fuel; you also know the law as well as I do: 'Any stowaway discovered in an 30 EDS shall be jettisoned immediately following discovery.' "

There was the sound of a sharply indrawn breath from the girl. "*What does he mean?*"

"The stowaway is a girl."

"*What?*"

"She wanted to see her brother. She's only a kid and she didn't know what she was really doing."

"I see." All the curtness was gone from the commander's voice. "So you called me in the hope I could do something?" Without waiting for an answer he went on, "I'm sorry—I can do nothing. This cruiser 40 must maintain its schedule; the life of not one person but the lives of many depend on it. I know how you feel but I'm powerless to help

you. You'll have to go through with it. I'll have you connected with
Ship's Records."

The communicator faded to a faint rustle of sound, and he turned
back to the girl. She was leaning forward on the bench, almost rigid, her
eyes fixed wide and frightened.

"What did he mean, to go through with it? To jettison me . . . to go
through with it—what did he mean? Not the way it sounded . . . he
couldn't have. What did he mean—what did he really mean?"

Her time was too short for the comfort of a lie to be more than a
cruelly fleeting delusion.   10

"He meant it the way it sounded."

"*No!*" She recoiled from him as though he had struck her, one hand
half upraised as though to fend him off and stark unwillingness to believe
in her eyes.

"It will have to be."

"No! You're joking—you're insane! You can't mean it!"

"I'm sorry." He spoke slowly to her, gently. "I should have told you
before—I should have, but I had to do what I could first; I had to call the
Stardust. You heard what the commander said."

"But you can't—if you make me leave the ship, I'll *die.*"   20

"I know."

She searched his face, and the unwillingness to believe left her eyes,
giving way slowly to a look of dazed horror.

"You—know?" She spoke the words far apart, numb and wonderingly.

"I know. It has to be like that."

"You mean it—you really mean it." She sagged back against the wall,
small and limp like a little rag doll, and all the protesting and disbelief
gone. "You're going to do it—you're going to make me die?"

"I'm sorry," he said again. "You'll never know how sorry I am. It
has to be that way and no human in the universe can change it."   30

"You're going to make me die and I didn't do anything to die for—I
didn't *do* anything—"

He sighed, deep and weary. "I know you didn't, child. I know you
didn't."

"EDS." The communicator rapped brisk and metallic. "This is Ship's
Records. Give us all information on subject's identification disk."

He got out of his chair to stand over her. She clutched the edge of
the seat, her upturned face white under the brown hair and the lipstick
standing out like a blood-red cupid's bow.

"*Now?*"   40

"I want your identification disk," he said.

She released the edge of the seat and fumbled at the chain that suspended the plastic disk from her neck with fingers that were trembling and awkward. He reached down and unfastened the clasp for her, then returned with the disk to his chair.

"Here's your data, Records: Identification Number T837—"

"One moment," Records interrupted. "This is to be filed on the gray card, of course?"

"Yes."

"And the time of execution?"

"I'll tell you later."

"Later? This is highly irregular; the time of the subject's death is required before—"

He kept the thickness out of his voice with an effort. "Then we'll do it in a highly irregular manner—you'll hear the disk read first. The subject is a girl and she's listening to everything that's said. Are you capable of understanding that?"

There was a brief, almost shocked silence, then Records said meekly, "Sorry. Go ahead."

He began to read the disk, reading it slowly to delay the inevitable for as long as possible, trying to help her by giving her what little time he could to recover from her first horror and let it resolve into the calm of acceptance and resignation.

"Number T8374 dash Y54. Name, Marilyn Lee Cross. Sex, female. Born July 7, 2160." *She was only eighteen.* "Height, five-three. Weight, a hundred and ten." *Such a slight weight, yet enough to add fatally to the mass of the shell-thin bubble that was an EDS.* "Hair, brown. Eyes, blue. Complexion, light. Blood type, O." *Irrelevant data.* "Destination, Port City, Mimir." *Invalid data.*

He finished and said, "I'll call you later," then turned once again to the girl. She was huddled back against the wall, watching him with a look of numb and wondering fascination.

"They're waiting for you to kill me, aren't they? They want me dead, don't they? You and everybody on the cruiser want me dead, don't you?" Then the numbness broke and her voice was that of a frightened and bewildered child. "Everybody wants me dead and I didn't *do* anything. I didn't hurt anyone—I only wanted to see my brother."

"It's not the way you think—it isn't that way at all," he said. "Nobody wants it this way; nobody would ever let it be this way if it was humanly possible to change it."

"Then why is it? I don't understand. Why is it?"

"This ship is carrying kala fever serum to Group One on Woden. Their own supply was destroyed by a tornado. Group Two—the crew your brother is in—is eight thousand miles away across the Western Sea, and their helicopters can't cross it to help Group One. The fever is invariably fatal unless the serum can be had in time, and the six men in Group One will die unless this ship reaches them on schedule. These little ships are always given barely enough fuel to reach their destination, and if you stay aboard your added weight will cause it to use up all its fuel before it reaches the ground. It will crash then, and you and I will die, and so will the six men waiting for the fever serum."

It was a full minute before she spoke, and as she considered his words, the expression of numbness left her eyes.

"Is that it?" she asked at last. "Just that the ship doesn't have enough fuel?"

"Yes."

"I can go alone or I can take seven others with me—is that the way it is?"

"That's the way it is."

"And nobody wants me to have to die?"

"Nobody."

"Then maybe—Are you sure nothing can be done about it? Wouldn't people help me if they could?"

"Everyone would like to help you, but there is nothing anyone can do. I did the only thing I could do when I called the *Stardust*."

"And it won't come back—but there might be other cruisers, mightn't there? Isn't there any hope at all that there might be someone, somewhere, who could do something to help me?"

She was leaning forward a little in her eagerness as she waited for his answer.

"No."

The word was like the drop of a cold stone and she again leaned back against the wall, the hope and eagerness leaving her face. "You're sure—you *know* you're sure?"

"I'm sure. There are no other cruisers within forty light-years; there is nothing and no one to change things."

She dropped her gaze to her lap and began twisting a pleat of her skirt between her fingers, saying no more as her mind began to adapt itself to the grim knowledge.

It was better so; with the going of all hope would go the fear; with the going of all hope would come resignation. She needed time and she could have so little of it. How much?

The EDS's were not equipped with hull-cooling units; their speed had to be reduced to a moderate level before entering the atmosphere. They were decelerating at .10 gravity, approaching their destination at a far higher speed than the computers had calculated on. The *Stardust* had been quite near Woden when she launched the EDS; their present velocity was putting them nearer by the second. There would be a critical point, soon to be reached, when he would have to resume deceleration. When he did so, the girl's weight would be multiplied by the gravities of deceleration, would become, suddenly, a factor of paramount importance, the factor the computers had been ignorant of when they determined the amount of fuel the EDS should have. She would have to go when deceleration began; it could be no other way. When would that be—how long could he let her stay?

"How long can I stay?"   10

He winced involuntarily from the words that were so like an echo of his own thoughts. How long? He didn't know; he would have to ask the ship's computers. Each EDS was given a meager surplus of fuel to compensate for unfavorable conditions within the atmosphere, and relatively little fuel was being consumed for the time being. The memory banks of the computers would still contain all data pertaining to the course set for the EDS; such data would not be erased until the EDS reached its destination. He had only to give the computers the new data— the girl's weight and the exact time at which he had reduced the deceleration to .10.   20

"Barton." Commander Delhart's voice came abruptly from the communicator as he opened his mouth to call the *Stardust*. "A check with Records shows me you haven't completed your report. Did you reduce the deceleration?"

So the commander knew what he was trying to do.

"I'm decelerating at point ten," he answered. "I cut the deceleration at seventeen fifty and the weight is a hundred and ten. I would like to stay at point ten as long as the computers say I can. Will you give them the question?"

It was contrary to regulations for an EDS pilot to make any changes in 30 the course or degree of deceleration the computers had set for him, but the commander made no mention of the violation. Neither did he ask the reason for it. It was not necessary for him to ask; he had not become commander of an interstellar cruiser without both intelligence and an understanding of human nature. He said only, "I'll have that given to the computers."

The communicator fell silent and he and the girl waited, neither of them speaking. They would not have to wait long; the computers would give the answer within moments of the asking. The new factors would be fed into the steel maw of the first bank, and the electrical impulses would go through the complex circuits. Here and there a relay might 40 click, a tiny cog turn over, but it would be essentially the electrical impulses that found the answer; formless, mindless, invisible, determining with utter precision how long the pale girl beside him might live. Then five little segments of metal in the second bank would trip in rapid succession against an inked ribbon and a second steel maw would spit out the slip of paper that bore the answer.

The chronometer on the instrument board read 18:10 when the commander spoke again.

"You will resume deceleration at nineteen ten."

She looked toward the chronometer, then quickly away from it. "Is that when . . . when I go?" she asked. He nodded and she dropped her eyes to her lap again.   10

"I'll have the course correction given to you," the commander said. "Ordinarily I would never permit anything like this, but I understand your position. There is nothing I can do, other than what I've just done, and you will not deviate from these new instructions. You will complete your report at nineteen ten. Now—here are the course corrections."

The voice of some unknown technician read them to him, and he wrote them down on the pad clipped to the edge of the control board. There would, he saw, be periods of deceleration when he neared the atmosphere when the deceleration would be five gravities—and at five gravities one hundred ten pounds would become five hundred fifty 20 pounds.

The technician finished and he terminated the contact with a brief acknowledgement. Then, hesitating a moment, he reached out and shut off the communicator. It was 18:13 and he would have nothing to report until 19:10. In the meantime, it somehow seemed indecent to permit others to hear what she might say in her last hour.

He began to check the instrument readings, going over them with unnecessary slowness. She would have to accept the circumstances, and there was nothing he could do to help her into acceptance; words of sympathy would only delay it.   30

It was 18:20 when she stirred from her motionlessness and spoke.

"So that's the way it has to be with me?"

He swung around to face her. "You understand now, don't you? No one would ever let it be like this if it could be changed."

"I understand," she said. Some of the color had returned to her face and the lipstick no longer stood out so vividly red. "There isn't enough fuel for me to stay. When I hid on this ship I got into something I didn't know anything about and now I have to pay for it."

She had violated a man-made law that said KEEP OUT, but the penalty was not for men's making or desire and it was a penalty men could not 40 revoke. A physical law had decreed: *h amount of fuel will power an EDS with a mass of m safely to its destination;* and a second physical law had decreed: *h amount of fuel will not power an EDS with a mass of m plus x safely to its destination.*

EDS's obeyed only physical laws, and no amount of human sympathy for her could alter the second law.

"But I'm afraid. I don't want to die—not now. I want to live, and nobody is doing anything to help me; everybody is letting me go ahead and acting just like nothing was going to happen to me. I'm going to die and nobody *cares*."

"We all do," he said. "I do and the commander does and the clerk in Ship's Records; we all care and each of us did what little he could to help you. It wasn't enough—it was almost nothing—but it was all we could do." 10

"Not enough fuel—I can understand that," she said, as though she had not heard his own words. "But to have to die for it. *Me* alone . . ."

How hard it must be for her to accept the fact. She had never known danger of death; had never known the environments where the lives of men could be as fragile and fleeting as sea foam tossed against a rocky shore. She belonged on gentle Earth, in that secure and peaceful society where she could be young and gay and laughing with the others of her kind; where life was precious and well guarded and there was always the assurance that tomorrow would come. She belonged in that world of soft winds and a warm sun, music and moonlight and gracious manners, and not on the hard, bleak frontier. 20

"How did it happen to me so terribly quickly? An hour ago I was on the *Stardust*, going to Mimir. Now the *Stardust* is going on without me and I'm going to die and I'll never see Gerry and Mama and Daddy again—I'll never see anything again."

He hesitated, wondering how he could explain it to her so she would really understand and not feel she had somehow been the victim of a reasonlessly cruel injustice. She did not know what the frontier was like; she thought in terms of safe, secure Earth. Pretty girls were not jettisoned on Earth; there was a law against it. On Earth her plight would have filled the newscasts and a fast black patrol ship would have been racing to her rescue. Everyone, everywhere, would have known of Marilyn Lee Cross, and no effort would have been spared to save her life. But this was not Earth and there were no patrol ships; only the *Stardust*, leaving them behind at many times the speed of light. There was no one to help her, there would be no Marilyn Lee Cross smiling from the newscasts tomorrow. Marilyn Lee Cross would be but a poignant memory for an EDS pilot and a name on a gray card in Ship's Records. 30

"It's different here; it's not like back on Earth," he said. "It isn't that no one cares; it's that no one can do anything to help. The frontier is big, 40 and here along its rim the colonies and exploration parties are scattered so thin and far between. On Woden, for example, there are only sixteen men—sixteen men on an entire world. The exploration parties, the survey crews, the little first colonies—they're all fighting alien environments, trying to make a way for those who will follow after. The environments fight back, and those who go first usually make mistakes only once. There is no margin of safety along the rim of the frontier; there can't be until the way is made for the others who will come later, until the new worlds are tamed and settled. Until then men will have to pay the penalty for making mistakes, with no one to help them, because there is no one *to* help them."

"I was going to Mimir," she said. "I didn't know about the frontier; I was only going to Mimir and *it's* safe."

"Mimir is safe, but you left the cruiser that was taking you there."

She was silent for a little while. "It was all so wonderful at first; there was plenty of room for me on this ship and I would be seeing Gerry so soon. I didn't know about the fuel, didn't know what would happen to me . . ."

Her words trailed away, and he turned his attention to the viewscreen, not wanting to stare at her as she fought her way through the black horror of fear toward the calm gray of acceptance.

Woden was a ball, enshrouded in the blue haze of its atmosphere, swimming in space against the background of star-sprinkled dead blackness. The great mass of Manning's Continent sprawled like a gigantic hourglass in the Eastern Sea, with the western half of the Eastern Continent still visible. There was a thin line of shadow along the right-hand edge of the globe, and the Eastern Continent was disappearing into it as the planet turned on its axis. An hour before, the entire continent had been in view; now a thousand miles of it had gone into the thin edge of shadow and around to the night that lay on the other side of the world. The dark blue spot that was Lotus Lake was approaching the shadow. It was somewhere near the southern edge of the lake that Group Two had their camp. It would be night there soon, and quick behind the coming of night the rotation of Woden on its axis would put Group Two beyond the reach of the ship's radio.

He would have to tell her before it was too late for her to talk to her brother. In a way, it would be better for both of them should they not do so, but it was not for him to decide. To each of them the last words would be something to hold and cherish, something that would cut like the blade of a knife yet would be infinitely precious to remember, she for her own brief moments to live and he for the rest of his life.

He held down the button that would flash the grid lines on the viewscreen and used the known diameter of the planet to estimate the distance the southern tip of Lotus Lake had yet to go until it passed beyond radio range. It was approximately five hundred miles. Five hundred miles; thirty minutes—and the chronometer read 18:30. Allowing for error in estimating, it would not be later than 19:05 that the turning of Woden would cut off her brother's voice.

The first border of the Western Continent was already in sight along the left side of the world. Four thousand miles across it lay the shore of the Western Sea and the camp of Group One. It had been in the Western 10 Sea that the tornado had originated, to strike with such fury at the camp and destroy half their prefabricated buildings, including the one that housed the medical supplies. Two days before, the tornado had not existed; it had been no more than great gentle masses of air out over the calm Western Sea. Group One had gone about their routine survey work, unaware of the meeting of air masses out at sea, unaware of the force the union was spawning. It had struck their camp without warning—a thundering, roaring destruction that sought to annihilate all that lay before it. It had passed on, leaving the wreckage in its wake. It had destroyed the labor of months and had doomed six men to die and then, 20 as though its task was accomplished, it once more began to resolve into gentle masses of air. But, for all its deadliness, it had destroyed with neither malice nor intent. It had been a blind and mindless force, obeying the laws of nature, and it would have followed the same course with the same fury had men never existed.

Existence required order, and there was order: the laws of nature, irrevocable and immutable. Men could learn to use them, but men could not change them. The circumference of a circle was always pi times the diameter, and no science of man would ever make it otherwise. The combination of chemical A with chemical B under condition C invariably 30 produced reaction D. The law of gravitation was a rigid equation, and it made no distinction between the fall of a leaf and the ponderous circling of a binary star system. The nuclear conversion process powered the cruisers that carried men to the stars; the same process in the form of a nova would destroy a world with equal efficiency. The laws *were*, and the universe moved in obedience to them. Along the frontier were arrayed all the forces of nature, and sometimes they destroyed those who were fighting their way outward from Earth. The men of the frontier had long ago learned the bitter futility of cursing the forces that would destroy them, for the forces were blind and deaf; the futility of looking to the 40 heavens for mercy, for the stars of the galaxy swung in their long, long sweep of two hundred million years, as inexorably controlled as they by the laws that knew neither hatred nor compassion. The men of the frontier knew—but how was a girl from Earth to fully understand? *H amount of fuel will not power an EDS with a mass of m plus x safely to its destination.* To himself and her brother and parents she was a sweet-faced girl in her teens; to the laws of nature she was x, the unwanted factor in a cold equation.

She stirred again on the seat. "Could I write a letter? I want to write to Mama and Daddy. And I'd like to talk to Gerry. Could you let me talk to him over your radio there?"

"I'll try to get him," he said.   10

He switched on the normal-space transmitter and pressed the signal button. Someone answered the buzzer almost immediately.

"Hello. How's it going with you fellows now—is the EDS on its way?"

"This isn't Group One; this is the EDS," he said. "Is Gerry Cross there?"

"Gerry? He and two others went out in the helicopter this morning and aren't back yet. It's almost sundown, though, and he ought to be back right away—in less than an hour at the most."

"Can you connect me through to the radio in his 'copter?"   20

"Huh-uh. It's been out of commission for two months—some printed circuits went haywire and we can't get any more until the next cruiser stops by. Is it something important—bad news for him, or something?"

"Yes—it's very important. When he comes in, get him to the transmitter as soon as you possibly can."

"I'll do that; I'll have one of the boys waiting at the field with a truck. Is there anything else I can do?"

"No, I guess that's all. Get him there as soon as you can and signal me."

He turned the volume to an inaudible minimum, an act that would 30 not affect the functioning of the signal buzzer, and unclipped the pad of paper from the control board. He tore off the sheet containing his flight instructions and handed the pad to her, together with pencil.

"I'd better write to Gerry too," she said as she took them. "He might not get back to camp in time."

She began to write, her fingers still clumsy and uncertain in the way they handled the pencil, and the top of it trembling a little as she poised it between words. He turned back to the viewscreen, to stare at it without seeing it.

She was a lonely little child trying to say her last goodbye, and she 40 would lay out her heart to them. She would tell them how much she loved them and she would tell them not to feel bad about it, that it was only something that must happen eventually to everyone and she was not afraid. The last would be a lie and it would be there to read between the sprawling, uneven lines: a valiant little lie that would make the hurt all the greater for them.

Her brother was of the frontier and he would understand. He would not hate the EDS pilot for doing nothing to prevent her going; he would know there had been nothing the pilot could do. He would understand, though the understanding would not soften the shock and pain when he learned his sister was gone. But the others, her father and mother—they would not understand. They were of Earth and they would think in the manner of those who had never lived where the safety margin of life was a thin, thin line—and sometimes not at all. What would they think of the faceless, unknown pilot who had sent her to her death?

They would hate him with cold and terrible intensity, but it really didn't matter. He would never see them, never know them. He would have only the memories to remind him; only the nights of fear, when a blue-eyed girl in gypsy sandals would come in his dreams to die again . . . .

He scowled at the viewscreen and tried to force his thoughts into less emotional channels. There was nothing he could do to help her. She had unknowingly subjected herself to the penalty of a law that recognized neither innocence nor youth nor beauty, that was incapable of sympathy or leniency. Regret was illogical—and yet, could knowing it to be illogical ever keep it away?

She stopped occasionally, as though trying to find the right words to tell them what she wanted them to know, then the pencil would resume its whispering to the paper. It was 18:37 when she folded the letter in a square and wrote a name on it. She began writing another, twice looking up at the chronometer, as though she feared the black hand might reach its rendezvous before she had finished. It was 18:45 when she folded it as she had done the first letter and wrote a name and address on it.

She held the letters out to him. "Will you take care of these and see that they're enveloped and mailed?"

"Of course." He took them from her hand and placed them in a pocket of his gray uniform shirt.

"These can't be sent off until the next cruiser stops by, and the *Stardust* will have long since told them about me, won't it?" she asked. He nodded and she went on: "That makes the letters not important in one way, but in another way they're very important—to me, and to them."

"I know. I understand, and I'll take care of them."

She glanced at the chronometer, then back to him. "It seems to move faster all the time, doesn't it?"

He said nothing, unable to think of anything to say, and she asked, "Do you think Gerry will come back to camp in time?"

"I think so. They said he should be in right away."

She began to roll the pencil back and forth between her palms. "I hope he does. I feel sick and scared and I want to hear his voice again and maybe I won't feel so alone. I'm a coward and I can't help it."

"No," he said, "you're not a coward. You're afraid, but you're not a coward." 10

"Is there a difference?"

He nodded. "A lot of difference."

"I feel so alone. I never did feel like this before; like I was all by myself and there was nobody to care what happened to me. Always, before, there were Mama and Daddy there and my friends around me. I had lots of friends, and they had a going-away party for me the night before I left."

Friends and music and laughter for her to remember—and on the viewscreen Lotus Lake was going into the shadow.

"Is it the same with Gerry?" she asked. "I mean, if he should make 20 a mistake, would he have to die for it, all alone and with no one to help him?"

"It's the same with all, along the frontier; it will always be like that so long as there is a frontier."

"Gerry didn't tell us. He said the pay was good, and he sent money home all the time because Daddy's little shop just brought in a bare living, but he didn't tell us it was like this."

"He didn't tell you his work was dangerous?"

"Well—yes. He mentioned that, but we didn't understand. I always thought danger along the frontier was something that was a lot of fun; 30 an exciting adventure, like in the three-D shows." A wan smile touched her face for a moment. "Only it's not, is it? It's not the same at all, because when it's real you can't go home after the show is over."

"No," he said. "No, you can't."

Her glance flicked from the chronometer to the door of the air lock, then down to the pad and pencil she still held. She shifted her position slightly to lay them on the bench beside her, moving one foot out a little. For the first time he saw that she was not wearing Vegan gypsy sandals, but only cheap imitations; the expensive Vegan leather was some kind of grained plastic, the silver buckle was gilded iron, the jewels were colored 40 glass. *Daddy's little shop just brought in a bare living.* She must have left college in her second year, to take the course in linguistics that would enable her to make her own way and help her brother provide for her parents, earning what she could by part-time work after classes were over. Her personal possessions on the *Stardust* would be taken back to her parents—they would neither be of much value nor occupy much storage space on the return voyage.

"Isn't it—" she stopped, and he looked at her questioningly. "Isn't it cold in here?" she asked, almost apologetically. "Doesn't it seem cold to you?"

"Why, yes," he said. He saw by the main temperature gauge that the room was at precisely normal temperature. "Yes, it's colder than it 10 should be."

"I wish Gerry would get back before it's too late. Do you really think he will, and you didn't just say so to make me feel better?"

"I think he will—they said he would be in pretty soon." On the viewscreen Lotus Lake had gone into the shadow but for the thin blue line of its western edge, and it was apparent he had overestimated the time she would have in which to talk to her brother. Reluctantly, he said to her, "His camp will be out of radio range in a few minutes; he's on that part of Woden that's in the shadow"—he indicated the viewscreen—"and the turning of Woden will put him beyond contact. There may not be much time left when 20 he comes in—not much time to talk to him before he fades out. I wish I could do something about it—I would call him right now if I could."

"Not even as much time as I will have to stay?"

"I'm afraid not."

"Then—" She straightened and looked toward the air lock with pale resolution. "Then I'll go when Gerry passes beyond range. I won't wait any longer after that—I won't have anything to wait for."

Again there was nothing he could say.

"Maybe I shouldn't wait at all. Maybe I'm selfish—maybe it would be better for Gerry if you just told him about it afterward." 30

There was an unconscious pleading for denial in the way she spoke and he said, "He wouldn't want you to do that, to not wait for him."

"It's already coming dark where he is, isn't it? There will be all the long night before him, and Mama and Daddy don't know yet that I won't ever be coming back like I promised them I would. I've caused everyone I love to be hurt, haven't I? I didn't want to—I didn't intend to."

"It wasn't your fault," he said. "It wasn't your fault at all. They'll know that. They'll understand."

"At first I was so afraid to die that I was a coward and thought only of myself. Now I see how selfish I was. The terrible thing about dying like 40 this is not that I'll be gone but that I'll never see them again; never be able to tell them that I didn't take them for granted; never be able to tell them

I knew of the sacrifices they made to make my life happier, that I knew all the things they did for me and that I loved them so much more than I ever told them. I've never told them any of those things. You don't tell them such things when you're young and your life is all before you—you're so very afraid of sounding sentimental and silly. But it's so different when you have to die—you wish you had told them while you could and you wish you could tell them you're sorry for all the little mean things you ever did or said to them. You wish you could tell them that you didn't really mean to ever hurt their feelings and for them to only remember that you always loved them far more than you ever let them know." 10

"You don't have to tell them that," he said. "They will know—they've always known it."

"Are you sure?" she asked. "How can you be sure? My people are strangers to you."

"Wherever you go, human nature and human hearts are the same."

"And they will know what I want them to know—that I love them?"

"They've always known it, in a way far better than you could ever put in words for them."

"I keep remembering the things they did for me, and it's the little things they did that seem to be the most important to me, now. Like 20 Gerry—he sent me a bracelet of fire rubies on my sixteenth birthday. It was beautiful—it must have cost him a month's pay. Yet I remember him more for what he did the night my kitten got run over in the street. I was only six years old and he held me in his arms and wiped away my tears and told me not to cry, that Flossy was gone for just a little while, for just long enough to get herself a new fur coat, and she would be on the foot of my bed the very next morning. I believed him and quit crying and went to sleep dreaming about my kitten coming back. When I woke up the next morning, there was Flossy on the foot of my bed in a brand-new white fur coat, just like he had said she would be. It wasn't until a long time later that Mama told me Gerry 30 had got the pet-shop owner out of bed at four in the morning and, when the man got mad about it, Gerry told him he was either going to go down and sell him the white kitten right then or he'd break his neck."

"It's always the little things you remember people by; all the little things they did because they wanted to do them for you. You've done the same for Gerry and your father and mother; all kinds of things that you've forgotten about, but that they will never forget."

"I hope I have. I would like for them to remember me like that."

"They will."

"I wish—" She swallowed. "The way I'll die—I wish they wouldn't 40 ever think of that. I've read how people look who die in space—their insides all ruptured and exploded and their lungs out between their teeth and then, a few seconds later, they're all dry and shapeless and horribly ugly. I don't want them to ever think of me as something dead and horrible like that."

"You're their own, their child and their sister. They could never think of you other than the way you would want them to, the way you looked the last time they saw you."

"I'm still afraid," she said. "I can't help it, but I don't want Gerry to know it. If he gets back in time, I'm going to act like I'm not afraid at all and—"

The signal buzzer interrupted her, quick and imperative.   10

"Gerry!" She came to her feet. "It's Gerry now!"

He spun the volume control knob and asked, "Gerry Cross?"

"Yes," her brother answered, an undertone of tenseness to his reply. "The bad news—what is it?"

She answered for him, standing close behind him and leaning down a little toward the communicator, her hand resting small and cold on his shoulder.

"Hello, Gerry." There was only a faint quaver to betray the careful casualness of her voice. "I wanted to see you—"

"Marilyn!" There was sudden and terrible apprehension in the way   20 he spoke her name. "What are you doing on that EDS?"

"I wanted to see you," she said again. "I wanted to see you, so I hid on this ship—"

"You *hid* on it?"

"I'm a stowaway . . . I didn't know what it would mean—"

"*Marilyn!*" It was the cry of a man who calls, hopeless and desperate, to someone already and forever gone from him. "What have you done?"

"I . . . it's not—" Then her own composure broke and the cold little hand gripped his shoulder convulsively. "Don't, Gerry—I only wanted to see you; I didn't intend to hurt you. Please, Gerry, don't feel like that—"   30

Something warm and wet splashed on his wrist, and he slid out of the chair, to help her into it and swing the microphone down to her level.

"Don't feel like that. Don't let me go knowing you feel like that—"

The sob she had tried to hold back choked in her throat, and her brother spoke to her. "Don't cry, Marilyn." His voice was suddenly deep and infinitely gentle, with all the pain held out of it. "Don't cry, Sis—you mustn't do that. It's all right, honey—everything is all right."

"I—" Her lower lip quivered and she bit into it. "I didn't want you to feel that way—I just wanted us to say goodbye, because I have to go in a minute."   40

"Sure—sure. That's the way it'll be, Sis. I didn't mean to sound the way I did." Then his voice changed to a tone of quick and urgent demand. "EDS—have you called the *Stardust*? Did you check with the computers?"

"I called the *Stardust* almost an hour ago. It can't turn back, there are no other cruisers within forty light-years, and there isn't enough fuel."

"Are you sure that the computers had the correct data—sure of everything?"

"Yes—do you think I could ever let it happen if I wasn't sure? I did everything I could do. If there was anything at all I could do now, I would do it."

"He tried to help me, Gerry." Her lower lip was no longer trembling 10 and the short sleeves of her blouse were wet where she had dried her tears. "No one can help me and I'm not going to cry any more and everything will be all right with you and Daddy and Mama, won't it?"

"Sure—sure it will. We'll make out fine."

Her brother's words were beginning to come in more faintly, and he turned the volume control to maximum. "He's going out of range," he said to her. "He'll be gone within another minute."

"You're fading out, Gerry," she said. "You're going out of range. I wanted to tell you—but I can't now. We must say goodbye so soon—but maybe I'll see you again. Maybe I'll come to you in your dreams with 20 my hair in braids and crying because the kitten in my arms is dead; maybe I'll be the touch of a breeze that whispers to you as it goes by; maybe I'll be one of those gold-winged larks you told me about, singing my silly head off to you; maybe, at times, I'll be nothing you can see, but you will know I'm there beside you. Think of me like that, Gerry; always like that and not—the other way."

Dimmed to a whisper by the turning of Woden, the answer came back:

"Always like that, Marilyn—always like that and never any other way."

"Our time is up, Gerry—I have to go now. Good—" Her voice broke in mid-word and her mouth tried to twist into crying. She pressed her hand 30 hard against it and when she spoke again the words came clear and true:

"Goodbye, Gerry."

Faint and ineffably poignant and tender, the last words came from the cold metal of the communicator:

"Goodbye, little sister . . ."

She sat motionless in the hush that followed, as though listening to the shadow-echoes of the words as they died away, then she turned away from the communicator, toward the air lock, and he pulled down the black lever beside him. The inner door of the air lock slid swiftly open, to reveal the bare little cell that was waiting for her, and she walked to it. 40

She walked with her head up and the brown curls brushing her shoulders, with the white sandals stepping as sure and steady as the fractional gravity would permit and the gilded buckles twinkling with little lights of blue and red and crystal. He let her walk alone and made no move to help her, knowing she would not want it that way. She stepped into the air lock and turned to face him, only the pulse in her throat to betray the wild beating of her heart.

"I'm ready," she said.

He pushed the lever up and the door slid its quick barrier between them, enclosing her in black and utter darkness for her last moments of life. It clicked as it locked in place and he jerked down the red lever. There was a slight waver to the ship as the air gushed from the lock, a 10 vibration to the wall as though something had bumped the outer door in passing, then there was nothing and the ship was dropping true and steady again. He shoved the red lever back to close the door on the empty air lock and turned away, to walk to the pilot's chair with the slow steps of a man old and weary.

Back in the pilot's chair he pressed the signal button of the normal-space transmitter. There was no response; he had expected none. Her brother would have to wait through the night until the turning of Woden permitted contact through Group One.

It was not yet time to resume deceleration, and he waited while the 20 ship dropped endlessly downward with him and the drives purred softly. He saw that the white hand of the supplies-closet temperature gauge was on zero. A cold equation had been balanced and he was alone on the ship. Something shapeless and ugly was hurrying ahead of him, going to Woden, where her brother was waiting through the night, but the empty ship still lived for a little while with the presence of the girl who had not known about the forces that killed with neither hatred nor malice. It seemed, almost, that she still sat, small and bewildered and frightened, on the metal box beside him, her words echoing hauntingly clear in the void she had left behind her: 30

I didn't do anything to die for . . . I didn't do anything . . .

REVIEWING THE STORY _____

THE MAIN IDEA

1. "The Cold Equations" of the title refer to the fact that
   (a) the temperature inside the EDS must remain cold.
   (b) scientists who deal with equations are heartless.
   (c) the laws of nature cannot be changed no matter what the situation.
   (d) space journeys are not for young girls.

DETAILS

2. An EDS is chiefly designed for

    (a) intergalactic travel through hyperspace.

    (b) close attack with blasters on enemy ships.

    (c) short emergency rescue missions in normal space.

    (d) detection and jettison of stowaways.

3. A tornado on Woden had destroyed

    (a) the only EDS on the planet.

    (b) the supply of serum.

    (c) a priceless collection of green kala midges.

    (d) the radio of exploration Group One.

4. Why is a stowaway a problem on an EDS?

    (a) There is not enough food on board for two persons.

    (b) The stowaway may be sick with the fever carried by the green kala midges.

    (c) The supply of oxygen on the ship has been precisely calculated for only one person.

    (d) The added weight causes the ship to use up too much fuel and crash.

5. Even though the pilot believes it won't help, he first calls

    (a) his superior back on Earth.

    (b) Commander Delhart on the *Stardust*.

    (c) the girl's brother on Woden.

    (d) the clerk in Ship's Records.

6. The girl and her brother

    (a) were both highly trained scientists.

    (b) came from a poor family on Earth.

    (c) used their wealth to tour the galaxies.

    (d) did not care for each other.

ORDER OF EVENTS

7. Choose the letter that gives the order in which the events happen.

    (1) The pilot discovers the girl on the EDS.

    (2) The *Stardust* receives a call for help from Woden.

    (3) The pilot calls the *Stardust* on his radio.

    (4) The girl and her brother talk on the radio.

        (a) 2-1-3-4   **(b)** 4-3-2-1   **(c)** 1-2-3-4   **(d)** 4-1-3-2

CAUSE AND EFFECT

8. As soon as the girl is discovered hiding on the EDS, she is destined to die because of the lack of extra **(a)** fuel **(b)** food **(c)** oxygen **(d)** time.

9. The pilot reduces the rate of deceleration of the EDS in order to

   (a) save the girl from certain death.
   (b) make the girl's trip more comfortable.
   (c) give the girl more time to live.
   (d) reach Woden sooner.

INFERENCES

10. Pilot Barton and Commander Delhart are both men who are

    (a) self-disciplined but kind.
    (b) cold and calculating.
    (c) romantic and impulsive.
    (d) ambitious but fair.

11. The story takes place in the year

    (a) 1998   **(b)** 2000   **(c)** 2160   **(d)** 2178.

    (*Hint*: See page 34.)

PREDICTING OUTCOMES

12. If the pilot were to meet Gerry Cross on Woden, the girl's brother would probably

    (a) accuse him of murder.
    (b) ask where Marilyn was.
    (c) understand and forgive him.
    (d) hate him forever.

BUILDING YOUR VOCABULARY

1. He was an EDS pilot, *inured* to the sight of death, long since accustomed to it and to viewing the dying of another man with an objective lack of emotion . . . .

   a. Inured (page 27, lines 11-13) means **(a)** upset by **(b)** used to **(c)** injured by **(d)** partial to.

    b. The BEST strategy for answering part *a* is to

        (a) skim the rest of the paragraph.

        (b) study the rest of the sentence for context clues.

        (c) look for other uses of the word in the story.

        (d) note the spelling of *inured*.

2. Additional fuel would be used . . ., *infinitesimal* increments of fuel that would not be missed until the ship had almost reached its destination.

    Infinitesimal (page 29, lines 5-8) means extremely **(a)** large **(b)** small **(c)** energetic **(d)** valuable.

3. It seemed he could hear the whisper of a *furtive* movement inside the closet, then nothing.

    Furtive (page 29, lines 23-24) means **(a)** secret **(b)** distant **(c)** rapid **(d)** wild.

4. Marilyn Lee Cross would be but a *poignant* memory for an EDS pilot . . . .

    Something *poignant* (page 38, lines 39-40) is **(a)** frightening **(b)** fast fading **(c)** deeply emotional **(d)** pointless.

5. The signal buzzer interrupted her, quick and *imperative*.

    Imperative (page 46, line 10) means **(a)** soothing **(b)** commanding **(c)** musical **(d)** amusing.

STUDYING THE WRITER'S CRAFT

1. A *metaphor* is a figure of speech that compares two things without the use of *like* or *as*. Consider this example from the story (page 30, lines 7-9): "She obeyed, his silence making the smile fade into the meek and guilty expression of a pup that has been caught in mischief and knows it must be punished."

    a. How does the comparison of the girl to a puppy influence our feelings about her?

    b. What is the effect of comparing the punishment of a mischievous puppy to the punishment the girl must face?

2. The story is told through the pilot, in the ***third-person point of view*** ("he"). Why do you think the author decided to tell the story through the perceptions and thoughts of the pilot rather than those of the girl?

3. In a short story, the use of *suspense* first hooks us and then keeps us reading. Suspense makes us wonder, "What will happen next? How will things work out?"

   a. How is suspense used in the opening pages of the story (page 27, line 1, to page 29, line 40)?

   b. What is the element of suspense in the pilot's radio call to the girl's brother (page 41, line 7, to page 46, line 12)?

   c. What crucial question keeps us in suspense through most of the story?

ACTIVITIES FOR LISTENING, SPEAKING, WRITING

1. Imagine that you are a movie or TV critic. Choose a movie or TV show about space travel that you have seen, and write a brief review of it for your school paper. Does the movie or TV show deal with the problems and dangers of space travel? Discuss this point in your review.

2. In "The Cold Equations," the pilot really has no choices. At best, he can only delay the inevitable. In real life, however, people in charge often must make hard choices. During wartime, for example, military doctors with limited medical facilities must decide quickly who can be saved and who is beyond medical help. This kind of life-or-death decision is called *triage*. In peacetime, too, advances in medical technology and limited resources may lead to a kind of triage. For example, there may be many patients needing organ transplants but relatively few available organs. Which patients will be chosen? Who decides? And how? Be prepared to discuss this difficult topic of triage with your classmates.

3. "The Cold Equations" poses a problem for which there is no satisfactory solution. Using fictitious names, write a brief sketch or story about a problem in your life or the life of someone else for which there seems to be no solution. How does the hero or heroine of your sketch or story cope with such a problem?

Wait It Out

by Larry Niven

Have I made a mistake? It won't kill me if I have. It could drive me mad, though.

Of the nine planets in our solar system, Pluto is the smallest, the coldest, and the most distant from the Sun. Imagine the horror of being marooned on such a planet! That's the nightmare facing the narrator of this brief tale of space travel to Pluto.

In the following story, three space travelers have flown three billion miles from Earth to explore this frozen lump of rock and ice. From the orbiting Earth-return vehicle, the two-man landing craft dropped to the surface of Pluto. Then disaster struck. The landing craft became stuck in the ice of the planet.

What would you do in such a fix? What could anybody do? If there is any way to survive such an ordeal, can you guess what it might be? Read on!

Like many other science-fiction writers, Larry Niven thinks and writes on a grand scale. Many of his individual short stories and novels form parts of a huge saga of future human history—the Known Space series. His best-known novels in this series are the *World of Ptavvs* (1966) and *Ringworld* (1970).

Also like other science-fiction writers, Niven has created a number of short stories and novels with coauthors. Most successful of these collaborations are the highly popular novels written with Jerry Pournelle, including *The Mote in God's Eye* (1974) and *Lucifer's Hammer* (1977).

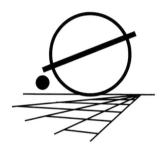

Night on Pluto. Sharp and distinct, the horizon line cuts across my field of vision. Below that broken line is the dim gray-white of snow seen by starlight. Above, space-blackness and space-bright stars. From behind a jagged row of frozen mountains the stars pour up in singletons and clusters and streamers of cold white dots. Slowly they move, but visibly, just fast enough for a steady eye to capture their motion.

Something wrong there. Pluto's rotation period is long: 6.39 days. Time must have slowed for me.

It should have stopped.

I wonder if I may have made a mistake.

The planet's small size brings the horizon close. It seems even closer without a haze of atmosphere to fog the distances. Two sharp peaks protrude into the star swarm like the filed front teeth of a cannibal warrior. In the cleft between those peaks shines a sudden bright point.

I recognize the Sun, though it shows no more disk than any other, dimmer star. The sun shines as a cold point between the frozen peaks; it pulls free of the rocks and shines in my eyes . . .

The Sun is gone, the starfield has shifted. I must have passed out.

It figures.

10

Have I made a mistake? It won't kill me if I have. It could drive me mad, though . . .

I don't feel mad. I don't feel anything, not pain, not loss, not regret, not fear. Not even pity. Just: *what a situation.*

Gray-white against gray-white: the landing craft, short and wide and conical, stands half-submerged in an icy plain below the level of my eyes. Here I stand, looking east, waiting.

Take a lesson: this is what comes of not wanting to die.

Pluto was not the most distant planet. It had stopped being that in 1979, ten years ago. Now Pluto was at perihelion, as close to the Sun— 10 and to Earth—as it would ever get. To ignore such an opportunity would have been sheer waste.

And so we came, Jerome and Sammy and I, in an inflated plastic bubble poised on an ion jet. We'd spent a year and a half in that bubble. After so long together, with so little privacy, perhaps we should have hated each other. We didn't. The UN psycho team must have chosen well.

But—just to be out of sight of the others, even for a few minutes. Just to have something to *do,* something that was not predictable. A new world could hold infinite surprises. As a matter of fact, so could our 20 laboratory-tested hardware. I don't think any of us really trusted the Nerva-K under our landing craft.

Think it through. For long trips in space, you use an ion jet giving low thrust over long periods of time. The ion motor on our own craft had been decades in use. Where gravity is materially lower than Earth's, you land on dependable chemical rockets. For landings on Earth and Venus, you use heat shields and the braking power of the atmosphere. For landing on the gas giants—but who would want to?

The Nerva-class fission rockets are used only for takeoff from Earth, where thrust and efficiency count. Responsiveness and maneuverability 30 count for too much during a powered landing. And a heavy planet will always have an atmosphere for braking.

Pluto didn't.

For Pluto, the chemical jets to take us down and bring us back up were too heavy to carry all that way. We needed a highly maneuverable Nerva-type atomic rocket motor using hydrogen for reaction mass.

And we had it. But we didn't trust it.

Jerome Glass and I went down, leaving Sammy Cross in orbit. He griped about that, of course. He'd started that back at the Cape and kept it up for a year and a half. But someone had to stay. Someone had to be 40 aboard the Earth-return vehicle, to fix anything that went wrong, to relay communications to Earth, and to fire the bombs that would solve Pluto's one genuine mystery.

We never did solve that one. Where *does* Pluto get all that mass? The planet's a dozen times as dense as it has any right to be. We could have solved that with the bombs, the same way they solved the mystery of the makeup of the Earth, sometime in the last century. They mapped the patterns of earthquake ripples moving through the Earth's bulk. But those ripples were from natural causes, like the Krakatoa[1] eruption. On Pluto the bombs would have done it better.

A bright star-sun blazes suddenly between two fangs of mountain. I wonder if they'll know the answers, when my vigil ends.

The sky jumps and steadies, and—

I'm looking east, out over the plain where we landed the ship. The plain and the mountains behind seem to be sinking like Atlantis:[2] an illusion created by the flowing stars. We slide endlessly down the black sky, Jerome and I and the mired ship.

The Nerva-K behaved perfectly. We hovered for several minutes to melt our way through various layers of frozen gases and get ourselves something solid to land on. Condensing volatiles steamed around us and boiled below, so that we settled in a soft white glow of fog lit by the hydrogen flame.

Black wet ground appeared below the curve of the landing skirt. I let the ship drop carefully, carefully . . . and we touched.

It took us an hour to check the ship and get ready to go outside. But who would be first? This was no idle matter. Pluto would be the solar system's last outpost for most of future history, and the statue to the first man on Pluto would probably remain untarnished forever.

Jerome won the toss. All for the sake of a turning coin, Jerome's would be the first name in the history books. I remember the grin I forced! I wish I could force one now. He was laughing and talking of marble statues as he went through the lock.

There's irony in that, if you like that sort of thing.

I was screwing down my helmet when Jerome started shouting obscenities into the helmet mike. I cut the checklist short and followed him out.

One look told it all.

The black wet dirt beneath our landing skirt had been dirty ice, water ice mixed haphazardly with lighter gases and ordinary rock. The heat

1. **Krakatoa:** volcano in Indonesia that erupted in 1883.
2. **Atlantis:** according to legend, an island or continent that sank into the Atlantic Ocean.

draining out of the Nerva jet had melted that ice. The rocks within the ice had sunk, and so had the landing vehicle, so that when the water froze again it was halfway up the hull. Our landing craft was sunk solid in the ice.

We could have done some exploring before we tried to move the ship. When we called Sammy, he suggested doing just that. But Sammy was up there in the Earth-return vehicle, and we were down here with our landing vehicle mired in the ice of another world.

We were terrified. Until we got clear we would be good for nothing, and we both knew it.

I wonder why I can't remember the fear.   10

We did have one chance. The landing vehicle was designed to move about on Pluto's surface; and so she had a skirt instead of landing jacks. Half a gravity of thrust would have given us a ground effect, safer and cheaper than using the ship like a ballistic missile. The landing skirt must have trapped gas underneath when the ship sank, leaving the Nerva-K engine in a bubble cavity.

We could melt our way out.

I know we were as careful as two terrified men could be. The heat rose in the Nerva-K, agonizingly slow. In flight there would have been a coolant effect as cold hydrogen fuel ran through the pile. We couldn't use 20 that. But the environment of the motor was terribly cold. The two factors might compensate, or—

Suddenly dials went wild. Something had cracked from the savage temperature differential. Jerome used the damper rods without effect. Maybe they'd melted. Maybe wiring had cracked, or resistors had become superconductors in the cold. Maybe the pile—but it doesn't matter now.

I wonder why I can't remember the fear.

Sunlight—

And a logy, dreamy feeling. I'm conscious again. The same stars rise in formation over the same dark mountains.   30

Something heavy is nosing up against me. I feel its weight against my back and the backs of my legs. What is it? Why am I not terrified?

It slides around in front of me, questing. It looks like a huge amoeba, shapeless and translucent, with darker bodies showing within it. I'd guess it's about my own weight.

Life on Pluto! But how? Superfluids? Helium II contaminated by complex molecules? In that case the beast had best get moving; it will need shade come sunrise. Sunside temperature on Pluto is all of 50° Absolute.[3]

---

3. **Absolute** (also called *Kelvin*): temperature scale used to measure extremely low temperatures. (A temperature of 50° Absolute is about –376° Fahrenheit.)

No, come back! It's leaving, flowing down toward the splash crater. Did my thoughts send it away? Nonsense. It probably didn't like the taste of me. It must be terribly slow, that I can watch it move. The beast is still visible, blurred because I can't look directly at it, moving downhill toward the landing vehicle and the tiny statue to the first man to die on Pluto.

After the fiasco with the Nerva-K, one of us had to go down and see how much damage had been done. That meant tunneling down with the flame of a jet backpack, then crawling under the landing skirt. We didn't talk about the implications. We were probably dead. The man who went down into the bubble cavity was even more probably dead; but 10 what of it? Dead is dead.

I feel no guilt. I'd have gone myself if I'd lost the toss.

The Nerva-K had spewed fused bits of the fission pile all over the bubble cavity. We were trapped for good. Rather, I was trapped, and Jerome was dead. The bubble cavity was a hell of radiation.

Jerome had been swearing softly as he went in. He came out perfectly silent. He'd used up all the good words on lighter matters, I think.

I remember I was crying, partly from grief and partly from fear. I remember that I kept my voice steady in spite of it. Jerome never knew. What he guessed is his own affair. He told me the situation, he told me 20 goodbye, and then he strode out onto the ice and took off his helmet. A fuzzy white ball engulfed his head, exploded outward, then settled to the ground in microscopic snowflakes.

But all that seems infinitely remote. Jerome stands out there with his helmet clutched in his hands: a statue to himself, the first man on Pluto. A frost of recondensed moisture conceals his expression.

Sunrise. I hope the amoeba—

That was wild. The sun stood poised for an instant, a white point-source between twin peaks. Then it streaked upward—and the spinning sky jolted to a stop. No wonder I didn't catch it before. It happened so fast. 30

A horrible thought. What has happened to me could have happened to Jerome! I wonder—

There was Sammy in the Earth-return vehicle, but he couldn't get down to me. I couldn't get up. The life system was in good order, but sooner or later I would freeze to death or run out of air.

I stayed with the landing vehicle about thirty hours, taking ice and soil samples, analyzing them, delivering the data to Sammy via laser beam; delivering also high-minded last messages, and feeling sorry for myself. On my trips outside I kept passing Jerome's statue. For a corpse, and one which has not been prettified by the post-surgical skills of an 40 embalmer, he looks good. His frost-dusted skin is indistinguishable from marble, and his eyes are lifted toward the stars in poignant yearning. Each time I passed him I wondered how I would look when my turn came.

"You've got to find an oxygen layer," Sammy kept saying.

"Why?"

"To keep you alive! Sooner or later they'll send a rescue ship. You can't give up now!"

I'd already given up. There was oxygen, but there was no such layer as Sammy kept hoping for. There were veins of oxygen mixed with other things, like veins of gold ore in rock. Too little, too finely distributed.

"Then use the water ice! That's only poetic justice, isn't it? You can 10 get the oxygen out by electrolysis!"[4]

But a rescue ship would take years. They'd have to build it from scratch, and redesign the landing vehicle too. Electrolysis takes power, and heat takes power. I had only the batteries.

Sooner or later I'd run out of power. Sammy couldn't see this. He was more desperate than I was. I didn't run out of last messages; I stopped sending them because they were driving Sammy crazy.

I passed Jerome's statue one time too many, and an idea came.

This is what comes of not wanting to die.

In Nevada, three billion miles from here, half a million corpses lie 20 frozen in vaults surrounded by liquid nitrogen. Half a million dead men wait for an earthly resurrection, on the day medical science discovers how to unfreeze them safely, how to cure what was killing each one of them, how to cure the additional damage done by ice crystals breaking cell walls all through their brains and bodies.

Half a million fools? But what choice did they have? They were dying.

I was dying.

A man can stay conscious for tens of seconds in vacuum. If I moved fast, I could get out of my suit in that time. Without that insulation to protect me, Pluto's black night would suck warmth from my body in 30 seconds. At 50° Absolute, I'd stay in frozen storage until one version or another of the Day of Resurrection.

Sunlight—

—And stars. No sign of the big blob that found me so singularly tasteless yesterday. But I could be looking in the wrong direction.

I hope it got to cover.

I'm looking east, out over the splash plain. In my peripheral vision the ship looks unchanged and undamaged.

---

4. **electrolysis:** use of an electric current to break down a compound into its component elements—for example, water into hydrogen and oxygen.

My suit lies beside me on the ice. I stand on a peak of black rock, poised in my silvered underwear, looking eternally out at the horizon. Before the cold touched my brain I found a last moment in which to assume a heroic stance. Go east, young man. Wouldn't you know I'd get my directions mixed? But the fog of my breathing-air hid everything, and I was moving in terrible haste.

Sammy Cross must be on his way home now. He'll tell them where I am.

Stars pour up from behind the mountains. The mountains and the splash plain and Jerome and I sink endlessly beneath the sky.   10

My corpse must be the coldest in history. Even the hopeful dead of Earth are only stored at liquid nitrogen temperatures. Pluto's night makes that look torrid, after the 50° Absolute heat of day seeps away into space.

A superconductor is what I am. Sunlight raises the temperature too high, switching me off like a machine at every dawn. But at night my nervous system becomes a superconductor. Currents flow; thoughts flow; sensations flow. Sluggishly. The one hundred and fifty-three hours of Pluto's rotation flash by in what feels like fifteen minutes. At that rate I can wait it out.

I stand as a statue and a viewpoint. No wonder I can't get emotional 20 about anything. Water is a rock here, and my glands are contoured ice within me. But I feel sensations: the pull of gravity, the pain in my ears, the tug of vacuum over every square inch of my body. The vacuum will not boil my blood. But the tensions are frozen into the ice of me, and my nerves tell me so. I feel the wind whistling from my lips, like an exhalation of cigarette smoke.

This is what comes of not wanting to die. What a joke if I got my wish!

Do you suppose they'll find me? Pluto's small for a planet. For a place to get lost in, a small planet is all too large. But there's the ship.

Though it seems to be covered with frost. Vaporized gases recon- 30 densed on the hull. Gray-white on gray-white, a lump on a dish of re-frozen ice. I could stand here forever waiting for them to pick my ship from its surroundings.

Stop that.

Sunlight—

Stars rolling up the sky. The same patterns, endlessly rolling up from the same points. Does Jerome's corpse live the same half-life I live now? He should have stripped, as I did. I wish I'd thought to wipe the ice from his eyes!

I wish that superfluid blob would come back.   40

Damn. It's *cold*.

REVIEWING THE STORY

THE MAIN IDEA

1. In this story, the narrator, or speaker
   (a) leaves Jerome and Sammy on Pluto.
   (b) solves the mystery of Pluto's great density.
   (c) succeeds in rejoining the Earth-return vehicle.
   (d) figures out how to stay alive until he is rescued.

DETAILS

2. The narrator is (a) an unnamed astronaut (b) Sammy Cross (c) Jerome Glass (d) Larry Niven.

3. As the story opens, the narrator is standing
   (a) inside the landing craft.
   (b) back on Earth.
   (c) upon a rock on Pluto.
   (d) in the Earth-return vehicle orbiting Pluto.

4. Pluto is
   (a) hot both night and day.
   (b) cold both night and day.
   (c) the planet closest to the Earth.
   (d) one of the largest planets.

5. The landing craft can't get free from the ice because of a breakdown in
   (a) communications with Earth.
   (b) cooperation among the three astronauts.
   (c) the oxygen supply.
   (d) the Nerva-K engine.

6. The narrator's idea for surviving on Pluto comes from
   (a) remembering frozen corpses back on Earth.
   (b) seeing the superfluid amoeba-like blob.
   (c) adopting a suggestion from Sammy Cross in the Earth-return vehicle.
   (d) taking Jerome Glass's last words of advice.

ORDER OF EVENTS

7. Choose the letter of the event that takes place FIRST in the story.

   (a) The narrator takes off his space suit outside.
   (b) Jerome goes out onto the ice and removes his helmet.
   (c) They try to melt their way out of the ice.
   (d) They toss a coin to decide who will be first on Pluto.

CAUSE AND EFFECT

8. Jerome Glass goes outside and takes off his helmet because

   (a) he decides to sacrifice himself to save the narrator.
   (b) Sammy Cross orders him to do so.
   (c) he has been exposed to a lethal dose of radiation.
   (d) he wants to get a better look at the superfluid blob.

9. The narrator becomes conscious at night because

   (a) warmth from the amoeba thaws out his frozen nervous system.
   (b) his space suit no longer operates in sunlight.
   (c) the extreme cold turns his nervous system into a superconductor.
   (d) Pluto faces the Earth at that time.

INFERENCES

10. The narrator's comment that the superfluid amoeba-like blob "will need shade come sunrise" because the daytime "temperature on Pluto is all of 50° Absolute" is (a) serious (b) humorous (c) impatient (d) sad.

11. The story takes place in (a) 1979 (b) 1989 (c) 1999 (d) 2009. (*Hint*: See page 55.)

PREDICTING OUTCOMES

12. For the narrator to be rescued, he would have to be

   (a) brought back to Earth.
   (b) given artificial respiration.
   (c) cured of radioactive poisoning.
   (d) safely thawed out.

BUILDING YOUR VOCABULARY _____

1. I wonder if they'll know the answers, when my *vigil* ends.

   A *vigil* (page 56, line 11) is a(an)
   (a) period of watchful waiting.
   (b) lifetime.
   (c) moment of prayer.
   (d) ordeal.

2. The black wet dirt beneath our landing skirt had been dirty ice, water ice mixed *haphazardly* with lighter gases and ordinary rock.

   Haphazardly (page 56, lines 36-37) means (a) thoroughly (b) randomly (c) fortunately (d) dangerously.

3. It looks like a huge amoeba, shapeless and *translucent*, with darker bodies showing within it.

   Trans- means "across or through" and *lucent* means "light." You can combine these facts with the rest of the sentence to infer that when something is *translucent* (page 57, lines 33-34), it
   (a) can be set on fire.
   (b) can be lifted easily.
   (c) contains darker bodies.
   (d) can be seen through.

4. After the *fiasco* with the Nerva-K, one of us had to go down and see how much damage had been done.

   A *fiasco* (page 58, lines 6-7) is a(an) (a) introduction (b) great success (c) total failure (d) false image.

5. Pluto's night makes that look *torrid*, after the 50° Absolute heat of day seeps away into space.

   Something *torrid* (page 60, lines 12-13) is (a) frightening (b) cold (c) hot (d) dark.

STUDYING THE WRITER'S CRAFT _____

1. Writers often use *foreshadowing* to hint at what will happen later in the story. How does each of the following foreshadow a later event?

   a. I don't think any of us really trusted the Nerva-K under our landing craft. (page 55, lines 21-22) *b.* He [Jerome] was laughing and talking of marble statues as he went through the lock. (page 56, lines 30-31)

c. This is what comes of not wanting to die. (page 55, line 8; page 59, line 19; page 60, line 27)

2. Despite the narrator's desperate situation, the **mood** of the story is neither bleak nor depressing. Mention some of the humorous touches that help keep the mood light.

3. Look again at the several references to the strange amoeba-like creature the narrator sees on Pluto. (page 57, lines 31-38; page 58, lines 1-5 and 27; page 59, lines 34-36; page 60, line 40) What do these references add to the **characterization** of the narrator? What trait in him do they suggest?

ACTIVITIES FOR LISTENING, SPEAKING, WRITING

1. Listen while two or more of your classmates debate the following question: "Given the situation of the narrator in 'Wait It Out,' would you choose instant death, as Jerome Glass did, or a period of suspended animation that could last for years or even forever, as the narrator did? Explain the reasons for your decision." Take notes on the debate, and be prepared to tell which side made the better argument, and why.

2. Looking beyond the story, you would assume that Sammy Cross begins the long voyage home in the Earth-return vehicle. Alone for a year and a half in the inflated plastic bubble, he keeps a diary of his thoughts and feelings. He records what has happened and his hopes and fears for the future. Imagine that you are Sammy, and write one or more entries for this diary.

3. Even a happy ending can have its own bizarre twist. Suppose that some fifty years later a rescue team finds the narrator on Pluto, successfully restores him to life, and carries him back to Earth. In his frozen sleep, he has not aged a day. His family and friends on Earth, however, are now fifty years older. (His children—if he had any—would probably be older than he is.) For a newspaper or magazine, write a brief human-interest article about an interview you had with the narrator. Describe what happened to him back on Earth and how he feels about it. Give your article a striking headline.

Exploring Other Worlds and Protecting This One: The Connection

by Carl Sagan

Other planets provide important insights about what dumb things not to do to Earth.

In the following article, the eminent space scientist and author Carl Sagan argues that planetary exploration can teach us important lessons about our own planet. Describing three global disasters that could overtake us, he explains how understanding other planets may help us save our own.

So far, the exploration of other planets, starting with Mars, has been limited to robots. Some day, this robotic exploration may give way to human exploration. Would you want to be one of the explorers sent to other planets? Why or why not?

Few scientists are better equipped than Carl Sagan to make the case for space exploration. For thirty years, he has written and lectured widely on the subject. He created and presented the educational television series *Cosmos*, and he has written works such as *Broca's Brain* (1979) and *Contact* (1985).

Dr. Sagan is a professor of astronomy and space sciences at Cornell University. He advises many scientific organizations, including the National Aeronautics and Space Administration (NASA), the National Academy of Science, and the Smithsonian Institution. He also serves as President of The Planetary Society, from whose publication, *The Planetary Report*, the article in this book has been reprinted.

The *Apollo* images of Earth from space revealed plainly the fragility and vulnerability of our lovely little world, and powerfully assisted the coming of age of a global ecological consciousness. Such pictures by themselves may be worth the whole cost of the space program, because their meaning has reached so many. But what is not so widely understood is how much vital and urgent information we have gained about our own world from robotic exploration of other worlds.

If we are stuck on one world, we are limited to a single case; we do not know what else is possible. Then like a linguist who knows only English, or a physicist who knows about gravity only from falling bodies 10 on Earth, our insights are narrow and our predictive abilities severely circumscribed. But when we explore other worlds, our perspective widens. We gain a new understanding of worlds in general, including our own.

Robotic exploration of other worlds has already opened our eyes in many fields of Earth science, including the study of volcanoes, earthquakes and weather. It may turn out to have profound implications for biology because all life on Earth is built on a common biochemical master plan. The discovery of a single extraterrestrial organism—even something as humble as a bacterium—would revolutionize biology. But the connection between exploring other worlds and protecting our own is most evident in the study of Earth's climate and the burgeoning threat to the climate that our technology now represents. Other planets provide important insights about what dumb things not to do to Earth.

Three environmental catastrophes, or potential catastrophes, have been uncovered accidentally, mainly in the last two decades: ozonosphere depletion, greenhouse warming, and nuclear winter. I want briefly to sketch some of the ways in which planetary exploration aided and deep- 10 ened these findings.

THINNING OZONE SHIELD

It was disquieting to discover that an inert material with all sorts of practical functions—it serves as the working fluid in refrigerators and air conditioners, as propellant for deodorants and other products in aerosol cans and as lightweight foamy packaging for fast foods, to name only a few—can pose a danger to life on Earth. Who would have figured it?

The molecules in question are called chlorofluorocarbons (CFCs). They are extremely chemically inert, which means they are invulnerable— until they find themselves up in the ozone layer, where they are dissoci- 20 ated[1] by sunlight. The chlorine atoms thus liberated deplete the ozone and let more ultraviolet light from the Sun reach the ground.

This increased ultraviolet intensity ushers in a ghastly procession of potential consequences involving not just skin cancer, but the weakening of the human immune system and, most dangerous of all, the destruction of agriculture and of photosynthetic microorganisms at the base of the food chain on which most life on Earth depends.

The principal manufacturer of this material, the Dupont company (which gave it the brand name Freon)—after years of pooh-poohing the concern of environmentalists, after taking out full-page ads in newspapers 30 and scientific magazines claiming that the uproar all came from wild extrapolations from inadequate data, that nobody had actually demonstrated any peril—that company has now announced that it will rapidly phase out all its CFC production. The precipitating event seems to have been the discovery in 1986 by British scientists of a hole in the Antarctic ozone layer. There is now good evidence of thinning of the ozone layer at other latitudes as well.

---

1. **dissociated:** broken down into simpler parts.

Who discovered that CFCs posed a threat to the ozone layer? Was it Dupont exercising corporate responsibility? Nope. Was it the Environmental Protection Agency protecting us? Nope. Was it the Department of Defense defending us? Nope. It was two ivory-tower, white-coated university scientists working in 1974 on something else—Sherwood Rowland and Mario Molina of the University of California, Irvine.

Their work used reaction rate constants of chemical reactions involving chlorine and other halogens, determined in part with NASA support. Why NASA? Because Venus has chlorine and fluorine molecules in its atmosphere—as discovered by US spacecraft and ground-based observations—and planetary aeronomers wanted to understand what's happening there. 10

THANK YOU, VENUS

Confirming theoretical work on ozone depletion was done with a big computer model by a group led by Michael McElroy at Harvard. How is it they had all these branching networks of halogen chemical kinetics[2] in their computer ready to go? Because they were working on the halogen chemistry of the atmosphere of Venus. Venus helped make the discovery that the Earth's ozone layer is in danger. (Such serendipity, by the way, is found in many discoveries in science.)

There is an absolutely unexpected connection between the atmospheric photochemistries of two planets, and suddenly a very practical result emerges from the most blue-sky, abstract kind of work, understanding the upper atmosphere of Venus.

There is also a Mars connection to ozone depletion on Earth. *Viking* found the surface of Mars to be lifeless and remarkably deficient even in simple organic molecules. This deficiency is widely understood as due to the lack of ozone in the Martian atmosphere. Ultraviolet light from the Sun strikes the surface of Mars unimpeded; if any organic matter were there, it would be quickly destroyed by solar ultraviolet light or the oxidation products of solar ultraviolet light. Thus part of the reason that the topmost layers of Mars are antiseptic is that Mars has an ozone hole of planetary dimensions—a possibly useful cautionary tale for us, who are busily making holes in our ozone layer.

CO_2[3] AND THE GREENHOUSE EFFECT

Now let's look at global warming from the increasing greenhouse effect, which derives largely from carbon dioxide generated by the burning of fossil fuels—but also from the buildup of other infrared-absorbing gases (oxides of nitrogen, methane, those same CFCs and some other molecules). Some of the important recent work on global warming has been done by James Hansen and his colleagues at the Goddard Institute for Space Sciences, a NASA facility in New York City.

Hansen and his colleagues point out that over the last hundred years the five warmest years in terms of average global temperature have been in the 1980s. If their current projections prove correct, and world temperatures continue to be driven up by the increasing levels of carbon

2. **kinetics** (ki-NET-iks): study of motion and the forces affecting it.
3. **CO_2:** carbon dioxide.

dioxide and other gases in Earth's atmosphere, then 1990 will be the warmest year in the last 120,000.[4]

Some of the consequences projected by various climatologists to the middle and end of the next century include the conversion of the Soviet Ukraine and the American Midwest, the breadbasket of the world, to something approaching scrub deserts. The slow volume expansion of sea water, the melting of glacial and polar ice and later the collapse of the West Antarctic ice sheet would cause the inundation[5] of every coastal city on the planet. Now that's serious. Mitigating this warming will be very expensive.   10

Hansen has played a major role before committees of the House and Senate, convincing them to take the threat of global warming seriously. How did Hansen get involved with the issue of Earth's climatic future in the first place? As a graduate student at the University of Iowa, he wrote a doctoral thesis that attempted (mistakenly, we now know) to disprove the contention that Venus was hot because of a massive greenhouse effect there. Venus got Hansen thinking about the greenhouse effect.

Those who are skeptical about carbon dioxide greenhouse warming might profitably note the massive greenhouse on Venus, where the atmosphere is primarily carbon dioxide, the surface pressure is about 90   20 times that on Earth, and the surface temperature is about 900 degrees Fahrenheit (480 degrees Celsius). No one proposes that Venus' runaway greenhouse effect was caused by Venusians who burned too much coal, drove fuel-inefficient autos or cut down their forests. That's not the point. But the climatological history of our planetary neighbor, an otherwise Earthlike planet on which the surface became hot enough to melt tin or lead, is worth considering—especially by those who say that the increasing greenhouse effect on Earth will be self-correcting, that we don't really have to worry about it.

NUCLEAR WINTER   30

Nuclear winter is the darkening and cooling of the Earth, mainly from fine smoke particles injected into the atmosphere from the burning of cities and petroleum facilities that would follow even a "small" nuclear war.

There has been a vigorous scientific debate on just how serious nuclear winter is likely to be. The debate has now largely converged. Most

---

4. *Editor's Note:* The 1992 *World Almanac* did, in fact, list 1990 as the warmest year since 1880, with an average global temperature of 59.81 degrees.
5. **inundation** (in-un-DAY-shun): flooding.

three-dimensional general circulation models now get nearly the same answer provided they use the same starting conditions. That answer is close to the results first announced in 1982/1983 by a team of five scientists, to which I'm proud to belong, called TTAPS (for Richard P. Turco, Owen B. Toon, Thomas Ackerman, James Pollack and myself). Of the five TTAPS scientists, three are nearly full-time planetary scientists, and the other two have published many papers in planetary science.

The earliest intimation of nuclear winter came during the *Mariner 9* mission to Mars, when there was a global dust storm and we were unable to see the surface of the planet; the infrared spectrometer on *Mariner 9* 10 found the high atmosphere to be warmer and the surface colder than it ought to have been. We sat down and tried to calculate how that could come about. Eventually this line of inquiry led us from dust storms on Mars to nuclear winter on Earth.

PLANETARY PERSPECTIVE

Planetary science provides a global perspective, a big interdisciplinary picture that turns out to be very helpful in finding and attempting to define these looming climate catastrophes. When you cut your teeth studying other worlds, you develop a point of view—one very useful in understanding this world. There are probably other such catastrophes 20 still to be uncovered. When they emerge, I think it likely that planetary science will play an important role in discovering and assessing them.

When I look at the evidence, I find that planetary exploration is of the most practical and urgent utility for us here on Earth. Even if we were not concerned about exploration, even if we did not have a nanogram of adventuresome spirit in us, even if we were only concerned for ourselves in the narrowest sense, planetary exploration would be a superb investment. NASA ought to make this case.

REVIEWING THE ARTICLE _____

THE MAIN IDEA

1. Which of the following headlines best summarizes the main idea of the article?
   (a) Venus and the Greenhouse Effect
   (b) Earth Studies Solve Puzzles of Planets
   (c) Planetary Probes Help in Protecting Earth
   (d) NASA's Role in Space Exploration

DETAILS

2. The layer of atmospheric ozone surrounding the Earth is referred to as the "ozone shield" because it
   (a) renders chlorofluorocarbon molecules harmless.
   (b) keeps the oxygen we breathe from escaping into outer space.
   (c) protects the Earth from being struck by meteorites.
   (d) blocks dangerous ultraviolet rays emitted by the Sun.

3. The ozone layer is damaged by (a) ultraviolet rays. (b) carbon dioxide. (c) chlorofluorocarbons. (d) fine smoke particles.

4. The greenhouse effect involves (a) improvements in agriculture. (b) darkening and cooling of the Earth. (c) increases in skin cancer. (d) global warming.

5. Two global consequences of the greenhouse effect are
   (a) skin cancer and weakening of the human immune system.
   (b) improvements in agriculture and benefits to the food chain.
   (c) creation of deserts and coastal flooding.
   (d) darkening and cooling of the Earth.

6. A global dust storm on Mars led scientists to realize the possibility of a
   (a) nuclear winter on Earth.
   (b) massive greenhouse effect on Mars.
   (c) serious threat to the ozone shield.
   (d) failure of the *Mariner 9* space mission to Mars.

ORDER OF EVENTS

7. Choose the letter that gives the order in which the events happen.
   (1) As more ultraviolet rays reach Earth, living creatures are harmed.
   (2) Chlorine atoms from chlorofluorocarbons (CFCs) damage the Earth's ozone shield.
   (3) Sunlight breaks down CFCs, releasing chlorine atoms.
   (a) 2-3-1   (b) 3-2-1   (c) 1-3-2   (d) 1-2-3

CAUSE AND EFFECT

8. One cause of the greenhouse effect is
   (a) burning coal and oil.
   (b) fighting a nuclear war.

(c) allowing more ultraviolet radiation to reach the Earth.

(d) exploring other planets.

9. According to Dr. Sagan, the most practical effect of planetary exploration has been the

(a) discovery of extraterrestrial organisms.

(b) banning of even "small" nuclear wars.

(c) understanding of potential climatic catastrophes on Earth.

(d) understanding of climatic conditions on other planets.

INFERENCES

10. The three discoveries described in the article were made by

(a) the Department of Defense.

(b) corporate researchers.

(c) atomic scientists.

(d) planetary scientists.

11. After rereading the last paragraph of the article, you can infer that Dr. Sagan would like to see

(a) greater support for planetary exploration.

(b) less funding for NASA.

(c) more manned space flights than robotic ones.

(d) an increase in the U.S. nuclear arsenal.

PREDICTING OUTCOMES

12. Dr. Sagan suggests that if we continue to make holes in our ozone layer, the Earth may become as lifeless as **(a)** Venus **(b)** Mars **(c)** Mercury **(d)** the Moon.

BUILDING YOUR VOCABULARY

1. But the connection between exploring other worlds and protecting our own is most evident in the study of Earth's climate and the *burgeoning* threat to the climate that our technology now represents.

Burgeoning (page 67, lines 2-5) means **(a)** long recognized **(b)** slowly decreasing **(c)** rapidly growing **(d)** secret.

2. It was *disquieting* to discover that an inert material with all sorts of practical functions . . . can pose a danger to life on Earth.

    a. Something *disquieting* (page 67 lines 13-17 is **(a)** noisy **(b)** disturbing **(c)** silent **(d)** reassuring.

    b. The BEST strategy for answering part *a* is to

        (a) analyze the word into its parts: *dis-* (not) + *quieting.*

        (b) look for other uses of the word in the article.

        (c) reread the paragraph containing *disquieting.*

        (d) reread the entire section on ozone depletion.

3. The chlorine atoms thus liberated *deplete* the ozone and let more ultraviolet light from the Sun reach the ground.

The prefix *de-* appears in such words as *deactivate* (to make *not* active) and *devalue* (to make *less* in value). The root *plete* appears in such words as *complete* (full or perfect) and *replete* (abundantly full). From these clues, you can infer that *deplete* (page 67, lines 21-22) means to **(a)** increase **(b)** decrease **(c)** repeat **(d)** free.

4. Thus part of the reason that the topmost layers of Mars are *antiseptic* is that Mars has an ozone hole of planetary dimensions . . . .

The word *antiseptic* usually means free of germs. In the context of this sentence, however, *antiseptic* (page 69, lines 19-21) means **(a)** full of germs **(b)** poisonous **(c)** without life **(d)** extremely hot.

5. The earliest *intimation* of nuclear winter came during the *Mariner 9* mission to Mars . . . .

An *intimation* (page 71, lines 8-9) is a(an)

(a) explanation or interpretation.

(b) warning or caution.

(c) suggestion or hint.

(d) origin or source.

STUDYING THE WRITER'S CRAFT   _____

1. By seeing how Carl Sagan organizes his article, you can learn useful strategies for organizing your own writing.

    a. In which lines on page 67 does Dr. Sagan announce the parts into which he will organize his article?

    b. What device does he use throughout the article to help the reader follow the sequence of topics?

    c. In which lines on page 71 does he summarize and conclude the main idea developed in the article?

2. The article by Dr. Sagan contains many scientific and technical terms and concepts. Yet the author's *tone* does not "sound" dry and formal.

   a. How do the following excerpts from the article help keep the author's "tone of voice" informal?

   (1) Other planets provide important insights about what dumb things not to do to Earth. (page 67, lines 5-6)

   (2) Who would have figured it? (page 67, line 17)

   (3) Now let's look at global warming . . . . (page 69, line 24)

   (4) Now that's serious. (page 70, line 9)

   b. What other examples of informality or humor can you find in the article?

3. As a piece of expository writing, the article does more than inform. It also seeks to convince readers that even though space exploration costs billions of dollars, it is still worth pursuing. In which two sentences at the beginning and end of the article does the author explicitly make this point?

ACTIVITIES FOR LISTENING, SPEAKING, WRITING

1. In a brief composition, explain how the accompanying cartoon reflects the OPPOSITE of a "global ecological consciousness."

2. If you were a Congressional representative, would you vote for or against spending on space exploration? Write a brief statement of your decision. Then support that decision with facts and reasons. Be prepared to present your ideas to your classmates.

3. In a few paragraphs, tell how important you think the "adventuresome spirit" is in space travel. Give reasons for your point of view.

TIME TRAVEL
Theme 2

T ime travel seems a logical extension of space travel. If you can take a trip from here to there, why not from now to then? In a sense, we all experience a kind of time travel every night. We go to bed, close our eyes, and—presto!—it's tomorrow morning. Such time travel is the basis of "The Sliced-Crosswise Only-on-Tuesday World." In this story, people are "frozen" in time while time itself moves forward.

Like space travel, time travel can move in many "directions." In working out the plot of a time-travel story, therefore, the science-fiction writer has a rich variety of choices. Travel from the future back to the present takes place in "Of Time and Third Avenue." The story "Absolutely Inflexible" develops an ingenious cycle of two-way time travel, from future to past and past to future.

In addition to the three forms of time travel just mentioned, others are possible. How many of these other forms, or "directions," of time travel can you imagine?

Time travel involves a basic problem, often called the "time-travel paradox." If you could travel into the past, for example, could you make changes that would affect the future—your present? Suppose that you kept your great-grandfather from meeting and marrying your great-grandmother. Would you never be born?

Because of such mind-boggling possibilities, some people argue that we will never be able to travel in time. Yet the latest theories of modern science leave the door open to time travel. You can take a peek through that open door in the article "Is Time Travel Possible?"

The Sliced-Crosswise Only-on-Tuesday World

by Philip José Farmer

All his life, he had known only Tuesdays. Would Wednesday rush at him, roaring, like a tidal wave? Pick him up and hurl him against the reefs of a strange time?

In this tragicomic tale set in the next century, science has discovered how to deal with overpopulation. People are permitted to live in only one day of the week. For the other six days, they are stored away in a state of suspended animation.

To explain this bizarre arrangement, Farmer invents several devices and gives them appropriate names. At the end of a designated day, people living in that day are exposed to the rays of a *somnium*. This device gives them all the sleep and dreams they need in just four hours. Upon awakening, they enter tall gray *stoners*, upright cylinders made of indestructible *eternium*. Here they remain as if frozen in time until their designated day comes around again.

Thanks to this amazing technology, science has solved the problem of overpopulation. What science hasn't solved, however, are the problems that come from falling in love. Pity poor Tom Pym, a Tuesday man who falls passionately in love with a beautiful young woman from Wednesday. Is it possible for Tom to get into Wednesday? And if he does, can you guess what happens?

Philip José Farmer

Author of numerous novels and short stories, Farmer is widely known to science-fiction fans for his Tier World and Riverworld series. These two groups of novels, written in the 1960s and 1970s, imaginatively blend fantasy, folklore, and history. As characters in some of his novels, Farmer introduces actual historical persons or famous characters from fiction. Some of Farmer's best work, however, appears in his treatment of standard science-fiction themes, as in this story of time travel.

Getting into Wednesday was almost impossible.

Tom Pym had thought about living on other days of the week. Almost everybody with any imagination did. There were even TV shows speculating on this. Tom Pym had even acted in two of these. But he had no genuine desire to move out of his own world. Then his house burned down.

This was on the last day of the eight days of spring. He awoke to look out the door at the ashes and the firemen. A man in a white asbestos suit motioned for him to stay inside. After fifteen minutes, another man in a suit gestured that it was safe. He pressed the button by the door, and 10 it swung open. He sank down in the ashes to his ankles; they were a trifle warm under the inch-thick coat of water-soaked crust.

There was no need to ask what had happened, but he did, anyway.

The fireman said, "A short-circuit, I suppose. Actually, we don't know. It started shortly after midnight, between the time that Monday quit and we took over."

Tom Pym thought that it must be strange to be a fireman or a policeman. Their hours were so different, even though they were still limited by the walls of midnight.

By then the others were stepping out of their stoners or "coffins" as 20 they were often called. That left sixty still occupied.

They were due for work at 08:00. The problem of getting new clothes and a place to live would have to be put off until off-hours, because the TV studio where they worked was behind in the big special it was due to put on in 144 days.

They ate breakfast at an emergency center. Tom Pym asked a grip,[1] if he knew of any place he could stay. Though the government would find one for him, it might not look very hard for a convenient place.

The grip told him about a house only six blocks from his former house. A makeup man had died, and as far as he knew the vacancy had not been filled. Tom got onto the phone at once, since he wasn't needed at that moment, but the office wouldn't be open until ten, as the recording informed him. The recording was a very pretty girl with red hair, tourmaline eyes, and a very sexy voice. Tom would have been more impressed if he had not known her. She had played in some small parts in two of his shows, and the maddening voice was not hers. Neither was the color of her eyes.

At noon he called again, got through after a ten-minute wait, and asked Mrs. Bellefield if she would put through a request for him. Mrs. Bellefield reprimanded him for not having phoned sooner; she was not sure that anything could be done today. He tried to tell her his circumstances and then gave up. Bureaucrats! That evening he went to a public emergency place, slept for the required four hours while the inductive field speeded up his dreaming, woke up, and got into the upright cylinder of eternium. He stood for ten seconds, gazing out through the transparent door at other cylinders with their still figures, and then he pressed the button. Approximately fifteen seconds later he became unconscious.

He had to spend three more nights in the public stoner. Three days of fall were gone; only five left. Not that that mattered in California so much. When he had lived in Chicago, winter was like a white blanket being shaken by a madwoman. Spring was a green explosion. Summer was a bright roar and a hot breath. Fall was the topple of a drunken jester in garish motley.

The fourth day, he received notice that he could move into the very house he had picked. This surprised and pleased him. He knew of a dozen who had spent a whole year—forty-eight days or so—in a public station while waiting. He moved in the fifth day with three days of spring to enjoy. But he would have to use up his two days off to shop for clothes, bring in groceries and other goods, and get acquainted with his housemates. Sometimes, he wished he had not been born with the compulsion to act. TV'ers worked five days at a stretch, sometimes six, while a plumber, for instance, only put in three days out of seven.

1. **grip:** stagehand.

The house was as large as the other, and the six extra blocks to walk would be good for him. It held eight people per day, counting himself. He moved in that evening, introduced himself, and got Mabel Curta, who worked as a secretary for a producer, to fill him in on the household routine. After he made sure that his stoner had been moved into the stoner room, he could relax somewhat.

Mabel Curta had accompanied him into the stoner room, since she had appointed herself his guide. She was a short, overly curved woman of about thirty-five (Tuesday time). She had been divorced three times, and marriage was no more for her unless, of course, Mr. Right came along. 10 Tom was between marriages himself, but he did not tell her so.

"We'll take a look at your bedroom," Mabel said. "It's small but it's soundproofed, thank God."

He started after her, then stopped. She looked back through the doorway and said, "What is it?"

"This girl . . ."

There were sixty-three of the tall gray eternium cylinders. He was looking through the door of the nearest at the girl within.

"Wow! Really beautiful!"

If Mabel felt any jealousy, she suppressed it.   20

"Yes, isn't she!"

The girl had long, black, slightly curly hair, a face that could have launched him a thousand times times a thousand times, a figure that had enough but not too much, and long legs. Her eyes were open; in the dim light they looked a purplish-blue. She wore a thin silvery dress.

The plate by the top of the door gave her vital data. Jennie Marlowe. Born 2031 A.D., San Marino, California. She would be twenty-four years old. Actress. Unmarried. Wednesday's child.

"What's the matter?" Mabel said.

"Nothing."   30

How could he tell her that he felt sick in his stomach from a desire that could never be satisfied? Sick from beauty?

For will in us is over-ruled by fate.
Who ever loved, that loved not at first sight?

"What?" Mabel said, and then, after laughing, "You must be kidding?"

She wasn't angry. She realized that Jennie Marlowe was no more competition than if she were dead. She was right. Better for him to busy himself with the living of this world. Mabel wasn't too bad, cuddly, really. 40

They went downstairs afterward after 18:00 to the TV room. Most of the others were there, too. Some had their earplugs in; some were looking at the screen but talking. The newscast was on, of course. Everybody was filling up on what had happened last Tuesday and today. The Speaker of the House was retiring after his term was up. His days of usefulness were over and his recent ill health showed no signs of disappearing. There was a shot of the family graveyard in Mississippi with the pedestal reserved for him. When science someday learned how to rejuvenate, he would come out of stonerment.

"That'll be the day!" Mabel said. She squirmed on his lap.

"Oh, I think they'll crack it," he said. "They're already on the track; they've succeeded in stopping the aging of rabbits." 10

"I don't mean that," she said. "Sure, they'll find out how to rejuvenate people. But then what? You think they're going to bring them all back? With all the people they got now and then they'll double, maybe triple, maybe quadruple, the population? You think they won't just leave them standing there?" She giggled, and said, "What would the pigeons do without them?"

He squeezed her waist. At the same time, he had a vision of himself squeezing *that* girl's waist. Hers would be soft enough but with no hint of fat.

Forget about her. Think of now. Watch the news. 20

A Mrs. Wilder had stabbed her husband and then herself with a kitchen knife. Both had been stonered immediately after the police arrived, and they had been taken to the hospital. An investigation of a work slowdown in the county government offices was taking place. The complaints were that Monday's people were not setting up the computers for Tuesday's. The case was being referred to the proper authorities of both days. The Ganymede base reported that the Great Red Spot of Jupiter was emitting weak but definite pulses that did not seem to be random.

The last five minutes of the program was a précis devoted to outstanding events of the other days. Mrs. Cuthmar, the housemother, turned 30 the channel to a situation comedy with no protests from anybody.

Tom left the room, after telling Mabel that he was going to bed early. He had a hard day tomorrow.

He tiptoed down the hall and the stairs and into the stoner room. The lights were soft, there were many shadows, and it was quiet. The sixty-three cylinders were like ancient granite columns of an underground chamber of a buried city. Fifty-five faces were white blurs behind the clear metal. Some had their eyes open; most had closed them while waiting for the field radiated from the machine in the base. He looked through Jennie Marlowe's door. He felt sick again. Out of his reach; never for him. 40 Wednesday was only a day away. No, it was only a little less than four and a half hours away.

He touched the door. It was slick and only a little cold. She stared at him. Her right forearm was bent to hold the strap of a large purse. When the door opened, she would step out, ready to go. Some people took their showers and fixed their faces as soon as they got up from their sleep and then went directly into the stoner. When the field was automatically radiated at 05:00, they stepped out a minute later, ready for the day.

He would like to step out of his "coffin," too, at the same time.

But he was barred by Wednesday.

He turned away. He was acting like a sixteen-year-old kid. He had been sixteen about one hundred and six years ago, not that that made any difference. Physiologically, he was thirty.

As he started up to the second floor, he almost turned around and went back for another look. But he took himself by his neck-collar and pulled himself up to his room. There he decided he would get to sleep at once. Perhaps he would dream about her. If dreams were wish-fulfillments, they would bring her to him. It still had not been "proved" that dreams always expressed wishes, but it had been proved that man deprived of dreaming did go mad. And so the somniums radiated a field that put man into a state in which he got all the sleep, and all the dreams, that he needed within a four-hour period. Then he was awakened and a little later went into the stoner where the field suspended all atomic and subatomic activity. He would remain in that state forever unless the activating field came on.

He slept, and Jennie Marlowe did not come to him. Or, if she did, he did not remember. He awoke, washed his face, went down eagerly to the stoner, where he found the entire household standing around, talking, laughing. Then they would step into their cylinders, and a silence like that at the heart of a mountain would fall.

He had often wondered what would happen if he did not go into the stoner. How would he feel? Would he be panicked? All his life, he had known only Tuesdays. Would Wednesday rush at him, roaring, like a tidal wave? Pick him up and hurl him against the reefs of a strange time?

What if he made some excuse and went back upstairs and did not go back down until the field had come on? By then, he could not enter. The door to his cylinder would not open again until the proper time. He could still run down to the public emergency stoners only three blocks away. But if he stayed in his room, waiting for Wednesday?

Such things happened. If the breaker of the law did not have a reasonable excuse, he was put on trial. It was a felony second only to murder to "break time," and the unexcused were stonered. All felons, sane or insane, were stonered. Or *mañanaed,*[2] as some said. The *mañanaed* criminal waited in immobility and unconsciousness, preserved unharmed until science had techniques to cure the insane, the neurotic, the criminal, the sick. *Mañana.*

"What was it like in Wednesday?" Tom had asked a man who had been unavoidably left behind because of an accident.

"How would I know? I was knocked out except for about fifteen minutes. I was in the same city, and I had never seen the faces of the ambulance men, of course, but then I've never seen them here. They stonered me and left me in the hospital for Tuesday to take care of."   10

He must have it bad, he thought. Bad. Even to think of such a thing was crazy. Getting into Wednesday was almost impossible. Almost. But it could be done. It would take time and patience, but it could be done.

He stood in front of his stoner for a moment. The others said, "See you! So long! Next Tuesday!" Mabel called, "Good night, lover!"

"Good night," he muttered.

"What?" she shouted.

"Good night!"

He glanced at the beautiful face behind the door. Then he smiled. He had been afraid that she might hear him say good night to a woman 20 who called him lover.

He had ten minutes yet. The intercom alarms were whooping. Get going, everybody! Time to take the six-day trip! Run! Remember the penalties!

He remembered, but he wanted to leave a message. The recorder was on a table. He activated it, and said, "Dear *Miss* Jennie Marlowe. My name is Tom Pym, and my stoner is next to yours. I am an actor, too; in fact, I work at the same studio as you. I know this is presumptuous of me, but I have never seen anybody so beautiful. Do you have a talent to match your beauty? I would like to see some run-offs of your shows. 30 Would you please leave some in room five? I'm sure the occupant won't mind. Yours, Tom Pym."

He ran it back. It was certainly bald enough, and that might be just what was needed. Too flowery or too pressing would have made her leery. He had commented on her beauty twice but not overstressed it. And the appeal to her pride in her acting would be difficult to resist. Nobody knew better than he about that.

He whistled a little on his way to the cylinder. Inside, he pressed the button and looked at his watch. Five minutes to midnight. The light on the huge screen above the computer in the police station would not 40

2. **mañanaed:** tomorrowed, from the Spanish word *mañana,* tomorrow.

be flashing for him. Ten minutes from now, Wednesday's police would step out of their stoners in the precinct station, and they would take over their duties.

There was a ten-minute hiatus between the two days in the police station. Anything could happen in these few minutes and it sometimes did. But a price had to be paid to maintain the walls of time.

He opened his eyes. His knees sagged a little and his head bent. The activation was a million microseconds fast—from eternium to flesh and blood almost instantaneously and the heart never knew that it had been stopped for such a long time. Even so, there was a little delay in the muscles' response to a standing position.

He pressed the button, opened the door, and it was as if his button had launched the day. Mabel had made herself up last night so that she looked dawn-fresh. He complimented her and she smiled happily. But he told her he would meet her for breakfast. Halfway up the staircase, he stopped, and waited until the hall was empty. Then he sneaked back down and into the stoner room. He turned on the recorder.

A voice, husky but also melodious, said, "Dear Mister Pym. I've had a few messages from other days. It was fun to talk back and forth across the abyss between the worlds, if you don't mind my exaggerating a little. But there is really no sense in it, once the novelty has worn off. If you become interested in the other person, you're frustrating yourself. That person can only be a voice in a recorder and a cold waxy face in a metal coffin. I wax poetic. Pardon me. If the person doesn't interest you, why continue to communicate? There is no sense in either case. And I *may* be beautiful. Anyway, I thank you for the compliment, but I am also sensible.

"I should have just not bothered to reply. But I want to be nice; I didn't want to hurt your feelings. So please don't leave any more messages."

He waited while silence was played. Maybe she was pausing for effect. Now would come a chuckle or a low honey-throated laugh, and she would say, "However, I don't like to disappoint my public. The run-offs are in your room."

The silence stretched out. He turned off the machine and went to the dining room for breakfast.

Siesta time at work was from 14:40 to 14:45. He lay down on the bunk and pressed the button. Within a minute he was asleep. He did dream of Jennie this time; she was a white shimmering figure solidifying out of the darkness and floating toward him. She was even more beautiful than she had been in her stoner.

The shooting ran overtime that afternoon so that he got home just in time for supper. Even the studio would not dare keep a man past his supper hour, especially since the studio was authorized to serve food only at noon.

He had time to look at Jennie for a minute before Mrs. Cuthmar's voice screeched over the intercom. As he walked down the hall, he thought, "I'm getting barnacled on her. It's ridiculous. I'm a grown man. Maybe . . . maybe I should see a psycher."

Sure, make your petition, and wait until a psycher has time for you. Say about three hundred days from now, if you are lucky. And if the psycher doesn't work out for you, then petition for another, and wait six hundred days.   10

Petition. He slowed down. Petition. What about a request, not to see a psycher, but to move? Why not? What did he have to lose? It would probably be turned down, but he could at least try.

Even obtaining a form for the request was not easy. He spent two nonwork days standing in line at the Center City Bureau before he got the proper forms. The first time, he was handed the wrong form and had to start all over again. There was no line set aside for those who wanted to change their days. There were not enough who wished to do this to justify such a line. So he had to queue up before the Miscellaneous Office counter of the Mobility Section of the Vital Exchange Department of the   20 Interchange and Cross Transfer Bureau. None of these titles had anything to do with emigration to another day.

When he got his form the second time, he refused to move from the office window until he had checked the number of the form and asked the clerk to double-check. He ignored the cries and the mutterings behind him. Then he went to one side of the vast room and stood in line before the punch machines. After two hours, he got to sit down at a small rolltop desk-shaped machine, above which was a large screen. He inserted the form into the slot, looked at the projection of the form, and punched buttons to mark the proper spaces opposite the proper questions. After   30 that, all he had to do was to drop the form into a slot and hope it did not get lost. Or hope he would not have to go through the same procedure because he had improperly punched the form.

That evening, he put his head against the hard metal and murmured to the rigid face behind the door, "I must really love you to go through all this. And you don't even know it. And, worse, if you did, you might not care one bit."

To prove to himself that he had kept his gray stuff,[3] he went out with Mabel that evening to a party given by Sol Voremwolf, a producer. Voremwolf

---

3. **gray stuff:** intelligence. The brain is sometimes referred to as "gray matter" or "little gray cells."

had just passed a civil service examination giving him an A-13 rating. This meant that, in time, with some luck and the proper pull, he would become an executive vice-president of the studio.

The party was a qualified success. Tom and Mabel returned about half an hour before stoner time.

He put Mabel off with an excuse, and went down to the stoner room ahead of the others. Not that that would do him any good if he wanted to get stonered early. The stoners only activated within narrow time limits.

He leaned against the cylinder and patted the door. "I tried not to think about you all evening. I wanted to be fair to Mabel, it's not fair to go out with her and think about you all the time."

All's fair in love . . .

He left another message for her, then wiped it out. What was the use? Besides, he knew that his speech was a little thick. He wanted to appear at his best for her.

Why should he? What did she care for him?

The answer was, he did care, and there was no reason or logic connected with it. He loved this forbidden, untouchable, far-away-in-time, yet-so-near woman.

Mabel had come in silently. She said, "You're sick!"

Tom jumped away. Now why had he done that? He had nothing to be ashamed of. Then why was he so angry with her? His embarrassment was understandable but his anger was not.

Mabel laughed at him, and he was glad. Now he could snarl at her. He did so, and she turned away and walked out. But she was back in a few minutes with the others. It would soon be midnight.

By then he was standing inside the cylinder. A few seconds later, he left it, pushed Jennie's backward on its wheels, and pushed his around so that it faced hers. He went back in, pressed the button, and stood there. The double doors only slightly distorted his view. But she seemed even more removed in distance, in time, and in unattainability.

Three days later, well into winter, he received a letter. The box inside the entrance hall buzzed just as he entered the front door. He went back and waited until the letter was printed and had dropped out from the slot. It was the reply to his request to move to Wednesday.

Denied. Reason: he had no reasonable reason to move.

That was true. But he could not give his real motive. It would have been even less impressive than the one he had given. He had punched the box opposite No. 12. REASON: TO GET INTO AN ENVIRONMENT WHERE MY TALENTS WILL BE MORE LIKELY TO BE ENCOURAGED.

He cursed and he raged. It was his human, his civil right to move into any day he pleased. That is, it should be his right. What if a move did cause much effort? What if it required a transfer of his I.D. and all the records connected with him from the moment of his birth? What if . . . ?

He could rage all he wanted to, but it would not change a thing. He was stuck in the world of Tuesday.

Not yet, he muttered. Not yet. Fortunately, there is no limit to the number of requests I can make in my own day. I'll send out another. They think they can wear me out, huh? Well, I'll wear them out. Man against the machine. Man against the system. Man against the bureaucracy and the hard cold rules. 10

Winter's twenty days had sped by. Spring's eight days rocketed by. It was summer again. On the second day of the twelve days of summer, he received a reply to his second request.

It was neither a denial nor an acceptance. It stated that if he thought he would be better off psychologically in Wednesday because his astrologer said so, then he would have to get a psycher's critique of the astrologer's analysis. Tom Pym jumped into the air and clicked his sandaled heels together. Thank God that he lived in an age that did not classify astrologers as charlatans! The people—the masses—had protested that 20 astrology was a necessity and that it should be legalized and honored. So laws were passed, and because of that, Tom Pym had a chance.

He went down to the stoner room and kissed the door of the cylinder and told Jennie Marlowe the good news. She did not respond, though he thought he saw her eyes brighten just a little. That was, of course, only his imagination, but he liked his imagination.

Getting a psycher for a consultation and getting through the three sessions took another year, another forty-eight days. Doctor Sigmund Traurig was a friend of Doctor Stelhela, the astrologer, and so that made things easier for Tom. 30

"I've studied Doctor Stelhela's chart carefully and analyzed carefully your obsession for this woman," he said. "I agree with Doctor Stelhela that you will always be unhappy in Tuesday, but I don't quite agree with him that you will be happier in Wednesday. However, you have this thing going for this Miss Marlowe, so I think you should go to Wednesday. But only if you sign papers agreeing to see a psycher there for extended therapy."

Only later did Tom Pym realize that Doctor Traurig might have wanted to get rid of him because he had too many patients. But that was an uncharitable thought. 40

He had to wait while the proper papers were transmitted to Wednesday's authorities. His battle was only half-won. The other officials could turn him down. And if he did get to his goal, then what? She could reject him without giving him a second chance.

It was unthinkable, but she could.

He caressed the door and then pressed his lips against it.

"Pygmalion could at least touch Galatea,"[4] he said. "Surely, the gods—the big dumb bureaucrats—will take pity on me, who can't even touch you. Surely."

The psycher had said that he was incapable of a true and lasting bond with a woman, as so many men were in this world of easy-come-easy-go liaisons. He had fallen in love with Jennie Marlowe for several reasons. She may have resembled somebody he had loved when he was very young. His mother, perhaps? No? Well, never mind. He would find out in Wednesday—perhaps. The deep, the important, truth was that he loved Miss Marlowe because she could never reject him, kick him out, or become tiresome, complain, weep, yell, insult, and so forth. He loved her because she was unattainable and silent.

"I love her as Achilles must have loved Helen when he saw her on top of the walls of Troy,"[5] Tom said.

"I wasn't aware that Achilles was ever in love with Helen of Troy," Doctor Traurig said drily.

"Homer never said so, but I *know* that he must have been! Who could see her and *not* love her?"

"How would I know? I never saw her! If I had suspected these delusions would intensify . . ."

"I am a poet!" Tom said.

"Overimaginative, you mean! Hmmm. She must be a douser! I don't have anything particular to do this evening. I'll tell you what . . . my curiosity is aroused . . . I'll come down to your place tonight and take a look at this fabulous beauty, your Helen of Troy."

Doctor Traurig appeared immediately after supper, and Tom Pym ushered him down the hall and into the stoner room at the rear of the big house as if he were a guide conducting a famous critic to a just-discovered Rembrandt.

The doctor stood for a long time in front of the cylinder. He hmmmed several times and checked her vital-data plate several times. Then he turned and said, "I see what you mean, Mr. Pym. Very well. I'll give the go-ahead."

---

4. **Pygmalion** (pig-MAYL-yun) . . . **Galatea** (gal-eh-TEE-eh): Pygmalion was a king of ancient Greece who fell in love with a female statue he had sculpted. In answer to his prayers, the goddess Aphrodite brought Galatea to life.

5. **Achilles** (uh-KIL-eez), a Greek hero, and **Helen**, a queen of Troy, are important characters in the *Iliad*, Homer's epic poem about the Trojan War.

"Ain't she something?" Tom said on the porch. "She's out of this world, literally and figuratively, of course."

"Very beautiful. But I believe that you are facing a great disappointment, perhaps heartbreak, perhaps, who knows, even madness, much as I hate to use that unscientific term."

"I'll take the chance," Tom said. "I know I sound nuts, but where would we be if it weren't for nuts? Look at the man who invented the wheel, at Columbus, at James Watt, at the Wright brothers, at Pasteur, you name them."

"You can scarcely compare these pioneers of science with their passion for truth with you and your desire to marry a woman. But, as I have observed, she is strikingly beautiful. Still, that makes me exceedingly cautious. Why isn't she married? What's wrong with her?" 10

"For all I know, she may have been married a dozen times!" Tom said. "The point is, she isn't now! Maybe she's disappointed and she's sworn to wait until the right man comes along. Maybe . . ."

"There's no maybe about it, you're neurotic," Traurig said. "But I actually believe that it would be more dangerous for you *not* to go to Wednesday than it would be *to* go."

"Then you'll say yes!" Tom said, grabbing the doctor's hand and shaking it. 20

"Perhaps. I have some doubts."

The doctor had a faraway look. Tom laughed and released the hand and slapped the doctor on the shoulder. "Admit it! You were really struck by her! You'd have to be dead not to!"

"She's all right," the doctor said. "But you must think this over. If you do go there and she turns you down, you might go off the deep end, much as I hate to use such a poetical term."

"No, I won't. I wouldn't be a bit the worse off. Better off, in fact. I'll at least get to see her in the flesh."

Spring and summer zipped by. Then, a morning he would never forget, the letter of acceptance. With it, instructions on how to get to Wednesday. These were simple enough. He was to make sure that the technicians came to his stoner sometime during the day and readjusted the timer within the base. He could not figure out why he could not just stay out of the stoner and let Wednesday catch up to him, but by now he was past trying to fathom the bureaucratic mind. 30

He did not intend to tell anyone at the house, mainly because of Mabel. But Mabel found out from someone at the studio. She wept when she saw him at supper time, and she ran upstairs to her room. He felt bad, but he did not follow to console her. 40

That evening, his heart beating hard, he opened the door to his stoner. The others had found out by then; he had been unable to keep the business to himself. Actually, he was glad that he had told them. They seemed happy for him. Finally, Mabel came downstairs, wiping her eyes, and she said she wished him luck, too. She had known that he was not really in love with her. But she did wish someone would fall in love with her just by looking inside her stoner.

When she found out that he had gone to see Doctor Traurig, she said, "He's a very influential man. Sol Voremwolf had him for his analyst. He says he's even got influence on other days. He edits the *Psyche Cross-currents*, you know, one of the few periodicals read by other people."

Other, of course, meant those who lived in Wednesdays through 10 Mondays.

Tom said he was glad he had gotten Traurig. Perhaps he had used his influence to get the Wednesday authorities to push through his request so swiftly. The walls between the worlds were seldom broken, but it was suspected that the very influential did it when they pleased.

Now, quivering, he stood before Jennie's cylinder again. The last time, he thought, that I'll see her stonered. Next time, she'll be warm, colorful, touchable flesh.

"*Ave atque vale!*"[6] he said aloud. The others cheered. Mabel said, "How corny!" They thought he was addressing them, and perhaps he 20 had included them.

He stepped inside the cylinder, closed the door, and pressed the button. He would keep his eyes open, so that . . .

And today was Wednesday. Though the view was exactly the same, it was like being on Mars.

He pushed open the door and stepped out. The seven people had faces he knew and names he had read on their plates. But he did not know them.

He started to say hello, and then he stopped.

Jennie Marlowe's cylinder was gone.   30

He seized the nearest man by the arm.

"Where's Jennie Marlowe?"

"Let go. You're hurting me. She's gone. To Tuesday."

"*Tuesday! Tuesday?*"

"Sure. She'd been trying to get out of here for a long time. She had something about this day being unlucky for her. She was unhappy, that's for sure. Just two days ago, she said her application had finally been accepted. Apparently, some Tuesday psycher had used his influence. He came down and saw her in her stoner and that was it, brother."

The walls and the people and the stoners seemed to be distorted. 40

6. *Ave atque vale!* (Latin): Hail and farewell!

Time was bending itself this way and that. He wasn't in Wednesday; he wasn't in Tuesday. He wasn't in *any* day. He was stuck inside himself at some crazy date that should never have existed.

"She can't do that!"

"Oh, no! She just did that!"

"But . . . you can't transfer more than once!"

"That's her problem."

It was his, too.

"I should never have brought him down to look at her!" Tom said. "The swine! The unethical swine!"   10

Tom Pym stood there for a long time, and then he went into the kitchen. It was the same environment, if you discounted the people. Later, he went to the studio and got a part in a situation play which was, really, just like all those in Tuesday. He watched the newscaster that night. The President of the U.S.A. had a different name and face, but the words of his speech could have been those of Tuesday's President. He was introduced to a secretary of a producer; her name wasn't Mabel, but it might as well have been.

The difference here was that Jennie was gone, and oh, what a world of difference it made to him.

REVIEWING THE STORY

THE MAIN IDEA

1. Which popular saying best expresses the main idea of the story?
    (a) Time is money.
    (b) To err is human, to forgive divine.
    (c) All's fair in love and war.
    (d) All the world loves a lover.

DETAILS

2. The story is set in
    (a) Great Britain.
    (b) the United States of America.
    (c) a type of spaceship called a *stoner*.
    (d) another planet.

3. The time of the story is in the middle of the (a) 19th century (b) 20th century (c) 21st century (d) 22nd century.

4. The hero, Tom Pym, is a **(a)** psycher **(b)** firefighter **(c)** TV actor **(d)** criminal.

5. Tom obtains help in moving to Wednesday from
   (a) Mabel Curta.
   (b) Jennie Marlowe.
   (c) Sol Voremwolf.
   (d) Sigmund Traurig.

6. When Tom arrives in Wednesday, he discovers that
   (a) Dr. Traurig has arrived there before him.
   (b) Mabel Curta has come with him.
   (c) Jennie Marlowe has moved to Tuesday.
   (d) he is no longer in love with Jennie.

ORDER OF EVENTS

7. Choose the letter that gives the order in which the events happen.
   (1) Dr. Traurig goes to look at Jennie.
   (2) Tom falls in love with Jennie.
   (3) Jennie moves to Tuesday.
   (4) Tom applies for a transfer to Wednesday.
       (a) 1-2-3-4   **(b)** 2-4-1-3   **(c)** 4-3-2-1   **(d)** 2-4-3-1

CAUSE AND EFFECT

8. Tom has to find other living quarters because
   (a) he loses his job.
   (b) it is his turn to move.
   (c) he is reported to the authorities.
   (d) his house burns down.

9. As a result of severe overcrowding in the world of the future, people
   (a) no longer have children.
   (b) do not marry.
   (c) live in one-day shifts.
   (d) move frequently.

INFERENCES

10. We can infer that in Tom Pym's world, people no longer
    (a) have to obey the laws.
    (b) want to obey the laws.

(c) commit any crimes.

(d) are executed for any crimes.

11. Perhaps Dr. Traurig arranges for Jennie to move to Tuesday because he

(a) is in love with her.

(b) wants to keep Tom from moving to Wednesday.

(c) hopes that Jennie will become his patient.

(d) plans to move to Wednesday himself.

PREDICTING OUTCOMES

12. If Tom were to ask Dr. Traurig for help in returning to Tuesday, the psycher would probably **(a)** agree **(b)** refuse **(c)** ask Jennie **(d)** tell Mabel Curta.

BUILDING YOUR VOCABULARY _____

1. Mrs. Bellefield *reprimanded* him for not having phoned sooner; she was not sure that anything could be done today.

   From the context of the sentence, you can tell that the OPPOSITE of *reprimanded* (page 81, lines 17-19) is **(a)** scolded **(b)** reproached **(c)** praised **(d)** rebuked.

2. When science someday learned how to *rejuvenate*, he would come out of stonerment.

   You have seen the prefix *re-*, the root *juven*, and the suffix *-ate* in such words as *reread*, *juvenile*, and *activate*. From this analysis, you can figure out that to *rejuvenate* (page 83, lines 6-7) must mean to

   (a) cure a disease.

   (b) reform a criminal.

   (c) encourage young people to reread actively.

   (d) make young again.

3. I know this is *presumptuous* of me, but I have never seen anybody so beautiful.

   If *presume* means "to do something without permission," someone who is *presumptuous* (page 85, lines 28-29)

   (a) acts shyly.

   (b) goes beyond what is proper.

(c) behaves selfishly.

(d) seems highly critical.

4. Man against the *bureaucracy* and the hard cold rules.

A *bureaucracy* (page 89, lines 10-11) is associated with **(a)** freedom **(b)** inefficient rules **(c)** bold new ways **(d)** furniture.

5. He could not figure out why he could not just stay out of the stoner and let Wednesday catch up with him, but by now he was past trying to *fathom* the bureaucratic mind.

A *fathom* is a unit of length (about six feet) used for measuring the depth of water. As used in this sentence, to *fathom* (page 91, lines 34-36) means

(a) to understand by getting to the bottom of something.

(b) to take the linear measure of something.

(c) to avoid something by letting it pass by you.

(d) to find fault with something.

STUDYING THE WRITER'S CRAFT

1. A good fiction writer works hard to earn the reader's belief in the world of the story. Even in a tale of the future like this one, the author strives to create *verisimilitude*—literally, "truth-likeness."

   a. What are some of the technical details in the story that tell us we are in a world of the future?

   b. Which of these details—if any—does the author explain?

   c. How well do you think these details contribute to the verisimilitude of the story?

2. The story of Tom Pym contains a number of literary flourishes, or bits of fancy writing. (For one example, see page 81, lines 29-31.) Especially in its last few pages, the story also contains literary allusions, or references to works of literature. (For example, on page 90, line 5, Tom says, "Pygmalion could at least touch Galatea.")

   a. Mention a few other literary flourishes and allusions in the story.

   b. Do they seem appropriate to Tom Pym? Explain.

3. This is a story with a surprise ending. Yet a skillful writer prepares subtle hints for the reader—*foreshadowing*—to make the surprise ending appear somehow inevitable. Does Philip José Farmer provide any anticipatory clues to his surprise ending? If so, what are they?

ACTIVITIES FOR LISTENING, SPEAKING, WRITING

1. Suppose that Tom Pym, now stuck in Wednesday, decides to leave a tape recording for Jennie Marlowe, now living in Tuesday. What would he say? Write a message from Tom to Jennie that does justice to Tom's feelings.

2. Imagine that Tom also decides to make a tape recording for Dr. Traurig. What would he say? Before you write this message, think not only about Tom's feelings, but also about his possible motives for trying to communicate with the psycher.

3. Although the story is set in the future, it is, in some respects, an old-fashioned tale of love at first sight. Do you believe in love at first sight? What is the difference between love and attraction? Between love and infatuation? What do you think is necessary to make a love relationship last? Be prepared to discuss your answers to these questions with your classmates.

Of Time and Third Avenue

by Alfred Bester

You have placed us in an extremely dangerous position. I have been sent to find a solution.

Who wouldn't like to know what the future will bring? For thousands of years, we humans have consulted oracles, soothsayers, prophets, diviners, and seers. To try to predict the future, we have had our palms read and our dreams interpreted. Our futures have also been read by means of crystal balls, tea leaves, and horoscopes. "If only we could foretell the future," we assure ourselves, "what wealth and power would be ours!"

Oliver Wilson Knight, the young man in the following story, has just such an opportunity. But there is a catch! At the heart of this ingenious story is the time-travel paradox. A time traveler who goes into the past could conceivably change the future (his or her present), perhaps in disastrous ways. Similarly, a person who knows the future might be able to alter it in equally destructive ways. Yet Oliver Wilson Knight may think such risks are worth taking for the sake of knowing the future. What do you think he does? What would you do?

As you read, it may help to know that this story was first published in 1951, when 1990 seemed far in the future. Be prepared, too, for some strange speech from Mr. Boyne, who may be a time traveler from the future.

Alfred Bester

Alfred Bester has made his living by writing for television, radio, magazines, and even comic books. For his own enjoyment, however, he writes science fiction. His two most popular science-fiction novels, written in the 1950s, are *The Demolished Man* (1952) and *The Stars My Destination* (1956). In the short story "Of Time and Third Avenue," he gives time travel, a favorite theme in many of his stories, an unexpected twist.

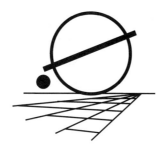

What Macy hated about the man was the fact that he squeaked. Macy didn't know if it was the shoes, but he suspected the clothes. In the back room of his tavern, under the poster that asked: "WHO FEARS MENTION THE BATTLE OF THE BOYNE?" Macy inspected the stranger. He was tall, slender, and very dainty. Although he was young, he was almost bald. There was fuzz on top of his head and over his eyebrows. When he reached into his jacket for a wallet, Macy made up his mind. It was the clothes that squeaked.

"MQ,[1] Mr. Macy," the stranger said in a staccato voice. "Very good. For rental of this back room including exclusive utility for one chronos—" 10

"One whatos?" Macy asked nervously.

"Chronos. The incorrect word? Oh, yes. Excuse me. One hour."

"You're a foreigner," Macy said. "What's your name? I bet it's Russian."

"No. Not foreign," the stranger answered. His frightening eyes whipped around the back room. "Identify me as Boyne."

"Boyne!" Macy echoed incredulously.

"MQ. Boyne." Mr. Boyne opened a wallet like an accordion, ran his fingers through various colored papers and coins, then withdrew a hundred-dollar bill. He jabbed it at Macy and said, "Rental fee for one hour. As agreed. One hundred dollars. Take it and go." 20

---

1. **MQ:** probably the stranger's equivalent for "OK." (What other strange words and expressions does he use later in the story?)

Impelled by the thrust of Boyne's eyes, Macy took the bill and staggered out to the bar. Over his shoulder he quavered, "What'll you drink?"

"Drink? Alcohol? Never!" Boyne answered.

He turned and darted to the telephone booth, reached under the pay phone and located the lead-in wire. From a side pocket he withdrew a small glittering box and clipped it to the wire. He tucked it out of sight, then lifted the receiver.

"Coordinates west seventy-three—fifty-eight—fifteen," he said rapidly, "north forty—forty-five—twenty. Disband sigma. You're ghosting . . ." After a pause he continued: "Stet. Stet! Transmission clear. I want 10 a fix on Knight. Oliver Wilson Knight. Probability to four significant figures. You have the coordinates. . . . Ninety-nine, point nine eight oh seven? MQ. Stand by. . . ."

Boyne poked his head out of the booth and peered toward the tavern door. He waited with steely concentration until a young man and a pretty girl entered. Then he ducked back to the phone. "Probability fulfilled. Oliver Wilson Knight in contact. MQ. Luck my Para." He hung up and was sitting under the poster as the couple wandered toward the back room.

The young man was about twenty-six, of medium height and inclined 20 to be stocky. His suit was rumpled, his seal-brown hair was rumpled, and his friendly face was crinkled by good-natured creases. The girl had black hair, soft blue eyes, and a small private smile. They walked arm in arm and liked to collide gently when they thought no one was looking. At this moment they collided with Mr. Macy.

"I'm sorry, Mr. Knight," Macy said. "You and the young lady can't sit back there this afternoon. The premises have been rented."

Their faces fell. Boyne called, "Quite all right, Mr. Macy. All correct. Happy to entertain Mr. Knight and friend as guests."

Knight and the girl turned to Boyne uncertainly. Boyne smiled and 30 patted the chair alongside him. "Sit down," he said. "Charmed, I assure you."

The girl said, "We hate to intrude, but this is the only place in town where you can get genuine stone ginger beer."

"Already aware of the fact, Miss Clinton." To Macy he said, "Bring ginger beer and go. No other guests. These are all I'm expecting."

Knight and the girl stared at Boyne in astonishment as they sat down slowly. Knight placed a wrapped parcel of books on the table. The girl took a breath and said, "You know me, Mr. . . . ?"

"Boyne. As in Boyne, Battle of. Yes, of course. You are Miss Jane 40 Clinton. This is Mr. Oliver Wilson Knight. I rented premises particularly to meet you this afternoon."

"This supposed to be a gag?" Knight asked, a dull flush appearing on his cheeks.

"Ginger beer," answered Boyne gallantly as Macy arrived, deposited bottles and glasses, and departed in haste.

"You couldn't know we were coming here," Jane said. "We didn't know ourselves . . . until a few minutes ago."

"Sorry to contradict, Miss Clinton," Boyne smiled. "The probability of your arrival at longitude seventy-three—fifty-eight—fifteen, latitude forty—forty-five—twenty was ninety-nine point nine eight oh seven per cent. No one can escape four significant figures."   10

"Listen," Knight began angrily, "if this is your idea of—"

"Kindly drink ginger beer and listen to my idea, Mr. Knight." Boyne leaned across the table with galvanic intensity. "This hour has been arranged with difficulty and much cost. To whom? No matter. You have placed us in an extremely dangerous position. I have been sent to find a solution."

"Solution for what?" Knight asked.

Jane tried to rise. "I . . . I think we'd b-better be go—"

Boyne waved her back, and she sat down like a child. To Knight he said, "This noon you entered premises of J. D. Craig and Company, dealer   20
in printed books. You purchased, through transfer of money, four books. Three do not matter, but the fourth—" he tapped the wrapped parcel emphatically—"that is the crux of this encounter."

"What are you talking about?" Knight exclaimed.

"One bound volume consisting of collected facts and statistics."

"The almanac?"

"The almanac."

"What about it?"

"You intended to purchase a 1950 almanac."

"I bought the '50 almanac."   30

"You did not!" Boyne blazed. "You bought the almanac for 1990."

"What?"

"The *World Almanac* for 1990," Boyne said clearly, "is in this package. Do not ask how. There was a mistake that has already been disciplined. Now the error must be adjusted. That is why I am here. It is why this meeting was arranged. You cognate?"

Knight burst into laughter and reached for the parcel. Boyne leaned across the table and grasped his wrist. "You must not open it, Mr. Knight."

"All right." Knight leaned back in his chair. He grinned at Jane and sipped ginger beer. "What's the payoff on the gag?"   40

"I must have the book, Mr. Knight. I would like to walk out of this tavern with the almanac under my arm."

"You would, eh?"

"I would."

"The 1990 almanac?"

"Yes."

"If," said Knight, "there was such a thing as a 1990 almanac, and if it was in that package, wild horses couldn't get it away from me."

"Why, Mr. Knight?"

"Don't be an idiot. A look into the future? Stock market re-ports . . . horse races . . . politics. It'd be money from home. I'd be rich."

"Indeed yes." Boyne nodded sharply. "More than rich. Omnipotent. 10 The small mind would use the almanac from the future for small things only. Wagers on the outcome of games and elections. And so on. But the intellect of dimensions—*your* intellect—would not stop there."

"You tell me." Knight grinned.

"Deduction. Induction. Inference." Boyne ticked the points off on his fingers. "Each fact would tell you an entire history. Real-estate investment, for example. What lands to buy and sell. Population shifts and census reports would tell you. Transportation. Lists of marine disasters and rail-road wrecks would tell you whether rocket travel has replaced the train and ship." 20

"Has it?" Knight chuckled.

"Flight records would tell you which company's stock should be bought. Lists of postal receipts would tell you which are the cities of the future. The Nobel Prize winners would tell you which scientists and what new inventions to watch. Armament budgets would tell you which fac-tories and industries to control. Cost-of-living reports would tell you how best to protect your wealth against inflation or deflation. Foreign-ex-change rates, stock exchange reports, bank suspensions and life-insurance indexes would provide the clues to protect you against any and all dis-asters." 30

"That's the idea," Knight said. "That's for me."

"You really think so?"

"I know so. Money in my pocket. The world in my pocket."

"Excuse me," Boyne said keenly, "but you are only repeating the dreams of childhood. You want wealth. Yes. But only won through en-deavor—your own endeavor. There is no joy in success as an unearned gift. There is nothing but guilt and unhappiness. You are aware of this already."

"I disagree," Knight said.

"Do you? Then why do you work? Why not steal? Rob? Burgle? 40 Cheat others of their money to fill your own pockets?"

"But I . . ." Knight began, and then stopped.

"The point is well taken, eh?" Boyne waved his hand impatiently. "No, Mr. Knight. Seek a mature argument. You are too ambitious and healthy to wish to steal success."

"Then I'd just want to know if I would be successful."

"Ah? Stet. You wish to thumb through the pages looking for your name. You want reassurance. Why? Have you no confidence in yourself? You are a promising young attorney. Yes. I know that. It is part of my data. Has not Miss Clinton confidence in you?"

"Yes," Jane said in a loud voice. "He doesn't need reassurance from a book." 10

"What else, Mr. Knight?"

Knight hesitated, sobering in the face of Boyne's overwhelming intensity. Then he said, "Security."

"There is no such thing. Life is insecurity. You can find safety only in death."

"You know what I mean," Knight muttered. "The knowledge that life is worth planning. There's the H-bomb."

Boyne nodded quickly. "True. It is a crisis. But then, I'm here. The world will continue. I am proof."

"If I believe you." 20

"And if you do not?" Boyne blazed. "You do not want security. You want courage." He nailed the couple with a contemptuous glare. "There is in this country a legend of pioneer forefathers from whom you are supposed to inherit courage in the face of odds. D. Boone, E. Allen, S. Houston, A. Lincoln, G. Washington and others. Fact?"

"I suppose so," Knight muttered. "That's what we keep telling ourselves."

"And where is the courage in you? Pfui! It is only talk. The unknown terrifies you. Danger does not inspire you to fight, as it did D. Crockett; it makes you whine and reach for the reassurance in this book. Fact?" 30

"But the H-bomb . . ."

"It is a danger. Yes. One of many. What of that? Do you cheat at solhand?"

"Solhand?"

"Your pardon." Boyne reconsidered, impatiently snapping his fingers at the interruption to the white heat of his argument. "It is a game played singly against chance relationships in an arrangement of cards. I forget your noun."

"Oh!" Jane's face brightened. "Solitaire."

"Quite right. Solitaire. Thank you, Miss Clinton." Boyne turned his 40 frightening eyes on Knight. "Do you cheat at solitaire?"

"Occasionally."

"Do you enjoy games won by cheating?"

"Not as a rule."

"They are thisney, yes? Boring. They are tiresome. Pointless. Null-coordinated. You wish you had won honestly."

"I suppose so."

"And you will suppose so after you have looked at this bound book. Through all your pointless life you will wish you had played honestly the game of life. You will verdash that look. You will regret. You will totally recall the pronouncement of our great poet-philosopher Trynbyll who summed it up in one lightning, skazon line. *'The Future is Tekon,'* 10 said Trynbyll. Mr. Knight, do not cheat. Let me implore you to give me the almanac."

"Why don't you take it away from me?"

"It must be a gift. We can rob you of nothing. We can give you nothing."

"That's a lie. You paid Macy to rent this back room."

"Macy was paid, but I gave him nothing. He will think he was cheated, but you will see to it that he is not. All will be adjusted without dislocation."

"Wait a minute—"   20

"It has all been carefully planned. I have gambled on you, Mr. Knight. I am depending on your good sense. Let me have the almanac. I will disband—reorient—and you will never see me again. Vorloss verdash! It will be a bar adventure to narrate for friends. Give me the almanac!"

"Hold the phone," Knight said. "This is a gag. Remember? I—"

"Is it?" Boyne interrupted. "Is it? Look at me."

For almost a minute the young couple stared at the bleached white face with its deadly eyes. The half-smile left Knight's lips, and Jane shuddered involuntarily. There was chill and dismay in the back room.

"This can't be happening!" Knight glanced helplessly at Jane. "He's 30 got me believing. You?"

Jane nodded jerkily.

"What should we do? If everything he says is true, we can refuse and live happily ever after."

"No," Jane said in a choked voice. "There may be money and success in that book, but there's divorce and death too. Give him the book."

"Take it," Knight said faintly.

Boyne rose instantly. He picked up the parcel and went into the phone booth. When he came out, he had three books in one hand and a smaller parcel made up of the original wrapping in the other. He placed 40 the books on the table and stood for a moment, smiling down.

"My gratitude," he said. "You have eased a precarious situation. It is only fair you should receive something in return. We are forbidden to transfer anything that might divert existing phenomena streams, but at least I can give you one token of the future."

He backed away, bowed curiously, and said, "My service to you both." Then he turned and started out of the tavern.

"Hey!" Knight called. "The token?"

"Mr. Macy has it," Boyne answered and was gone.

The couple sat at the table for a few blank moments like sleepers slowly awakening. Then, as reality began to return, they stared at each other and burst into laughter.   10

"He really had me scared," Jane said.

"Talk about Third Avenue characters. What an act. What'd he get out of it?"

"Well . . . he got your almanac."

"But it doesn't make sense." Knight began to laugh again. "All that business about paying Macy but not giving him anything. And I'm supposed to see that he isn't cheated. And the mystery token of the future . . ."

The tavern door burst open and Macy shot through the saloon into the back room. "Where is he?" Macy shouted. "Where's the thief? Boyne, 20 he calls himself. More likely his name is Dillinger."

"Why, Mr. Macy!" Jane exclaimed. "What's the matter?"

"Where is he?" Macy pounded on the door of the men's room. "Come out, ye blaggard!"

"He's gone," Knight said. "He left just before you got back."

"And you, Mr. Knight!" Macy pointed a trembling finger at the young lawyer. "You, to be party to thievery and racketeers. Shame on you!"

"What's wrong?" Knight asked.

"He paid me one hundred dollars to rent this back room," Macy 30 cried in anguish. "One hundred dollars. I took the bill over to Bernie the pawnbroker, being cautious-like, and he found out it's a forgery. It's a counterfeit."

"Oh, no." Jane laughed. "That's too much. Counterfeit?"

"Look at this," Mr. Macy shouted, slamming the bill down on the table.

Knight inspected it closely. Suddenly he turned pale and the laughter drained out of his face. He reached into his inside pocket, withdrew a checkbook and began to write with trembling fingers.

"What on earth are you doing?" Jane asked.   40

"Making sure that Macy isn't cheated," Knight said. "You'll get your hundred dollars, Mr. Macy."

"Oliver! Are you insane? Throwing away a hundred dollars ..."

"And I won't be losing anything either," Knight answered. "All will be adjusted without dislocation! They're diabolical. Diabolical!"

"I don't understand."

"Look at the bill," Knight said in a shaky voice. "Look closely."

It was beautifully engraved and genuine in appearance. Benjamin Franklin's benign features gazed up at them mildly and authentically; but in the lower right-hand corner was printed: "Series 1980 D." And underneath that was signed: "Oliver Wilson Knight, Secretary of the Treasury."

REVIEWING THE STORY

THE MAIN IDEA

1. Mr. Boyne convinces the two young people that life must be lived with
   (a) caution and security.
   (b) wealth and power.
   (c) courage and confidence.
   (d) guilt and unhappiness.

DETAILS

2. Boyne has rented the back room of a tavern in order to
   (a) discuss business with Macy.
   (b) be alone.
   (c) meet a young couple there.
   (d) sell a rare book to a young couple.

3. The story takes place in (a) 1950 (b) 1980 (c) 1990 (d) the 21st century.

4. Oliver Wilson Knight is a promising young (a) politician (b) doctor (c) lawyer (d) writer.

5. Knight has accidentally obtained a
   (a) counterfeit $100 bill.
   (b) rare book from the past.
   (c) history of the Battle of the Boyne.
   (d) book of facts from the future.

6. In the end, Knight decides to
   (a) give what Boyne wants to Macy.
   (b) give Boyne what he wants.

(c) sell Boyne what he wants.

(d) trade with Boyne for information about the future.

ORDER OF EVENTS

7. Choose the letter of the event that happens LAST in the story.

(a) Boyne goes into the phone booth with the parcel of books.

(b) Knight gives Macy a check for $100.

(c) Knight purchases four books.

(d) Boyne rents the back room for $100.

CAUSE AND EFFECT

8. Boyne's appearance in the tavern on Third Avenue is caused by a

(a) mistake made by Macy.

(b) threat to the past.

(c) threat to the future.

(d) call for help from Jane Clinton.

9. When Jane and Oliver look into Boyne's eyes, they feel (a) frightened (b) angry (c) sad (d) sleepy.

INFERENCES

10. We can infer that Boyne comes from (a) another planet (b) the past (c) a foreign country (d) the future.

11. When Knight tells Jane Clinton, "And I won't be losing anything either" (page 106, line 2), he apparently thinks that

(a) Macy will give back the $100 check to him.

(b) his own future success is assured.

(c) the $100 bill is indeed counterfeit.

(d) Boyne was lying after all.

PREDICTING OUTCOMES

12. If Oliver Knight had decided to keep and use the almanac he bought, he might have endangered

(a) the book dealer J. D. Craig and Company.

(b) Macy and his tavern on Third Avenue.

(c) history up to 1950.

(d) the world of the future.

BUILDING YOUR VOCABULARY

1. "MQ, Mr. Macy," the stranger said in a *staccato* voice.

   Staccato (page 99, line 9) speech is **(a)** smooth and flowing **(b)** extremely loud **(c)** abrupt and broken **(d)** foreign.

2. Boyne leaned across the table with *galvanic* intensity.

   a. A word similar in meaning to *galvanic* (page 101, lines 12-13) is **(a)** detached **(b)** lazy **(c)** galactic **(d)** electric.

   b. Which is the BEST strategy for answering part *a*?
      (a) Analyze the word *galvanic* into its parts.
      (b) Eliminate inappropriate choices by pairing each one with *intensity*.
      (c) Reread the paragraph in which the word appears.
      (d) Look for an earlier use of the word in the story.

3. "Indeed yes." Boyne nodded sharply. "More than rich. *Omnipotent*."

   An *omnipotent* (page 102, line 10) person is **(a)** all-powerful **(b)** extremely rich **(c)** very poor **(d)** all-suffering.

4. He nailed the couple with a *contemptuous* glare.

   a. A synonym for *contemptuous* (page 103, line 22) is **(a)** contemplative **(b)** affectionate **(c)** scornful **(d)** hopeful.

   b. The BEST strategy for answering part *a* is to
      (a) reread the entire conversation between Boyne and Knight up to the sentence in which the word appears.
      (b) reread only the paragraph in which the word appears.
      (c) look for clues in the names listed later in the paragraph containing the word.
      (d) replace the italicized word with each choice and judge its appropriateness in the context of the sentence.

5. You have eased a *precarious* situation.

   The BEST meaning of *precarious* (page 104, line 42) is
   (a) variously colored.
   (b) prematurely old.
   (c) firmly established.
   (d) dangerously unstable.

STUDYING THE WRITER'S CRAFT _____

1. In the first few paragraphs of the story, Alfred Bester establishes Boyne as an alien character.

    a. How does Boyne's physical appearance seem strange?

    b. How does Boyne's speech suggest someone who may be "out of this world"?

    c. At what point in the story did you feel certain that Boyne was some sort of alien, either of space or time? Explain your answer.

2. A fiction writer may choose to *characterize* one of the persons in a story partly through his or her impact on others.

    a. How does Boyne affect Macy? Give evidence for your answer from the story.

    b. How does Boyne affect Jane Clinton? Explain.

    c. How does Boyne affect Oliver Knight during the course of the story? Explain.

3. A short story gets its energy from *conflict*, or the struggle between opposing forces. It gives pleasure to its readers by the satisfactory *resolution* (working out) of the conflict.

    a. Which two characters in the story are in obvious external conflict with each other? Why?

    b. What is the resolution of this conflict?

    c. What is the nature of the less-obvious internal conflict within Oliver Knight?

    d. How is Knight's conflict resolved? What helps resolve it?

ACTIVITIES FOR LISTENING, SPEAKING, WRITING

1. Suppose that Knight had decided to keep and use the 1990 almanac. What do you think would have happened to him? to Jane? to Boyne? Write a brief alternate ending to the story. Tell what you think happens to the three characters and why it happens.

2. Boyne was sent from the future to the past on a mission of the utmost importance. Imagine that he has now returned with the 1990 almanac to his world of the future and must file a report. Write Boyne's report for him. (Don't forget to date it.)

3. In groups of three, at your teacher's direction, take the parts of Boyne, Knight, and Jane. Read aloud from the story only the material within quotation marks from page 100, lines 31-32 (Boyne: "Sit down. Charmed, I assure you") to page 104, line 37 (Knight: "Take it"). After this dramatic reading, discuss with your classmates how well you think this part of the story works as a play.

Absolutely Inflexible

by Robert Silverberg

But you knew you were going on a one-way trip to the future, and you're subject to whatever that future wants to do with you, since there's no way of getting back.

If you think that time travel would be all fun and adventure, think again! The story that follows explores the darker side of time travel. Commenting on "Absolutely Inflexible," Robert Silverberg has wondered if it may not be true that "time travel is a risky business, best left alone. Certainly, that's the theme of this excursion into paradox."

Both one-way and two-way time travel appear in this ingenious story. As you will see, each type of time travel carries its own danger. Suppose you had a chance for two-way time travel. Would you go? And if you chose to go, would you travel to the past or to the future? Find out how Absolutely Inflexible Mahler answers these questions for himself.

Robert Silverberg

Two prestigious awards are made for the best works of science fiction published each year. They are like the Oscars given for excellence in motion pictures. Since 1953, science-fiction fans at the annual World Science Fiction Convention have voted for writers to be honored with the *Hugo Award*. (The award was named after Hugo Gernsbach, who edited *Amazing Stories*. Started in 1926, this was the first science-fiction magazine published in the United States. Gernsbach also coined the term "science fiction.") Since 1966, a second award has been given by members of the Science Fiction Writers of America. This is the *Nebula Award*.

For many of his science-fiction novels and short stories, Robert Silverberg won both Hugo and Nebula awards. He wrote hundreds of books, both fiction and nonfiction, some under his own name, some under pseudonyms, and some in collaboration with other authors. Since the 1960s, he also edited a great many anthologies of science fiction. Both as writer and editor, Silverberg is astonishingly prolific.

The detector over in one corner of Mahler's little office gleamed a soft red. He indicated it with a weary gesture of his hand to the sad-eyed time-jumper who sat slouched glumly across the desk from him, looking cramped and uncomfortable in the bulky space suit he was compelled to wear.

"You see," Mahler said, tapping his desk. "They've just found another one. We're constantly bombarded with you people. When you get to the Moon, you'll find a whole Dome full of them. I've sent over four 10 thousand there myself since I took over the Bureau. And that was eight years ago—in 2776. An average of five hundred a year. Hardly a day goes by without someone dropping in on us."

"And not one has been set free," the time-jumper said. "Every time-traveler who's come here has been packed off to the Moon immediately. Every one."

"Every one," Mahler said. He peered through the thick shielding, trying to see what sort of man was hidden inside the space suit. Mahler often wondered about the men he condemned so easily to the Moon. This one was small of stature, with wispy locks of white hair pasted to his high forehead by perspiration. Evidently he had been a scientist, a respected man of his time, perhaps a happy father (although very few of the time-jumpers were family men). Perhaps he possessed some bit of scientific knowledge which would be invaluable to the twenty-eighth century; perhaps not. It did not matter. Like all the rest, he would have to be sent to the Moon, to live out his remaining days under the grueling, primitive conditions of the Dome.

"Don't you think that's a little cruel?" the other asked. "I came here with no malice, no intent to harm whatsoever. I'm simply a scientific observer from the past. Driven by curiosity, I took the Jump. I never expected that I'd be walking into life imprisonment."

"I'm sorry," Mahler said, getting up. He decided to end the interview; he had to get rid of this jumper because there was another coming right up. Some days they came thick and fast, and this looked like one of them. But the efficient mechanical tracers never missed one.

"But can't I live on Earth and stay in this space suit?" the time-jumper asked, panicky now that he saw his interview with Mahler was coming to an end. "That way I'd be sealed off from contact at all times."

"Please don't make this any harder for me," Mahler said. "I've explained to you why we must be absolutely inflexible about this. There cannot—must not—be any exceptions. It's two centuries since last there was any occurrence of disease on Earth. In all this time we've lost most of the resistance acquired over the previous countless generations of disease. I'm risking my life coming so close to you, even with the space suit sealing you off."

Mahler signaled to the tall, powerful guards waiting in the corridor, grim in the casings that protected them from infection. This was always the worst moment.

"Look," Mahler said, frowning with impatience. "You're a walking death trap. You probably carry enough disease germs to kill half the world. Even a cold, a common cold, would wipe out millions now. Resistance to disease has simply vanished over the past two centuries; it isn't needed, with all diseases conquered. But you time-travelers show up loaded with potentialities for all the diseases the world used to have. And we can't risk having you stay here with them."

"But I'd—"

"I know. You'd swear by all that's holy to you or to me that you'd never leave the confines of the space suit. Sorry. The word of the most honorable man doesn't carry any weight against the safety of the lives of Earth's billions. We can't take the slightest risk by letting you stay on Earth. It's unfair, it's cruel, it's everything else. You had no idea you would walk into something like this. Well, it's too bad for you. But you knew you were going on a one-way trip to the future, and you're subject to whatever that future wants to do with you, since there's no way of getting back."

Mahler began to tidy up the papers on his desk in a way that signaled finality. "I'm terribly sorry, but you'll just have to see our way of thinking about it. We're frightened to death at your very presence here. We can't allow you to roam Earth, even in a space suit. No; there's nothing 10 for you but the Moon. I have to be absolutely inflexible. Take him away," he said, gesturing to the guards. They advanced on the little man and began gently to ease him out of Mahler's office.

Mahler sank gratefully into the pneumochair and sprayed his throat with laryngogel. These long speeches always left him exhausted, his throat feeling raw and scraped. Someday I'll get throat cancer from all this talking, Mahler thought. And that'll mean the nuisance of an operation. But if I don't do this job, someone else will have to.

Mahler heard the protesting screams of the time-jumper impassively. In the beginning he had been ready to resign when he first witnessed the 20 inevitable frenzied reaction of jumper after jumper as the guards dragged them away, but eight years had hardened him.

They had given him the job because he was hard, in the first place. It was a job that called for a hard man. Condrin, his predecessor, had not been the same sort of man Mahler was, and for that reason Condrin was now himself on the Moon. He had weakened after heading the Bureau a year, and had let a jumper go; the jumper had promised to secrete himself at the tip of Antarctica, and Condrin, thinking that Antarctica was as safe as the Moon, had foolishly released him. That was when they called Mahler in. In eight years Mahler had sent four thousand men to the Moon. 30 (The first was the runaway jumper, intercepted in Buenos Aires after he had left a trail of disease down the hemisphere from Appalachia to the Argentine Protectorate. The second was Condrin.)

It was getting to be a tiresome job, Mahler thought. But he was proud to hold it. It took a strong man to do what he was doing. He leaned back and awaited the arrival of the next jumper.

The door slid smoothly open as the burly body of Dr. Fournet, the Bureau's chief medical man, broke the photoelectronic beam. Mahler glanced up. Fournet carried a time-rig dangling from one hand.

"Took this away from our latest customer," Fournet said. "He told 40 the medic who examined him that it was a two-way rig, and I thought I'd bring it to show you."

Mahler came to full attention quickly. A two-way rig? Unlikely, he thought. But it would mean the end of the dreary jumper prison on the Moon if it were true. Only how could a two-way rig exist?

He reached out and took it from Fournet. "It seems to be a conventional twenty-fourth-century type," he said.

"But notice the extra dial here," Fournet said, pointing. Mahler peered and nodded.

"Yes. It *seems* to be a two-way rig. But how can we test it? And it's not really very probable," Mahler said. "Why should a two-way rig suddenly show up from the twenty-fourth century, when no other traveler's 10 had one? We don't even have two-way time-travel ourselves, and our scientists don't think it's possible. Still," he mused, "it's a nice thing to dream about. We'll have to study this a little more closely. But I don't seriously think it'll work. Bring him in, will you?"

As Fournet turned to signal the guards, Mahler asked him, "What's his medical report, by the way?"

"From here to here," Fournet said somberly. "You name it, he's carrying it. Better get him shipped off to the Moon as soon as possible. I won't feel safe until he's off this planet." The big medic waved to the guards.

Mahler smiled. Fournet's overcautiousness was proverbial in the Bu- 20 reau. Even if a jumper were to show up completely free from disease, Fournet would probably insist that he was carrying everything from asthma to leprosy.

The guards brought the jumper into Mahler's office. He was fairly tall, Mahler saw, and young. It was difficult to see his face clearly through the dim plate of the protective space suit all jumpers were compelled to wear, but Mahler could tell that the young time-jumper's face had much of the lean, hard look of Mahler's own. It seemed that the jumper's eyes had widened in surprise as he entered the office, but Mahler was not sure. 30

"I never dreamed I'd find you here," the jumper said. The transmitter of the space suit brought his voice over deeply and resonantly. "Your name is Mahler, isn't it?"

"That's right," Mahler agreed.

"To go all these years—and find you. Talk about improbabilities!"

Mahler ignored him, declining to take up the gambit. He had found it was good practice never to let a captured jumper get the upper hand in conversation. His standard procedure was firmly to explain to the jumper the reasons why it was imperative that he be sent to the Moon, and then send him, as quickly as possible. 40

"You say this is a two-way time-rig?" Mahler asked, holding up the flimsy-looking piece of equipment.

"That's right," the other agreed. "Works both ways. If you pressed the button, you'd go straight back to 2360 or thereabouts."

"Did you build it?"

"Me? No, hardly," said the jumper. "I found it. It's a long story, and I don't have time to tell it. In fact, if I tried to tell it, I'd only make things ten times worse than they are, if that's possible. No. Let's get this over with, shall we? I know I don't stand much of a chance with you, and I'd just as soon make it quick."

"You know, of course, that this is a world without disease—" Mahler began sonorously.

"And that you think I'm carrying enough germs of different sorts to wipe out the whole world. And therefore you have to be absolutely inflexible with me. All right. I won't try to argue with you. Which way is the Moon?"

Absolutely inflexible. The phrase Mahler had used so many times, the phrase that summed him up so neatly. He chuckled to himself; some of the younger technicians must have tipped the jumper off about the usual procedure, and the jumper was resigned to going peacefully, without bothering to plead. It was just as well.

Absolutely inflexible.

Yes, Mahler thought, the words fit him well. He was becoming a stereotype in the Bureau. Perhaps he was the only Bureau chief who had never relented and let a jumper go. Probably all the others, bowed under the weight of the hordes of curious men flooding in from the past, had finally cracked and taken the risk. But not Mahler; not Absolutely Inflexible Mahler. He knew the deep responsibility that rode on his shoulders, and he had no intention of failing what amounted to a sacred trust. His job was to find the jumpers and get them off Earth as quickly and as efficiently as possible. Every one. It was a task that required unsoftening inflexibility.

"This makes my job much easier," Mahler said. "I'm glad I won't have to convince you of the necessity of my duty."

"Not at all," the other agreed. "I understand. I won't even waste my breath. You have good reasons for what you're doing, and nothing I say can alter them." He turned to the guards. "I'm ready. Take me away."

Mahler gestured to them, and they led the jumper away. Amazed, Mahler watched the retreating figure, studying him until he could no longer be seen.

If they were all like that, Mahler thought.

I could have gotten to like that one. That was a sensible man—one of the few. He knew he was beaten, and he didn't try to argue in the face of absolute necessity. It's too bad he had to go; he's the kind of man I'd like to find more often these days.

But I mustn't feel sympathy, Mahler told himself.

He had performed his job so well so long because he had managed to suppress any sympathy for the unfortunates he had to condemn. Had there been someplace else to send them—back to their own time, preferably—he would have been the first to urge abolition of the Moon prison. But, with no place else to send them, he performed his job efficiently and automatically.

He picked up the jumper's time-rig and examined it. A two-way rig would be the solution, of course. As soon as the jumper arrives, turn him around and send him back. They'd get the idea soon enough. Mahler 10 found himself wishing it were so: he often wondered what the jumpers stranded on the Moon must think of him.

A two-way rig could change the world completely; its implications were staggering. With men able to move with ease backward and forward in time, past, present, and future would blend into one mind-numbing new entity. It was impossible to conceive of the world as it would be, with free passage in either direction.

But even as Mahler fondled the confiscated time-rig, he realized something was wrong. In the six centuries since the development of time-travel, no one had yet developed a known two-way rig. And, more important, 20 there were no documented reports of visitors from the future. Presumably, if a two-way rig existed, such visitors would have been commonplace.

So the jumper had been lying, Mahler thought with regret. The two-way rig was an impossibility. He had merely been playing a game with his captors. This *couldn't* be a two-way rig, because the past held no record of anyone's going back.

Mahler examined the rig. There were two dials on it, one the conventional forward dial and the other indicating backward travel. Whoever had prepared this hoax had gone to considerable extent to document it. *Why?*

Could it be that the jumper had told the truth? Mahler wished he 30 could somehow test the rig in his hands; there was always that one chance that it might actually work, that he would no longer have to be the rigid dispenser of justice, Absolutely Inflexible Mahler.

He looked at it. As a time machine, it was fairly crude. It made use of the standard distorter pattern, but the dial was the clumsy wide-range twenty-fourth-century one; the vernier system, Mahler reflected, had not been introduced until the twenty-fifth.

Mahler peered closer to read the instruction label. PLACE LEFT HAND HERE, it said. He studied it carefully. The ghost of a thought wandered into his mind; he pushed it aside in horror, but it recurred. It would be 40 so simple. What if—?

No.

But—
PLACE LEFT HAND HERE.
He reached out tentatively with his left hand.
Just a bit—
No.
PLACE LEFT HAND HERE.
He touched his hand gingerly to the indicated place. There was a little crackle of electricity. He let go, quickly, and started to replace the time-rig on his desk when the desk abruptly faded out from under him.

The air was foul and grimy. Mahler wondered what had happened 10 to the Conditioner. Then he looked around.

Huge grotesque ugly buildings raised to the sky. Black, despairing clouds of smoke overhead. The harsh screech of an industrial society.

He was in the middle of an immense city, with streams of people rushing past him on the street at a furious pace. They were all small, stunted creatures, angry-looking, their faces harried, neurotic. It was the same black, frightened expression Mahler had seen so many times on the faces of jumpers escaping to what they hoped might be a more congenial future.

He looked at the time-rig clutched in one hand, and knew what had 20 happened.

The two-way rig.

It meant the end of the Moon prisons. It meant a complete revolution in civilization. But he had no further business back in this age of nightmare. He reached down to activate the time-rig.

Abruptly someone jolted him from behind. The current of the crowd swept him along, as he struggled to regain his control over himself. Suddenly a hand reached out and grabbed the back of his neck.

"Got a card, Hump?"

He whirled to face an ugly, squinting-eyed man in a dull-brown 30 uniform with a row of metallic buttons.

"Hear me? Where's your card, Hump? Talk up or you get Spotted."

Mahler twisted out of the man's grasp and started to jostle his way quickly through the crowd, desiring nothing more than a moment to set the time-rig and get out of this disease-ridden squalid era. As he shoved people out of his way, they shouted angrily at him.

"There's a Hump!" someone called. "Spot him!"

The cry became a roar. "Spot him! Spot him!"

Wherever—whenever—he was, it was no place to stay in long. He turned left and went pounding down a side street, and now it was a 40 full-fledged mob that dashed after him, shouting wildly.

"Send for the Crimers!" a deep voice boomed. "They'll Spot him!"

Someone caught up to him, and without looking Mahler reached behind and hit out, hard. He heard a dull grunt of pain, and continued running. The unaccustomed exercise was tiring him rapidly.

An open door beckoned. He stepped inside, finding himself inside a machine store of sorts, and slammed the door shut. They still had manual doors, a remote part of his mind observed coldly.

A salesman came toward him. "Can I help you, sir? The latest models, right here."

"Just leave me alone," Mahler panted, squinting at the time-rig. The salesman watched uncomprehendingly as Mahler fumbled with the little dial.

There was no vernier. He'd have to chance it and hope he hit the right year. The salesman suddenly screamed and came to life, for reasons Mahler would never understand. Mahler averted him and punched the stud viciously.

It was wonderful to step back into the serenity of twenty-eighth-century Appalachia. Small wonder so many time-jumpers come here, Mahler reflected, as he waited for his overworked heart to calm down. Almost anything would be preferable to *then*.

He looked around the quiet street for a Convenience where he could repair the scratches and bruises he had acquired during his brief stay in the past. They would scarcely be able to recognize him at the Bureau in his present battered condition, with one eye nearly closed, a great livid welt on his cheek, and his clothing hanging in tatters.

He sighted a Convenience and started down the street, pausing at the sound of a familiar soft mechanical whining. He looked around to see one of the low-running mechanical tracers of the Bureau purring up the street toward him, closely followed by two Bureau guards, clad in their protective casings.

Of course. He had arrived from the past, and the detectors had recorded his arrival, as they would that of any time-traveler. They never missed.

He turned and walked toward the guards. He failed to recognize either one, but this did not surprise him; the Bureau was a vast and wide-ranging organization, and he knew only a handful of the many guards who accompanied the tracers. It was a pleasant relief to see the tracer; the use of tracers had been instituted during his administration, so at least he knew he hadn't returned too early along the time stream.

"Good to see you," he called to the approaching guards. "I had a little accident in the office."

They ignored him and methodically unpacked a space suit from the storage trunk of the mechanical tracer. "Never mind talking," one said. "Get into this."

He paled. "But I'm no jumper," he said. "Hold on a moment, fellows. This is all a mistake. I'm Mahler—head of the Bureau. Your boss."

"Don't play games with us, fellow," the taller guard said, while the other forced the space suit down over Mahler. To his horror, Mahler saw that they did not recognize him at all.

"If you'll just come peacefully and let the Chief explain everything to you, without any trouble—" the short guard said.   10

"But I *am* the Chief," Mahler protested. "I was examining a two-way time-rig in my office and accidentally sent myself back to the past. Take this thing off me and I'll show you my identification card; that should convince you."

"Look, fellow, we don't want to be convinced of anything. Tell it to the Chief if you want. Now, are you coming, or do we bring you?"

There was no point, Mahler decided, in trying to prove his identity to the clean-faced young medic who examined him at the Bureau office. That would only add more complications, he realized. No; he would wait until he reached the office of the Chief.   20

He saw now what had happened: apparently he had landed somewhere in his own future, shortly after his own death. Someone else had taken over the Bureau, and he, Mahler, was forgotten. (Mahler suddenly realized with a little shock that at this very moment his ashes were probably reposing in an urn at the Appalachia Crematorium.)

When he got to the Chief of the Bureau, he would simply and calmly explain his identity and ask for permission to go back the ten or twenty or thirty years to the time in which he belonged, and where he could turn the two-way rig over to the proper authorities and resume his life from his point of departure. And when that happened, the jumpers would no 30 longer be sent to the Moon, and there would be no further need for Absolutely Inflexible Mahler.

But, he realized, if I've already done this, then why is there still a Bureau now? An uneasy fear began to grow in him.

"Hurry up and finish that report," Mahler told the medic.

"I don't know what the rush is," the medic said. "Unless you like it on the Moon."

"Don't worry about me," Mahler said confidently. "If I told you who I am, you'd think twice about—"

"Is this thing your time-rig?" the medic asked boredly, interrupting. 40

"Not really. I mean—yes, yes it is," Mahler said. "And be careful with it. It's the world's only two-way rig."

"Really, now?" said the medic. "Two ways, eh?"

"Yes. And if you'll take me in to your Chief—"

"Just a minute. I'd like to show this to the Head Medic."

In a few moments the medic returned. "All right, let's go to the Chief now. I'd advise you not to bother arguing; you can't win. You should have stayed where you came from."

Two guards appeared and jostled Mahler down the familiar corridor to the brightly lit little office where he had spent eight years. Eight years on the other side of the fence.

As he approached the door of what had once been his office, he carefully planned what he would say to his successor. He would explain the accident, demonstrate his identity as Mahler, and request permission to use the two-way rig to return to his own time. The Chief would probably be belligerent at first, then curious, finally amused at the chain of events that had ensnarled Mahler. And, of course, he would let him go, after they had exchanged anecdotes about their job, the job they both held at the same time and across a gap of years. Mahler swore never again to touch a time machine, once he got back. He would let others undergo the huge job of transmitting the jumpers back to their own eras.

He moved forward and broke the photoelectronic beam. The door to the Bureau Chief's office slid open. Behind the desk sat a tall, powerful-looking man, lean, hard.

Me.

Through the dim plate of the space suit into which he had been stuffed, Mahler saw the man behind the desk. Himself. Absolutely Inflexible Mahler. The man who had sent four thousand men to the Moon, without exception, in the unbending pursuit of his duty.

And if he's Mahler—

Who am I?

Suddenly Mahler saw the insane circle complete. He recalled the jumper, the firm, deep-voiced, unafraid time-jumper who had arrived claiming to have a two-way rig and who had marched off to the Moon without arguing. Now Mahler knew who that jumper was.

But how did the cycle start? Where did the two-way rig come from in the first place? He had gone to the past to bring it to the present to take it to the past to—

His head swam. There was no way out. He looked at the man behind the desk and began to walk toward him, feeling a wall of circumstance growing around him, while he, in frustration, tried impotently to beat his way out.

It was utterly pointless to argue. Not with Absolutely Inflexible Mahler. It would just be a waste of breath. The wheel had come full circle, and he was as good as on the Moon. He looked at the man behind the desk with a new, strange light in his eyes.

"I never dreamed I'd find you here," the jumper said. The transmitter of the space suit brought his voice over deeply and resonantly.

REVIEWING THE STORY

THE MAIN IDEA

1. The title "Absolutely Inflexible" refers to
   (a) life in the Dome on the Moon.
   (b) Condrin as Bureau Chief.
   (c) Dr. Fournet, the Bureau's chief medical man.
   (d) Mahler's character and job performance.

DETAILS

2. According to the story, time-jumpers pose a threat to Mahler's world because they
   (a) may bring scientific knowledge from another age.
   (b) carry diseases to which people have lost resistance.
   (c) could change things through the time-travel paradox.
   (d) may cause overpopulation on Earth.

3. At the beginning of the story, the date is (a) 2360 (b) 2500 (c) 2776 (d) 2784.

4. As Bureau Chief, Mahler must send time-jumpers
   (a) to a hospital.
   (b) back to the past.
   (c) to prison on the Moon.
   (d) on to the future.

5. When the story opens, Mahler believes that time travel can be
   (a) only one way.
   (b) two way.
   (c) helpful to his people.
   (d) easily reversible.

6. Returning from his trip in time, Mahler meets
   (a) Condrin, his predecessor.
   (b) Absolutely Inflexible Mahler.

(c) the short, white-haired time-jumper.

(d) a stranger who has succeeded him as Chief of the Bureau.

ORDER OF EVENTS

7. Choose the letter that gives the order in which the events happen.

(1) Mahler becomes Bureau Chief.

(2) Mahler tests a two-way time-rig.

(3) Condrin is sent to the Moon.

(4) The sad-eyed time-jumper pleads with Mahler.

(a) 1-3-4-2   (b) 3-4-1-2   (c) 3-1-4-2   (d) 2-1-3-4

CAUSE AND EFFECT

8. Mahler's first trip in time is caused by his

(a) impatience with the sad-eyed time-jumper.

(b) need to prove his absolute inflexibility.

(c) curiosity and wish to give up being absolutely inflexible.

(d) desire to escape from the Moon.

9. The effect of Mahler's time travel is to

(a) end the need for a Moon prison.

(b) convince scientists that two-way travel exists.

(c) bring all time travel to an end.

(d) change nothing at all.

INFERENCES

10. Mahler's use of the two-way time-rig is

(a) required by his job as Bureau Chief.

(b) partly accidental.

(c) a matter of historical record.

(d) the only way to avoid new diseases.

11. The time-jumper with the two-way rig knows that Mahler is absolutely inflexible because the time-jumper is

(a) Condrin, Mahler's predecessor.

(b) the sad-eyed jumper Mahler sent to the Moon.

(c) Mahler himself.

(d) Dr. Fournet, the Bureau's chief medical man.

PREDICTING OUTCOMES

12. After the story ends, the Mahler behind the desk, who unwittingly sent himself to the Moon, probably
    (a) gives the rig back to Dr. Fournet.
    (b) has copies of the two-way rig made for others to use.
    (c) accidentally uses the rig himself.
    (d) gives the rig back to its original owner.

BUILDING YOUR VOCABULARY _____

1. I've explained to you why we must be absolutely *inflexible* about this.

   A person who is absolutely *inflexible* (page 113, lines 23-24) would never (a) lie (b) yield (c) forget (d) persevere.

2. Mahler heard the protesting screams of the time-jumper *impassively*.
   a. *Impassively* (page 114, line 19) means
      (a) with deep sympathy.
      (b) with great difficulty.
      (c) without understanding.
      (d) without emotion.
   b. The BEST strategy for answering part *a* is to
      (a) read the paragraph before the one containing the word *impassively*.
      (b) read the sentence in which *impassively* appears.
      (c) read the sentence after the one in which *impassively* appears.
      (d) remember the physical description of the time-jumper.

3. . . . the jumper was *resigned* to going peacefully, without bothering to plead.

   In this context, *resigned* (page 116, lines 18-19) means
   (a) voluntarily gave up a job or office.
   (b) submitted without protest.
   (c) determined never to give in.
   (d) signed a paper promising peaceful behavior.

4. They were all small, stunted creatures, angry-looking, their faces *harried*, neurotic.

   Faces that look *harried* (page 118, lines 15-16) are
   (a) marked by stress and anxiety.
   (b) always in a hurry.

(c) covered with hair.

(d) cheerful and happy.

5. The Chief would probably be *belligerent* at first, then curious, finally amused at the chain of events that had ensnarled Mahler.

   The word that means the OPPOSITE of *belligerent* (page 121, lines 13-15) is **(a)** antagonistic **(b)** unfriendly **(c)** hostile **(d)** sympathetic.

STUDYING THE WRITER'S CRAFT

1. A *metaphor* is a figure of speech in which a word or phrase is used to suggest a comparison with an actual object or action. Unlike a *simile* (see page 24), a metaphor does not use the word *like* or *as*. By using metaphors, you can pack a great deal of meaning and feeling into a single word or phrase. *Example*: "We're constantly *bombarded* with you people." (page 112, line 9) The metaphorical use of *bombarded* compares time-jumpers (people) with bombs. During an aerial bombardment, bombs are both numerous and destructive. This is just what Mahler thinks and feels about the thousands of time-jumpers he has exiled to the Moon.

   In each of the following sentences, tell what two things are being compared in the italicized metaphor.

   a. The word of the most honorable man doesn't *carry any weight* against the safety of the lives of Earth's billions. (page 113, line 42 to page 114, line 2)

   b. A two-way rig could change the world completely; its implications were *staggering*. (page 117, lines 13-14)

   c. The *ghost* of a thought *wandered* into his mind; he pushed it aside in horror, but it recurred. (page 117, lines 39-40)

2. A good writer uses complete and correct sentences. There may be times, however, when incomplete sentences—sentence fragments—are more effective. Reread the paragraph on page 118, lines 12-13 ("Huge grotesque . . . society"). Which sentences are fragments? Do you think that sentence fragments work better than complete sentences at this particular point in the story? Explain why or why not. (*Hint*: Consider Mahler's state of mind at this moment.)

3. A story writer must create *verisimilitude* (the appearance of being genuine) for a fictitious world. Robert Silverberg has invented a num-

ber of technical details and a routine procedure to explain the detection and handling of time-jumpers in Mahler's world. Describe these details and the procedure.

ACTIVITIES FOR LISTENING, SPEAKING, WRITING

1. Imagine that a time-travel company is sponsoring an essay contest. The winner of the contest gets a free trip to the past and back. Write a brief essay telling what period in the past you would like to visit and why. To compete successfully against the other contestants, you'll have to write a good, convincing essay.

2. According to Mahler, "In the six centuries since the development of time-travel, no one had yet developed a known two-way rig." (page 117, lines 19-20) Mahler soon learns, however, that a working two-way rig has been developed. Why does nobody else ever learn of the existence of this extraordinary device? Be prepared to discuss this crucial question with your classmates.

3. Working with your classmates, prepare a list of things you would seal up in a time capsule to show people of the future what life in your time was like. The capsule is to be buried underground until the people of the 28th century, Mahler's time, unearth it. As a friendly gesture, include some written messages to these people who will be alive seven centuries from now. Also write instructions as to where the time capsule is located, when it was buried, and when it is to be opened. For safekeeping, where would you put these instructions?

Is Time Travel Possible?

by Mark Davidson

Einstein[1] himself, only four weeks before his death, confided in a letter to a friend that modern physics had converted him to the ancient belief that "the distinction between past, present and future is only a stubbornly persistent illusion."

When science-fiction writers describe the actual mechanisms of time travel, they are deliberately vague. This is certainly true of the three stories in this theme. Considering the present state of time travel, you can understand why these writers are a bit fuzzy about how it works.

Is real time travel, then, only a fantasy? Will it always remain nothing but a clever idea in science fiction? Some tentative but intriguing answers are emerging from three areas of scientific study: particle physics,[2] astronomy, and space travel.

In the following article, Mark Davidson, a California university teacher and science writer, surveys the evidence for and against time travel. Read the article and then decide for yourself: Is time travel possible?

---

1. **Einstein:** Albert Einstein (1879–1955), world-famous German-American physicist.
2. **particle physics:** the study of subatomic units of matter or energy, such as electrons, protons, and neutrons.

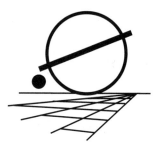

Contrary to the old warning that time waits for no one, time slows down when you are on the move. It also slows down more as you move faster, which means astronauts someday may survive so long in space that they would return to an Earth of the distant future. If you could move at the speed of light, 186,282 miles a second, your time would stand still. If you could move faster than light, outpacing your shadow, your time would move backward.

TIME STRETCHING

Although no form of matter yet discovered moves as fast or faster than light, scientific experiments have confirmed that accelerated motion causes a voyager's time to be stretched. Einstein predicted this in 1905, when he introduced the concept of relative time as part of his Special Theory of Relativity. A search is now under way to confirm the suspected existence of particles of matter that move faster than light and therefore possibly might serve as our passports to the past.

Einstein employed a definition of time, for experimental purposes, as that which is measured by a clock. He regarded a clock as anything that measured a uniformly repeating physical process. In accordance with his definition, time and time's relativity are measurable by any sundial, hourglass, metronome, alarm clock, or an atomic clock that can measure a billionth of a second because its "tick" is based on the uniformly repeating wobble of the spinning-top motion of electrons.

With atomic-clock application of Einstein's definition of time, scientists have demonstrated that an ordinary airplane flight is like a brief visit to the Fountain of Youth. In 1972, for example, scientists who took four atomic clocks on an airplane trip around the world discovered that the moving clocks moved slightly slower than atomic clocks which had remained on the ground. If you fly around the world, preferably going eastward to gain the advantage of the added motion of the Earth's rotation, the atomic clocks show that you'll return younger than you would have been if you had stayed home. Frankly, you'll be younger by only 40 billionths of a second. Such an infinitesimal saving of time hardly makes up for all the hours you age while waiting at airports, but *any* saving of time proves that time can be stretched. Moreover, atomic clocks have demonstrated that the stretching of time, or "time dilation," increases with speed.   10

Here is an example of what you can expect if tomorrow's space-flight technology—employing the energy of thermonuclear fusion, matter-antimatter annihilation, or whatever—enables you to move at ultra-high speeds. Imagine you're an astronaut with a twin who stays home. If you travel back and forth to the nearest star at about half the speed of light, you'll be gone for eighteen Earth years. When you return, your twin will be eighteen years older, but you'll have aged only sixteen years. Your body will be two years younger than your twin's because time aboard the flying spaceship will have moved slower than time on Earth. You will have aged normally, but you will have been in a slower time zone. If your 20 spaceship moves at about 90 percent of light-speed, you'll age only 50 percent as much as your twin. If you whiz along at 99.86 percent of light-speed, you'll age only 5 percent as much. These examples of time-stretching, of course, cannot be tested with any existing spacecraft. Yet, they are based on mathematical projections of relativity science, as confirmed by the atomic-clock experiments.

Speed is not the only factor that slows time; so does gravity. Einstein determined in his General Theory of Relativity (the 1915 sequel to his 1905 Special Theory of Relativity) that the force of an object's gravity "curves" the space in the object's gravitational field. When gravity curves 30 space, Einstein reasoned, gravity also must curve time, because space and time are linked in a space-time continuum. The concept of the space-time continuum, developed by one of Einstein's former professors, simply means that time and space must be considered together because time is a fourth dimension of space.

Numerous atomic-clock experiments have confirmed Einstein's calculation that, the closer you are to the Earth's center of gravity, which is the Earth's core, the slower you will age. In one of these experiments, an atomic clock was taken from the National Bureau of Standards in Washington, D.C., near sea level, and moved to mile-high Denver. The results 40 demonstrated that people in Denver age more rapidly by a tiny amount than people in Washington.

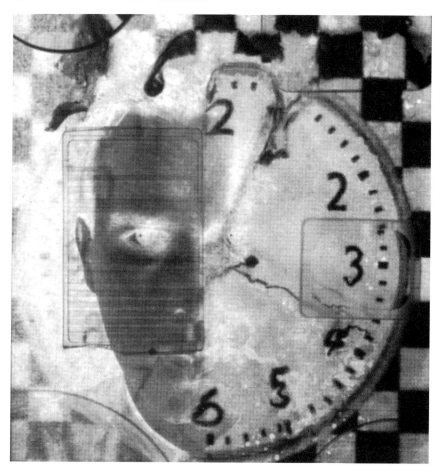

If you would like gravity's space-time warp to extend your life, get a home at the beach and a job as a deep-sea diver. Avoid living in the mountains or working in a skyscraper. If you're taking airplane trips to slow your aging, make sure you fly fast enough to cancel out the gravity-reduction effect of being high above the Earth's surface. That advice, like the advice about flying around the world, will enable you to slow your aging by only a few billionths of a second.

Nevertheless, those tiny fractions of a second add up to more proof that time-stretching is a reality. The proof involving gravity suggests that you could have an unforgettable rendezvous with a black hole, where gravity is believed to be so powerful that it imprisons light. In a black hole—a huge, burned-out star that has collapsed into infinite density and, therefore, infinite gravity—the object's extreme warp of space-time would make your time stand still. Granted, a black hole would be an awfully dark and dreary place to spend eternity, but think of all the time you'd have to redecorate.

TIME REVERSAL

Though time reversal is a highly debatable theory, particle physicists have discovered a phenomenon that indicates it may be an everyday occurrence for the creatures of inner space. To appreciate this discovery, imagine that you use your VCR to watch a movie scene of a car crash in reverse. The reversed scene of the crash is obviously unrealistic, and you have no trouble realizing that you're watching the scene in reverse.

Now, pretend that you could watch a movie scene of a crash be- 10 tween an electron and a positron, resulting in their becoming two photons. If you were able to reverse this crash with your VCR, according to scientific calculations, you'd see the two photons become an electron and a positron. Both scenes are equally authentic, and scientists say you would have absolutely no way of telling which scene is moving forward in time and which is moving backward. The same is true of the identity-switching games of protons and neutrons and other inner-space phenomena.

Scientists conclude from this "principle of time reversal invariance" that the distinction between the past and the future does not exist in the 20 domain of inner space. "It is conceivable," physicist Richard Morris deduces, "that this result is telling us something about the nature of time that we have not yet grasped. Time, after all, is one of those elusive things that we all think we understand, but which may contain mysteries that we have not yet fathomed."

Nay-sayers generally concede that we could travel to the past if we were able to move faster than light. However, they insist that nature has protected the past from the possible interferences of time-travelers by establishing light-speed as the universal speed limit, a traffic law so strict that nature won't even let you combine the speed of light with 30 a moving object. If a flying plane fires a rocket, the rocket zooms off at the combined velocity of the rocket and the plane. If the plane fires a beam of light, the light-beam velocity will not be affected at all by the velocity of the plane. Moreover, no known material object is allowed to move as fast as light. The nay-sayers note that nature increases your mass as you increase your speed. More mass means more inertia, which means more resistance to a change in the rate of motion, or a change from non-motion to motion. An object as small as a particle of dust, moving almost as fast as light, would acquire the mass, and therefore the inertia, of an entire planet. The object still would be the size of a dust particle, but it would weigh at least as much as Earth. At the very instant before any object would accelerate to light-speed, it would be stricken with infinite inertia—a condition you may have experienced on mornings when you knew that getting out of bed simply was impossible.

JOURNEY TO THE FUTURE

If we did discover a source of energy that would enable us to travel beyond light-speed, we might have access not only to the past, but also, in a sort of Rip Van Winkle sense, to the future. Suppose you went on a super-light-speed trek to the Spiral Nebula in the Andromeda Galaxy. That location is separated from Earth by 1,500,000 light-years, the distance light travels in 1,500,000 years. Suppose you make the round trip in just a few moments, also taking some precaution to avoid getting whisked back to the past. If all goes well, you'll return to the Earth 3,000,000 years into its future, because that's how much Earth time will have elapsed.

If that possibility doesn't give you future shock, imagine you're such a speedy space-traveler that you're able to survive out there for some billions of Earth years. You might have it made, some cosmologists (astronomers who study the universe as a whole) contend, because by then the universe may have stopped expanding. Most cosmologists now believe that our universe has been expanding ever since it was hatched in a Big Bang explosion about 15,000,000,000 years ago. If you wait enough billions of years before you return from your space voyage, you may enter an era called the "Big Crunch" by cosmologists like John A. Wheeler of the University of Texas.

During the "Big Crunch," if it ever happens, astronomical history would move in reverse. After billions of years of expansion, cooling, and entropy (loss of energy), gravity would cause the universe to contract and consequently begin regaining its lost heat and energy. According to some "Big Crunch" scenarios, plants will become seeds and people will live their lives from the grave to the cradle. You would be in a world where youth no longer is wasted on the young. Granted, you may not enjoy the fact that every television show will be a rerun, and you'd have to watch every show in reverse, but don't worry. Just sit back and watch television be un-invented.

Some cosmologists speculate that the "Big Crunch" could be part of an endless cycle of cosmic expansion and contraction, fulfilling legendary prophecies of "eternal recurrence." Many of today's scientific speculations about time are echoes of age-old debates about what makes time tick. Einstein himself, only four weeks before his death, confided in a letter to a friend that modern physics had converted him to the ancient belief that "the distinction between past, present and future is only a stubbornly persistent illusion."

Time, like destiny, is an abstraction. It cannot be seen, touched, smelled, or tasted. It seems to have no existence apart from the events it measures, but something tells us that time is out there, somewhere. "When we pursue the meaning of time," according to the time-obsessed 10 English novelist-playwright J.B. Priestley, "we are like a knight on a quest, condemned to wander through innumerable forests, bewildered and baffled, because the magic beast he is looking for is the horse he is riding."

What about our quest for particles that travel faster than light? If we find them, will we be able to harness their energy to tour the past? If we return to our past, will we be forced to repeat our blunders and suffer the same consequences? Or will we be able to use our hindsight to make everything turn out better the second time around?

Will we ever be able to take instant trips to the distant future, the 20 way people do in the movies, with a twist of a dial and a "zap! zap!" of sound effects? If such trips are impossible because the script for the future has yet to be written, will we be able to witness the distant future by stretching the time of our lives sufficiently to wait for it?

In short, was the Mad Hatter right when he told Alice that time is a "he," and that "if you only kept on good terms with him, he'd do almost anything you liked with the clock"? One cannot resist the temptation to respond that only time will tell.

REVIEWING THE ARTICLE _____

THE MAIN IDEA

1. Which of the following titles best expresses the main idea of the article?
   (a) Time Travel in Science Fiction
   (b) Theoretical and Experimental Support for the Possibility of Time Travel
   (c) The Speed of Light: Nature's Permanent Barrier to Time Travel
   (d) The "Big Crunch" as the Key to Time Travel

DETAILS

2. According to paragraph 2 on page 128, Einstein's Special Theory of Relativity (1905) predicted a relationship between time and
   (a) a clock.
   (b) the expanding universe.
   (c) inner-space phenomena.
   (d) accelerated motion.

3. A 1972 experiment that flew atomic clocks around the world demonstrated that as the speed of an object increases, time
   (a) continues at its regular rate.
   (b) speeds up greatly.
   (c) slows down slightly.
   (d) stands still.

4. A person living at sea level and a person living in Denver would age at different rates because of differences in
   (a) average temperature.
   (b) gravity.
   (c) air pollution.
   (d) life style.

   (*Hint*: See the last four paragraphs in the section on "Time Stretching.")

5. In a black hole of infinite gravity, time would (a) slow down (b) speed up (c) continue unchanged (d) stand still.

6. According to paragraph 1 on page 131, time reversal may be possible in (a) outer space (b) inner space (c) atomic clocks (d) black holes.

ORDER OF EVENTS

7. Some cosmologists believe that if the "Big Crunch" comes (see page 132), events will
   (a) continue to move forward in time as we experience time now.
   (b) move backward in time.
   (c) be frozen in time.
   (d) disappear completely because of the destruction of the Earth.

CAUSE AND EFFECT

8. Critics of time travel (nay-sayers) argue that objects in the real world cannot travel to the past because they are unable to move faster than **(a)** a rocket **(b)** light **(c)** sound **(d)** an atomic clock.

9. One effect of living in the era of the "Big Crunch" is that you would grow **(a)** younger **(b)** older **(c)** stronger **(d)** wiser.

INFERENCES

10. If you were driving your car during the time of the "Big Crunch," the car would be moving **(a)** forward **(b)** backward **(c)** faster **(d)** more slowly.

11. From the article, we may infer that humans
    - **(a)** can never travel in time.
    - **(b)** will certainly be able to travel in time someday.
    - **(c)** can travel only into the future someday.
    - **(d)** might be able to travel in time someday.

PREDICTING OUTCOMES

12. The consequences of time travel are
    - **(a)** sure to be disastrous.
    - **(b)** full of benefits for humanity.
    - **(c)** possible to predict with current data.
    - **(d)** impossible to predict.

BUILDING YOUR VOCABULARY

1. Here is an example of what you can expect if tomorrow's space-flight technology—employing the energy of thermonuclear fusion, matter-antimatter *annihilation*, or whatever—enables you to move at ultra-high speeds.

   The root of *annihilation* (page 129, lines 11-14) is *nihil*, meaning "nothing" or "zero." (Our words *nil* and *null* come from this root.) The suffix *-ation* means "action of" or "process of." From these clues, you can infer that *annihilation* of an object causes it to
    - **(a)** expand infinitely.
    - **(b)** cease to exist.
    - **(c)** grow older.
    - **(d)** become heavier.

2. Yet, they [examples of time-stretching] are based on mathematical *projections* of relativity science, as confirmed by the atomic-clock experiments.

   Of the following four meanings of *projections* (page 129, lines 24-26), which one makes the BEST sense in the sentence from the article?
   (a) things that stick out from a surface
   (b) images displayed on a screen
   (c) predictions based on present data
   (d) assumptions that other people think or feel one's own thoughts or feelings

3. The proof involving gravity suggests that you could have an unforgettable *rendezvous* with a black hole, where gravity is believed to be so powerful that it imprisons light.

   A *rendezvous* (page 130, lines 10-12) is a(an) (a) explosion (b) accident (c) meeting (d) remembering.

4. Both scenes are equally *authentic*, and scientists say you would have absolutely no way of telling which scene is moving forward in time and which is moving backward.

   The BEST synonym for *authentic* (page 131, lines 14-16) is (a) genuine (b) impressive (c) timely (d) autocratic.

5. You might have it made, some *cosmologists* (astronomers who study the universe as a whole) contend, because by then the universe may have stopped expanding.
   a. *Cosmologists* (page 132, lines 20-22) are scientists who study
      (a) the solar system.
      (b) individual stars.
      (c) entire galaxies.
      (d) the entire universe.
   b. The BEST strategy for answering part *a* is to
      (a) analyze the word into its component parts.
      (b) skim the paragraph containing the word.
      (c) read the definition in parentheses.
      (d) read the following sentence, in which the word recurs.

STUDYING THE WRITER'S CRAFT

1. Which paragraph in the article serves as a summary of the entire article? Explain your answer.

2. Good expository writing contains both *abstract concepts* and *concrete examples*. The concrete examples help readers visualize and understand the abstract concepts.

Abstract Concept: "Nature won't even let you combine the speed of light with a moving object."

Concrete Example: "If a flying plane fires a rocket, the rocket zooms off at the combined velocity of the rocket and the plane. If the plane fires a beam of light, the light-beam velocity will not be affected at all by the velocity of the plane." (page 131, lines 31-34)

Expressions such as "for example," "for instance," "suppose," and "imagine" often signal the use of concrete examples.

Using page and line references, identify two or more uses of abstract concepts combined with concrete examples in the article.

3. How does the author of the article use *tone* to prevent the difficulty of the concepts from becoming too heavy a burden for the reader? (*Hint*: Look at the last sentence in each of the three sections of the article.)

ACTIVITIES FOR LISTENING, SPEAKING, WRITING

1. Listen and take notes while two or more of your classmates debate the following question: "Is time travel possible—yes or no?" After reading the article, what do you think? Be prepared to tell which side of the debate made the better argument and to share your own views on time travel with your classmates.

2. Science-fiction movies and television dramas often employ time travel in their plots. Write and organize a set of notes in outline form on the use of time travel in a motion picture or television drama you have seen. Your notes should serve as the basis for a brief talk on the topic. How was time travel explained—if at all—in the example you chose? What device was used to make it plausible? How convincing was the explanation or device? Be prepared to talk with your classmates about your materials.

3. The applications of science and technology can help or harm humanity. Suppose that time travel were to become a reality. Write an essay showing either how it might help people or how it might hurt them. Use concrete examples to make your abstract concepts clear and interesting.

ROBOTS AND ARTIFICIAL INTELLIGENCE
Theme 3

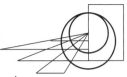

Every human invention from a crude stone ax to a nuclear reactor can be used to help or harm people. Prehistoric man could swing a stone ax to chop wood or to bash out the brains of his neighbor. A nuclear reactor can produce peaceful energy or deadly atomic bombs. For this reason, people have always harbored mixed feelings about their own technology.

Science-fiction writers often reflect these mixed feelings about technology in their works. The author of "Robbie" takes an optimistic view of machines in this story of a devoted family robot and the little girl who loves him. In "Dial F for Frankenstein," a brief tale of artificial intelligence, the author takes a darker view of technology. With "Instinct," the tables are turned as the author gives us a robot's view of human beings.

The machines that appear as characters in science-fiction stories are of three types. Perhaps best known are *robots*, machines that can perform one or more of the physical and mental tasks ordinarily done by humans. These would include the metallic creatures in "Robbie" and "Instinct" and the complex artificial intelligence in "Dial F for Frankenstein." A more intimate blend of machine and human occurs in *cyborgs*, humans in whom one or more mechanical or electronic parts have been implanted for enhanced capabilities. You may already have seen cyborgs in movies such as *The Terminator* and *Robocop*. Most complex of all are *androids*, artificial creatures so like humans that they can sometimes pass for them.

How far along have we actually come in our attempt to reinforce or even replace ourselves with machines? Robots already perform many tasks in our automated factories. Modern medicine has already turned some of us into cyborgs through the use of prosthetic limbs, artificial hearts, and respirators that breathe for us. Someday, modern biology may even enable us to create androids.

Do all these advances in technology mean that we are close to being replaced by clever machines? The answer seems to be: Not so easily or so soon! For an account of just one of the many skills a robot will need before it can function as a human being, read the article "Smart Skin."

Robbie

by Isaac Asimov

*In a minute she had returned, a frightened little girl. "Mamma,
Robbie isn't in his room. Where is he?"*

Some science-fiction authors depict science and technology as if they were
threatening monsters. Early in his career as a writer of science fiction,
Isaac Asimov rejected this negative view of science and technology. He
decided to write a series of stories about robots that would show them
in a positive light. To this end, he developed what has come to be known
as Asimov's Three Laws of Robotics:

1. A robot may not injure a human being, or, through inaction, allow a
   human being to come to harm.

2. A robot must obey the orders given it by human beings except when
   such orders would conflict with the First Law.

3. A robot must protect its own existence as long as such protection
   does not conflict with the First and Second Laws.

   The story that follows, "Robbie," appeared in a science-fiction magazine in 1940. It was the first of a series of twelve robot stories by Asimov,
all based on the preceding three laws. As you read "Robbie," ask yourself:
How does the story illustrate the three robotic laws?

Until his death in 1992, Asimov wrote both science fact and science fiction from expert knowledge and long experience. He had a Ph.D. in chemistry from Boston University and taught there briefly as a professor of biochemistry. Starting in 1939, he became one of the founding fathers of modern science fiction.

A prolific author, Asimov is best known for his science-fiction stories and novels about robots and his *Foundation* series, a sweeping history of the future. He was also the editor of many collections of the works of other science-fiction writers. In addition, he wrote numerous books for the general reader on subjects as diverse as science, the Bible, humor, history, and Shakespeare. Turning out more than ten books a year, he wrote an astonishing total of nearly 500 books. No wonder that his works seem to fill half the shelves in a public library!

"Ninety-eight—ninety-nine—*one hundred*." Gloria withdrew her chubby little forearm from before her eyes and stood for a moment, wrinkling her nose and blinking in the sunlight. Then, trying to watch in all directions at once, she withdrew a few cautious steps from the tree against which she had been leaning.

She craned her neck to investigate the possibilities of a clump of bushes to the right and then withdrew farther to obtain a better angle for viewing its dark recesses. The quiet was profound except for the incessant buzzing of insects and the occasional chirrup of some hardy bird, braving the midday sun.

Gloria pouted, "I bet he went inside the house, and I've told him a million times that that's not fair."

With tiny lips pressed together tightly and a severe frown crinkling her forehead, she moved determinedly toward the two-story building up past the driveway.

10

Too late she heard the rustling sound behind her, followed by the distinctive and rhythmic clump-clump of Robbie's metal feet. She whirled about to see her triumphing companion emerge from hiding and make for the home-tree at full speed.

Gloria shrieked in dismay. "Wait, Robbie! That wasn't fair, Robbie! You promised you wouldn't run until I found you." Her little feet could make no headway at all against Robbie's giant strides. Then, within ten feet of the goal, Robbie's pace slowed suddenly to the merest of crawls, and Gloria, with one final burst of wild speed, dashed pantingly past him to touch the welcome bark of home-tree first. 10

Gleefully, she turned on the faithful Robbie, and with the basest of ingratitude, rewarded him for his sacrifice, by taunting him cruelly for a lack of running ability.

"Robbie can't run," she shouted at the top of her eight-year-old voice. "I can beat him any day. I can beat him any day." She chanted the words in a shrill rhythm.

Robbie didn't answer, of course—not in words. He pantomimed running, instead, inching away until Gloria found herself running after him as he dodged her narrowly, forcing her to veer in helpless circles, little arms outstretched and fanning at the air. 20

"Robbie," she squealed, "stand still!" —And the laughter was forced out of her in breathless jerks.

—Until he turned suddenly and caught her up, whirling her round, so that for her the world fell away for a moment with a blue emptiness beneath, and green trees stretching hungrily downward toward the void. Then she was down in the grass again, leaning against Robbie's leg and still holding a hard, metal finger.

After a while, her breath returned. She pushed uselessly at her disheveled hair in vague imitation of one of her mother's gestures and twisted to see if her dress were torn. 30

She slapped her hand against Robbie's torso, "Bad boy! I'll spank you!"

And Robbie cowered, holding his hands over his face so that she had to add, "No, I won't, Robbie. I won't spank you. But anyway, it's my turn to hide now because you've got longer legs and you promised not to run till I found you."

Robbie nodded his head—a small parallelepiped[1] with rounded edges and corners attached to a similar but much larger parallelepiped that served as torso by means of a short, flexible stalk—and obediently

1. **parallelepiped:** six-faced solid figure made up of parallelograms, four-sided flat figures with opposite sides that are equal and parallel.

faced the tree. A thin, metal film descended over his glowing eyes and from within his body came a steady, resonant ticking.

"Don't peek now—and don't skip any numbers," warned Gloria, and scurried for cover.

With unvarying regularity, seconds were ticked off, and at the hundredth, up went the eyelids, and the glowing red of Robbie's eyes swept the prospect. They rested for a moment on a bit of colorful gingham that protruded from behind a boulder. He advanced a few steps and convinced himself that it was Gloria who squatted behind it.

Slowly, remaining always between Gloria and home-tree, he ad- 10 vanced on the hiding place, and when Gloria was plainly in sight and could no longer even theorize to herself that she was not seen, he extended one arm toward her, slapping the other against his leg so that it rang again. Gloria emerged sulkily.

"You peeked!" she exclaimed, with gross unfairness. "Besides I'm tired of playing hide-and-seek. I want a ride."

But Robbie was hurt at the unjust accusation, so he seated himself carefully and shook his head ponderously from side to side.

Gloria changed her tone to one of gentle coaxing immediately, "Come on, Robbie. I didn't mean it about the peeking. Give me a ride."   20

Robbie was not to be won over so easily, though. He gazed stubbornly at the sky, and shook his head even more emphatically.

"Please, Robbie, please give me a ride." She encircled his neck with rosy arms and hugged tightly. Then, changing moods in a moment, she moved away. "If you don't, I'm going to cry," and her face twisted appallingly in preparation.

Hard-hearted Robbie paid scant attention to this dreadful possibility, and shook his head a third time. Gloria found it necessary to play her trump card.[2]

"If you don't," she exclaimed warmly, "I won't tell you any more 30 stories, that's all. Not one—"

Robbie gave in immediately and unconditionally before this ultimatum, nodding his head vigorously until the metal of his neck hummed. Carefully, he raised the little girl and placed her on his broad, flat shoulders.

Gloria's threatened tears vanished immediately and she crowed with delight. Robbie's metal skin, kept at a constant temperature of seventy by the high resistance coils within, felt nice and comfortable, while the beautifully loud sound her heels made as they bumped rhythmically against his chest was enchanting.

"You're an air-coaster, Robbie, you're a big, silver air-coaster. Hold 40

2. **trump card:** winning card.

out your arms straight. —You *got* to, Robbie, if you're going to be an air-coaster."

The logic was irrefutable. Robbie's arms were wings catching the air currents and he was a silver 'coaster.

Gloria twisted the robot's head and leaned to the right. He banked sharply. Gloria equipped the 'coaster with a motor that went "Br-r-r" and then with weapons that went "Powie" and "Sh-sh-shshsh." Pirates were giving chase and the ship's blasters were coming into play. The pirates dropped in a steady rain.

"Got another one. —Two more," she cried.   10

·   Then "Faster, men," Gloria said pompously, "we're running out of ammunition." She aimed over her shoulder with undaunted courage and Robbie was a blunt-nosed spaceship zooming through the void at maximum acceleration.

Clear across the field he sped, to the patch of tall grass on the other side, where he stopped with a suddenness that evoked a shriek from his flushed rider, and then tumbled her onto the soft, green carpet.

Gloria gasped and panted, and gave voice to intermittent whispered exclamations of "That was *nice!*"

Robbie waited until she had caught her breath and then pulled gen-   20
tly at a lock of hair.

"You want something?" said Gloria, eyes wide in an apparently artless perplexity that fooled her huge "nursemaid" not at all. He pulled the curl harder.

"Oh, I know. You want a story."

Robbie nodded rapidly.

"Which one?"

Robbie made a semi-circle in the air with one finger.

The little girl protested, "*Again?* I've told you Cinderella a million times. Aren't you tired of it? —It's for babies."   30

Another semi-circle.

"Oh, well," Gloria composed herself, ran over the details of the tale in her mind (together with her own elaborations, of which she had several) and began:

"Are you ready? Well—once upon a time there was a beautiful little girl whose name was Ella. And she had a terribly cruel stepmother and two very ugly and *very* cruel step-sisters and—"

Gloria was reaching the very climax of the tale—midnight was striking and everything was changing back to the shabby originals lickety-split, while Robbie listened tensely with burning eyes—when the   40
interruption came.

"Gloria!"

It was the high-pitched sound of a woman who has been calling not once, but several times; and had the nervous tone of one in whom anxiety was beginning to overcome impatience.

"Mamma's calling me," said Gloria, not quite happily. "You'd better carry me back to the house, Robbie."

Robbie obeyed with alacrity, for somehow there was that in him which judged it best to obey Mrs. Weston, without as much as a scrap of hesitation. Gloria's father was rarely home in the daytime except on Sunday—today, for instance—and when he was, he proved a genial and un- 10 derstanding person. Gloria's mother, however, was a source of uneasiness to Robbie and there was always the impulse to sneak away from her sight.

Mrs. Weston caught sight of them the minute they rose above the masking tufts of long grass and retired inside the house to wait.

"I've shouted myself hoarse, Gloria," she said, severely. "Where were you?"

"I was with Robbie," quavered Gloria. "I was telling him Cinderella, and I forgot it was dinner-time."

"Well, it's a pity Robbie forgot, too." Then, as if that reminded her 20 of the robot's presence, she whirled upon him. "You may go, Robbie. She doesn't need you now." Then, brutally, "And don't come back till I call you."

Robbie turned to go, but hesitated as Gloria cried out in his defense, "Wait, Mamma, you got to let him stay. I didn't finish Cinderella for him. I said I would tell him Cinderella and I'm not finished."

"Gloria!"

"Honest and truly, Mamma, he'll stay so quiet, you won't even know he's here. He can sit on the chair in the corner, and he won't say a word,—I mean he won't *do* anything. Will you, Robbie?" 30

Robbie, appealed to, nodded his massive head up and down once.

"Gloria, if you don't stop this at once, you shan't see Robbie for a whole week."

The girl's eyes fell, "All right! But Cinderella is his favorite story and I didn't finish it. —And he likes it so much."

The robot left with a disconsolate step and Gloria choked back a sob.

George Weston was comfortable. It was a habit of his to be comfortable on Sunday afternoons. A good, hearty dinner below the hatches; a nice, soft, dilapidated couch on which to sprawl; a copy of the *Times*; slippered feet and shirtless chest;—how could anyone *help* but be com- 40 fortable?

He wasn't pleased, therefore, when his wife walked in. After ten years of married life, he still was so unutterably foolish as to love her, and there was no question that he was always glad to see her—still Sunday afternoons just after dinner were sacred to him and his idea of solid comfort was to be left in utter solitude for two or three hours. Consequently, he fixed his eye firmly upon the latest reports of the Lefebre-Yoshida expedition to Mars (this one was to take off from Lunar Base and might actually succeed) and pretended she wasn't there.

Mrs. Weston waited patiently for two minutes, then impatiently for two more, and finally broke the silence.   10

"George!"

"Hmpph?"

"George, I say! *Will* you put down that paper and look at me?"

The paper rustled to the floor and Weston turned a weary face toward his wife, "What is it, dear?"

"You know what it is, George. It's Gloria and that terrible machine."

"What terrible machine?"

"Now don't pretend you don't know what I'm talking about. It's that robot Gloria calls Robbie. He doesn't leave her for a moment."

"Well, why should he? He's not supposed to. And he certainly isn't 20 a terrible machine. He's the best darn robot money can buy and I'm sure he set me back half a year's income. He's worth it, though—darn sight cleverer than half my office staff."

He made a move to pick up the paper again, but his wife was quicker and snatched it away.

"You listen to *me*, George. I won't have my daughter entrusted to a machine—and I don't care how clever it is. It has no soul, and no one knows what it may be thinking. A child just isn't *made* to be guarded by a thing of metal."

Weston frowned, "When did you decide this? He's been with Gloria 30 two years now and I haven't seen you worry till now."

"It was different at first. It was a novelty; it took a load off me, and—and it was a fashionable thing to do. But now I don't know. The neighbors—"

"Well, what have the neighbors to do with it? Now, look. A robot is infinitely more to be trusted than a human nursemaid. Robbie was constructed for only one purpose really—to be the companion of a little child. His entire 'mentality' has been created for the purpose. He just can't help being faithful and loving and kind. He's a machine—*made so*. That's more than you can say for humans."   40

"But something might go wrong. Some—some—" Mrs. Weston was a bit hazy about the insides of a robot, "some little jigger will come loose and the awful thing will go berserk and—and—" She couldn't bring herself to complete the quite obvious thought.

"Nonsense," Weston denied, with an involuntary nervous shiver. "That's completely ridiculous. We had a long discussion at the time we bought Robbie about the First Law of Robotics. You *know* that it is impossible for a robot to harm a human being; that long before enough can go wrong to alter that First Law, a robot would be completely inoperable. It's a mathematical impossibility. Besides I have an engineer from U. S. Robots here twice a year to give the poor gadget a complete overhaul. Why, there's no more chance of anything at all going wrong with Robbie than there is of you or I suddenly going looney—considerably less, in fact. Besides, how are you going to take him away from Gloria?"

He made another futile stab at the paper, and his wife tossed it angrily into the next room.

"That's just it, George! She won't play with anyone else. There are dozens of little boys and girls that she should make friends with, but she won't. She won't go *near* them unless I make her. That's no way for a little girl to grow up. You want her to be normal, don't you? You want her to be able to take her part in society."

"You're jumping at shadows, Grace. Pretend Robbie's a dog. I've seen hundreds of children who would rather have their dog than their father."

"A dog is different, George. We *must* get rid of that horrible thing. You can sell it back to the company. I've asked, and you can."

"You've *asked?* Now look here, Grace, let's not go off the deep end. We're keeping the robot until Gloria is older and I don't want the subject brought up again." And with that he walked out of the room in a huff.

Mrs. Weston met her husband at the door two evenings later. "You'll have to listen to this, George. There's bad feeling in the village."

"About what?" asked Weston. He stepped into the washroom and drowned out any possible answer by the splash of water.

Mrs. Weston waited. She said, "About Robbie."

Weston stepped out, towel in hand, face red and angry, "What are you talking about?"

"Oh, it's been building up and building up. I've tried to close my eyes to it, but I'm not going to any more. Most of the villagers consider Robbie dangerous. Children aren't allowed to go near our place in the evenings."

"We trust *our* child with the thing."

"Well, people aren't reasonable about these things."

"Then who needs them?"

"Saying that doesn't solve the problem. I've got to do my shopping down there. I've got to meet them every day. And it's even worse in the city these days when it comes to robots. New York has just passed an ordinance keeping all robots off the streets between sunset and sunrise."

"All right, but they can't stop us from keeping a robot in our home. —Grace, this is one of your campaigns. I recognize it. But it's no use. The answer is still, no! We're keeping Robbie!"

Ten times in the ensuing week, he cried, "Robbie stays,—and that's *final!*" and each time it was weaker and accompanied by a louder and more agonized groan. 10

Came the day at last, when Weston approached his daughter guiltily and suggested a "beautiful" visivox show in the village.

Gloria clapped her hands happily, "Can Robbie go?"

"No, dear," he said, and winced at the sound of his voice, "they won't allow robots at the visivox—but you can tell him all about it when you get home." He stumbled all over the last few words and looked away.

Gloria came back from town bubbling over with enthusiasm, for the visivox had been a gorgeous spectacle indeed.

She waited for her father to maneuver the jet-car into the sunken garage. "Wait till I tell Robbie, Daddy. He would have liked it like any- 20 thing. —Especially when Francis Fran was backing away so-o-o quietly, and backed right into one of the Leopard-Men and had to run." She laughed again, "Daddy, are there really Leopard-Men on the Moon?"

"Probably not," said Weston absently. "It's just funny make-believe." He couldn't take much longer with the car. He'd have to face it.

Gloria ran across the lawn. "Robbie. —Robbie!"

Then she stopped suddenly at the sight of a beautiful collie which regarded her out of serious brown eyes as it wagged its tail on the porch.

"Oh, what a nice dog!" Gloria climbed the steps, approached cautiously and patted it. "Is it for me, Daddy?" 30

Her mother had joined them. "Yes, it is, Gloria. Isn't it nice—soft and furry. It's very gentle. It *likes* little girls."

"Can he play games?"

"Surely. He can do any number of tricks. Would you like to see some?"

"Right away. I want Robbie to see him, too. —*Robbie!*" She stopped, uncertainly, and frowned, "I'll bet he's just staying in his room because he's mad at me for not taking him to the visivox. You'll have to explain to him, Daddy. He might not believe me, but he knows if you say it, it's so."

Weston's lips grew tighter. He looked toward his wife but could not 40 catch her eye.

Gloria turned precipitously and ran down the basement steps, shouting as she went, "Robbie— Come and see what Daddy and Mamma brought me. They brought me a dog, Robbie."

In a minute she had returned, a frightened little girl. "Mamma, Robbie isn't in his room. Where is he?" There was no answer and George Weston coughed and was suddenly extremely interested in an aimlessly drifting cloud. Gloria's voice quavered on the verge of tears, "Where's Robbie, Mamma?"

Mrs. Weston sat down and drew her daughter gently to her, "Don't feel bad, Gloria. Robbie has gone away, I think."

"Gone *away*? Where? Where's he gone away, Mamma?"   10

"No one knows, darling. He just walked away. We've looked and we've looked and we've looked for him, but we can't find him."

"You mean he'll never come back again?" Her eyes were round with horror.

"We may find him soon. We'll keep looking for him. And meanwhile you can play with your nice new doggie. Look at him! His name is Lightning and he can—"

But Gloria's eyelids had overflown, "I don't want the nasty dog—I want Robbie. I want you to find me Robbie." Her feelings became too deep for words, and she spluttered into a shrill wail.   20

Mrs. Weston glanced at her husband for help, but he merely shuffled his feet morosely and did not withdraw his ardent stare from the heavens, so she bent to the task of consolation, "Why do you cry, Gloria? Robbie was only a machine, just a nasty old machine. He wasn't alive at all."

"He was *not* no machine!" screamed Gloria, fiercely and ungrammatically. "He was a *person* just like you and me and he was my *friend*. I want him back. Oh, Mamma, I want him back."

Her mother groaned in defeat and left Gloria to her sorrow.

"Let her have her cry out," she told her husband. "Childish griefs are never lasting. In a few days, she'll forget that awful robot ever existed."   30

But time proved Mrs. Weston a bit too optimistic. To be sure, Gloria ceased crying, but she ceased smiling, too, and the passing days found her ever more silent and shadowy. Gradually, her attitude of passive unhappiness wore Mrs. Weston down and all that kept her from yielding was the impossibility of admitting defeat to her husband.

Then, one evening, she flounced into the living room, sat down, folded her arms and looked boiling mad.

Her husband stretched his neck in order to see her over his newspaper, "What now, Grace?"

"It's that child, George. I've had to send back the dog today. Gloria   40 positively couldn't stand the sight of him, she said. She's driving me into a nervous breakdown."

Weston laid down the paper and a hopeful gleam entered his eye, "Maybe— Maybe we ought to get Robbie back. It might be done, you know. I can get in touch with—"

"No!" she replied, grimly. "I won't hear of it. We're not giving up that easily. My child shall *not* be brought up by a robot if it takes years to break her of it."

Weston picked up his paper again with a disappointed air. "A year of this will have me prematurely gray."

"You're a big help, George," was the frigid answer. "What Gloria needs is a change of environment. Of course she can't forget Robbie here. 10 How can she when every tree and rock reminds her of him? It is really the *silliest* situation I have ever heard of. Imagine a child pining away for the loss of a robot."

"Well, stick to the point. What's the change in environment you're planning?"

"We're going to take her to New York."

"The city! In August! Say, do you know what New York is like in August? It's unbearable."

"Millions do bear it."

"They don't have a place like this to go to. If they didn't have to 20 stay in New York, they wouldn't."

"Well, *we* have to. I say we're leaving now—or as soon as we can make the arrangements. In the city, Gloria will find sufficient interests and sufficient friends to perk her up and make her forget that machine."

"Oh, Lord," he groaned, "those frying pavements!"

"We have to," was the unshaken response. "Gloria has lost five pounds in the last month and my little girl's health is more important to me than your comfort."

"It's a pity you didn't think of your little girl's health before you 30 deprived her of her pet robot," he muttered—but to himself.

Gloria displayed immediate signs of improvement when told of the impending trip to the city. She spoke little of it, but when she did, it was always with lively anticipation. Again, she began to smile and to eat with something of her former appetite.

Mrs. Weston hugged herself for joy and lost no opportunity to triumph over her still skeptical husband.

"You see, George, she helps with the packing like a little angel, and chatters away as if she hadn't a care in the world. It's just as I told you—all we need do is substitute other interests."   40

"Hmpph," was the skeptical response, "I hope so."

Preliminaries were gone through quickly. Arrangements were made for the preparation of their city home and a couple were engaged as housekeepers for the country home. When the day of the trip finally did come, Gloria was all but her old self again, and no mention of Robbie passed her lips at all.

In high good-humor the family took a taxi-gyro[3] to the airport (Weston would have preferred using his own private 'gyro, but it was only a two-seater with no room for baggage) and entered the waiting liner.

"Come, Gloria," called Mrs. Weston. "I've saved you a seat near the 10 window so you can watch the scenery."

Gloria trotted down the aisle cheerily, flattened her nose into a white oval against the thick clear glass, and watched with an intentness that increased as the sudden coughing of the motor drifted backward into the interior. She was too young to be frightened when the ground dropped away as if let through a trap-door and she herself suddenly became twice her usual weight, but not too young to be mightily interested. It wasn't until the ground had changed into a tiny patchwork quilt that she withdrew her nose, and faced her mother again.

"Will we soon be in the city, Mamma?" she asked, rubbing her chilled 20 nose, and watching with interest as the patch of moisture which her breath had formed on the pane shrank slowly and vanished.

"In about half an hour, dear." Then, with just the faintest trace of anxiety, "Aren't you glad we're going? Don't you think you'll be very happy in the city with all the buildings and people and things to see? We'll go to the visivox every day and see shows and go to the circus and the beach and—"

"Yes, Mamma," was Gloria's unenthusiastic rejoinder. The liner passed over a bank of clouds at the moment, and Gloria was instantly absorbed in the unusual spectacle of clouds underneath one. Then they 30 were over clear sky again, and she turned to her mother with a sudden mysterious air of secret knowledge.

"I know why we're going to the city, Mamma."

"Do you?" Mrs. Weston was puzzled. "Why, dear?"

"You didn't tell me because you wanted it to be a surprise, but I know." For a moment, she was lost in admiration at her own acute penetration, and then she laughed gaily. "We're going to New York so we can find Robbie, aren't we? —With detectives."

The statement caught George Weston in the middle of a drink of water, with disastrous results. There was a sort of strangled gasp, a geyser

3. **taxi-gyro:** a passenger autogyro, an early version of the helicopter.

of water, and then a bout of choking coughs. When all was over, he stood there, a red-faced, water-drenched and very, very annoyed person.

Mrs. Weston maintained her composure, but when Gloria repeated her question in a more anxious tone of voice, she found her temper rather bent.

"Maybe," she retorted, tartly. "Now sit and be still, for Heaven's sake."

New York City, 1998 A.D., was a paradise for the sightseer more than ever in its history. Gloria's parents realized this and made the most of it.

On direct orders from his wife, George Weston arranged to have his 10 business take care of itself for a month or so, in order to be free to spend the time in what he termed "dissipating Gloria to the verge of ruin." Like everything else Weston did, this was gone about in an efficient, thorough, and businesslike way. Before the month had passed, nothing that could be done had not been done.

She was taken to the top of the half-mile-tall Roosevelt Building, to gaze down in awe upon the jagged panorama of rooftops that blended far off in the fields of Long Island and the flatlands of New Jersey. They visited the zoos where Gloria stared in delicious fright at the "real live lion" (rather disappointed that the keepers fed him raw steaks, instead 20 of human beings, as she had expected), and asked insistently and per-emptorily to see "the whale."

The various museums came in for their share of attention, together with the parks and the beaches and the aquarium.

She was taken halfway up the Hudson in an excursion steamer fitted out in the archaism[4] of the mad Twenties. She travelled into the strato-sphere on an exhibition trip, where the sky turned deep purple and the stars came out and the misty earth below looked like a huge concave bowl. Down under the waters of the Long Island Sound she was taken in a glass-walled sub-sea vessel, where in a green and wavering world, 30 quaint and curious sea-things ogled her and wiggled suddenly away.

On a more prosaic level, Mrs. Weston took her to the department stores where she could revel in another type of fairyland.

In fact, when the month had nearly sped, the Westons were con-vinced that everything conceivable had been done to take Gloria's mind once and for all off the departed Robbie—but they were not quite sure they had succeeded.

The fact remained that wherever Gloria went, she displayed the most

---

4. **archaism** (ar-KAY-izm): something from the past that is outdated, no longer in use.

absorbed and concentrated interest in such robots as happened to be present. No matter how exciting the spectacle before her, nor how novel to her girlish eyes, she turned away instantly if the corner of her eye caught a glimpse of metallic movement.

Mrs. Weston went out of her way to keep Gloria away from all robots.

And the matter was finally climaxed in the episode at the Museum of Science and Industry. The Museum had announced a special "children's program" in which exhibits of scientific witchery scaled down to the child mind were to be shown. The Westons, of course, placed it upon their list of "absolutely."   10

It was while the Westons were standing totally absorbed in the exploits of a powerful electromagnet that Mrs. Weston suddenly became aware of the fact that Gloria was no longer with her. Initial panic gave way to calm decision and, enlisting the aid of three attendants, a careful search was begun.

Gloria, of course, was not one to wander aimlessly, however. For her age, she was an unusually determined and purposeful girl, quite full of the maternal genes in that respect. She had seen a huge sign on the third floor, which had said, "This Way to the Talking Robot." Having spelled it out to herself and having noticed that her parents did not seem to wish 20 to move in the proper direction, she did the obvious thing. Waiting for an opportune moment of parental distraction, she calmly disengaged herself and followed the sign.

The Talking Robot was a *tour de force*,[5] a thoroughly impractical device, possessing publicity value only. Once an hour, an escorted group stood before it and asked questions of the robot engineer in charge in careful whispers. Those the engineer decided were suitable for the robot's circuits were transmitted to the Talking Robot.

It was rather dull. It may be nice to know that the square of 14 is 196, that the temperature at the moment is 72 degrees Fahrenheit, and 30 the air pressure 30.02 inches of mercury, that the atomic weight of sodium is 23, but one doesn't really need a robot for that. One especially does not need an unwieldy, totally immobile mass of wires and coils spreading over 25 square yards.

Gloria gazed attentively at this large thing with the wheels. For a moment, she hesitated in dismay. It didn't look like any robot she had ever seen.

Cautiously and doubtfully she raised her treble voice, "Please, Mr. Robot, sir, are you the Talking Robot, sir?" She wasn't sure, but it seemed

5. *tour de force:* feat of great skill or cleverness.

to her that a robot that actually talked was worth a great deal of politeness.

There was an oily whir of gears and a mechanically-timbred voice boomed out in words that lacked accent and intonation, "I—am—the—robot—that—talks."

Gloria stared at it ruefully. It *did* talk, but the sound came from inside somewheres. There was no *face* to talk to. She said, "Can you help me, Mr. Robot, sir?"

The Talking Robot, was designed to answer questions, and only such questions as it could answer had ever been put to it. It was quite confident 10 of its ability, therefore, "I—can—help—you."

"Thank you, Mr. Robot, sir. Have you seen Robbie?"

"Who—is—Robbie?"

"He's a robot, Mr. Robot, sir." She stretched to tiptoes. "He's about so high, Mr. Robot, sir, only higher, and he's very nice. He's got a head, you know. I mean you haven't, but he has, Mr. Robot, sir."

The Talking Robot had been left behind, "A—robot?"

"Yes, Mr. Robot, sir. A robot just like you, except he can't talk, of course, and—looks like a real person."

"A—robot—like—me?"   20

"Yes, Mr. Robot, sir."

To which the Talking Robot's only response was an erratic splutter and an occasional incoherent sound. The radical generalization offered it, i.e., its existence, not as a particular object, but as a member of a general group, was too much for it. Loyally, it tried to encompass the concept and half a dozen coils burnt out. Little warning signals were buzzing.

Gloria stood waiting, with carefully concealed impatience, for the machine's answer when she heard the cry behind her of "There she is," and recognized that cry as her mother's.   30

"What are you doing here, you bad girl?" cried Mrs. Weston, anxiety dissolving at once into anger. "Do you know you frightened your mamma and daddy almost to death? Why did you run away?"

The robot engineer had also dashed in, tearing his hair, and demanding who of the gathering crowd had tampered with the machine. "Can't anybody read signs?" he yelled. "You're not allowed in here without an attendant."

Gloria raised her grieved voice over the din, "I only came to see the Talking Robot, Mamma. I thought he might know where Robbie was because they're both robots." And then, as the thought of Robbie was 40 suddenly brought forcefully home to her, she burst into a sudden storm of tears, "And I *got* to find Robbie, Mamma. I *got* to."

Mrs. Weston strangled a cry, and said, "Oh, good Heavens. Come home, George. This is more than I can stand."

That evening, George Weston left for several hours, and the next morning, he approached his wife with something that looked suspiciously like smug complacence.

"I've got an idea, Grace."

"About what?" was the gloomy, uninterested query.

"About Gloria."

"You're not going to suggest buying back that robot?"

"No, of course not."   10

"Then go ahead. I might as well listen to you. Nothing *I've* done seems to have done any good."

"All right. Here's what I've been thinking. The whole trouble with Gloria is that she thinks of Robbie as a *person* and not as a *machine*. Naturally, she can't forget him. Now if we managed to convince her that Robbie was nothing more than a mess of steel and copper in the form of sheets and wires with electricity its juice of life, how long would her longings last? It's the psychological attack, if you see my point."

"How do you plan to do it?"

"Simple. Where do you suppose I went last night? I persuaded 20 Robertson of U. S. Robots and Mechanical Men Corporation to arrange for a complete tour of his premises tomorrow. The three of us will go, and by the time we're through, Gloria will have it drilled into her that a robot is *not* alive."

Mrs. Weston's eyes widened gradually and something glinted in her eyes that was quite like sudden admiration, "Why, George, that's a *good* idea."

And George Weston's vest buttons strained. "Only kind I have," he said.

Mr. Struthers was a conscientious General Manager and naturally 30 inclined to be a bit talkative. The combination, therefore, resulted in a tour that was fully explained, perhaps even overabundantly explained, at every step. However, Mrs. Weston was not bored. Indeed, she stopped him several times and begged him to repeat his statements in simple language so that Gloria might understand. Under the influence of this appreciation of his narrative powers, Mr. Struthers expanded genially and became ever more communicative, if possible.

George Weston, himself, showed a gathering impatience.

"Pardon me, Struthers," he said, breaking into the middle of a lecture on the photoelectric cell, "haven't you a section of the factory where only 40 robot labor is employed?"

"Eh? Oh, yes! Yes, indeed!" He smiled at Mrs. Weston. "A vicious circle in a way, robots creating more robots. Of course, we are not making a general practice out of it. For one thing, the unions would never let us. But we can turn out a very few robots using robot labor exclusively, merely as a sort of scientific experiment. You see," he tapped his pince-nez[6] into one palm argumentatively, "what the labor unions don't real-ize—and I say this as a man who has always been very sympathetic with the labor movement in general—is that the advent of the robot, while involving some dislocation to begin with, will, inevitably—"

"Yes, Struthers," said Weston, "but about that section of the factory 10 you speak of—may we see it? It would be very interesting, I'm sure."

"Yes! Yes, of course!" Mr. Struthers replaced his pince-nez in one convulsive movement and gave vent to a soft cough of discomfiture. "Follow me, please."

He was comparatively quiet while leading the three through a long corridor and down a flight of stairs. Then, when they had entered a large well-lit room that buzzed with metallic activity, the sluices opened and the flood of explanation poured forth again.

"There you are!" he said with pride in his voice. "Robots only! Five men act as overseers and they don't even stay in this room. In five years, 20 that is, since we began this project, not a single accident has occurred. Of course, the robots here assembled are comparatively simple, but . . ."

The General Manager's voice had long died to a rather soothing murmur in Gloria's ears. The whole trip seemed rather dull and point-less to her, though there *were* many robots in sight. None were even remotely like Robbie, though, and she surveyed them with open con-tempt.

In this room, there weren't any people at all, she noticed. Then her eyes fell upon six or seven robots busily engaged at a round table halfway across the room. They widened in incredulous surprise. It was a big room. 30 She couldn't see for sure, but one of the robots looked like—looked like— it *was!*

"*Robbie!*" Her shriek pierced the air, and one of the robots about the table faltered and dropped the tool he was holding. Gloria went almost mad with joy. Squeezing through the railing before either parent could stop her, she dropped lightly to the floor a few feet below, and ran toward her Robbie, arms waving and hair flying.

And the three horrified adults, as they stood frozen in their tracks, saw what the excited little girl did not see,—a huge, lumbering tractor bearing blindly down upon its appointed track. 40

---

6. **pince-nez** (PANTS-nay): eyeglasses clipped to the nose by a small spring.

It took split-seconds for Weston to come to his senses, and those split-seconds meant everything, for Gloria could not be overtaken. Although Weston vaulted the railing in a wild attempt, it was obviously hopeless. Mr. Struthers signalled wildly to the overseers to stop the tractor, but the overseers were only human and it took time to act.

It was only Robbie that acted immediately and with precision.

With metal legs eating up the space between himself and his little mistress, he charged down from the opposite direction. Everything then happened at once. With one sweep of an arm, Robbie snatched up Gloria, slackening his speed not one iota, and, consequently, knocking every 10 breath of air out of her. Weston, not quite comprehending all that was happening, felt, rather than saw, Robbie brush past him, and came to a sudden bewildered halt. The tractor intersected Gloria's path half a second after Robbie had, rolled on ten feet further and came to a grinding, long-drawn-out stop.

Gloria regained her breath, submitted to a series of passionate hugs on the part of both her parents and turned eagerly toward Robbie. As far as she was concerned, nothing had happened except that she had found her friend.

But Mrs. Weston's expression had changed from one of relief to one 20 of dark suspicion. She turned to her husband, and, despite her disheveled and undignified appearance, managed to look quite formidable, "*You* engineered this, *didn't* you?"

George Weston swabbed at a hot forehead with his handkerchief. His hand was unsteady, and his lips could curve only into a tremulous and exceedingly weak smile.

Mrs. Weston pursued the thought, "Robbie wasn't designed for engineering or construction work. He couldn't be of any use to them. You had him placed there deliberately so that Gloria would find him. You know you did." 30

"Well, I did," said Weston. "But, Grace, how was I to know the reunion would be so violent? And Robbie has saved her life; you'll have to admit that. You *can't* send him away again."

Grace Weston considered. She turned toward Gloria and Robbie and watched them abstractedly for a moment. Gloria had a grip about the robot's neck that would have asphyxiated any creature but one of metal, and was prattling nonsense in half-hysterical frenzy. Robbie's chrome-steel arms (capable of bending a bar of steel two inches in diameter into a pretzel) wound about the little girl gently and lovingly, and his eyes glowed a deep, deep red. 40

"Well," said Mrs. Weston, at last, "I guess he can stay with us until he rusts."

REVIEWING THE STORY

THE MAIN IDEA

1. The main idea of "Robbie" is that a robot may not
   (a) allow itself to be harmed.
   (b) harm another robot, except when ordered to do so by a human being.
   (c) harm a human being or allow one to be harmed.
   (d) cause harm to any living thing.

DETAILS

2. The story begins
   (a) in New York City in 1940.
   (b) in a village not far from New York City in 1998.
   (c) in a village two centuries from now.
   (d) in a place and time not identified.

3. One human trait that Robbie lacks is (a) sight (b) hearing (c) speech (d) loyalty.

4. To answer question 3, you would have to notice that Robbie
   (a) had to be guided to find Gloria.
   (b) responded only to written commands.
   (c) used pantomime and hand signals to communicate.
   (d) abandoned Gloria for several months.

5. Mr. and Mrs. Weston take Gloria on a vacation to
   (a) take her mind off Robbie.
   (b) convince her that Robbie was only a machine.
   (c) reward her for agreeing to give up Robbie.
   (d) look for the missing Robbie.

6. Near the end of the story, Robbie
   (a) outwits the Talking Robot.
   (b) is just a mess of metal and wires.
   (c) rescues Mrs. Weston.
   (d) saves Gloria's life.

ORDER OF EVENTS

7. Choose the letter of the event that happens FIRST in the story.
   (a) The Westons fly to New York City.
   (b) Gloria plays hide-and-seek with Robbie.
   (c) Mr. Weston arranges a tour of U.S. Robots.
   (d) Gloria speaks with the Talking Robot.

CAUSE AND EFFECT

8. Mr. Weston gets rid of Robbie because
   (a) Gloria wants a dog instead.
   (b) the robot is too expensive to keep.
   (c) his wife persuades him to do so.
   (d) he realizes that the robot could harm Gloria.

9. As a result of Robbie's disappearance, Gloria becomes (a) happy (b) angry (c) sad (d) proud.

INFERENCES

10. Although Robbie is a robot that cannot speak, we can infer from the story that he has
    (a) writing talent.
    (b) an interest in sports.
    (c) a robot wife and children.
    (d) feelings.

11. The story suggests that Robbie will
    (a) always protect himself first.
    (b) risk his own destruction to protect Gloria.
    (c) loyally protect all of the Weston family.
    (d) never hurt another robot.

PREDICTING OUTCOMES

12. If Gloria had ordered Robbie to do something that might harm her, the robot would probably
    (a) obey her at once.
    (b) read her the Three Laws of Robotics.
    (c) refuse to obey.
    (d) destroy himself.

BUILDING YOUR VOCABULARY _____

1. And Robbie *cowered*, holding his hands over his face . . . .

   When the robot *cowered* (page 143, line 33), he

   (a) showed that he was no coward.
   (b) shrank away as if afraid.
   (c) uttered sad little sounds.
   (d) spun rapidly around.

2. The logic was *irrefutable*.

   a. The root word in *irrefutable* (page 145, line 3) is (a) *refute* (b) *table*
   (c) *able* (d) none of these.

   b. The word *irrefutable* means

   (a) unrelated to anything.
   (b) easily challenged.
   (c) impossible to understand.
   (d) impossible to disprove.

3. Robbie obeyed with *alacrity* for somehow there was that in him which judged it best to obey Mrs. Weston, without as much as a scrap of hesitation.

   a. Something done with *alacrity* (page 146, lines 7-9) is done

   (a) with a loud cry.
   (b) at once.
   (c) after a pause.
   (d) tearfully.

   b. The BEST strategy for answering part *a* is to

   (a) break the word down into prefix, root, and suffix.
   (b) look for an earlier use of the word.
   (c) note the pronunciation of the word.
   (d) reread the sentence containing the word.

4. He made another *futile* stab at the paper, and his wife tossed it angrily into the next room.

   The word *futile* (page 148, lines 13-14) means (a) furious (b) ineffective (c) useful (d) skillful.

5. On a more *prosaic* level, Mrs. Weston took her to the department stores where she could revel in another type of fairyland.

   The word *prosaic* (page 153, lines 32-33) means (a) ordinary (b) poetic (c) expensive (d) powerful.

STUDYING THE WRITER'S CRAFT _____

1. In the first section of the story (page 142, line 1, to page 145, line 37), we meet the two main characters, Gloria and Robbie. The author *characterizes* them by obeying a basic rule for writing fiction: "Don't tell. Show!"

    a. Before we are *told* that Gloria is eight years old (page 143, line 14), several clues *show* us that she is a little girl. Mention at least three of these clues.

    b. Before we are *told* that Robbie is a robot (page 145, line 5), numerous clues *show* us that fact. Mention at least six of these clues.

    c. The author never *tells* us how Gloria feels about Robbie and how Robbie "feels" about her. Nevertheless, the actions of the two characters and Gloria's words clearly *show* us the nature of that relationship. How would you describe their relationship? Give evidence for your answer from the first section of the story.

2. The *plot* is the series of related actions or events that make up a story. A good plot contains three important elements: *conflict, suspense*, and a satisfying *resolution*.

    a. What is the chief conflict in the story?

    b. What central question creates suspense in the story?

    c. How is the conflict resolved and the suspense relieved?

3. An author must choose a story's *point of view* with care. In "Robbie," Isaac Asimov uses an *omniscient* (or "all-knowing") *point of view*. Instead of having one of the characters tell the story from the *first-person point of view* (using the first-person pronoun "I"), the narrator is the author, who is outside the story and knows everything.

    a. Why do you think Asimov didn't choose the first-person point of view with Robbie as the narrator?

    b. Why didn't Asimov choose Gloria to be the narrator? (*Hint:* From which scenes in the story is she absent? How would having Gloria tell the story spoil some of the story's suspense?)

ACTIVITIES FOR LISTENING, SPEAKING, WRITING

1. Would you like to own a robot like Robbie? What would you ask a personal robot to do for you? What burdens or responsibilities might owning your own robot impose on you? In a brief composition, tell why you would or would not want to own a robot like Robbie.

2. Robbie's favorite story is "Cinderella." If you don't already know this famous fairy tale, listen while one of your classmates or your teacher briefly tells the story. With your classmates, discuss the possibility that "Robbie" is a modern version of "Cinderella." Although some male and female roles may be reversed, there are correspondences. Which character in the Asimov story could stand for Cinderella? Which one for the prince? For the wicked stepmother? For the fairy godmother? In what other ways are the two stories similar?

3. New developments in technology, such as the use of robots in manufacturing, can replace human workers with machines. In a fully automated factory, for example, one robot may do the work once performed by many workers. These workers have become unemployed because of technology—a problem called *technological unemployment*.

   a. Early in the Industrial Revolution, workers responded violently to the problem of technological unemployment. Look up *General Lud* and the *Luddites* in an encyclopedia or other reference work. Take notes on what you have read, and be ready to share your findings with your classmates.

   b. How would you feel if a robot took over your job (or a relative's job), did it better and for much less money? What do you think the government, factory owners, and workers should do if and when this happens? Discuss this issue with your classmates.

Dial F for Frankenstein

by Arthur C. Clarke

What would this supermind actually do? *Would it be friendly—hostile—indifferent? Would it even know that we exist . . . ?*

We all stand to benefit from today's complex computer networks. Without these electronic communication networks, modern medical research, military defense, publishing, and banking wouldn't be possible.

Like all the bright gifts of progress, however, these communication systems have a potential for harm. Computer viruses can spread like wildfire through interlinked computers, wiping out their programs. Computer networks can threaten personal privacy. Even the secrets of businesses and governments may not be safe from the computer's growing capacity for electronic search and capture.

All these potential threats are mild compared to the disaster in Clarke's 1965 short story "Dial F for Frankenstein." The timing of the disaster—December 1, 1975—was clearly wrong. But how impossible is the disaster itself? Read on and make your own decision.

Arthur C. Clarke

You may have heard of the British author Arthur C. Clarke only because of the filmscript he wrote for *2001: A Space Odyssey* (1968). Readers of science fiction know him better as the author of such excellent novels as *Childhood's End* (1953), *The City and the Stars* (1956), and *Rendezvous with Rama* (1973). The latter novel won both Hugo and Nebula awards.

Clarke's interests also include astronomy, space travel, and communications. In 1945, he published an article explaining how instant world communication could be achieved by bouncing microwave signals off artificial satellites orbiting the Earth. At the time, this idea was pure science fiction. Twenty years later, however, the International Telecommunication Satellite Organization (INTELSAT) orbited the first communication satellite. Today, people around the world are linked in global networks of microwave signals relayed through artificial satellites. Clarke's science fiction has become science fact.

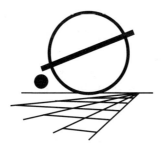

A t 0150 Greenwich mean time on December 1, 1975, every telephone in the world started to ring. A quarter of a billion people picked up their receivers to listen for a few seconds with annoyance or perplexity. Those who had been awakened in the middle of the night assumed that some far-off friend was calling over the satellite telephone network that had gone into service, with such a blaze of publicity, the day before. But there was no voice on the line, only a sound that to many seemed like the roaring of the sea—to others, like the vibrations of harp strings in the wind. And there were many more, in that moment, who recalled a secret sound of childhood—the noise of blood pulsing through the veins, heard 10 when a shell is cupped over the ear. Whatever it was, it lasted no more than twenty seconds; then it was replaced by the dialing tone.

The world's subscribers cursed, muttered, "Wrong number," and hung up. Some tried to dial a complaint, but the line seemed busy. In a few hours, everyone had forgotten the incident—except those whose duty it was to worry about such things.

At the Post Office Research Station, the argument had been going on all morning and had got nowhere. It continued unabated through the lunch break, when the hungry engineers poured into the little café across the road.

"I still think," said Willy Smith, the solid-state electronics man, "that it was a temporary surge of current, caused when the satellite network was switched in."

"It was obviously *something* to do with the satellites," agreed Jules 10 Reyner, circuit designer. "But why the time delay? They were plugged in at midnight; the ringing was two hours later—as we all know to our cost." He yawned violently.

"What do *you* think, Doc?" asked Bob Andrews, computer programmer. "You've been very quiet all morning. Surely you've got some idea?"

Dr. John Williams, head of the mathematics division, stirred uneasily.

"Yes," he said, "I have. But you won't take it seriously."

"That doesn't matter. Even if it's as crazy as those science fiction yarns you write under a pseudonym, it may give us some leads."

Williams blushed, but not very hard. Everyone knew about his sto- 20 ries, and he wasn't ashamed of them. After all, they *had* been collected in book form. (Remainder at five shillings;[1] he still had a couple of hundred copies.)

"Very well," he said, doodling on the tablecloth. "This is something I've been wondering about for years. Have you ever considered the analogy between an automatic telephone exchange and the human brain?"

"Who hasn't thought of it?" scoffed one of his listeners. "That idea must go back to Graham Bell."

"Possibly; I never said it was original. But I do say it's time we started taking it seriously." He squinted balefully at the fluorescent 30 tubes above the table; they were needed on this foggy winter day. "What's wrong with the lights? They've been flickering for the last five minutes."

"Don't bother about that; Maisie's probably forgotten to pay her electricity bill. Let's hear more about your theory."

"Most of it isn't theory; it's plain fact. We know that the human brain is a system of switches—neurons—interconnected in a very elaborate fashion by nerves. An automatic telephone exchange is also a system of switches—selectors, and so forth—connected together with wires."

1. **Remainder at five shillings:** book sold at a great discount. A shilling is a former British unit of money equal to one-twentieth of a pound. (*See footnote 4 on page 168.*)

"Agreed," said Smith. "But that analogy won't get you very far. Aren't there about fifteen billion neurons in the brain? That's a lot more than the number of switches in an autoexchange."

Williams's answer was interrupted by the scream of a low-flying jet; he had to wait until the café had ceased to vibrate before he could continue.

"Never heard them fly *that* low," Andrews grumbled. "Thought it was against regulations."

"So it is, but don't worry—London Airport Control will catch him."

"I doubt it," said Reyner. "That *was* London Airport, bringing in a 10 Concorde on ground approach. But I've never heard one so low, either. Glad I wasn't aboard."

"Are we, or are we *not*, going to get on with this blasted discussion?" demanded Smith.

"You're right about the fifteen billion neurons in the human brain," continued Williams, unabashed. "And *that's* the whole point. Fifteen billion sounds a large number, but it isn't. Round about the 1960s, there were more than that number of individual switches in the world's autoexchanges. Today, there are approximately five times as many."

"I see," said Reyner very slowly. "And as of yesterday, they've all 20 become capable of full interconnection, now that the satellite links have gone into service."

"Precisely."

There was silence for a moment, apart from the distant clanging of a fire-engine bell.

"Let me get this straight," said Smith. "Are you suggesting that the world telephone system is now a giant brain?"

"That's putting it crudely—anthropomorphically.[2] I prefer to think of it in terms of critical size." Williams held his hands out in front of him, fingers partly closed. 30

"Here are two lumps of U-235;[3] nothing happens as long as you keep them apart. But bring them together"—he suited the action to the words—"and you have something *very* different from one bigger lump of uranium. You have a hole half a mile across.

"It's the same with our telephone networks; until today they've been largely independent, autonomous. But now we've suddenly multiplied the connecting links—the networks have all merged together—and we've reached criticality."

2. **anthropomorphically:** giving human characteristics to nonhuman objects or animals.
3. **U-235:** form of uranium, a radioactive element used in atom bombs.

"And just what does criticality mean in this case?" asked Smith.

"For want of a better word—consciousness."

"A weird sort of consciousness," said Reyner. "What would it use for sense organs?"

"Well, all the radio and TV stations in the world would be feeding information into it, through their landlines. *That* should give it something to think about! Then there would be all the data stored in all the computers; it would have access to that—and to the electronic libraries, the radar tracking systems, the telemetering in the automatic factories. Oh, it would have enough sense organs! We can't begin to imagine its picture of the world, 10 but it would certainly be infinitely richer and more complex than ours."

"Granted all this, because it's an entertaining idea," said Reyner, "what could it *do* except think? It couldn't go anywhere; it would have no limbs."

"Why should it want to travel? It would already be everywhere! And every piece of remotely controlled electrical equipment on the planet could act as a limb."

"Now I understand that time delay," interjected Andrews. "It was conceived at midnight, but it wasn't born until one-fifty this morning. The noise that woke us all up was—its birth cry." 20

His attempt to sound facetious was not altogether convincing, and nobody smiled. Overhead, the lights continued their annoying flicker, which seemed to be getting worse. Then there was an interruption from the front of the café as Jim Small of Power Supplies made his usual boisterous entry.

"Look at this, fellows," he grinned, waving a piece of paper in front of his colleagues. "I'm rich. Ever seen a bank balance like *that?*"

Dr. Williams took the proffered statement, glanced down the columns, and read the balance aloud: "Credit 999,999,897.87 pounds."[4]

"Nothing very odd about that," he continued above the general 30 amusement. "I'd say it means the computer's made a slight mistake. That sort of thing was happening all the time just after the banks converted to the decimal system."

"I know, I know," said Jim, "but don't spoil my fun. I'm going to frame this statement—and what would happen if I drew a check for a few million on the strength of this? Could I sue the bank if it bounced?"

"Not on your life," answered Reyner. "I'll take a bet that the banks thought of *that* years ago and protected themselves somewhere down in the small print. But by the way—when did you get that statement?"

---

4. **pound:** the basic monetary unit of the United Kingdom and several other countries.

"In the noon delivery; it comes straight to the office, so that my wife doesn't have a chance of seeing it."

"Hmm—that means it was computed early this morning. Certainly after midnight . . ."

"What are you driving at? And why all the long faces?"

No one answered him; he had started a new hare, and the hounds were in full cry.

"Does anyone here know about automated banking systems?" asked Willy Smith. "How are they tied together?"

"Like everything else these days," said Bob Andrews. "They're all 10 in the same network—the computers talk to one another all over the world. It's a point for you, John. If there was real trouble, that's one of the first places I'd expect it. Besides the phone system itself, of course."

"No one answered the question I asked before Jim came in," complained Reyner. "What would this supermind actually *do*? Would it be friendly—hostile—indifferent? Would it even know that we exist, or would it consider the electronic signals it's handling to be the only reality?"

"I see you're beginning to believe me," said Williams with a certain grim satisfaction. "I can only answer your question by asking another. What does a newborn baby do? It starts looking for food." He 20 glanced up at the flickering lights. "My God," he said slowly, as if a thought had just struck him. "There's only one food it would need—electricity."

"This nonsense has gone far enough," said Smith. "What the devil's happened to our lunch? We gave our orders twenty minutes ago."

Everyone ignored him.

"And then," said Reyner, taking up where Williams had left off, "it would start looking around and stretching its limbs. In fact, it would start to play, like any growing baby."

"And babies *break* things," said someone softly. 30

"It would have enough toys, heaven knows. That Concorde that went over just now. The automated production lines. The traffic lights in our streets."

"Funny you should mention that," interjected Small. "Something's happened to the traffic outside—it's been stopped for the last ten minutes. Looks like a big jam."

"I guess there's a fire somewhere—I heard an engine."

"I've heard two—and what sounded like an explosion over toward the industrial estate. Hope it's nothing serious."

"Maisie!!! What about some candles? We can't see a thing!" 40

"I've just remembered—this place has an all-electric kitchen. We're going to get cold lunch, if we get any lunch at all."

"At least we can read the newspaper while we're waiting. Is that the latest edition you've got there, Jim?"

"Yes—haven't had time to look at it yet. Hmm—there *do* seem to have been a lot of odd accidents this morning—railway signals jammed—water main blown up through failure of relief valve—dozens of complaints about last night's wrong numbers—"

He turned the page and became suddenly silent.

"What's the matter?"

Without a word, Small handed over the paper. Only the front page made sense. Throughout the interior, column after column was a mass 10 of printer's pi[5]—with, here and there, a few incongruous advertisements making islands of sanity in a sea of gibberish. They had obviously been set up as independent blocks and had escaped the scrambling that had overtaken the text around them.

"So this is where long-distance typesetting and autodistribution have brought us," grumbled Andrews. "I'm afraid Fleet Street's[6] been putting too many eggs in one electronic basket."

"So have we all, I'm afraid," said Williams very solemnly. "So have we all."

"If I can get a word in edgeways, in time to stop the mob hysteria 20 which seems to be infecting this table," said Smith loudly and firmly, "I'd like to point out that there's nothing to worry about—even if John's ingenious fantasy is correct. We only have to switch off the satellites—and we'll be back where we were yesterday."

"Prefrontal lobotomy,"[7] muttered Williams. "I'd thought of that."

"Eh? Oh, yes—cutting out slabs of the brain. That would certainly do the trick. Expensive, of course, and we'd have to go back to sending telegrams to each other. But civilization would survive."

From not too far away, there was a short, sharp explosion.

"I don't like this," said Andrews nervously. "Let's hear what the old 30 BBC's got to say—the one o'clock news has just started."

He reached into his briefcase and pulled out a transistor radio.

"—unprecedented number of industrial accidents, as well as the unexplained launching of three salvos of guided missiles from military installations in the United States. Several airports have had to suspend operations owing to the erratic behavior of their radars, and the banks and stock exchanges have closed because their information-processing systems have become completely unreliable." ("You're telling me," mut-

5. **printer's pi** (*also* **pie**): a confused jumble of printer's type.
6. **Fleet Street:** London street where newspaper and printing offices were located.
7. **prefrontal lobotomy:** operation that removes tissue from the frontal lobes of the brain to relieve certain mental disorders.

tered Small, while the others shushed him.) "One moment, please—there's a news flash coming through. . . . Here it is. We have just been informed that all control over the newly installed communication satellites has been lost. They are no longer responding to commands from the ground. According to—"

The BBC went off the air; even the carrier wave died. Andrews reached for the tuning knob and twisted it round the dial. Over the whole band, the ether was silent.

Presently Reyner said, in a voice not far from hysteria, "That prefrontal lobotomy was a good idea, John. Too bad that baby's already 10 thought of it."

Williams rose slowly to his feet.

"Let's get back to the lab," he said. "There must be an answer somewhere."

But he knew already that it was far, far too late. For Homo sapiens, the telephone bell had tolled.

REVIEWING THE STORY

THE MAIN IDEA

1. Which of the following figurative statements best expresses the main idea of the story?

   (a) It's never too late to polish up your dreams.
   (b) Monsters are merely the thoughts of evil men.
   (c) Progress may prove to be our worst disease.
   (d) Science is the surgeon to cure all ills.

DETAILS

2. The men in the story are all

   (a) telephone operators.
   (b) science-fiction writers.
   (c) research engineers.
   (d) newspaper reporters.

3. As the story opens, the men are

   (a) waiting for lunch in a café.
   (b) reading the newspaper in a library.
   (c) attending a conference at the library.
   (d) listening to news reports on the radio.

4. During the course of the story, the fluorescent lights **(a)** become brighter **(b)** flicker and go out **(c)** explode **(d)** remain unchanged.

5. The man with a theory about what is happening is **(a)** Willy Smith **(b)** Jules Reyner **(c)** John Williams **(d)** Jim Small.

6. His theory is that the new global telephone system has acquired **(a)** a conscience **(b)** consciousness **(c)** confusion **(d)** unconsciousness.

ORDER OF EVENTS

7. Choose the letter of the event that happens LAST in the story.
   (a) A jet airplane seems to be out of control.
   (b) Telephones ring all over the world.
   (c) All the radio stations go dead.
   (d) Jim Small shows off a huge error in his bank statement.

CAUSE AND EFFECT

8. The strange events in the story appear to have been caused by the
   (a) operations of military installations in the United States.
   (b) opening of the worldwide satellite telephone network.
   (c) science-fiction stories of Dr. John Williams.
   (d) failure of Maisie to pay her electricity bill.

9. A major effect of the strange new problem is that
   (a) the human brain is breaking down.
   (b) lunch will be late and cold.
   (c) people will have to communicate by telegram.
   (d) electrical devices are all failing.

INFERENCES

10. At the start of the story, the ringing of telephones all over the world seems to be
    (a) the first official test of the new satellite telephone network.
    (b) the result of dialing wrong numbers.
    (c) the result of secret childhood memories.
    (d) an unexplained and perplexing oddity.

11. By the end of the story, the evidence suggests that
    (a) a foreign country has conspired to conquer the world.
    (b) the satellite telephone network has taken control of the world.

(c) the five men have a plan to save the world.

(d) the satellite telephone network has run out of electrical power.

PREDICTING OUTCOMES

12. What will happen if the military attempts to launch missiles to destroy the orbiting communication satellites?

(a) The missiles will malfunction.

(b) The satellites will be destroyed.

(c) The global telephone network will shut down.

(d) Every telephone in the world will ring again.

BUILDING YOUR VOCABULARY _____

1. Have you ever considered the *analogy* between an automatic telephone exchange and the human brain?

   An *analogy* (page 166, lines 25-26) is a **(a)** conversation **(b)** contrast **(c)** similarity **(d)** false argument.

2. "You're right about the fifteen billion neurons in the human brain," continued Williams, *unabashed*.

   Describing Dr. Williams as *unabashed* (page 167, lines 15-16) suggests that he

   (a) has not been hit hard.

   (b) is not upset.

   (c) does not understand Smith's earlier question.

   (d) wants to hurt Smith.

3. It's the same with our telephone networks; until today they've been largely independent, *autonomous*.

   a. The phrase closest in meaning to *autonomous* (page 167, lines 35-36) is **(a)** closely connected **(b)** self-contained **(c)** fast-acting **(d)** extremely expensive.

   b. The word in this sentence that gives the BEST clue to the meaning of *autonomous* is **(a)** networks **(b)** today **(c)** largely **(d)** independent.

4. "Now I understand that time delay," *interjected* Andrews.

   Interjected (page 168, line 18) means

   (a) said in a sad, dejected tone.

   (b) thought but not said aloud.

(c) spoken after a long delay.

(d) inserted or interrupted.

5. Dr. Williams took the *proffered* statement, glanced down the columns, and read the balance aloud: "Credit 999,999,897.87 pounds."

A synonym for *proffered* (page 168, lines 28-29) is (a) preferred (b) profitable (c) offered (d) offensive.

STUDYING THE WRITER'S CRAFT

1. By occasionally using **figurative language**, Arthur C. Clarke makes abstract ideas more colorful and interesting for his readers. Referring to Jim Small, for example, Clarke writes: "No one answered him; he had started a new hare, and the hounds were in full cry." (page 169, lines 6-7)

   a. In this **metaphor**, what does the hare represent?

   b. Who are the hounds?

   c. How would you translate the metaphorical statement into a literal statement?

   d. Which do you find more effective: the metaphorical statement or the literal statement?

2. In addition to the five men in the story, there is one other important "character," who never appears.

   a. Who or what is this "character"?

   b. What clues do the title and the last sentence of the story provide about the nature of this "character" and what it will probably do?

3. Which is more important in this story—**characterization** (the development of characters) or the exploration of an idea? Explain your answer with evidence from the story.

ACTIVITIES FOR LISTENING, SPEAKING, WRITING

1. During the half day in which the story takes place, the new artificial intelligence is born and begins "to play, like any growing baby." At first, it breaks things. Suppose, though, that this supermind matures extremely rapidly—*before* it destroys humanity. As an "adult," what might it do? What kind of relationship could develop between it and the human race? Write a very short science-fiction story or sketch in which you answer these questions.

2. Listen and take notes on a separate sheet of paper while your teacher reads aloud a passage about artificial intelligence. (This passage appears in a separate Answer Key accompanying this book.) Then use your notes and your memory of what you have just heard to write a brief summary of the topic discussed in the passage. Be sure to state the main idea clearly. Provide as many supporting details as you can. Give your summary a title.

3. You may have noticed that most of "Dial F for Frankenstein" consists of dialogue. How would this story work as a play? At your teacher's direction, work in a small group to adapt a part of the story as a play. Read your adaptation aloud to the rest of the class.

Instinct

by Lester del Rey

For a long time, he sat quietly with the book on his lap, wondering what it would be like to have instincts. . . . Man should have implanted one instinct in a robot's brain, at least, just to show what it was like.

It is a million years since Man lived on Earth. Only the robots he created have survived him. Slowly, over the centuries, the robots built new robots, developed advanced technology, and expanded throughout the universe. But they have carefully refrained from improving themselves. Until the robots can discover what caused Man to die out, they are afraid to change themselves from the way Man first constructed them.

Robot bioengineers have a theory about the extinction of Man. Perhaps he was the victim of some special inborn trait, something no robot has—*instinct*. To test this theory, the robot scientists are using a new technique of gene-building to try to re-create Man. So far, all of their experiments have ended in failure.

In this slyly humorous tale, Lester del Rey gives us a robot's-eye view of humanity. In some respects, it's a view that is a bit wacky. The robots are, after all, like human scientists trying to reconstruct the daily life of dinosaurs. But what if one day they succeed?

Lester del Rey

Early in his career, Lester del Rey contributed a great deal of short fiction to *Astounding*, the influential science-fiction magazine edited by John W. Campbell from 1937 to 1971. Del Rey's best novel, *Nerves* (1956), tells of an accident in a nuclear power plant. He wrote many books for children under various pseudonyms, such as Philip St. John and Edson McCann. In later years, he turned from science fiction to the writing of fantasy fiction.

Besides his work as an author, del Rey also served as an editor. In the 1970s, he edited a number of popular collections of science-fiction stories and fantasy stories.

Senthree waved aside the slowing scooter and lengthened his stride down the sidewalk; he had walked all the way from the rocket port, and there was no point to a taxi now that he was only a few blocks from the bio-labs. Besides, it was too fine a morning to waste in riding. He sniffed at the crisp, clean fumes of gasoline appreciatively and listened to the music of his hard heels slapping against the concrete.

It was good to have a new body again. He hadn't appreciated what life was like for the last hundred years or so. He let his eyes rove across the street toward the blue flame of a welding torch and realized how long it had been since his eyes had really appreciated the delicate beauty of such a flame. The wise old brain in his chest even seemed to think better now.

It was worth every stinking minute he'd spent on Venus. At times like this, one could realize how good it was to be alive and to be a robot.

Then he sobered as he came to the old bio-labs. Once there had been plans for a fine new building instead of the old factory in which he had started it all four hundred years ago. But somehow, there'd never been time for that. It had taken almost a century before they could master the

10

technique of building up genes and chromosomes into the zygote[1] of a simple fish that would breed with the natural ones. Another century had gone by before they produced Oscar, the first artificially made pig. And there they seemed to have stuck. Sometimes it seemed to Senthree that they were no nearer re-creating Man than they had been when they started.

He dilated the door and went down the long hall, studying his reflection in the polished walls absently. It was a good body. The black enamel was perfect and every joint of the metal case spelled new techniques and luxurious fitting. But the old worries were beginning to settle. He grunted at Oscar LXXII, the lab mascot, and received an answering grunt. The pig came over to root at his feet, but he had no time for that. He turned into the main lab room, already taking on the worries of his job.

It wasn't hard to worry as he saw the other robots. They were clustered about some object on a table, dejection on every gleaming back. Senthree shoved Ceofor and Beswun aside and moved up. One look was enough. The female of the eleventh couple lay there in the strange stiffness of protoplasm that had died, a horrible grimace on her face.

"How long—and what happened to the male?" Senthree asked.

Ceofor swung to face him quickly. "Hi, boss. You're late. Hey, new body!"

Senthree nodded, as they came grouping around, but his words were automatic as he explained about falling in the alkali pool on Venus and ruining his worn body completely. "Had to wait for a new one. And then the ship got held up while we waited for the Arcturus superlight ship to land. They'd found half a dozen new planets to colonize, and had to spread the word before they'd set down. Now, what about the creatures?"

"We finished educating about three days ago," Ceofor told him. Ceofor was the first robot trained in Senthree's technique of gene-building and the senior assistant. "Expected you back then, boss. But . . . well, see for yourself. The man is still alive, but he won't be long."

Senthree followed them back to another room and looked through the window. He looked away quickly. It had been another failure. The man was crawling about the floor on hands and knees, falling half the time to his stomach, and drooling. His garbled mouthing made no sense.

"Keep the news robots out," he ordered. It would never do to let the public see this. There was already too much of a cry against homovivifying,[2] and the crowds were beginning to mutter something about it being unwise to mess with vanished life forms. They seemed actually afraid of the legendary figure of Man.

1. **zygote:** cell formed by union of male and female germ cells.
2. **homovivifying:** literally, "bringing man (human beings) to life."

"What luck on Venus?" one of them asked, as they began the job of carefully dissecting the body of the female failure to look for the reason behind the lack of success.

"None. Just another rumor. I don't think Man ever established self-sufficient colonies. If he did, they didn't survive. But I found something else—something the museum would give a fortune for. Did my stuff arrive?"

"You mean that box of tar? Sure, it's over there in the corner."

Senthree let the yielding plastic of his mouth smile at them as he strode toward it. They had already ripped off the packing, and now he reached up for a few fine wires in the tar. It came off as he pulled, loosely repacked over a thin layer of wax. At that, he'd been lucky to sneak it past customs. This was the oldest, crudest, and biggest robot discovered so far—perhaps one of the fabulous Original Models. It stood there rigidly, staring out of its pitted, expressionless face. But the plate on its chest had been scraped carefully clean, and Senthree pointed it out to them.

MAKEPEACE ROBOT, SER. 324MD2991. SURGEON.

"A mechanic for Man bodies," Beswun translated. "But that means . . ."

"Exactly." Senthree put it into words. "It must know how Man's body was built—if it has retained any memory. I found it in a tarpit by sheer accident, and it seems to be fairly well preserved. No telling whether there were any magnetic fields to erode memories, of course, and it's all matted inside. But if we can get it to working . . ."

Beswun took over. He had been trained as a physicist before the mysterious lure of the bio-lab had drawn him here. Now he began wheeling the crude robot away. If he could get it into operation, the museum could wait. The re-creation of Man came first!

Senthree pulled X-ray lenses out of a pouch and replaced the normal ones in his eyes before going over to join the robots who were beginning dissection. Then he switched them for the neutrino detector lenses that had made this work possible. The neutrino was the only particle that could penetrate the delicate protoplasmic cells without ruining them and yet permit the necessary millions of times magnification. It was a fuzzy image, since the neutrino spin made such an insignificant field for the atomic nuclei to work on that few were deflected. But through them, he could see the vague outlines of the pattern within the cells. It was as they had designed the original cell—there had been no reshuffling of genes in handling. He switched to his micromike hands and began the delicate work of tracing down the neuron connections. There was only an occasional mutter as one of the robots beside him switched to some new investigation.

The female should have lived! But somewhere, in spite of all their care, she had died. And now the male was dying. Eleven couples—eleven failures. Senthree was no nearer finding the creators of his race than he had been centuries before.

Then the radio in his head buzzed its warning and he let it cut in, straightening from his work. "Senthree."

"The Director is in your office. Will you report at once?"

What did old Emptinine want . . . or wait again, there'd been a selection while he was on Venus investigating the rumors of Man. Some young administrator—Arpeten—had the job now.   10

Ceofor looked up guiltily, obviously having tuned in. "I should have warned you. We got word three days ago he was coming, but forgot it in reviving the couple. Trouble?"

Senthree shrugged, screwing his normal lenses back in and trading to the regular hands. They couldn't have found out about the antique robot. They had been seen by nobody else. It was probably just sheer curiosity over some rumor that they were reviving the couple. If his appropriation[3] hadn't been about exhausted, Senthree would have told him where to go; but now was hardly the time, with a failure on one hand and a low credit balance on the other. He polished his new head 20 quickly with the aid of one of the walls for a mirror and headed toward his office.

But Arpeten was smiling. He got to his feet as the bio-lab chief entered, holding out a well-polished hand. "Dr. Senthree. Delighted. And you've got an interesting place here. I've already seen most of it. And that pig—they tell me it's a descendant of a boar out of your test tubes."

"Incubation wombs. But you're right—the seventy-second generation."

"Fascinating." Arpeten must have been reading too much of that book *Proven Points to Popularity* they'd dug up in the ruins of Hudson ten 30 years before, but it had worked. He was the Director. "But tell me. Just what good are pigs?"

Senthree grinned, in spite of himself. "Nobody knows. Men apparently kept a lot of them, but so far as I can see they are completely useless. They're clever, in a way. But I don't think they were pets. Just another mystery."

"Umm. Like men. Maybe you can tell me what good Man will be. I've been curious about that since I saw your appropriations. But nobody can answer."

---

3. **appropriation:** grant of money to fund a project.

"It's in the records," Senthree told him sharply. Then he modified his voice carefully. "How well do you know your history? I mean about the beginning."

"Well . . ."

He probably knew some of it, Senthree thought. They all got part of it as legends. He leaned back in his seat now, though, as the biochemist began the old tale of the beginning as they knew it. They knew that there had been Man a million years before them. And somebody—Asimov or Asenion, the record wasn't quite clear—had apparently created the first robot. They had improved it up to about the present level. Then there had been some kind of a contest in which violent forces had ruined the factories, most of the robots, and nearly all of the Men. It was believed from the fragmentary records that a biological weapon had killed the rest of man, leaving only the robots.

Those first robots, as they were now known, had had to start on a ruined world from scratch—a world where mines were exhausted, and factories were gone. They'd learned to get metals from the seas, and had spent years and centuries slowly rebuilding the machines to build new robots. There had been only two of them when the task was finished, and they had barely time enough to run one new robot off and educate him sketchily. Then they had discharged finally, and he had taken up rebuilding the race. It was almost like beginning with no history and no science. Twenty millennia had passed before they began to rebuild a civilization of their own.

"But why did Man die?" Senthree asked. "That's part of the question. And are we going to do the same? We know we are similar to Man. Did he change himself in some way that ruined him? Can we change ourselves safely? You know that there are a thousand ways we could improve ourselves. We could add anti-gravity, and get rid of our cumbersome vehicles. We could add more arms. We could eliminate our useless mouths and talk by radio. We could add new circuits to our brains. But we don't dare. One school says that nobody can build a better race than itself, so Man must have been better than we are—and if he made us this way, there was a reason. Even if the psychologists can't understand some of the circuits in our brains, they don't dare touch them.

"We're expanding through the universe—but we can't even change ourselves to fit the new planets. And until we can find the reasons for Man's disappearance, that makes good sense. We know he was planning to change himself. We have bits of evidence. And he's dead. To make it worse, we have whole reels of education tape that probably contain all the answers—but information is keyed to Man's brain, and we can't respond to it. Give us a viable Man, and he can interpret that. Or we can find out by comparison what we can and cannot do. I maintain we can do a lot."

Arpeten shook his head doubtfully. "I suppose you think you know why he died!"

"I think so, yes. Instinct! That's a built-in reaction, an unlearned thought. Man had it. If a man heard a rattlesnake, he left the place in a hurry, even though he'd never heard it before. Response to that sound was built into him. No tape impressed it, and no experience was needed. We know the instincts of some of the animals, too—and one of them is to struggle and kill—like the ants who kill each other off. I think Man 10 did just that. He couldn't get rid of his instincts when they were no longer needed, and they killed him. He *should* have changed—and we can change. But I can't tell that from animals. I need intelligent life, to see whether instinct or intelligence will dominate. And robots don't have instincts—I've looked for even one sign of something not learned individually, and can't find it. It's the one basic difference between us. Don't you see, Man is the whole key to our problem of whether we can change or not without risking extermination?"

"Umm." The director sounded noncommittal. "Interesting theory. But how are you going to know you have Man?"   20

Senthree stared at the robot with more respect. He tried to explain, but he had never been as sure of that himself as he might. Theoretically, they had bones and bits of preserved tissue. They had examined the gene pattern of these, having learned that the cells of the individual contain the same pattern as that of the zygote. And they had other guides—Man's achievements, bits of his literature. From these, some working theories could be made. But he couldn't be quite sure—they'd never really known whether man's pigment was dark brown, pinkish orange, white, or what; the records they had seemed to disagree on this.

"We'll know when we get an intelligent animal with instinct," he 30 said at last. "It won't matter exactly whether he is completely like Man or not. At least it will give us a check on things we must know. Until then, we'll have to go on trying. You might as well know that the last experiment failed, though it was closer. But in another hundred years . . ."

"So." Arpeten's face became bland, but he avoided the look of Senthree. "I'm afraid not. At least for a while. That's what I came about, you know. We've just had word of several new planets around Arcturus, and it will take the major allocation of our funds to colonize these. New robots must be built, new ships—oh, you know. And we're retrenching a bit on other things. Of course, if you'd succeeded . . . but perhaps it's 40 better you failed. You know how the sentiment against reviving Man has grown."

Senthree growled bitterly. He'd seen how it was carefully nurtured—though he had to admit it seemed to be easy to create. Apparently most of the robots were afraid of Man—felt he would again take over, or something. Superstitious fools.

"How much longer?" he asked.

"Oh, we won't cut back what you have, Dr. Senthree. But I'm afraid we simply can't allocate more funds. When this is finished, I was hoping to make you biological investigator, incidentally, on one of the planets. There'll be work enough. . . . Well, it was a pleasure." He shook hands again, and walked out, his back a gleaming ramrod of efficiency and 10 effectiveness.

Senthree turned back, his new body no longer moving easily. It could already feel the harsh sands and unknown chemical poisons of investigating a new planet—the futile, empty carding of new life that could have no real purpose to the robots. No more appropriations! And they had barely enough funds to meet the current bills.

Four hundred years—and a ship to Arcturus had ended it in three months. Instinct, he thought again—given life with intelligence and instinct together for one year, and he could settle half the problems of his race, perhaps. But robots could not have instincts. Fifty years of study 20 had proven that.

Beswun threw up a hand in greeting as he returned, and he saw that the dissection was nearly complete, while the antique robot was activated. A hinge on its ludicrous jaw was moving, and rough, grating words were coming out. Senthree turned to the dissecting bench, and then swung back as he heard them.

"Wrong . . . wrong," it was muttering. "Can not live. Is not good brain. No pineal. Medulla good, but not good cerebrum. Fissures wrong. Maybe pituitary disfunction? No. How can be?" It probed doubtfully and set the brain aside. "Mutation maybe. Very bad. Need Milliken mike. See 30 nucleus of cells. Maybe just freak, maybe new disease."

Senthree's fingers were taut and stiff as he fished into his bag and came out with a set of lenses. Beswun shook his head and made a waiting sign. He went out at a run, to come back shortly with a few bits of metal and the shavings from machining still on his hands. "Won't fit—but these adapters should do it. There, 324MD2991. Now come over here where you can look at it over this table—that's where the—uh, rays are."

He turned back, and Senthree saw that a fine wire ran from one adapter. "He doesn't speak our bioterminology, Senthree. We'll have to see the same things he does. There—we can watch it on the screen. Now, 40 324MD2991, you tell us what is wrong and point it out. Are your hands steady enough for that?"

"Hands one-billionth inch accurate," the robot creaked; it was a meaningless noise, though they had found the unit of measure mentioned. But whatever it meant, the hands were steady enough. The microprobe began touching shadowy bunches of atoms, droning and grating. "Freak. Very bad freak. How he lived? Would stop trophoblast, not attach to uterus. Ketone—no ketone there. Not understand. How he live?"

Ceofor dashed for their chromosome blanks and began lettering in the complex symbols they used. For a second, Senthree hesitated. Then he caught fire and began making notes along with his assistant. It seemed to take hours; it probably did. The old robot had his memory intact, but 10 there were no quick ways for him to communicate. And at last, the antique grunted in disgust and turned his back on them. Beswun pulled a switch.

"He expects to be discharged when not in use. Crazy, isn't it?" the physicist explained. "Look, boss, am I wrong, or isn't that close to what we did on the eleventh couple?"

"Only a few genes different in three chromosomes. We *were* close. But—umm, that's ridiculous. Look at all the brain tissue he'd have—and a lot of it unconnected. And here—that would put an extra piece on where big and little intestines join—a perfect focal point for infection.[4] It isn't efficient biological engineering. And yet—umm—most animals do have 20 just that kind of engineering. I think the old robot was right—this would be Man!" He looked at their excited faces, and his shoulders sank. "But there isn't time. Not even time to make a zygote and see what it would look like. Our appropriations won't come through."

It should have been a bombshell, but he saw at once that they had already guessed it. Ceofor stood up slowly.

"We can take a look, boss. We've got the sperm from the male that failed—all we have to do is modify those three, instead of making up a whole cell. We might as well have some fun before we go out looking for sand fleas that secrete hydrofluoric acid and menace our colonies. Come 30 on, even in your new body I'll beat you to a finished cell!"

Senthree grinned ruefully, but he moved toward the creation booth. His hands snapped on the little time field out of pure habit as he found a perfect cell. The little field would slow time almost to zero within its limits, and keep any damage from occurring while he worked. It made his own work difficult, since he had to force the probe against that, but it was insulated to some extent by other fields.

Then his hands took over. For a time he worked and thought, but the feeling of the protoplasm came into them, and his hands were almost one with the life stuff, sensing its tiny responses, inserting another link 40

4. **extra piece . . . infection:** Senthree is referring to the appendix.

onto a chain, supplanting an atom of hydrogen with one of the hydroxyl radicals, wielding all the delicate chemical manipulation. He removed the defective genes and gently inserted the correct ones. Four hundred years of this work lay behind him—work he had loved, work which had meant the possible evolution of his race into all it might be.

It had become instinct to him—instinct in only a colloquial sense, however; this was learned response, and real instinct lay deeper than that, so deep that no reason could overcome it and that it was automatic even the first time. Only Man had had instinct and intelligence—stored some-how in this tiny cell that lay within the time field.   10

He stepped out, just as Ceofor was drawing back in a dead heat. But the younger robot inspected Senthree's cell, and nodded. "Less dis-turbance and a neater job on the nucleus—I can't see where you pierced the wall. Well, if we had thirty years—even twenty—we could have Man again—or a race. Yours is male and mine female. But there's no time. . . . Shall I leave the time field on?"

Senthree started to nod.

Then he swung to Beswun. "The time field. Can it be reversed?"

"You mean to speed time up within it? No, not with that model. Take a bigger one. I could build you one in half an hour. But who'd want   20 to speed up time with all the troubles you'd get? How much?"

"Ten thousand—or at least seven thousand times! The period is up tomorrow when disbursements have to be made. I want twenty years in a day."

Beswun shook his head. "No. That's what I was afraid of. Figure it this way: you speed things up ten thousand times and that means the molecules in there speed up just that much, literally. Now 273° times ten thousand—and you have more than two million degrees of temperature. And those molecules have energy! They come busting out of there. No, can't be done."   30

"How much can you do?" Senthree demanded.

Beswun considered. "Ten times—maybe no more than nine. That gives you all the refractories[5] would handle, if we set it up down in the old pit under the building—you know, where they had the annealing oven."

It wasn't enough; it would still take two years. Senthree dropped onto a seat, vagrantly wondering again how this queer brain of his that the psychologists studied futilely could make him feel tired when his body could have no fatigue. It was probably one of those odd circuits they didn't dare touch.   40

5. **refractories:** heat-resistant linings in furnaces.

"Of course, you can use four fields," Beswun stated slowly. "Big one outside, smaller one, still smaller, and smallest inside that. Fourth power of nine is about sixty-six hundred. That's close—raise that nine a little and you'd have your twenty years in a day. By the time it leaked from field to field, it wouldn't matter. Take a couple of hours."

"Not if you get your materials together and build each shell inside the other—you'll be operating faster each step then," Ceofor shouted. "Somebody'll have to go in and stay there a couple of our minutes toward the end to attach the educator tapes—and to revive the couple!"

"Take power," Beswun warned.   10

Senthree shrugged. Let it. If the funds they had wouldn't cover it, the Directorate would have to make it up, once it was used. Besides, once Man was created, they couldn't fold up the bio-labs. "I'll go in," he suggested.

"My job," Ceofor told him flatly. "You won the contest in putting the cells right."

Senthree gave in reluctantly, largely because the younger robot had more experience at reviving than he did. He watched Beswun assemble the complicated net of wires and become a blur as he seemed to toss the second net together almost instantly. The biochemist couldn't see the third 20 go up—it was suddenly there, and Beswun was coming out as it flashed into existence. He held up four fingers, indicating all nets were working.

Ceofor dashed in with the precious cells for the prepared incubators that would nurture the bodies until maturity, when they would be ready for the educators. His body seemed to blur, jerk, and disappear. And almost at once he was back.

Senthree stood watching for a moment more, but there was nothing to see. He hesitated again, then turned and moved out of the building. Across the street lay his little lodging place, where he could relax with his precious two books—almost complete—that had once been printed 30 by Man. Tonight he would study that strange bit of Man's history entitled *Gather, Darkness*, with its odd indications of a science that Man had once had which had surpassed even that of the robots now. It was pleasanter than the incomprehensibility of the mysteriously titled *Mein Kampf*.[6] He'd let his power idle, and mull over it, and consider again the odd behavior of male and female who made such a complicated business of mating. That was probably more instinct—Man, it seemed, was filled with instincts.

---

6. *Gather, Darkness:* a novel (1950) by Fritz Leiber about a tyrannical world of the future. *Mien Kampf*, written in 1924 by Adolf Hitler, dictator of Nazi Germany, is a book about his life and ideas.

For a long time, though, he sat quietly with the book on his lap, wondering what it would be like to have instincts. There must be many unpleasant things about it. But there were also suggestions that it could be pleasant. Well, he'd soon know by observation, even though he could never experience it. Man should have implanted one instinct in a robot's brain, at least, just to show what it was like.

He called the lab once, and Ceofor reported that all was doing nicely, and that both children were looking quite well. Outside the window, Senthree heard a group go by, discussing the latest bits of news on the Arcturus expedition. At least in that, Man had failed to equal the robots. 10 He had somehow died before he could find the trick of using identity exchange to overcome the limitation imposed by the speed of light.

Finally he fell to making up a speech that he could deliver to the Director, Arpeten, when success was in his hands. It must be very short— something that would stick in the robot's mind for weeks, but carrying everything a scientist could feel on proving that those who opposed him were wrong. Let's see. . . .

The buzzer on the telescreen cut through his thoughts, and he flipped it on to see Ceofor's face looking out. Senthree's spirits dropped abruptly as he stared at the younger robot. 20

"Failure? No!"

The other shook his head. "No. At least, I don't know. I couldn't give them full education. Maybe the tape was uncomfortable. They took a lot of it, but the male tore his helmet off and took the girl's off. Now they just sit there, rubbing their heads and staring around."

He paused, and the little darkened ridges of plastic over his eyes tensed. "The time speed-up is off. But I didn't know what to do."

"Let them alone until I get there. If it hurts them, we can give them the rest of it later. How are they otherwise?"

"I don't know. They look all right, boss." Ceofor hesitated, and his 30 voice dropped. "Boss, I don't like it. There's something wrong here. I can't quite figure out what it is, but it isn't the way I expected. Hey, the male just pushed the female off her seat. Do you think their destructive instinct . . . ? No, she's sitting down on the floor now, with her head against him, and holding one of his hands. Wasn't that part of the mating ritual in one of the books?"

Senthree started to agree, a bit of a smile coming onto his face. It looked as if instinct were already in operation.

But a strange voice cut him off. "Hey, you robots, when do we eat around here?" 40

They could talk! It must have been the male. And if it wasn't the polite thanks and gratitude Senthree had expected, that didn't matter.

There had been all kinds of Men in the books, and some were polite while others were crude. Perhaps forced education from the tapes without fuller social experience was responsible for that. But it would all adjust in time.

He started to turn back to Ceofor, but the younger robot was no longer there, and the screen looked out on a blank wall. Senthree could hear the loud voice crying out again, rough and harsh, and there was a shrill, whining sound that might be the female. The two voices blended with the vague mutter of robot voices until he could not make out the words.

He wasted no time in trying. He was already rushing down to the 10 street and heading toward the labs. Instinct—the male had already shown instinct, and the female had responded. They would have to be slow with the couple at first, of course—but the whole answer to the robot problems lay at hand. It would only take a little time and patience now. Let Arpeten sneer, and let the world dote on the Arcturus explorers. Today, biochemistry had been crowned king with the magic of intelligence combined with instinct as its power.

Ceofor came out of the lab at a run with another robot behind him. The young robot looked dazed, and there was another emotion Senthree could not place. The older biochemist nodded, and the younger one 20 waved quickly. "Can't stop now. They're hungry." He was gone at full speed.

Senthree realized suddenly that no adequate supply of fruit and vegetables had been provided, and he hadn't even known how often Man had to eat. Or exactly what. Luckily, Ceofor was taking care of that.

He went down the hall, hearing a tumult of voices, with robots apparently spread about on various kinds of hasty business. The main lab where the couple was seemed quiet. Senthree hesitated at the door, wondering how to address them. There must be no questioning now. 30 Today he would not force himself on them, nor expect them to understand his purposes. He must welcome them and make them feel at ease in this world, so strange to them with their prehistoric tape education. It would be hard at first to adjust to a world of only robots, with no other Man people. The matter of instinct that had taken so long could wait a few days more.

The door dilated in front of him and he stepped into the lab, his eyes turning to the low table where they sat. They looked healthy, and there was no sign of misery or uncertainty that he could see, though he could not be sure of that until he knew them better. He could not even 40 be sure it was a scowl on the male's face as the Man turned and looked at him.

"Another one, eh? OK, come up here. What you want?"

Then Senthree no longer wondered how to address the Man. He bowed low as he approached them, and instinct made his voice soft and apologetic as he answered.

"Nothing, Master. Only to serve you."

REVIEWING THE STORY

THE MAIN IDEA

1. Which of the following statements best expresses the main idea of the story?
   (a) Robots cannot re-create ancient life forms.
   (b) Instinct in humans turns out to be unrelated to intelligence.
   (c) Robots are essentially no different from humans.
   (d) Robots have been programmed with only one instinct: to obey humans.

DETAILS

2. Senthree is
   (a) the pilot of an interplanetary spaceship.
   (b) the chief of a biological research laboratory.
   (c) one of the Original Models of robots.
   (d) the first successfully re-created human.

3. Senthree tells the Director that he believes human beings may have been killed off by (a) instinct (b) robots (c) intelligence (d) extraterrestrials.

4. For a million years, no robot has tried to
   (a) explore and colonize other worlds.
   (b) create new humans.
   (c) build new robots.
   (d) change the basic makeup of robots.

5. Help in successfully creating humans comes from
   (a) a book entitled *Gather, Darkness*.
   (b) advice from Director Arpeten.
   (c) an antique robot Senthree found on Venus.
   (d) discoveries made in creating the pig Oscar LXXII.

6. Senthree believes that robots do not have (a) brains (b) instincts (c) intelligence (d) memories.

ORDER OF EVENTS

7. Choose the letter that gives the order in which the events happen.
   (1) The old robot 324MD2991 lends a hand.
   (2) Senthree returns in a new body from Venus.
   (3) The robots scramble to serve the new Man.
   (4) The new Director and Senthree discuss funding for the lab.
   (a) 4-3-2-1   **(b)** 3-1-2-4   **(c)** 2-4-1-3   **(d)** 1-2-3-4

CAUSE AND EFFECT

8. The robot biologists must succeed quickly in their experiment because they are running out of **(a)** genes **(b)** ideas **(c)** funds **(d)** robots.

9. By successfully re-creating humans, Senthree hopes to discover if robots
   (a) are better than Man.
   (b) were created by Man.
   (c) can safely change humans.
   (d) can safely change themselves.

INFERENCES

10. We can infer that robots
    (a) are not very intelligent.
    (b) live for many centuries.
    (c) reproduce sexually as humans do.
    (d) periodically wage violent wars.

11. Compared to human technology, the technology of the robots is **(a)** more advanced **(b)** less advanced **(c)** on the same level **(d)** impossible to evaluate.

PREDICTING OUTCOMES

12. If the twelfth attempt to create humans had failed, Senthree would probably have
    (a) become the new Director.
    (b) fired his senior assistant Ceofor.
    (c) realized that humans possessed both instinct and intelligence.
    (d) become biological investigator on another planet.

BUILDING YOUR VOCABULARY _____

1. The pig came over to *root* at his feet, but he had no time for that.

   Which of the following meanings of the verb *root* (page 178, line 11) makes the BEST sense in the sentence?
   (a) to plant in the ground
   (b) to poke or dig about
   (c) to cheer or encourage
   (d) to remove completely by force

2. His *garbled* mouthing made no sense.
   a. *Garbled* (page 178, line 34) means
      (a) cleansed or disinfected.
      (b) precise and careful.
      (c) high-pitched and angry.
      (d) mixed-up and confused.
   b. The BEST strategy for figuring out the meaning of *garbled* is to note the
      (a) rest of the sentence.
      (b) spelling of the word.
      (c) pronunciation of the word.
      (d) paragraph that follows.

3. Don't you see, Man is the whole key to our problem of whether we can change or not without risking *extermination*?
   a. The word *risking* suggests that, for the robots, *extermination* (page 182, lines 16-18) would be (a) desirable (b) undesirable (c) impossible (d) entertaining.
   b. To *exterminate* means to
      (a) change completely.
      (b) turn inside out.
      (c) kill off completely.
      (d) send far away.

4. We've just had word of several new planets around Arcturus, and it will take the major *allocation* of our funds to colonize these.

   Allocation (page 182, lines 37-38) is the act of
   (a) moving to an entirely new location.
   (b) setting apart or reserving for a specific purpose.
   (c) appealing for help from other people.
   (d) arguing in favor of space travel.

5. He went down the hall, hearing a *tumult* of voices, with robots apparently spread about on various kinds of hasty business.

The word that is LEAST similar in meaning to *tumult* (page 188, lines 27-28) is **(a)** hubbub **(b)** uproar **(c)** commotion **(d)** murmur.

STUDYING THE WRITER'S CRAFT

1. Small details can help make a fictitious world believable, even one a million years in the future. Used consistently, these details help create *verisimilitude*, or the appearance of being true.

   a. What consistent pattern or rule underlies the names of the robots: Senthree, Ceofor, Beswun, and Arpeten? Rewrite each name so as to reveal this pattern or rule. (*Hint:* Senthree = S.N.3.)

   b. What references to persons or books from our era do you find in the story? How do Senthree's comments on these small details add humorous touches to the story?

2. What is the *conflict* in the story over "homovivifying," or reviving Man? On which sides of this conflict are Senthree and Arpeten?

3. Lester del Rey uses *suspense* to keep the reader wondering how things will work out. What two crucial questions in the reader's mind create suspense in the story?

ACTIVITIES FOR LISTENING, SPEAKING, WRITING

1. Be prepared to discuss the following questions with your classmates: Who is more sympathetically treated in the story, robots or humans? Which ones seem more intelligent and more likeable? Use evidence from the story to support your viewpoint.

2. Look up the term *instinct* in one or more reference books. In your own words, write a brief explanation of what instincts are. Give at least one example of instinctive behavior in animals. Then tell whether or not you believe that Senthree's behavior at the end of the story is an example of true instinct. Explain your opinion.

3. Listen while two or more of your classmates discuss the following questions. Take notes and be ready to contribute your own ideas to the discussion. How are the robots in the story like real human beings? How are they different? If they were to exist in our world today, should they have the same rights as human beings? Explain your answer to the last question.

Smart Skin

by Shawna Vogel

Robots capable of functioning autonomously will need a "smart skin" to sense whether they should, say, grasp a wrench more firmly or ease up their death grip on a tomato.

Robots moved long ago out of the pages of science fiction and into the factories and research facilities of modern industrialized nations. Today, robots perform complex but repetitive manufacturing tasks. They also work well in places where human beings can't go, such as the radioactive core of a nuclear reactor or the surface of the planet Mars. These robots, however, have been designed to perform particular tasks that involve relatively few decisions.

In science fiction, robots function very much as humans do—often far better. How near are we to creating intelligent robots that can work as well as humans? In this case, the leap from science fiction to science fact may not prove so easy. For an account of just one of the many problems involved in creating independent robots who can "think" and make decisions, read the following article.

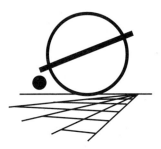

If we're ever to have the future promised us by "The Jetsons,"[1] we're at the very least going to need personal robots that can serve us breakfast. But to do that those robots will have to be able to sense the difference between a glass of orange juice and a soft-boiled egg, and to hold each with just enough pressure to keep it from either breaking or dropping to the floor. At the moment such a fine-tuned grip is beyond the capacity of any robot in existence.

Robots have no innate "feel" for the objects they are handling primarily because they lack one of our most useful sense organs: skin. That isn't to say they can't get a grip on things. Industrial robots can repeatedly   10 pick up objects like carburetors by exerting a preprogrammed pressure on them. But robots capable of functioning autonomously will need a "smart skin" to sense whether they should, say, grasp a wrench more firmly or ease up their death grip on a tomato.

One of the most sophisticated approaches to this goal is being developed at the University of Pisa by Italian engineer Danilo De Rossi, who has closely modeled an artificial skin on the inner and outer layers of human skin: the dermis and epidermis. His flexible, multilayered sheathing even has the same thickness as human skin—roughly that of a dime.   20

De Rossi's artificial dermis is made of a water-swollen conducting gel[2] sandwiched between two layers of electrodes that monitor the flow of electricity through the squishy middle. Like the all-natural human version, this dermis senses the overall pressure being exerted on an object. As pressure deforms the gel, the voltage between the electrodes changes; the harder the object being pressed, the greater the deforma-

1. **"The Jetsons":** animated-cartoon TV series of the 1960s about a family of the future.
2. **conducting gel:** a soft, elastic substance having the properties of both a liquid and a solid, which conducts, or transmits, electricity.

tion. By keeping tabs on how the voltage is changing, a skin-clad robot could thus distinguish between a rubber ball and a rock.

For resolving the finer details of surface texture, De Rossi has created an epidermal layer of sensor-studded sheets of plastic placed between thin sheets of rubber. The sensors are pinhead-size disks made of piezo-electric[3] substances, which emit an electric charge when subjected to pressure. These disks can sense texture as fine as the bumps on a braille manuscript.

Other researchers have developed texture-sensitive skins, but De Rossi's has a unique advantage. Because his disks respond to pressure from any direction—including forces pulling sideways across the surface of the skin—they can also sense friction. "No other sensor today can do that," says De Rossi. Most smart skins detect only pressure perpendicular to the surface and cannot feel lateral deformation. But a robot wearing 10 De Rossi's skin could easily feel the tug from a sticky piece of tape or, conversely, sense an alarming lack of friction when a greased motor bearing is slipping from its grasp.

Either of De Rossi's layers could be used separately to meet the specialized needs of industrial robots, but he envisions them as parts of an integrated skin for multipurpose mechanical hands. At the moment, however, De Rossi faces a small dilemma: his two layers are incompatible. The water essential to the working of the dermis invariably short-circuits[4] the sensitive epidermis. De Rossi will need to separate the two layers, but no matter what material he chooses he will probably have to compromise 20 among several ideals, such as extreme thinness, strength, and flexibility.

Even if he does manage to unite his layers, there will still be a number of hurdles to get over before a robot with artificial skin can become as adept as a human. Foremost among them is the basic question of how to coordinate all the tactile information transmitted. Robotics engineers still puzzle over how people use all the tactile messages conveyed by their hands to accomplish a feat as simple as threading a nut onto the end of a bolt.

REVIEWING THE ARTICLE

THE MAIN IDEA

1. The article discusses the problems of designing
   (a) industrial robots that perform repeated manufacturing tasks.
   (b) techniques for surgery on damaged human skin.
   (c) artificial skin for robots.
   (d) artificial skin for human burn victims.

3. **piezoelectric** (pee-AY-zoh): causing small variations in tiny currents as a result of mechanical stress.
4. **short-circuits** (verb): disrupts the flow of electricity by providing a shorter path.

DETAILS

2. To adjust its grip, a robot capable of functioning independently needs (a) feet (b) skin (c) ears (d) eyes.

3. Daniel De Rossi is
   (a) the author of the article.
   (b) a robot on "The Jetsons."
   (c) an Italian engineer.
   (d) a science-fiction author.

4. De Rossi is trying to imitate the inner and outer layers of human skin, which are called the
   (a) dermis and disks.
   (b) dermis and epidermis.
   (c) sensors and epidermis.
   (d) gel and electrodes.

5. De Rossi's outer layer of artificial skin can sense pressure
   (a) at a distance.
   (b) only perpendicular to the surface.
   (c) only sideways across the surface.
   (d) from any direction.

6. What form of energy has De Rossi used to give artificial skin its sense of touch? (a) chemical energy (b) heat energy (c) electrical energy (d) nuclear energy.

ORDER OF EVENTS

7. Two problems that De Rossi must solve in sequence are (1) eliminating the short circuits and then (2) coordinating all the
   (a) research of other scientists.
   (b) tactile information transmitted by the artificial skin.
   (c) information written about artificial skin.
   (d) new kinds of artificial skin.

CAUSE AND EFFECT

8. What causes the short circuits in the outer layer of artificial skin?
   (a) too much pressure on the skin
   (b) a shortage of electricity

(c) a piece of sticky tape

(d) water in the gel of the inner layer

9. As a result of wearing De Rossi's outer (epidermal) skin, a robot could detect (a) hardness (b) friction (c) size (d) heat.

INFERENCES

10. Skin, whether natural or artificial, is related to the sense of (a) touch (b) smell (c) sight (d) hearing.

11. The development of independent robots that can respond to change

(a) will never happen.

(b) will take more time.

(c) has been achieved in industrial robots.

(d) has been solved by De Rossi.

PREDICTING OUTCOMES

12. If you shook hands with a robot that had smart skin, the robot's hand would probably

(a) slide off your hand.

(b) adjust to the grip of your hand.

(c) crush your hand.

(d) change the grip of your hand.

BUILDING YOUR VOCABULARY _____

1. Robots have no *innate* "feel" for the objects they are handling primarily because they lack one of our most useful sense organs: skin.

The word *innate* (page 194, lines 8-9) means

(a) artificial or synthetic.

(b) native or inborn.

(c) delicate or sensitive.

(d) crude or rough.

2. De Rossi's artificial dermis is made of a water-swollen conducting gel sandwiched between two layers of electrodes that *monitor* the flow of electricity through the squishy middle.

a. The phrase that best expresses the meaning of the verb *monitor* (page 194, lines 21-23) in this sentence is

(a) reduce in volume.

(b) keep track of.

(c) disrupt.

(d) speed up.

b. The word or phrase in this paragraph that gives the BEST clue to the meaning of *monitor* is (a) deforms (b) distinguish (c) is changing (d) keeping tabs on.

3. Other researchers have developed texture-sensitive skins, but De Rossi's has a *unique* advantage.

a. An advantage that is *unique* (page 196, lines 5-6) is (a) unequaled (b) unknown (c) small (d) unfortunate.

b. The BEST clue to the meaning of *unique* may be found later in the same paragraph in sentence (a) 2 (b) 3 (c) 4 (d) 5.

4. The water essential to the working of the dermis *invariably* short-circuits the sensitive epidermis.

The word that is OPPOSITE in meaning to *invariably* (page 196, lines 18-19) is (a) always (b) constantly (c) never (d) perpetually.

5. Even if he does manage to unite his layers, there will still be a number of hurdles to get over before a robot with artificial skin can become as *adept* as a human.

Adept (page 196, lines 22-24) means (a) adult (b) expert (c) adequate (d) athletic.

STUDYING THE WRITER'S CRAFT

1. In writing about technical matters, an author may define unfamiliar terms by providing **context clues**. To define *dermis* and *epidermis*, for example, Shawna Vogel uses the rest of the sentence in which the words appear—their context—as a clue to their meanings. Thus, we learn that the *dermis* and *epidermis* (page 194, line 18) are, respectively, "the inner and outer layers of human skin." Write the part of the sentence that serves as a context clue to the meaning of each of the following terms:

a. *piezoelectric substances* (page 196, line 1-2)

b. *tactile messages* (page 196, line 25)

2. *Figurative language*, which often uses an implied comparison, can help make something clearer and more vivid.

   a. The term "smart skin" (title) is a form of figurative language called *personification*. A thing is given the attributes of a person. To what do we normally apply the adjective *smart*? To what is the robot's artificial skin being compared?

   b. The use of the word *sandwiched* in the phrase "gel sandwiched between two layers of electrodes" (page 194, line 22) involves a *metaphor*. In the implied comparison, what does the gel represent? What do the two layers of electrodes represent?

   c. The expression "there will still be a number of hurdles to get over" (page 196, lines 22-23) is another *metaphor*. To what are De Rossi and other robotic engineers being compared?

3. The article "Smart Skin" is tightly and logically organized. Each of the eight paragraphs helps develop the topic of creating smart skin. Working with a partner or in a small group, outline the article by writing a phrase to summarize the main point of each paragraph. [*Hint*: The first two paragraphs might be outlined thus: (1) Independent robots as a future goal (2) Need to develop artificial skin for such robots.] At your teacher's direction, compare your completed outline with those of your classmates.

ACTIVITIES FOR LISTENING, SPEAKING, WRITING

1. Smart skin would provide a robot with one important sense organ. What other sense organs do humans possess? Choose one of them, and get together with three or four other students to form a "think tank." Brainstorm ideas for equipping robots with the sense you've chosen. (How, for example, can you provide robots with sight?) Be creative. You might draw a design or explain your plans to the rest of the class.

2. From your reading of the article, how soon do you think robots will replace humans in the production of all goods and services—soon, late, or never? Write a brief composition explaining and supporting your opinion.

3. Recently an American electrical engineer patented a "robotic ant." This tiny six-legged machine, small enough to sneak undetected into secret government installations, could serve as a miniature spy. On a much larger scale, a personal robot might be built someday that

could serve as a soldier. Whether used as spies or soldiers, such robots might help some humans but hurt others. How does this use of robots fit in with Asimov's Three Laws of Robotics? (See page 141.) Be prepared to discuss this question with your classmates.

SPACE ALIENS, OR EXTRATERRESTRIALS
Theme 4

On October 30, 1938, millions of Americans were terrified by a radio report that huge and hostile creatures from Mars had invaded the Earth. The report turned out to be nothing more than a vivid radio drama by the talented Orson Welles and his Mercury Theatre group. However, this false alarm showed that vast numbers of people were ready to believe there is life in outer space. Even today, widespread belief in flying saucers and the immense popularity of the motion picture *E.T. The Extraterrestrial* (1982) attest to our continuing interest in space aliens.

Extraterrestrials appeared early in the pages of science fiction. At first they were merely bug-eyed monsters that had to be destroyed by the brave heroes of these primitive space operas. In time, however, science-fiction writers became less heavy-handed and more flexible in their treatment of extraterrestrials. What brought about this shift in attitude?

Strangely enough, some of the social forces that led to this change were the modern movements in civil rights, women's liberation, and environmentalism. All these movements fostered more tolerance for the differences of others and more respect for all living creatures, whether from planet Earth or the other side of the universe.

You can easily see this more sympathetic treatment of space aliens in the three stories that follow. "The Large Ant" turns the old formula of human hero and extraterrestrial villain upside down in a surprising encounter here on Earth. In "A Death in the House," a creature from outer space is treated with rare compassion. The story "Things" allows us to look at ourselves through the eyes of a tribe of peaceful extraterrestrials on another world.

What are the chances that space aliens really exist outside the pages of science fiction? In recent years, professional astronomers and the National Aeronautics and Space Administration (NASA) have decided to find out. They have joined forces in an ambitious long-term project called the Search for Extraterrestrial Intelligence, or SETI. For a debate about this controversial program, read the "Pro" and "Con" articles. Then decide for yourself if you think we'll ever hear from E.T.

The Large Ant

by Howard Fast

We don't look carefully at a thing that is horrible or repugnant to us. You can't look at anything through a screen of hatred.

What would you do if you were lying on your bed and suddenly, at the foot of the bed, you saw a strange creature looking at you? In that moment of shock, you'd have no time for calm reflection. What would your first impulsive reaction be? Fight? Flight? Or something else?

Would there be a typical human response in the first encounter with an alien creature from outer space? If so, would it be violent? Older science fiction answers, "Yes. It can be assumed that space aliens would be hostile and that we would fight back in self-defense." But whose assumption is that? And why?

In "The Large Ant," Howard Fast asks such questions. The answers, his story implies, could decide the fate of all humanity.

Howard Fast

Science fiction is only one of the many literary forms in the long and prolific career of Howard Fast. He has written highly successful novels, short stories, biographies, plays, screenplays, and even a weekly newspaper column. Among his best-selling historical novels are *Citizen Tom Paine* (1943), *Freedom Road* (1944), and *Spartacus* (1951). Thanks to translations of his works into more than eighty languages, Fast is one of the most popular contemporary authors in the world.

Fast's short science fiction may be sampled in collections such as *The General Zapped an Angel* (1970) and *A Touch of Infinity: Thirteen Stories of Fantasy and Science Fiction* (1973). Like most of his science fiction, "The Large Ant" offers a sympathetic yet unsparing account of what Fast has called "the follies of mankind."

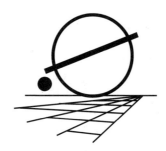

There have been all kinds of notions and guesses as to how it would end. One held that sooner or later there would be too many people; another that we would do each other in, and the atom bomb made that a very good likelihood. All sorts of notions, except the simple fact that we were what we were. We could find a way to feed any number of people and perhaps even a way to avoid wiping each other out with the bomb; those things we are very good at, but we have never been any good at changing ourselves or the way we behave.

I know. I am not a bad man or a cruel man; quite to the contrary, I am an ordinary, humane person, and I love my wife and my children and 10 I get along with my neighbors. I am like a great many other men, and I do the things they would do and just as thoughtlessly. There it is in a nutshell.

I am also a writer, and I told Lieberman, the curator, and Fitzgerald, the government man, that I would like to write down the story. They shrugged their shoulders. "Go ahead," they said, "because it won't make one bit of difference."

"You don't think it would alarm people?"

"How can it alarm anyone when nobody will believe it?"

"If I could have a photograph or two."

"Oh, no," they said then. "No photographs."

"What kind of sense does that make?" I asked them. "You are willing to let me write the story—why not the photographs so that people could believe me?"

"They still won't believe you. They will just say you faked the photographs, but no one will believe you. It will make for more con- 10 fusion, and if we have a chance of getting out of this, confusion won't help."

"What will help?"

They weren't ready to say that, because they didn't know. So here is what happened to me, in a very straightforward and ordinary manner.

Every summer, sometime in August, four good friends of mine and I go for a week's fishing on the St. Regis chain of lakes in the Adirondacks. We rent the same shack each summer; we drift around in canoes, and sometimes we catch a few bass. The fishing isn't very good, but we play cards well together, and we cook out and generally relax. This summer past, I had some things to do that couldn't be put off. I arrived three days 20 late, and the weather was so warm and even and beguiling that I decided to stay on by myself for a day or two after the others left. There was a small flat lawn in front of the shack, and I made up my mind to spend at least three or four hours at short putts. That was how I happened to have the putting iron next to my bed.

The first day I was alone, I opened a can of beans and a can of beer for my supper. Then I lay down in my bed with *Life on the Mississippi* and an eight-ounce chocolate bar. There was nothing I had to do, no telephone, no demands and no newspapers. At that moment, I was about as contented as any man can be in these nervous times.   30

It was still light outside, and enough light came in through the window above my head for me to read by. I was just reaching for the chocolate bar, when I looked up and saw it on the foot of my bed. The edge of my hand was touching the golf club, and with a single motion I swept the club over and down, struck it a savage and accurate blow, and killed it. That was what I referred to before. Whatever kind of a man I am, I react as a man does. I think that any man, black, white or yellow, in China, Africa or Russia, would have done the same thing.

First I found that I was sweating all over, and then I knew I was going to be sick. I went outside to vomit, recalling that this hadn't hap- 40 pened to me since 1943, on my way to Europe on a tub of a Liberty Ship. Then I felt better and was able to go back into the shack and look at it.

It was quite dead, but I had already made up my mind that I was not going to sleep alone in this shack.

I couldn't bear to touch it with my bare hands. With a piece of brown paper, I picked it up and dropped it into my fishing creel. That I put into the trunk case of my car, along with what luggage I carried. Then I closed the door of the shack, got into my car and drove back to New York. I stopped once along the road, just before I reached the Thruway, to nap in the car for a little over an hour. It was almost dawn when I reached the city, and I had shaved, had a hot bath and changed my clothes before my wife awoke.   10

During breakfast I explained that I was never much of a hand at the solitary business, and since she knew that, and since driving alone all night was by no means an extraordinary procedure for me, she didn't press me with any questions. I had two eggs and coffee. Then I went into my study and contemplated my fishing creel, which sat upon my desk.

My wife looked in, saw the creel, remarked that it had too ripe a smell, and asked me to remove it to the basement.

"I'm going to dress," she said. The kids were still at camp. "I have a date with Ann for lunch—I had no idea you were coming back. Shall I break it?"   20

"No, please don't. I can find things to do that have to be done."

Then I sat and stared at the creel some more, and finally I called the Museum, and asked who the curator of insects was. They told me his name was Bertram Lieberman, and I asked to talk to him. He had a pleasant voice. I told him that my name was Morgan, and that I was a writer, and he politely indicated that he had seen my name and read something that I had written. That is normal procedure when a writer introduces himself to a thoughtful person.

I asked Lieberman if I could see him, and he said that he had a busy morning ahead of him. Could it be tomorrow?   30

"I am afraid it has to be now," I said firmly.

"Oh? Some information you require."

"No. I have a specimen for you."

"Oh?" The "oh" was a cultivated, neutral interval. It asked and answered and said nothing. You have to develop that particular "oh."

"Yes. I think you will be interested."

"An insect?" he asked mildly.

"I think so."

"Oh? Large?"

"Quite large," I told him.   40

"Eleven o'clock? Can you be here then? On the main floor, to the right, as you enter."

"I'll be there," I said.

"One thing—dead?"

"Yes, it's dead."

"Oh?" again. "I'll be happy to see you at eleven o'clock, Mr. Morgan."

My wife was dressed now. She opened the door to my study and said firmly, "Do get rid of that fishing creel. It smells."

"Yes, darling. I'll get rid of it."

"I should think you'd want to take a nap after driving all night."

"Funny, but I'm not sleepy," I said. "I think I'll drop around to the museum." 10

My wife said that was what she liked about me, that I never tired of places like museums, police courts, and third-rate night clubs.

Anyway, aside from a racetrack, a museum is the most interesting and unexpected place in the world. It was unexpected to have two other men waiting for me, along with Mr. Lieberman, in his office. Lieberman was a skinny, sharp-faced man of about sixty. The government man, Fitzgerald, was small, dark-eyed, and wore gold-rimmed glasses. He was very alert, but he never told me what part of the government he represented. He just said "we," and it meant the government. Hopper, the third 20 man, was comfortable-looking, pudgy, and genial. He was a United States senator with an interest in entomology, although before this morning I would have taken better than even money that such a thing not only wasn't, but could not be.

The room was large and square and plainly furnished, with shelves and cupboards on all walls.

We shook hands, and then Lieberman asked me, nodding at the creel, "Is that it?"

"That's it."

"May I?" 30

"Go ahead," I told him. "It's nothing that I want to stuff for the parlor. I'm making you a gift of it."

"Thank you, Mr. Morgan," he said, and then he opened the creel and looked inside. Then he straightened up, and the other two men looked at him inquiringly.

He nodded. "Yes."

The senator closed his eyes for a long moment. Fitzgerald took off his glasses and wiped them industriously. Lieberman spread a piece of plastic on his desk, and then lifted the thing out of my creel and laid it on the plastic. The two men didn't move. They just sat where they were 40 and looked at it.

"What do you think it is, Mr. Morgan?" Lieberman asked me.

"I thought that was your department."

"Yes, of course. I only wanted your impression."

"An ant. That's my impression. It's the first time I saw an ant fourteen, fifteen inches long. I hope it's the last."

"An understandable wish," Lieberman nodded.

Fitzgerald said to me, "May I ask how you killed it, Mr. Morgan?"

"With an iron. A golf club, I mean. I was doing a little fishing with some friends up at St. Regis in the Adirondacks, and I brought the iron for my short shots. They're the worst part of my game, and when my friends left, I intended to stay on at our shack and do four or five hours of short putts. You see—" 10

"There's no need to explain," Hopper smiled, a trace of sadness on his face. "Some of our very best golfers have the same trouble."

"I was lying in bed, reading, and I saw it at the foot of my bed. I had the club—"

"I understand," Fitzgerald nodded.

"You avoid looking at it," Hopper said.

"It turns my stomach."

"Yes—yes, I suppose so."

Lieberman said, "Would you mind telling us why you killed it, Mr. Morgan?" 20

"Why?"

"Yes—why?"

"I don't understand you," I said. "I don't know what you're driving at."

"Sit down, please, Mr. Morgan," Hopper nodded. "Try to relax. I'm sure this has been very trying."

"I still haven't slept. I want a chance to dream before I say how trying."

"We are not trying to upset you, Mr. Morgan," Lieberman said. "We do feel, however, that certain aspects of this are very important. That is why I am asking you why you killed it. You must have had a reason. Did it seem about to attack you?" 30

"No."

"Or make any sudden motion toward you?"

"No. It was just there."

"Then why?"

"This is to no purpose," Fitzgerald put in. "We know why he killed it."

"Do you?"

"The answer is very simple, Mr. Morgan. You killed it because you are a human being." 40

"Oh?"

"Yes. Do you understand?"

"No, I don't."

"Then why did you kill it?" Hopper put in.

"I was scared to death. I still am, to tell the truth."

Lieberman said, "You are an intelligent man, Mr. Morgan. Let me show you something." He then opened the doors of one of the wall cupboards, and there were eight jars of formaldehyde and in each jar a specimen like mine—and in each case mutilated by the violence of its death. I said nothing. I just stared.

Lieberman closed the cupboard doors. "All in five days," he 10 shrugged.

"A new race of ants," I whispered stupidly.

"No. They're not ants. Come here!" He motioned me to the desk and the other two joined me. Lieberman took a set of dissecting instruments out of his drawer, used one to turn the thing over and then pointed to the underpart of what would be the thorax in an insect.

"That looks like part of him, doesn't it, Mr. Morgan?"

"Yes, it does."

Using two of the tools, he found a fissure and pried the bottom apart. It came open like the belly of a bomber; it was a pocket, a pouch, a 20 receptacle that the thing wore, and in it were four beautiful little tools or instruments or weapons, each about an inch and a half long. They were beautiful the way any object of functional purpose and loving creation is beautiful—the way the creature itself would have been beautiful, had it not been an insect and myself a man. Using tweezers, Lieberman took each instrument off the brackets that held it, offering each to me. And I took each one, felt it, examined it, and then put it down.

I had to look at the ant now, and I realized that I had not truly looked at it before. We don't look carefully at a thing that is horrible or repugnant to us. You can't look at anything through a screen of hatred. 30 But now the hatred and the fear were dilute, and as I looked, I realized it was not an ant although like an ant. It was nothing that I had ever seen or dreamed of.

All three men were watching me, and suddenly I was on the defensive. "I didn't know! What do you expect when you see an insect that size?"

Lieberman nodded.

"What *is* it?"

"We don't know," Hopper said. "We don't know what it is."

Lieberman pointed to the broken skull, from which a white sub- 40 stance oozed. "Brain material—a great deal of it."

"It could be a very intelligent creature," Hopper nodded.

Lieberman said, "It is an insect in developmental structure. We know very little about intelligence in our insects. It's not the same as what we call intelligence. It's a collective phenomenon—as if you were to think of the component parts of our bodies. Each part is alive, but the intelligence is a result of the whole. If that same pattern were to extend to creatures like this one—"

I broke the silence. They were content to stand there and stare at it.

"Suppose it were?"

"What?"

"The kind of collective intelligence you were talking about."   10

"Oh? Well, I couldn't say. It would be something beyond our wildest dreams. To us—well, what we are to an ordinary ant."

"I don't believe that," I said shortly, and Fitzgerald, the government man, told me quietly, "Neither do we. We guess."

"If it's that intelligent, why didn't it use one of those weapons on me?"

"Would that be a mark of intelligence?" Hopper asked mildly.

"Perhaps none of these are weapons," Lieberman said.

"Don't you know? Didn't the others carry instruments?"

"They did," Fitzgerald said shortly.

"Why? What were they?"   20

"We don't know," Lieberman said.

"But you can find out. We have scientists, engineers—this is an age of fantastic instruments. Have them taken apart!"

"We have."

"Then what have you found out?"

"Nothing."

"Do you mean to tell me," I said, "that you can find out nothing about these instruments—what they are, how they work, what their purpose is?"

"Exactly," Hopper nodded. "Nothing, Mr. Morgan. They are mean- 30 ingless to the finest engineers and technicians in the United States. You know the old story—suppose you gave a radio to Aristotle? What would he do with it? Where would he find power? And what would he receive with no one to send? It is not that these instruments are complex. They are actually very simple. We simply have no idea of what they can or should do."

"But there must be a weapon of some kind."

"Why?" Lieberman demanded. "Look at yourself, Mr. Morgan—a cultured and intelligent man, yet you cannot conceive a mentality that does not include weapons as a prime necessity. Yet a weapon is an unusual 40 thing, Mr. Morgan. An instrument of murder. We don't think that way, because the weapon has become the symbol of the world we inhabit. Is that civilized, Mr. Morgan? Or are the weapon and civilization in the ultimate sense incompatible? Can you imagine a mentality to which the concept of murder is impossible—or let me say absent? We see everything through our own subjectivity. Why shouldn't some other—this creature, for example—see the process of mentation[1] out of his subjectivity? So he approaches a creature of our world—and he is slain. Why? What explanation? Tell me, Mr. Morgan, what conceivable explanation could we offer a wholly rational creature for this—" pointing to the thing on his desk. "I am asking you the question most seriously. What explanation?"

"An accident?" I muttered.   10

"And the eight jars in my cupboard? Eight accidents?"

"I think, Dr. Lieberman," Fitzgerald said, "that you can go a little too far in that direction."

"Yes, you would think so. It's a part of your own background. Mine is as a scientist. As a scientist, I try to be rational when I can. The creation of a structure of good and evil, or what we call morality and ethics, is a function of intelligence—and unquestionably the ultimate evil may be the destruction of conscious intelligence. That is why, so long ago, we at least recognized the injunction, 'Thou shalt not kill!' even if we never gave more than lip service to it. But to a collective intelligence, such as this 20 might be a part of, the concept of murder would be monstrous beyond the power of thought."

I sat down. My hands were trembling. Hopper apologized. "We have been rather rough with you, Mr. Morgan. But over the past days, eight other people have done just what you did. We are caught in the trap of being what we are."

"But tell me—where do these things come from?"

"It almost doesn't matter where they come from," Hopper said hopelessly. "Perhaps from another planet—perhaps from inside this one—or the moon or Mars. That doesn't matter. Fitzgerald thinks they come from 30 a smaller planet, because their movements are apparently slow on earth. But Dr. Lieberman thinks that they move slowly because they have not discovered the need to move quickly. Meanwhile, they have the problem of murder and what to do with it. Heaven knows how many of them have died in other places—Africa, Asia, Europe."

"Then why don't you publicize this? Put a stop to it before it's too late!"

"We've thought of that," Fitzgerald nodded. "What then—panic, hysteria, charges that this is the result of the atom bomb? We can't change. We are what we are."   40

1. **mentation** (men-TAY-shun): the act of thinking or using the mind.

"They may go away," I said.

"Yes, they may," Lieberman nodded. "But if they are without the curse of murder, they may also be without the curse of fear. They may be social in the highest sense. What does society do with a murderer?"

"There are societies that put him to death—and there are other societies that recognize his sickness and lock him away, where he can kill no more," Hopper said. "Of course, when a whole world is on trial, that's another matter. We have atom bombs now and other things, and we are reaching out to the stars—"

"I'm inclined to think that they'll run," Fitzgerald put in. "They may just have that curse of fear, Doctor." 10

"They may," Lieberman admitted. "I hope so."

But the more I think of it the more it seems to me that fear and hatred are the two sides of the same coin. I keep trying to think back, to re-create the moment when I saw it standing at the foot of my bed in the fishing shack. I keep trying to drag out of my memory a clear picture of what it looked like, whether behind that chitinous[2] face and the two gently waving antennae there was any evidence of fear and anger. But the clearer the memory becomes, the more I seem to recall a certain wonderful dignity and repose. Not fear and not anger. 20

And more and more, as I go about my work, I get the feeling of what Hopper called "a world on trial." I have no sense of anger myself. Like a criminal who can no longer live with himself, I am content to be judged.

REVIEWING THE STORY _____

THE MAIN IDEA

1. The story deals with how human beings instinctively respond to something strange and unknown—with
   (a) love and kindness.
   (b) patience and curiosity.
   (c) fear and hatred.
   (d) suspicion and impatience.

DETAILS

2. The narrator of the story, Mr. Morgan, is a (a) scientist (b) government agent (c) U.S. senator (d) writer.

---

2. **chitinous** (KIT-n-us): made up of the hard outer shell that covers insects.

3. The narrator kills the large ant with a **(a)** gun **(b)** golf club **(c)** fishing creel **(d)** book.

4. Dr. Lieberman is a
    - **(a)** writer.
    - **(b)** government agent.
    - **(c)** U.S. senator interested in entomology.
    - **(d)** scientist specializing in insects.

5. In the past five days, eight other persons have
    - **(a)** reported peaceful contacts with extraterrestrials.
    - **(b)** been slain by one or more large ants.
    - **(c)** killed identical large ants.
    - **(d)** been arrested for murder.

6. Dr. Lieberman and the others suggest that the narrator's reaction to the large ant is
    - **(a)** highly unusual for a human being.
    - **(b)** typical of human beings.
    - **(c)** outrageous and immoral.
    - **(d)** nothing to worry about.

ORDER OF EVENTS

7. Choose the letter of the event that happens FIRST in the story.
    - **(a)** The narrator visits the museum.
    - **(b)** The narrator goes on vacation.
    - **(c)** The narrator is shown eight other large ants.
    - **(d)** The narrator kills the large ant.

CAUSE AND EFFECT

8. The narrator kills the large ant because he
    - **(a)** is angry at it.
    - **(b)** collects insects.
    - **(c)** feels frightened when he sees it.
    - **(d)** sees that it is about to attack him.

9. At first, the sight of the dead ant makes the narrator feel **(a)** curious **(b)** ill **(c)** angry **(d)** happy.

INFERENCES

10. The four little objects in the pouch or pocket of each large ant are
    (a) beautiful little tools.
    (b) instruments of high technology.
    (c) weapons of great power.
    (d) articles of unknown purpose.

11. By the end of the story, the narrator feels (a) guilty (b) proud (c) fearful (d) revengeful.

PREDICTING OUTCOMES

12. If the creature at the foot of the bed had looked like a tiny child, the narrator probably would have

    (a) screamed and run away.
    (b) killed it anyway.
    (c) thrown his book at it.
    (d) stared at it with surprise.

BUILDING YOUR VOCABULARY _____

1. I arrived three days late, and the weather was so warm and even and *beguiling* that I decided to stay on by myself for a day or two after the others left.

   In this sentence, the word *beguiling* (page 207, lines 20-22) means (a) cheating (b) monotonous (c) charming (d) breezy.

2. Hopper, the third man, was comfortable-looking, pudgy, and *genial*.

   a. In this sentence, *genial* (page 209, lines 20-21) means (a) friendly (b) like a genius (c) stern (d) firm-jawed.

   b. The BEST clue to the meaning of *genial* is to be found in

      (a) the sentence containing the word.
      (b) the preceding sentence.
      (c) the following sentence.
      (d) the name of the U.S. senator.

3. He then opened the doors of one of the wall cupboards, and there were eight jars of formaldehyde and in each jar a specimen like mine—and in each case *mutilated* by the violence of its death.

The BEST substitute for *mutilated* (page 211, lines 6-9) is **(a)** cruelly disappointed **(b)** extremely surprised **(c)** horribly injured **(d)** terribly discolored.

4. Lieberman took a set of dissecting instruments out of his drawer, used one to turn the thing over and then pointed to the underpart of what would be the *thorax* in an insect.

Even if you don't know just what a *thorax* (page 211, lines 14-16) is, you can use the context of the sentence to infer that it is a

(a) pocket, pouch, or receptacle.
(b) tool, instrument, or weapon.
(c) death spasm and rattle.
(d) section or part of the body.

5. We don't look carefully at a thing that is horrible or *repugnant* to us.

Something *repugnant* (page 211, lines 29-30) is LEAST likely to be **(a)** repulsive **(b)** appealing **(c)** offensive **(d)** revolting.

STUDYING THE WRITER'S CRAFT

1. The chronology, or time scheme, of this story is not simple or straightforward. To tell about earlier events, Howard Fast uses the *flashback* to the past, a familiar device in movies and fiction. This flashback appears within a *frame story* set in the present.

   a. Where does the flashback in the story begin?
   b. Where does the flashback end?
   c. Why do you think the author decided not to tell his story using only the flashback part? How does the frame around the flashback help the story?

2. A skilled fiction writer creates *suspense* by giving clues rather than openly telling readers what to expect.

   a. From the moment Morgan, the narrator, first sees the creature (page 207, line 32) until he gives Dr. Lieberman his impression of what it looks like (page 210, line 3), how does the narrator refer to the creature?
   b. What reactions of Morgan to the mere presence of the dead creature reinforce our feelings of horror and revulsion?
   c. How does the reaction of Morgan's wife to the contents of the fishing creel reinforce our sense of horror?

3. A skilled storyteller also lets readers infer things. Rather than constantly *tell* what is happening, the author simply *shows* people and events. It's up to the readers, then, to figure out things for themselves.

   a. What does the unexpected appearance of Fitzgerald, the government man, and Hopper, the U.S. senator, in the office of Dr. Bertram Lieberman suggest?

   b. Reread the three paragraphs in which Lieberman, Fitzgerald, and Hopper first react to the dead creature. (page 209, lines 33-41: "Thank you, Mr. Morgan," . . . looked at it.) Tell in your own words what Lieberman's nod and single word "Yes" mean. Also tell what you can infer from the reactions of the senator and the government man.

ACTIVITIES FOR LISTENING, SPEAKING, WRITING

1. Suppose a council of the antlike creatures meets somewhere in outer space. They must decide what to do with the human race. What would they say? What might they decide? If you were one of them, what would you suggest? Be ready to discuss this scenario with your classmates.

2. Tell what might have happened if the narrator had *not* killed the large ant. Use your imagination in a brief essay, story, or play to explore the question "What if . . . ?"

3. When Morgan insists that the creature must have had "a weapon of some kind," Dr. Lieberman responds as follows:

   "Why?" Lieberman demanded. "Look at yourself, Mr. Morgan—a cultured and intelligent man, yet you cannot conceive a mentality that does not include weapons as a prime necessity. Yet a weapon is an unusual thing, Mr. Morgan. An instrument of murder. We don't think that way, because the weapon has become the symbol of the world we inhabit. Is that civilized, Mr. Morgan? Or are the weapon and civilization in the ultimate sense incompatible?"

   Do you agree or disagree with the suggestion that weapons and human civilization cannot exist together, that they are ultimately incompatible? Why or why not? Be prepared to discuss your point of view with your classmates.

A Death in the House

by Clifford D. Simak

*It was a horrid-looking thing, green and shiny, with some purple
spots on it, and it was repulsive even twenty feet away. And it
stank.*

Whether writing about robots or aliens, Simak treats his nonhuman characters with sympathy and dignity. The following story of an encounter
between a human being and a space alien shows Simak at his humane
and gently humorous best.

When Old Mose Abrams finds an alien in the woods on his farm,
the creature is hurt or sick. Hideous as it is, Old Mose "was not the kind
of man who could bear to leave a sick thing out there in the woods."
What happens next changes Old Mose's life in strange and wonderful
ways.

As you read the story, ask yourself: "What did Old Mose have to
give up? What did he get in return? Was it a fair exchange?"

Clifford D. Simak

Early in his long career as a science-fiction writer, Simak was encouraged and influenced by the writer and editor John W. Campbell. As editor of the magazine *Astounding Science Fiction*, Campbell published some of Simak's best early fiction. Several of Simak's novels and short stories won Hugo or Nebula awards. For a lifetime of achievement, he was given the Grand Master Award of the Science Fiction Writers of America.

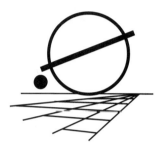

Old Mose Abrams was out hunting cows when he found the alien. He didn't know it was an alien, but it was alive and it was in a lot of trouble and Old Mose, despite everything the neighbors said about him, was not the kind of man who could bear to leave a sick thing out there in the woods.

It was a horrid-looking thing, green and shiny, with some purple spots on it, and it was repulsive even twenty feet away. And it stank.

It had crawled, or tried to crawl, into a clump of hazel brush, but hadn't made it. The head part was in the brush and the rest lay out there naked in the open. Every now and then the parts that seemed to be arms 10 and hands clawed feebly at the ground, trying to force itself deeper in the brush, but it was too weak; it never moved an inch.

It was groaning, too, but not too loud—just the kind of keening sound a lonesome wind might make around a wide, deep eave. But there was more in it than just the sound of winter wind; there was a frightened, desperate note that made the hair stand up on Old Mose's nape.

Old Mose stood there for quite a spell, making up his mind what he ought to do about it, and a while longer after that working up his courage, although most folks offhand would have said that he had plenty. But this was the sort of situation that took more than just ordinary screw- 20 up courage. It took a lot of foolhardiness.

But this was a wild, hurt thing and he couldn't leave it there, so he walked up to it and knelt down, and it was pretty hard to look at, though there was a sort of fascination in its repulsiveness that was hard to figure out—as if it were so horrible that it dragged one to it. And it stank in a way that no one had ever smelled before.

Mose, however, was not finicky. In the neighborhood, he was not well known for fastidity. Ever since his wife had died almost ten years before, he had lived alone on his untidy farm and the housekeeping that he did was the scandal of all the neighbor women. Once a year, if he got around to it, he sort of shoveled out the house, but the rest of the year he just let things accumulate.

So he wasn't as upset as some might have been with the way the 10 creature smelled. But the sight of it upset him, and it took him quite a while before he could bring himself to touch it, and when he finally did, he was considerably surprised. He had been prepared for it to be either cold or slimy, or maybe even both. But it was neither. It was warm and hard and it had a clean feel to it, and he was reminded of the way a green corn stalk would feel.

He slid his hand beneath the hurt thing and pulled it gently from the clump of hazel brush and turned it over so he could see its face. It hadn't any face. It had an enlargement at the top of it, like a flower on top of a stalk, although its body wasn't any stalk, and there was a fringe 20 around this enlargement that wiggled like a can of worms, and it was then that Mose almost turned around and ran.

But he stuck it out.

He squatted there, staring at the no-face with the fringe of worms, and he got cold all over and his stomach doubled up on him and he was stiff with fright—and the fright got worse when it seemed to him that the keening of the thing was coming from the worms.

Mose was a stubborn man. One had to be stubborn to run a runty farm like this. Stubborn and insensitive in a lot of ways. But not insensitive, of course, to a thing in pain. 30

Finally he was able to pick it up and hold it in his arms and there was nothing to it, for it didn't weigh much. Less than a half-grown shoat,[1] he figured.

He went up the woods path with it, heading back for home, and it seemed to him the smell of it was less. He was hardly scared at all, and he was warm again and not cold all over.

For the thing was quieter now and keening just a little. And although he could not be sure of it, there were times when it seemed as if the thing were snuggling up to him, the way a scared and hungry baby will snuggle to any grown person that comes and picks it up. 40

1. **shoat:** young hog; pig.

Old Mose reached the buildings and he stood out in the yard a minute, wondering whether he should take it to the barn or house. The barn, of course, was the natural place for it, for it wasn't human—it wasn't even as close to human as a dog or cat or sick lamb would be.

He didn't hesitate too long, however. He took it into the house and laid it on what he called a bed, next to the kitchen stove. He got it straightened out all neat and orderly and pulled a dirty blanket over it, and then went to the stove and stirred up the fire until there was some flame.

Then he pulled up a chair beside the bed and had a good, hard, wondering look at this thing he had brought home. It had quieted down 10 a lot and seemed more comfortable than it had out in the woods. He tucked the blanket snug around it with a tenderness that surprised himself. He wondered what he had that it might eat, and even if he knew, how he'd manage feeding it, for it seemed to have no mouth.

"But you don't need to worry none," he told it. "Now that I got you under a roof, you'll be all right. I don't know too much about it, but I'll take care of you the best I can."

By now it was getting on toward evening, and he looked out the window and saw that the cows he had been hunting had come home by themselves. 20

"I got to go get the milking done and the other chores," he told the thing lying on the bed, "but it won't take me long. I'll be right back."

Old Mose loaded up the stove so the kitchen would stay warm and he tucked the thing in once again, then got his milk pails and went down to the barn.

He fed the sheep and pigs and horses and he milked the cows. He hunted eggs and shut the chicken house. He pumped a tank of water.

Then he went back to the house.

It was dark now and he lit the oil lamp on the table, for he was against electricity. He'd refused to sign up when REA[2] had run out the 30 line, and a lot of the neighbors had gotten sore at him for being uncooperative. Not that he cared, of course.

He had a look at the thing upon the bed. It didn't seem to be any better, or any worse, for that matter. If it had been a sick lamb or an ailing calf, he could have known right off how it was getting on, but this thing was different. There was no way to tell.

He fixed himself some supper and ate it and wished he knew how to feed the thing. And he wished, too, that he knew how to help it. He'd got it under shelter and he had it warm, but was that right or wrong for something like this? He had no idea. 40

2. **REA:** Rural Electrification Administration.

He wondered if he should try to get some help, then felt squeamish about asking help when he couldn't say exactly what had to be helped. But then he wondered how he would feel himself if he were in a far, strange country, all played out and sick, and no one to get him any help because they didn't know exactly what he was.

That made up his mind for him and he walked over to the phone. But should he call a doctor or a veterinarian? He decided to call the doctor because the thing was in the house. If it had been in the barn, he would have called the veterinarian.

He was on a rural line and the hearing wasn't good and he was half- 10 way deaf, so he didn't use the phone too often. He had told himself at times it was nothing but another aggravation, and there had been a dozen times he had threatened to have it taken out. But now he was glad he hadn't.

The operator got old Doctor Benson and they couldn't hear one another too well, but Mose finally made the doctor understand who was calling and that he needed him and the doctor said he'd come.

With some relief, Mose hung up the phone and was just standing there, not doing anything when he was struck by the thought that there might be others of these things down there in the woods. He had no idea what they were or what they might be doing or where they might be 20 going, but it was pretty evident that the one upon the bed was some sort of stranger from a very distant place. It stood to reason that there might be more than one of them, for far traveling was a lonely business and anyone—or anything—would like to have some company along.

He got the lantern down off the peg and lit it and went stumping out the door. The night was black as a stack of cats and the lantern light was feeble, but that made not a bit of difference, for Mose knew this farm of his like the back of his hand.

He went down the path into the woods. It was a spooky place, but it took more than woods at night to spook Old Mose. At the place where 30 he had found the thing, he looked around, pushing through the brush and holding the lantern high so he could see a bigger area, but he didn't find another one of them.

He did find something else, though—a sort of outsize birdcage made of metal lattice work that had wrapped itself around an eight-inch hickory tree. He tried to pull it loose, but it was jammed so tight that he couldn't budge it.

He sighted back the way it must have come. He could see where it had plowed its way through the upper branches of the trees, and out beyond were stars, shining bleakly with the look of far away. 40

Mose had no doubt that the thing lying on his bed beside the kitchen stove had come in this birdcage contraption. He marveled some at that, but he didn't fret himself too much, for the whole thing was so unearthly that he knew he had little chance of pondering it out.

He walked back to the house and he scarcely had the lantern blown out and hung back on its peg than he heard a car drive up.

The doctor, when he came up to the door, became a little grumpy at seeing Old Mose standing there.

"You don't look sick to me," the doctor said. "Not sick enough to drag me clear out here at night."

"I ain't sick," said Mose.

"Well, then," said the doctor, more grumpily than ever, "what did you mean by phoning me?"

"I got someone who is sick," said Mose. "I hope you can help him. I would have tried myself, but I don't know how to go about it."

The doctor came inside and Mose shut the door behind him.

"You got something rotten in here?" asked the doctor.

"No, it's just the way he smells. It was pretty bad at first, but I'm getting used to it by now."

The doctor saw the thing lying on the bed and went over to it. Old Mose heard him sort of gasp and could see him standing there, very stiff and straight. Then he bent down and had a good look at the critter on the bed.

When he straightened up and turned around to Mose, the only thing that kept him from being downright angry was that he was so flabbergasted.

"Mose," he yelled, "what *is* this?"

"I don't know," said Mose. "I found it in the woods and it was hurt and wailing and I couldn't leave it there."

"You think it's sick?"

"I know it is," said Mose. "It needs help awful bad. I'm afraid it's dying."

The doctor turned back to the bed again and pulled the blanket down, then went and got the lamp so that he could see. He looked the critter up and down, and he prodded it with a skittish finger, and he made the kind of mysterious clucking sound that only doctors make.

Then he pulled the blanket back over it again and took the lamp back to the table.

"Mose," he said, "I can't do a thing for it."

"But you're a doctor!"

"A human doctor, Mose. I don't know what this thing is, but it isn't human. I couldn't even guess what is wrong with it, if anything. And I wouldn't know what could be safely done for it even if I could diagnose its illness. I'm not even sure it's an animal. There are a lot of things about it that argue it's a plant."

Then the doctor asked Mose straight out how he came to find it and Mose told him exactly how it happened. But he didn't tell him anything about the birdcage, for when he thought about it, it sounded so fantastic that he couldn't bring himself to tell it. Just finding the critter and having it here was bad enough, without throwing in the birdcage.

"I tell you what," the doctor said, "You got something here that's outside all human knowledge. I doubt there's ever been a thing like this seen on Earth before. I have no idea what it is and I wouldn't try to guess. If I were you, I'd get in touch with the university up at Madison. There might be someone there who could get it figured out. Even if they 10 couldn't, they'd be interested. They'd want to study it."

Mose went to the cupboard and got the cigar box almost full of silver dollars and paid the doctor. The doctor put the dollars in his pocket, joshing Mose about his eccentricity.

But Mose was stubborn about his silver dollars. "Paper money don't seem legal, somehow," he declared. "I like the feel of silver and the way it clinks. It's got authority."

The doctor left and he didn't seem as upset as Mose had been afraid he might be. As soon as he was gone, Mose pulled up a chair and sat down beside the bed.   20

It wasn't right, he thought, that the thing should be so sick and no one to help—no one who knew any way to help it.

He sat in the chair and listened to the ticking of the clock, loud in the kitchen silence, and the crackling of the wood burning in the stove.

Looking at the thing lying on the bed, he had an almost fierce hope that it could get well again and stay with him. Now that its birdcage was all banged up, maybe there'd be nothing it could do but stay. And he hoped it would, for already the house felt less lonely.

Sitting in the chair between the stove and bed, Mose realized how lonely it had been. It had not been quite so bad until Towser died. He 30 had tried to bring himself to get another dog, but he never had been able to. For there was no dog that would take the place of Towser, and it had seemed unfaithful to even try. He could have gotten a cat, of course, but that would remind him too much of Molly; she had been very fond of cats, and until the time she died, there had always been two or three of them underfoot around the place.

But now he was alone. Alone with his farm and his stubbornness and his silver dollars. The doctor thought, like all the rest of them, that the only silver Mose had was in the cigar box in the cupboard. There wasn't one of them who knew about the old iron kettle piled plumb full 40 of them, hidden underneath the floorboards of the living room. He chuckled at the thought of how he had them fooled. He'd give a lot to see his neighbors' faces if they could only know. But he was not the one to tell them. If they were to find it out, they'd have to find it out for themselves.

He nodded in the chair and finally he slept, sitting upright, with his chin resting on his chest and his crossed arms wrapped around himself as if to keep him warm.

When he woke, in the dark before the dawn, with the lamp flickering on the table and the fire in the stove burned low, the alien had died.

There was no doubt of death. The thing was cold and rigid, and the husk that was its body was rough and drying out—as a corn stalk in the field dries out, whipping in the wind once the growing had been ended. 10

Mose pulled the blanket up to cover it, and although this was early to do the chores, he went out by lantern light and got them done.

After breakfast he heated water and washed his face and shaved, and it was the first time in years he'd shaved any day but Sunday. Then he put on his one good suit and slicked down his hair and got the old jalopy out of the machine shed and drove into town.

He hunted up Eb Dennison, the town clerk, who also was the secretary of the cemetery association.

"Eb," he said, "I want to buy a lot."

"But you've got a lot," protested Eb.   20

"That plot," said Mose, "is a family plot. There's just room for me and Molly."

"Well, then," asked Eb, "why another one? You have no other members of the family."

"I found someone in the woods," said Mose. "I took him home and he died last night. I plan to bury him."

"If you found a dead man in the woods," Eb warned him, "you better notify the coroner and sheriff."

"In time I may," said Mose, not intending to. "Now how about that plot?"   30

Washing his hands of the affair entirely, Eb sold him the plot.

Having bought his plot, Mose went to the undertaking establishment run by Albert Jones.

"Al," he said, "there's been a death out at the house. A stranger I found out in the woods. He doesn't seem to have anyone and I aim to take care of it."

"You got a death certificate?" asked Al, who subscribed to none of the niceties affected by most funeral parlor operators.

"Well, no, I haven't."

"Was there a doctor in attendance?"   40

"Doc Benson came out last night."

"He should have made you out one. I'll give him a ring."

He phoned Doctor Benson and talked with him a while and got red around the gills. He finally slammed down the phone and turned to Mose.

"I don't know what you're trying to pull off," he fumed, "but Doc tells me this thing of yours isn't even human. I don't take care of dogs or cats or—"

"This ain't no dog or cat."

"I don't care what it is. It's got to be human for me to handle it. And don't go trying to bury it in the cemetery, because it's against the law."

Considerably discouraged, Mose left the undertaking parlor and trudged slowly up the hill toward the town's one and only church.   10

He found the minister in his study working on a sermon. Mose sat down in a chair and fumbled his battered hat around and around in his work-scarred hands.

"Parson," he said, "I'll tell you the story from first to last," and he did. He added, "I don't know what it is. I guess no one else does, either. But it's dead and in need of decent burial and that's the least that I can do. I can't bury it in the cemetery, so I suppose I'll have to find a place for it on the farm. I wonder if you could bring yourself to come out and say a word or two."

The minister gave the matter some deep consideration.   20

"I'm sorry, Mose," he said at last. "I don't believe I can. I am not sure at all the church would approve of it."

"This thing may not be human," said Old Mose, "but it is one of God's critters."

The minister thought some more, and did some wondering out loud, but made up his mind finally that he couldn't do it.

So Mose went down the street to where his car was waiting and drove home, thinking about what heels some humans are.

Back at the farm again, he got a pick and shovel and went into the garden, and there, in one corner of it, he dug a grave. He went out to the 30 machine shed to hunt up some boards to make the thing a casket, but it turned out that he had used the last of the lumber to patch up the hog pen.

Mose went to the house and dug around in a chest in one of the back rooms which had not been used for years, hunting for a sheet to use as a winding shroud, since there would be no casket. He couldn't find a sheet, but he did unearth an old white linen tablecloth. He figured that would do, so he took it to the kitchen.

He pulled back the blanket and looked at the critter lying there in death, and a sort of lump came into his throat at the thought of it—how 40 it had died so lonely and so far from home without a creature of its own to spend its final hours with. And naked, too, without a stitch of clothing and with no possession, with not a thing to leave behind as a remembrance of itself.

He spread the tablecloth out on the floor beside the bed and lifted the thing and laid it on the tablecloth. As he laid it down, he saw the pocket in it—if it was a pocket—a sort of slitted flap in the center of what could be its chest. He ran his hand across the pocket area. There was a lump inside it. He crouched for a long moment beside the body, wondering what to do.

Finally he reached his fingers into the flap and took out the thing that bulged. It was a ball, a little bigger than a tennis ball, made of cloudy glass—or, at least, it looked like glass. He squatted there, staring at it, 10 then took it to the window for a better look.

There was nothing strange at all about the ball. It was just a cloudy ball of glass and it had a rough, dead feel about it, just as the body had.

He shook his head and took it back and put it where he'd found it and wrapped the body securely in the cloth. He carried it to the garden and put it in the grave. Standing solemnly at the head of the grave, he said a few short words and then shoveled in the dirt.

He had meant to make a mound above the grave and he had intended to put up a cross, but at the last he didn't do either one of these. There would be snoopers. The word would get around, and they'd be 20 coming out and hunting for the spot where he had buried this thing he had found out in the woods. So there must be no mound to mark the place and no cross as well. Perhaps it was for the best, he told himself, for what could he have carved or written on the cross?

By this time it was well past noon and he was getting hungry, but he didn't stop to eat, because there were other things to do. He went out into the pasture and caught up Bess and hitched her to the stoneboat and went down into the woods.

He hitched her to the birdcage that was wrapped around the tree, and she pulled it loose as pretty as you please. Then he loaded it on the 30 stoneboat and hauled it up the hill and stowed it in the back of the machine shed, in the far corner by the forge.

After that, he hitched Bess to the garden plow and gave the garden a cultivating that it didn't need so it would be fresh dirt all over and no one could locate where he'd dug the grave.

He was just finishing the plowing when Sheriff Doyle drove up and got out of the car. The sheriff was a soft-spoken man, but he was no dawdler. He got right to the point.

"I hear," he said, "you found something in the woods."

"That I did," said Mose.   40

"I hear it died on you."

"Sheriff, you heard right."

"I'd like to see it, Mose."

"Can't. I buried it. And I ain't telling where."

"Mose," the sheriff said, "I don't want to make you trouble, but you did an illegal thing. You can't go finding people in the woods and just bury them when they up and die on you."

"You talk to Doc Benson?"

The sheriff nodded. "He said it wasn't any kind of thing he'd ever seen before. He said it wasn't human."

"Well, then," said Mose, "I guess that lets you out. If it wasn't human, there could be no crime against a person. And if it wasn't owned, there ain't any crime against property. There's been no one around to claim they owned the thing, is there?"

The sheriff rubbed his chin. "No, there hasn't. Maybe you're right. Where did you study law?"

"I never studied law. I never studied nothing. I just use common sense."

"Doc said something about the folks up at the university might want to look at it."

"I tell you, Sheriff," said Mose. "This thing came here from somewhere and it died. I don't know where it came from and I don't know what it was and I don't hanker none to know. To me it was just a living thing that needed help real bad. It was alive and it had its dignity and in death it commanded some respect. When the rest of you refused it decent burial, I did the best I could. And that is all there is to it."

"All right, Mose," the sheriff said, "if that's how you want it."

He turned around and stalked back to the car. Mose stood beside old Bess hitched to her plow and watched him drive away. He drove fast and reckless as if he might be angry.

Mose put the plow away and turned the horse back to the pasture, and by now it was time to do chores again.

He got the chores all finished and made himself some supper and after supper sat beside the stove, listening to the ticking of the clock, loud in the silent house, and the crackle of the fire.

All night long the house was lonely.

The next afternoon, as he was plowing corn, a reporter came and walked up the row with him and talked with him when he came to the end of the row. Mose didn't like this reporter much. He was too flip and he asked some funny questions, so Mose clammed up and didn't tell him much.

A few days later, a man showed up from the university and showed him the story the reporter had gone back and written. The story made fun of Mose.

"I'm sorry," the professor said. "Those newspapermen are unaccountable. I wouldn't worry too much about anything they write."

"I don't," Mose told him.

The man from the university asked a lot of questions and made quite a point about how important it was that he should see the body.

But Mose only shook his head. "It's at peace," he said. "I aim to leave it that way."

The man went away disgusted, but still quite dignified.

For several days there were people driving by and dropping in, the idly curious, and there were some neighbors Mose hadn't seen for 10 months. But he gave them all short shrift and in a little while they left him alone and he went on with his farming and the house stayed lonely.

He thought again that maybe he should get a dog, but he thought of Towser and he couldn't do it.

One day, working in the garden, he found the plant that grew out of the grave. It was a funny-looking plant and his first impulse was to root it out.

But he didn't do it, for the plant intrigued him. It was a kind he'd never seen before and he decided he would let it grow, for a while at least, to see what kind it was. It was a bulky, fleshy plant, with heavy, 20 dark-green, curling leaves, and it reminded him in some ways of the skunk cabbage that burgeoned in the woods come spring.

There was another visitor, the queerest of the lot. He was a dark and intense man who said he was the president of a flying saucer club. He wanted to know if Mose had talked with the thing he'd found out in the woods and seemed terribly disappointed when Mose told him he hadn't. He wanted to know if Mose had found a vehicle the creature might have traveled in and Mose lied to him about it. He was afraid, the wild way the man was acting, that he might demand to search the place, and if he had, he'd likely have found the birdcage hidden in the machine shed back 30 in the corner by the forge. But the man got to lecturing Mose about withholding vital information.

Finally Mose had taken all he could of it, so he stepped into the house and picked up the shotgun from behind the door. The president of the flying saucer club said goodbye rather hastily and got out of there.

Farm life went on as usual, with the corn laid by and the haying started, and out in the garden the strange plant kept on growing and now was taking shape. Old Mose couldn't believe his eyes when he saw the sort of shape it took, and he spent long evening hours just standing in the garden, watching it and wondering if his loneliness were playing tricks on him. 40

The morning came when he found the plant standing at the door and waiting for him. He should have been surprised, of course, but he really wasn't, for he had lived with it, watching it of eventide, and although he had not dared admit it even to himself, he had known what it was.

For here was the creature he'd found in the woods, no longer sick and keening, no longer close to death, but full of life and youth.

It was not the same entirely, though. He stood and looked at it and could see the differences—the little differences that might have been those between youth and age, or between a father and a son, or again the differences expressed in an evolutionary pattern.

"Good morning," said Mose, not feeling strange at all to be talking 10 to the thing. "It's good to have you back."

The thing standing in the yard did not answer him. But that was not important; he had not expected that it would. The one important point was that he had something he could talk to.

"I'm going out to do the chores," said Mose. "You want to tag along?"

It tagged along with him and it watched him as he did the chores and he talked to it, which was a vast improvement over talking to himself.

At breakfast he laid an extra plate for it and pulled up an extra chair, but it turned out the critter was not equipped to use a chair, for it wasn't hinged to sit.   20

Nor did it eat. That bothered Mose at first, for he was hospitable, but he told himself that a big, strong, strapping youngster like this one knew enough to take care of itself, and he probably didn't need to worry too much about how it got along.

After breakfast he went out to the garden, with the critter accompanying him, and sure enough, the plant was gone. There was a collapsed husk lying on the ground, the outer covering that had been the cradle of the creature at his side.

Then he went to the machine shed, and the creature saw the birdcage and rushed over to it and looked it over minutely. Then it turned around 30 to Mose and made a sort of pleading gesture.

Mose went over to it and laid his hands on one of the twisted bars and the critter stood beside him and laid its hands on, too, and they pulled together. It was no use. They could move the metal some, but not enough to pull it back in shape again.

They stood and looked at one another, although looking may not be the word, for the critter had no eyes to look with. It made some funny motions with its hands, but Mose couldn't understand. Then it lay down on the floor and showed him how the birdcage ribs were fastened to the base.

It took a while for Mose to understand how the fastening worked, 40 and he never did know exactly why it did. There wasn't, actually, any reason that it should work that way.

First you applied some pressure, just the right amount at the exact and correct angle, and the bar would move a little. Then you applied some more pressure, again the exact amount and at the proper angle, and the bar would move some more. You did this three times and the bar came loose, although there was no reason why it should.

Mose started a fire in the forge and shoveled in some coal and worked the bellows while the critter watched. But when he picked up the bar to put it in the fire, the critter got between him and the forge and wouldn't let him near. Mose realized then he couldn't—or wasn't sup-posed to—heat the bar to straighten it and he never questioned the entire 10 rightness of it. For, he told himself, this thing must surely know the proper way to do it.

So he took the bar over to the anvil and started hammering it back into shape again, cold, without the use of fire, while the critter tried to show him the shape it should be. It took quite a while, but finally it was straightened out to the critter's satisfaction.

Mose figured they'd have themselves a time getting the bar back in place again, but it slipped on as slick as could be.

Then they took off another bar and this one went faster, now that Mose had the hang of it. 20

But it was hard and grueling labor. They worked all day and only straightened out five bars.

It took four solid days to get the bars on the birdcage hammered into shape, and all the time the hay was waiting to be cut.

But it was all right with Mose. He had someone to talk to and the house had lost its loneliness.

When they got the bars back in place, the critter slipped into the cage and started fooling with a dingus on the roof of it that looked like a complicated basket. Mose, watching, figured that the basket was some sort of control. 30

The critter was discouraged. It walked around the shed looking for something and seemed unable to find it. It came back to Mose and made its despairing, pleading gesture. Mose showed it iron and steel; he dug into a carton where he kept bolts and clamps and bushings and scraps of metal and other odds and ends, finding brass and copper and even some aluminum, but it wasn't any of these.

And Mose was glad—a bit ashamed for feeling glad, but glad all the same.

For it had been clear to him that when the birdcage was all ready, the critter would be leaving him. It had been impossible for Mose to stand 40 in the way of the repair of the cage, or to refuse to help. But now that it apparently couldn't be, he found himself well pleased.

Now the critter would have to stay with him and he'd have someone to talk to and the house would not be lonely. It would be welcome, he told himself, to have folks again. The critter was almost as good a companion as Towser.

Next morning, while Mose was fixing breakfast, he reached up in the cupboard to get the box of oatmeal and his hand struck the cigar box, and it came crashing to the floor. It fell over on its side and the lid came open and the dollars went free-wheeling all around the kitchen.

Out of the corner of his eye, Mose saw the critter leaping quickly in pursuit of one of them. It snatched it up and turned to Mose, with the coin held between its fingers, and a sort of thrumming noise was coming out of the nest of worms on top of it.

It bent and scooped up more of them and cuddled them and danced a sort of jig, and Mose knew, with a sinking heart, that it had been silver the critter had been hunting.

So Mose got down on his hands and knees and helped the critter gather up all the dollars. They put them back into the cigar box, and Mose picked up the box and gave it to the critter.

The critter took it and hefted it and had a disappointed look. Taking the box over to the table, it took the dollars out and stacked them in neat piles and Mose could see it was very disappointed.

Perhaps, after all, Mose thought, it had not been silver the thing had been hunting for. Maybe it had made a mistake in thinking that the silver was some other kind of metal.

Mose got down the oatmeal and poured it into some water and put it on the stove. When it was cooked and the coffee was ready, he carried his breakfast to the table and sat down to eat.

The critter still was standing across the table from him, stacking and restacking the piles of silver dollars. And now it showed him with a hand held above the stacks, that it needed more of them. This many stacks, it showed him, and each stack so high.

Mose sat stricken, with a spoon full of oatmeal halfway to his mouth. He thought of all those other dollars, the iron kettle packed with them, underneath the floorboards in the living room. And he couldn't do it; they were the only thing he had—except the critter now. And he could not give them up so the critter could go and leave him too.

He ate his bowl of oatmeal without tasting it and drank two cups of coffee. And all the time the critter stood there and showed him how much more it needed.

"I can't do it for you," Old Mose said. "I've done all you can expect of any living being. I found you in the woods and I gave you warmth and shelter. I tried to help you, and when I couldn't, at least I gave you a place to die in. I buried you and protected you from all those other people and I did not pull you up when you started growing once again. Surely you can't expect me to keep on giving endlessly."

But it was no good. The critter could not hear him, and he did not convince himself.

He got up from the table and walked into the living room with the critter trailing him. He loosened the floorboards and took out the kettle, and the critter, when it saw what was in the kettle, put its arms around itself and hugged in happiness.

They lugged the money out to the machine shed, and Mose built a 10 fire in the forge and put the kettle in the fire and started melting down the hard-saved money.

There were times he thought he couldn't finish the job, but he did.

The critter got the basket out of the birdcage and put it down beside the forge and dipped out the molten silver with an iron ladle and poured it here and there into the basket, shaping it in place with careful hammer taps.

It took a long time, for it was exacting work, but finally it was done and the silver almost gone. The critter lugged the basket back into the birdcage and fastened it in place.   20

It was almost evening now and Mose had to go and do the chores. He half expected the thing might haul out the birdcage and be gone when he came back to the house. And he tried to be sore at it for its selfishness—it had taken from him and had not tried to pay him back—it had not, so far as he could tell, even tried to thank him. But he made a poor job of being sore at it.

It was waiting for him when he came from the barn carrying two pails full of milk. It followed him inside the house and stood around and he tried to talk to it. But he didn't have the heart to do much talking. He could not forget that it would be leaving, and the pleasure of its present 30 company was lost in his terror of the loneliness to come.

For now he didn't even have his money to help ward off the loneliness.

As he lay in bed that night, strange thoughts came creeping in upon him—the thought of an even greater loneliness than he had ever known upon this runty farm, the terrible, devastating loneliness of the empty wastes that lay between the stars, a driven loneliness while one hunted for a place or person that remained a misty thought one could not define, but which it was most important one should find.

It was a strange thing for him to be thinking, and quite suddenly he 40 knew it was no thought of his, but of this other that was in the room with him.

He tried to raise himself, he fought to raise himself, but he couldn't do it. He held his head up a moment, then fell back upon the pillow and went sound asleep.

Next morning, after Mose had eaten breakfast, the two of them went to the machine shed and dragged the birdcage out. It stood there, a weird alien thing, in the chill brightness of the dawn.

The critter walked up to it and started to slide between two of the bars, but when it was halfway through, it stepped out again and moved over to confront Old Mose.

"Goodbye, friend," said Mose. "I'll miss you." 10

There was a strange stinging in his eyes.

The other held out its hand in farewell, and Mose took it and there was something in the hand he grasped, something round and smooth that was transferred from its hand to his.

The thing took its hand away and stepped quickly to the birdcage and slid between the bars. The hands reached for the basket and there was a sudden flicker and the birdcage was no longer there.

Mose stood lonely in the barnyard, looking at the place where there was no birdcage and remembering what he had felt or thought—or been told?—the night before as he lay in bed. 20

Already the critter would be there, out between the stars, in that black and utter loneliness, hunting for a place or thing or person that no human mind could grasp.

Slowly Mose turned around to go back to the house, to get the pails and go down to the barn to get the milking done.

He remembered the object in his hand and lifted his still-clenched fist in front of him. He opened his fingers and the little crystal ball lay there in his palm—and it was exactly like the one he'd found in the slitted flap in the body he had buried in the garden. Except that one had been dead and cloudy and this one had the living glow of a distant-burning 30 fire.

Looking at it, he had the strange feeling of a happiness and comfort such as he had seldom known before, as if there were many people with him and all of them were friends.

He closed his hand upon it and the happiness stayed on—and it was all wrong, for there was not a single reason that he should be happy. The critter had left him and his money was all gone and he had no friends, but still he kept on feeling good.

He put the ball into his pocket and stepped spryly for the house to get the milking pails. He pursed up his whiskered lips and began to 40 whistle, and it had been a long, long time since he had even thought to whistle.

Maybe he was happy, he told himself, because the critter had not left without stopping to take his hand and try to say goodbye.

And a gift, no matter how worthless it might be, how cheap a trinket, still had a basic value in simple sentiment. It had been many years since anyone had bothered to give him a gift.

It was dark and lonely and unending in the depths of space with no Companion. It might be long before another was obtainable.

It perhaps was a foolish thing to do, but the old creature had been such a kind savage, so fumbling and so pitiful and eager to help. And one who travels far and fast must likewise travel light. There had been 10 nothing else to give.

REVIEWING THE STORY _____

THE MAIN IDEA

1. The main idea of the story deals with the need for
   (a) independence from one's neighbors.
   (b) security in one's old age.
   (c) taking care of oneself first.
   (d) companionship in life.

DETAILS

2. Touching the space alien reminds Mose of touching a (a) small pig (b) can of worms (c) green stalk of corn (d) metal birdcage.

3. What happens when Mose tries to bury the dead alien according to human customs?
   (a) Mose is arrested.
   (b) The alien is buried next to Molly, Mose's wife.
   (c) Everyone is helpful.
   (d) No one will help him.

4. On top of the dead alien's grave,
   (a) a spaceship lands.
   (b) a strange plant begins to grow.
   (c) Mose places a cross.
   (d) Mose puts the birdcage.

5. The control mechanism of the extraterrestrial's spacecraft cannot be repaired without **(a)** silver **(b)** gold **(c)** copper **(d)** iron.

6. The little crystal ball that the space alien leaves with Mose

   (a) permits Mose to see into the future.
   (b) provides a sense of companionship.
   (c) enables Mose to travel in outer space.
   (d) protects Mose against sickness and death.

ORDER OF EVENTS

7. Choose the letter that gives the order in which the events happen.
   (1) Mose finds the second alien at the door.
   (2) Mose buries the dead alien.
   (3) Mose gives the alien all his silver.
   (4) Mose receives the crystal ball as a gift.
      (a) 4-3-2-1 **(b)** 1-2-3-4 **(c)** 2-1-3-4 **(d)** 3-4-1-2

CAUSE AND EFFECT

8. Mose helps the alien because he
   (a) hopes to learn more about outer space.
   (b) wants a reward.
   (c) sympathizes with all living things.
   (d) is interested in UFOs and extraterrestrial beings.

9. As a result of taking the alien into his home, Mose
   (a) realizes how lonely he has been.
   (b) decides to get another dog.
   (c) understands how the alien's mind works.
   (d) learns to love his neighbors.

INFERENCES

10. In the last two paragraphs of the story, the person whose thoughts we are "hearing" is **(a)** the space alien **(b)** Mose **(c)** Doctor Benson **(d)** a new character.

11. The alien creature is NOT capable of some form of **(a)** speech **(b)** sign language **(c)** understanding **(d)** mental telepathy.

PREDICTING OUTCOMES

12. As long as Mose keeps the gift from the space alien, the old farmer probably will NOT

   (a) grow older.
   (b) have to die.
   (c) feel lonely.
   (d) be visited by other space aliens.

BUILDING YOUR VOCABULARY

1. It was groaning, too, but not too loud—just the kind of *keening* sound a lonesome wind might make around a wide, deep eave.

A *keening* sound (page 220, lines 13-14) can best be described as **(a)** sharp **(b)** cheerful **(c)** blustery **(d)** mournful.

2. Old Mose stood there for quite a *spell*, making up his mind what he ought to do about it . . . .

Which of the following definitions of *spell* (page 220, lines 17-18) BEST fits this sentence?

   (a) to read or write the letters of a word
   (b) to relieve, or take over, for another person
   (c) a period of time
   (d) a set of magical words.

3. Mose, however, was not *finicky*.

   a. The word *finicky* (page 221, line 4) means **(a)** fussy **(b)** fickle **(c)** filthy **(d)** flabby.

   b. Which is the BEST strategy for answering part *a*?

      (a) Look for context clues in the sentence containing the word.
      (b) Study the paragraph in which the word appears.
      (c) Search for other uses of the word in the story.
      (d) Analyze the word into its component parts.

4. He wondered if he should try to get some help, then felt *squeamish* about asking help when he couldn't say exactly what had to be helped.

A person who is *squeamish* (page 223, lines 1-2) feels **(a)** confident **(b)** like screaming **(c)** angry **(d)** ill at ease.

5. The doctor put the dollars in his pocket, joshing Mose about his *eccentricity*.

   Eccentricity (page 225, lines 13-14) means **(a)** stinginess **(b)** wealthiness **(c)** oddness **(d)** stubbornness.

STUDYING THE WRITER'S CRAFT

1. A key to the success of this story is the author's ***characterization*** of Old Mose Abrams.

   a. What faults do the neighbors find in Old Mose? Give evidence for your answer from the story.

   b. What admirable traits do you find in him? Again, give evidence from the story.

2. Another key to the strength of this story is the author's use of ***description***. Good descriptive writing appeals to the senses. The first eleven paragraphs, for example, contain a rich variety of ***sensory details:*** sight, sound, smell, and touch.

   a. Give at least one example of each type of sensory detail from the first eleven paragraphs.

   b. What other examples of sensory details can you find in the rest of the story? Mention a few of them.

3. Most of the story is told using the third-person ***point of view***, slanted through Mose. Thus, we see and hear, think and feel, through the mind and heart of the old farmer.

   a. Why do you think Simak chose *not* to use the first-person point of view with Mose as narrator? (With this point of view, the first sentence might read: "I was out hunting cows when I found the alien.")

   b. At the very end of the story, there is an abrupt shift in point of view. Where does this shift occur? What is the new point of view? Why do you think Simak chose to end the story this way?

ACTIVITIES FOR LISTENING, SPEAKING, WRITING

1. One of the most famous ***parables*** (teaching stories) of the New Testament is the story of the Good Samaritan. Read this parable in the Gospel of St. Luke, chapter 10, verses 25-37. What parallels do you see between the biblical story and the science-fiction story you have just read? Write a brief answer to this question.

2. The title "A Death in the House" may mean more than it literally says. What deaths have already taken place in Mose's house? To what death does the title refer? Why is it important that this latest death occurs in Mose's house rather than in his barn? What does this fact say about Mose? What does it say about human values and humane behavior? Write a set of notes that give your answers to these questions. Be prepared to share your thoughts with your classmates.

3. Suppose that the human characters in the story were alive today. What do you think Old Mose would be likely to do with someone who is homeless or who is sick with AIDS? What might some of the other characters in the story do with such a person? Be prepared to discuss these questions with your classmates.

Things

by Zenna Henderson

For gifts given, something always is taken. We have no wish to exchange our young men for a look at the Strangers.

You may find the story "Things" both puzzling and unsettling. Without explanation or other help, it plunges you into an alien world of unfamiliar words and customs. To stretch your imagination even further, the story asks you to look at our world, our people, and our *things* through the eyes of the folk of this alien world.

Don't worry about understanding every strange word or custom the author has invented in this story. Context clues will help you guess at the meanings of many of them. Further help will be found in the glossary at the back of this book.

As you read "Things," ask yourself: Who are the Strangers? Who are the people of the coveti? For the things given, what has been taken away?

Zenna Henderson

For most of her life, Zenna Henderson taught in elementary schools in the Arizona countryside. Some of her most popular science-fiction stories are set in that region. They tell of the People, an alien race with psychic powers who live in hiding from human beings. Where most science fiction focuses on science and technology, her writings explore personal and spiritual values. Many of Henderson's short stories were published in the magazine *Fantasy and Science Fiction*.

Viat came back from the camp of the Strangers, his crest shorn, the devi ripped from his jacket, his mouth slack and drooling and his eyes empty. He sat for a day in the sun of the coveti center, not even noticing when the eager children gathered and asked questions in their piping little voices. When the evening shadow touched him, Viat staggered to his feet and took two steps and was dead.

The mother came then, since the body was from her and could never be alien, and since the emptiness that was not Viat had flown from his eyes. She signed him dead by pinning on his torn jacket the kiom—the kiom she had fashioned the day he was born, since to be born is to 10 begin to die. He had not yet given his heart, so the kiom was still hers to bestow. She left the pelu softly alight in the middle of the kiom because Viat had died beloved. He who dies beloved walks straight and strong on the path to the Hidden Ones by the light of the pelu. Be the pelu removed, he must wander forever, groping in the darkness of the unlighted kiom.

So she pinned the kiom and wailed him dead.

There was a gathering together after Viat was given back to the Earth. Backs were bent against the Sun, and the coveti thought together for a morning. When the Sun pointed itself into their eyes, they shaded 20 them with their open palms and spoke together.

242

"The Strangers have wrought an evil thing with us." Dobi patted the dust before him. "Because of them, Viat is not. He came not back from the camp. Only his body came, breathing until it knew he would not return to it."

"And yet, it may be that the Strangers are not evil. They came to us in peace. Even, they brought their craft down on barrenness instead of scorching our fields." Deci's eyes were eager on the sky. His blood was hot with the wonder of a craft dropping out of the clouds, bearing Strangers. "Perhaps there was no need for us to move the coveti."

"True, true," nodded Dobi. "They may not be of themselves evil, but 10 it may be that the breath of them is death to us, or perhaps the falling of their shadows or the silent things that walk invisible from their friendly hands. It is best that we go not to the camp again. Neither should we permit them to find the coveti."

"Cry them not forbidden, yet!" cried Deci, his crest rippling, "we know them not. To taboo them now would not be fair. They may come bearing gifts—"

"For gifts given, something always is taken. We have no wish to exchange our young men for a look at the Strangers." Dobi furrowed the dust with his fingers and smoothed away the furrows as Viat had been 20 smoothed away.

"And yet," Veti's soft voice came clearly as her blue crest caught the breeze, "it may be that they will have knowledge for us that we have not. Never have we taken craft into the clouds and back."

"Yes, yes!" Deci's eyes embraced Veti, who held his heart. "They must have much knowledge, many gifts for us."

"The gift of knowledge is welcome," said Tefu in his low rumble. "But gifts in the hands have fangs and bonds."

"The old words!" cried Deci. "The old ways do not hold when new ways arrive!"   30

"True," nodded Dobi. "If the new is truly a way and not a whirlwind or a trail that goes no place. But to judge without facts is to judge in error. I will go to the Strangers."

"And I." Tefu's voice stirred like soft thunder.

"And I? And I?" Deci's words tumbled on themselves and the dust stirred with his hurried rising.

"Young—" muttered Tefu.

"Young eyes to notice what old eyes might miss," said Dobi. "Our path is yours." His crest rippled as he nodded to Deci.

"Deci!" Veti's voice was shaken by the unknown. "Come not again 40 as Viat came. The heart you bear with you is not your own."

"I will come again," cried Deci, "To fill your hands with wonders and delights." He gave each of her cupped palms a kiss to hold against his return.

Time is not hours and days, or the slanting and shortening of shadows. Time is a held breath and a listening ear.

Time incredible passed before the ripple through the grass, the rustle through reeds, the sudden sound of footsteps where it seemed no footsteps could be. The rocks seemed to part to let them through.

Dobi led, limping, slow of foot, flattened of crest, his eyes hidden in the shadow of his bent head. Then came Tefu, like one newly blind, groping, reaching, bumping, reeling until he huddled against the familiar 10 rocks in the fading sunlight.

"Deci?" cried Veti, parting the crowd with her cry. "Deci?"

"He came not with us," said Dobi. "He watched us go."

"Willingly?" Veti's hands clenched over the memory of his mouth. "Willingly? Or was there force?"

"Willingly?" The eyes that Tefu turned to Veti saw her not. They looked within at hidden things. "Force? He stayed. There were no bonds about him." He touched a wondering finger to one eye and then the other. "Open," he rumbled. "Where is the light?"

"Tell me," cried Veti. "Oh, tell me!"   20

Dobi sat in the dust, his big hands marking it on either side of him.

"They truly have wonders. They would give us many strange things for our devi." His fingers tinkled the fringing of his jacket. "Fabrics beyond our dreams. Tools we could use. Weapons that could free the land of every flesh-hungry kutu."

"And Deci? And Deci?" Veti voiced her fear again.

"Deci saw all and desired all. His devi were ripped off before the sun slid an arm's reach. He was like a child in a meadow of flowers, clutching, grabbing, crumpling, and finding always the next flower 30 fairer."

Wind came in the silence and poured itself around bare shoulders.

"Then he will return," said Veti, loosening her clenched hand. "When the wonder is gone."

"As Viat returned?" Tefu's voice rumbled. "As I have returned?" He held his hand before his eyes and dropped his fingers one by one. "How many fingers before you? Six? Four? Two?

"You saw the Strangers, before we withdrew the coveti. You saw the strange garments they wore, the shining roundness, the heavy glitter and thickness. Our air is not air for them. Without the garments, they 40 would die."

"If they are so well wrapped against the world, how could they hurt?" cried Veti. "They cannot hurt Deci. He will return."

"I returned," murmured Tefu. "I did but walk among them and the misting of their finished breath has done this to me. Only time and the Hidden Ones know if sight is through for me.

"One was concerned for me. One peered at me when first my steps began to waver. He hurried me away from the others and sat away from me and watched with me as the lights went out. He was concerned for me—or was studying me. But I am blind."

"And you?" asked Veti of Dobi. "It harmed you not?"   10

"I took care," said Dobi. "I came not close after the first meeting. And yet—" he turned the length of his thigh. From hip to knee the split flesh glinted like the raking of a mighty claw. "I was among the trees when a kutu screamed on the hill above me. Fire lashed out from the Strangers and it screamed no more. Startled, I moved the branches about me and—s-s-s-st!" His finger streaked beside his thigh.

"But Deci—"

Dobi scattered his dust handprint with a swirl of his fingers. "Deci is like a scavenging mayu. He follows, hand outstretched. 'Wait wait,' he cried when we turned to go. 'We can lead the world with these wonders.' 20

"Why should we lead the world? Now there is no first and no last. Why should we reach beyond our brothers to grasp things that dust will claim?"

"Wail him dead, Veti," rumbled Tefu. "Death a thousand ways surrounds him now. And if his body comes again, his heart is no longer with us. Wail him dead."

"Yes," nodded Dobi. "Wail him dead and give thanks that our coveti is so securely hidden that the Strangers can never come to sow among us the seeds of more Viats and Tefus.

"The Strangers are taboo. The coveti path is closed."

So Veti wailed him dead, crouching in the dust of the coveti path, 30 clutching in her hands the kiom Deci had given her with his heart.

Viat's mother sat with her an hour—until Veti broke her wail and cried, "Your grief is not mine. You pinned Viat's kiom. You folded his hands to rest. You gave him back to the earth. Wail not with me. I wail for an emptiness—for an unknowledge. For a wondering and a fearing. You know Viat is on the trail to the Hidden Ones. But I know not of Deci. Is he alive? Is he dying in the wilderness with no pelu to light him into the darkness? Is he crawling now, blind and maimed up the coveti trail? I wail a death with no hope. A hopelessness with no death. I wail alone."

And so she wailed past the point of tears, into the aching dryness 40 of grief. The coveti went about its doing, knowing she would live again when grief was spent.

Then came the day when all faces swung to the head of the coveti trail. All ears flared to the sound of Veti's scream and all eyes rounded to see Deci stagger into the coveti.

Veti flew to him, her arms outstretched, her heart believing before her mind could confirm. But Deci winced away from her touch and his face half snarled as his hand, shorn of three fingers and barely beginning to regenerate, motioned her away.

"Deci!" cried Veti, "Deci?"

"Let—let—me breathe." Deci leaned against the rocks. Deci who could outrun a kutu, whose feet had lightness and swiftness beyond all 10 others in the coveti. "The trail takes the breath."

"Deci!" Veti's hands still reached, one all unknowingly proffering the kiom. Seeing it, she laughed and cast it aside. The death mark with Deci alive before her? "Oh, Deci!" And then she fell silent as she saw his maimed hand, his ragged crest, his ravaged jacket, his seared legs—his eyes—His eyes! They were not the eyes of the Deci who had gone with eagerness to see the Strangers. He had brought the Strangers back in his eyes.

His breath at last came smoothly and he leaned to Veti, reaching as he did so, into the bundle by his side.

"I promised," he said, seeing Veti only. "I have come again to fill 20 your hands with wonder and delight."

But Veti's hands were hidden behind her. Gifts from Strangers are suspect.

"Here," said Deci, laying an ugly angled thing down in the dust before Veti. "Here is death to all kutus, be they six-legged or two. Let the Durlo coveti say again the Klori stream is theirs for fishing," he muttered. "Nothing is theirs now save by our sufferance. I give you power, Veti."

Veti moved back a pace.

"And here," he laid a flask of glass beside the weapon. "This is for dreams and laughter. This is what Viat drank of—but too much. They 30 call it water. It is a drink the Hidden Ones could envy. One mouthful and all memory of pain and grief, loss and unreachable dreams is gone.

"I give you forgetfulness, Veti."

Veti's head moved denyingly from side to side.

"And here." He pulled forth, carelessly, arms-lengths of shining fabric that rippled and clung and caught the sun. His eyes were almost Deci's eyes again.

Veti's heart was moved, woman-wise, to the fabric and her hands reached for it, since no woman can truly see a fabric unless her fingers taste its body, flow, and texture. 40

"For you, for beauty. And this, that you might behold yourself untwisted by moving waters." He laid beside the weapon and the water a square of reflecting brightness. "For you to see yourself as Lady over the world as I see myself Lord."

Veti's hands dropped again, the fabric almost untasted. Deci's eyes again were the eyes of a stranger.

"Deci, I waited not for *things*, these long days." Veti's hands cleansed themselves together from the cling of the fabric. Her eyes failed before Deci and sought the ground, jerking away from the strange things in the dust. "Come, let us attend to your hurts."

"But no! But see!" cried Deci. "With these strange things our coveti can rule all the valley and beyond and beyond!" 10

"Why?"

"Why?" echoed Deci. "To take all we want. To labor no more save to ask and receive. To have power—"

"Why?" Veti's eyes still questioned. "We have enough. We are not hungry. We are clothed against the changing seasons. We work when work is needed. We play when work is done. Why do we need more?"

"Deci finds quiet ways binding," said Dobi. "Rather would he have shouting and far, swift going. And sweat and effort and delicious fear pushing him into action. Soon come the kutu hunting days, Deci. Save your thirst for excitement until then." 20

"Sweat and effort and fear!" snarled Deci. "Why should I endure that when with this—" He snatched up the weapon and with one wave of his hand sheared off the top of Tefu's house. He spoke into the dying thunder of the discharge. "No kutu alive could unsheath its fangs after that, except as death draws back the sheath to mock its finished strength.

"And if so against a kutu," he muttered, "how much more so against the Durlo coveti?"

"Come, Deci," cried Veti. "Let us bind your wounds. As time will heal them, so time will heal your mind of these Strangers."

"I want no healing," shouted Deci, anger twisting his haggard face. 30 "Nor will you after the Strangers have been here and proffered you their wonders in exchange for this foolish fringing devi." Contempt tossed his head. "For the devi in our coveti, we could buy their sky craft, I doubt not."

"They will not come," said Dobi. "The way is hidden. No Stranger can ever find our coveti. We have but to wait until—"

"Until tomorrow!" Deci's crest tossed rebelliously, his voice louder than need be. Or perhaps it seemed so from the echoes it raised in every heart. "I told—"

"You told?" Stupidly, the echo took words.

"*You told?*" Disbelief sharpened the cry. 40

"You told!" Anger spurted into the words.

"I told!" cried Deci. "How else reap the benefits that the Strangers—"

"Benefits!" spat Dobi. "Death!" His foot spurned the weapon in the dust. "Madness!" The flask gurgled as it moved. "Vanity!" Dust clouded across the mirror and streaked the shining fabric. "For such you have betrayed us to death."

"But no!" cried Deci. "*I* lived. Death does not always come with the Strangers." Sudden anger roughened his voice. "It's the old ways! You want no change! But all things change. It is the way of living things. Progress—"

"All change is not progress," rumbled Tefu, his hands hiding his blindness.   10

"Like it or not," shouted Deci. "Tomorrow the Strangers come! You have your choice, all of you!" His arm circled the crowd. "Keep to your homes like Tefu or come forward with your devi and find with me a power, a richness—"

"Or move the coveti again," said Dobi. "Away from betrayal and foolish greed. We have a third choice."

Deci caught his breath.

"Veti?" his whisper pled. "Veti? We do not need the rest of the coveti. You and I together. We can wait for the strangers. Together we can have the world. With this weapon not one person in this coveti or any other 20 can withstand us. We can be the new people. We can have our own coveti, and take what we want—anything, anywhere. Come to me, Veti."

Veti looked long into his eyes. "Why did you come back?" she whispered with tears in her voice. Then anger leaped into her eyes. "*Why did you come back!*" There was the force of a scream in her harsh words. She darted suddenly to the rocks. She snatched the kiom from the dust where it had fallen. Before Deci knew what was happening, she whirled on him and pinned death upon his ragged jacket. Then with a swift, decisive twist, she tore away the pelu and dropped it to the dust.

Deci's eyes widened in terror, his hand clutched at the kiom but 30 dared not touch it.

"No!" he screamed, "No!"

Then Veti's eyes widened and her hands reached also for the kiom, but no power she possessed could undo what she had done and her scream rose with Deci's.

Then knowing himself surely dead and dead unbeloved, already entering the eternity of darkness of the unlighted kiom, Deci crumpled to the ground. Under his cheek was the hardness of the weapon, under his outflung hand, the beauty of the fabric, and the sunlight, bending through the water, giggled crazily on his chin.   40

One dead unbeloved is not as much as a crushed flower by the path. For the flower at least there is regret for its ended beauty.

So knowing Deci dead, the coveti turned from him. There was for memory of him only an uncertainty to Veti's feet and a wondering shock in Veti's eyes as she turned with the others to prepare to move the coveti.

The wind came and poured over the dust and the things and Deci. And Deci lay waiting for his own breath to stop.

REVIEWING THE STORY

THE MAIN IDEA

1. The *theme* of a story is an important message the writer expresses by means of the story's events and characters. Which statement best expresses the theme of this story?

    (a) Progress is achieved only through technology.
    (b) All living things seek new ways.
    (c) People are more important than things.
    (d) Things are more important than people.

DETAILS

2. The young woman Veti is the beloved of **(a)** Viat **(b)** Dobi **(c)** Deci **(d)** Tefu.

3. The Strangers are **(a)** space travelers **(b)** evil spirits **(c)** a rival tribe **(d)** the Hidden Ones.

4. The Strangers give their things in exchange for **(a)** coveti **(b)** devi **(c)** kiom **(d)** pelu.

5. The kiom is a **(a)** gift of the Strangers **(b)** flesh-eating beast **(c)** manner of speaking **(d)** mark of death.

6. Deci reveals to the Strangers the

    (a) source of the precious devi.
    (b) names of his people.
    (c) location of the coveti.
    (d) secret of the kiom and pelu.

ORDER OF EVENTS

7. Choose the letter of the event that happens LAST in the story.

    (a) Deci brings gifts from the Strangers.
    (b) Veti pins the kiom on Deci.

    (c) Veti wails Deci dead.

    (d) Viat returns from the camp of the Strangers.

CAUSE AND EFFECT

8. Viat died because he

    (a) was wounded by the weapons of the Strangers.

    (b) inhaled the Strangers' exhaust fumes.

    (c) was infected by the Strangers' germs.

    (d) had too much of the Strangers' drink.

9. As a result of his visit to the Strangers, Deci becomes **(a)** arrogant **(b)** suspicious **(c)** wise **(d)** gentle.

INFERENCES

10. We can infer that the devi the Strangers want are

    (a) religious symbols of death.

    (b) powerful gifts from the Strangers.

    (c) clothing ornaments of precious metal.

    (d) dwelling places of the people.

11. The people of the coveti do NOT possess

    (a) religious beliefs and customs.

    (b) the products of modern technology.

    (c) hunting and fishing skills.

    (d) clothing and ornaments.

PREDICTING OUTCOMES

12. Wearing the kiom without a pelu, Deci will probably

    (a) recover very slowly.

    (b) return to the Strangers.

    (c) die alone and unloved.

    (d) find the path to the Hidden Ones.

BUILDING YOUR VOCABULARY

1. To *taboo* them now would not be fair.

    a. The verb *taboo* (page 243, line 16) means to declare something **(a)** worthy **(b)** shameful **(c)** generous **(d)** forbidden.

b. The BEST clue to the meaning of *taboo* is in

  (a) the word itself.
  (b) the sentence in which the word appears.
  (c) the following sentence.
  (d) the paragraph in which the word appears.

2. Dobi *furrowed* the dust with his fingers and smoothed away the furrows as Viat had been smoothed away.

   The word closest in meaning to *furrowed* (page 243, lines 19-21) is **(a)** piled **(b)** grooved **(c)** felt **(d)** patted.

3. Is he crawling now, blind and *maimed* up the coveti trail?

   To be *maimed* (page 245, line 38) is to be **(a)** badly frightened **(b)** deaf **(c)** seriously wounded **(d)** almost insane.

4. But Deci winced away from her touch and his face half snarled as his hand, shorn of three fingers and barely beginning to *regenerate*, motioned her away.

   a. Something that can *regenerate* (page 246, lines 5-7) is able to **(a)** grow back again **(b)** bleed freely **(c)** feel pain **(d)** turn in all directions.

   b. The BEST strategy for answering part *a* is to

     (a) reread the sentence containing *regenerate*.
     (b) look for clues later in the story.
     (c) analyze the word into its parts.
     (d) reread the preceding paragraph.

5. Nothing is theirs now *save* by our sufferance.

   In this sentence, the word *save* (page 246, line 27, and page 247, line 12) means **(a)** rescue **(b)** except **(c)** put aside **(d)** avoid.

STUDYING THE WRITER'S CRAFT _____

1. In this story, the author frequently uses ***figurative language***.

   a. Tefu warns that, unlike the gift of knowledge, "gifts in the hands have fangs and bonds." What is he implying about gifts of things?

   b. Veti cries out to Deci, "The heart you bear with you is not your own." What does she mean by this?

   c. Describing the time in which Dobi, Tefu, and Deci are away at the camp of the Strangers, the author writes: "Time is not hours and days, or the slanting and shortening of shadows. Time is a held breath and a listening ear." (page 244, lines 3-4) In the second sentence, time is *personified*, or treated as if it were a person. Whom does time represent, or stand for, here?

2. Here are typical examples of the speech of the coveti people:

   a. He came not back from the camp.

   b. Cry them not forbidden, yet!

   c. Soon come the kutu hunting days.

   Rewrite each sentence in ordinary English. By comparing your versions with those in the story, you can tell that the speech of the coveti people sounds strangely formal and ceremonial. It resembles the old-fashioned language a preacher might use in a sermon. Find several other examples of typical coveti speech in the story and rewrite them in ordinary English.

3. The author names but does not directly explain several alien objects and customs. Instead, she leaves it up to the reader to figure out what they are. Using *context clues*, explain each of the following: devi, coveti, kiom, pelu.

ACTIVITIES FOR LISTENING, SPEAKING, WRITING

1. With the kiom pinned on him, Deci gives himself up for dead. Do you think that a person can die because of his or her belief in the power of a hex, or evil spell? Be prepared to discuss this question with your classmates.

2. Imagine that the Strangers must send a report on their initial contacts with the natives of this alien planet. What would they tell the people back on their home planet? Write such a report, adopting the point of view and the values of the Strangers, not the people of the coveti.

3. The "things" of the story (and its title) are all products of science and technology: weapons, alcoholic beverages, woven cloth, a mirror. The story implies that for gifts given by science and technology, something is always taken. What are some of the gifts of science and technology to people of our world? What thing or things may we have to give in exchange for these gifts? Write a composition containing your answers and explanations.

The Search for Extraterrestrial Intelligence (SETI): Two Views

Intuition may be wrong, but we don't know for sure that nobody is out there.

OR

The chances of Earthlings locating intelligence away from home are as close to zero as they can get.

Most scientists would concede that some form of life may exist elsewhere in the universe. Perhaps single-cell organisms wiggle about in the strange seas of another world. Colonies of purple algae or pink moss may cover the continents of a distant planet. Until we develop interstellar travel, however, we may never know about such forms of extraterrestrial life.

Some scientists are looking and listening for much more advanced forms of life out there. They are searching for signs of intelligent life beyond Earth. They seek evidence of living creatures capable of sending some form of message, some signal that they exist. To this end, scientists are utilizing new technologies to build powerful radio telescopes throughout the world. It is this search for extraterrestrial *intelligence* (SETI) that provokes controversy.

Is SETI a search we must make, a goal too possible and an adventure too exciting to miss? Or is it a fool's quest, a colossal waste of precious resources and money needed right here on Earth? Which viewpoint do you think is right?

Pro

by John P. Wiley, Jr.

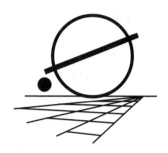

Somebody must be out there. On all those worlds circling red suns, blue suns, double suns, giant suns, pulsing suns: somewhere somebody is. Modern science stretches our intuition to the breaking point, or turns it upside down and inside out, and yet intuition is not always wrong simply because it is intuition. And intuition tells us that in a universe of billions of galaxies, each with billions of suns, there must be somebody else. If life can arise once, surely it can arise more than once.

Life elsewhere can reasonably be expected to be older than ours. The solar system we live in is only about 4.6 billion years old, a half or less than the age of the universe we see. The cosmos is filled with older stars 10 that would have older planets on which life could have arisen much longer ago than on Earth. The possibilities make the mind ache as much as do the distances involved.

Imagine ourselves walking around in 986 and speculating on what the next 1,000 years would bring. Could anyone have guessed at how much the human mind would come to understand of biology? It would be another 900 years before we even knew how diseases are transmitted. Would we have happily assented to the idea that the Earth is not the center of the universe, or that there are other galaxies? Today we smile, but can any of us guess what we will know in another 1,000 years? Not 20 to mention 10,000? My intuition fails. Yet if there are other civilizations out there, they may be not ten thousand, but ten million years older than ours. And if such a civilization developed the equivalent of open-heart

surgery, laser communications and space flight ten million years ago, what are they doing today?

As 1985 ended, scientists were looking back on a quarter century of looking for signs of such advanced civilizations with not a scintilla of evidence that any exist. During 120,000 hours of listening with the most sophisticated radio telescopes in seven different countries, we did not once hear "Breaker, breaker,"[1] strings of numbers, repeating patterns, any signals of any kind that stood out above the cosmic noise. For twenty-five years we have waited by the telephone and no one has called.

Astronomer Michael D. Papagiannis of Boston University recently reviewed the situation in *Nature*, the British science journal. He is president of Commission 51 of the International Astronomical Union: Search for Extraterrestrial Life. His vice presidents are N. S. Kardashev, a Russian, and Frank D. Drake, who in the spring of 1960 first turned a radio tele- 10 scope to a nearby star to listen for the signals of intelligent life.

According to Papagiannis, we have found nothing so far but we are about to launch our most sophisticated effort yet, and by about the year 2000 (let's make it 2001, in honor of Arthur C. Clarke) we will know a lot more about whether advanced civilizations abound in our galaxy. First Papagiannis reviews our most recent efforts, including some avenues that sound like they are straight out of science fiction. I had not realized that some have been searching with optical telescopes for artifacts, including automated probes, left in our solar system by civilizations from elsewhere. They specifically looked at the stable points in the Earth-Moon 20 and Earth-Sun gravitational systems, to see if we are being watched by a galactic equivalent of the television cameras stores use to keep an eye on us.

Astronomers in the United States and the Soviet Union have looked at stars that are unusually luminous at infrared wavelengths. They are looking for feats of astroengineering known as Dyson spheres, named for the Princeton physicist who first suggested them. To make a Dyson sphere, you simply dismantle all the planets around your star and reassemble the material in a hollow shell that envelops the star, catching large parts of its radiation (talk about an advanced civilization!). The trapped radiation 30 would be reemitted out the far side of the shell at infrared wavelengths.

Papagiannis himself is gearing up for an infrared search closer to home. Using data from the Infrared Astronomy Satellite, he is going to look for large artificial objects—things like space colonies and processing plants mining the raw materials in the asteroid belt—right here in our own solar system.

Most of the search, however, goes on with radio telescopes. Some are directed at specific places in the sky: nearby stars similar to the Sun

---

1. **"Breaker, breaker":** operator's code expression for "breaking into" a radio network—somewhat like "Hello."

have been a favorite from the first. But radio astronomers also check what Papagiannis calls magic places. The center of the galaxy, where stars are much closer together than they are in our neighborhood, way out in a spiral arm, seems an obvious place for a supercivilization and a pulsed beacon as a master navigational aid and communication channel.

Other searches swing across the entire sky. A radio telescope at Ohio State University has been searching much of the accessible sky since 1973, with some funding from NASA but dependent largely on the work of volunteers. Another whole-sky search, funded by the Planetary Society, has been conducted since March 1983 at the Oak Ridge Harvard-Smith- 10 sonian Observatory near Boston.

Now NASA is ready with the next generation of radios and signal detectors. Seeing how far we have come in just twenty-five years is exactly the kind of thing that makes me marvel at the thought of where we—or somebody else—will be in another 10,000 years. When Frank Drake first turned the Green Bank radio telescope toward the stars Epsilon Eridani and Tau Ceti that spring, he used a single-channel receiver. The new searches will be made with multichannel spectrum analyzers, instruments that can scan 8.4 million channels at the same time.

The new program is an all-California affair, centered at the NASA 20 Ames Research Center, the Jet Propulsion Laboratory, and Stanford University. Like previous efforts, it will be divided into a targeted search and an overall sky survey.

The targeted search will use large radio telescopes to look at 773 nearby stars of roughly the size and temperature of the Sun, as well as some other stars with unusual spectra.

The sky survey will use smaller radio telescopes, examining something on the order of a million sections of the sky. The whole thing could be done in five years but realistically will take more like ten, Papagiannis estimates. So if we start around 1990, we will finish up just about at the 30 turn of the century.

The search for extraterrestrial life has always been controversial. Scientists have argued that any advanced civilizations would have been here already. Since there are no signs that they have been here or are here, then they do not exist. Enrico Fermi put it simply a long time ago: "Where are they?"

The search is an old story. It is tedious (imagine looking through the computer printouts of 120,000 hours of telescope time). And, as Papagiannis says, ". . . we began to realize that none of us can claim to know how civilizations far more advanced than ours are likely to behave 40 and act."

The whole point is that we do not know that there is not a message. Intuition may be wrong, but we don't know for sure that nobody is out there. For the last twenty-five years, instead of just thinking about the question we have been doing something to answer it. We have moved from speculation to experiment. We are about to do a lot more. And wouldn't it be exciting if . . . ?

Con

by Frank Graham, Jr.

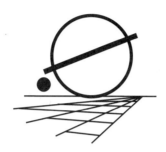

The gears are already in motion (symposia scheduled, calls for papers, even the planning of a World's Fair in Spain) to mark the quinque-centennial[2] of Columbus' arrival in the New World. The grand celebration will be, in essence, a reflection of the human impulse to reach out across time or space to other civilizations. We share the impulse, but are sometimes skeptical of the reaching out.

Consider a story in *The New York Times* about the approval of federal funds (perhaps a whopping $100 million over the next ten years) to listen for messages from "advanced civilizations" in space. Federal funding to detect signals from distant galaxies? In this time of the great budget crunch? We support pure research, but the Search for Extraterrestrial Intelligence (SETI) strikes us as catering to the UFO-chasers. Once upon a time, Senator William Proxmire routinely and aptly gave SETI's proponents not gold coins, but the Award of the Golden Fleece.[3]

What we're talking about here is not astronomy or mathematics but biology. Some astronomers, subjecting their guesstimate of the number of heavenly bodies out there to the laws of probability, calculate that there may be up to *100,000 advanced civilizations* in the Milky Way alone! From an evolutionary biologist's viewpoint, those projections are pure bunk.

2. **quinquecentennial:** 500th anniversary.
3. **Award of the Golden Fleece:** satirical "award" for scientific or military projects that, according to Senator Proxmire, waste taxpayers' money.

SETI's boosters apparently are unaware of how rare it is for *any* planet to produce the conditions needed to sustain life. Only one planet in our own solar system has done so. Yet this success (which, for all we know, is unique) required an almost incredibly precise blending of the beginnings of life at the optimum stage in our planet's development with suitable amounts of heat, light, oxygen, water, and atmospheric protection. Otherwise, life would have been doused at once. No one denies the possibility that life exists elsewhere. But the chance that it will evolve eventually into what *we* call intelligent life, capable of building technological wonders (as life improbably did on Earth after about 2.5 billion 10 years), is extremely remote. Biologists estimate that a billion species, most of them now extinct, have emerged on Earth. Most of them have got along quite nicely, living out their spans of time, without developing the kind of intelligence that sends signals to other worlds. One species managed it, but there was no guarantee that it would evolve in that direction, even under Earth's favorable conditions. Evolution is not goal-directed.

The chances of Earthlings locating intelligence away from home are as close to zero as they can get. A tidy explanation of why this is so was published last year by our most eminent evolutionary biologist, Ernst Mayr of Harvard, in an essay in his book *Toward a New Philosophy of* 20 *Biology.*

"Somehow, the supporters of SETI naively assume 'intelligence' means developing a technology capable of intragalactic or even intergalactic communication," Ernst Mayr wrote. "But such a development is highly improbable. For instance, Neanderthal Man, living 100,000 years ago, had a brain as big as ours. Yet his 'civilization' was utterly rudimentary. The wonderful civilizations of the Greeks, the Chinese, the Maya, or the Renaissance, although they were created by people who were for all intents and purposes physically identical with us, never developed such a technology, and neither did we until a few years ago. The assumption 30 that an intelligent extraterrestrial life must have the technology and mode of thinking of late twentieth-century Man is unbelievably naive."

Further, as Mayr pointed out, the timing of messages sent by the imagined spacelings would have to coincide to an almost miraculous degree with the setting up of our listening devices. Granted, some secondary benefits might accrue to us from such devices, but in this period of Gramm-Rudman,[4] the $100 million can surely be better used for grappling with cancer, or homelessness or our environmental ills.

Bill Proxmire, where are you now that we really need you?

---

4. **Gramm-Rudman:** 1985 law (sponsored by Senators Gramm, Rudman, and Hollings) requiring automatic spending cuts to hold down the federal deficit.

REVIEWING THE "PRO" AND "CON" ARTICLES _____

THE MAIN IDEA

1. The two authors have opposing views on
   (a) whether intelligent life is probable beyond Earth.
   (b) whether SETI will be successful.
   (c) whether SETI is worth funding.
   (d) all of the above.

DETAILS

2. According to the "Pro" article, compared to the age of the visible universe, our solar system is about (a) one billionth as old (b) half as old (c) the same age (d) slightly older.

3. The "Pro" writer says that the scientific search for extraterrestrial intelligence began in (a) 1960 (b) 1973 (c) 1985 (d) 1990.

4. Which article gives more information about the history of the search for extraterrestrial intelligence?
   (a) the "Pro" article
   (b) the "Con" article
   (c) Both give equal attention to the history of SETI.
   (d) Neither article discusses the history of SETI.

5. Some astronomers calculate that there may be up to 100,000 advanced civilizations in the Milky Way galaxy. The "Con" author believes that this calculation is
   (a) scientifically accurate.
   (b) probable but not yet proved.
   (c) completely possible.
   (d) absolutely ridiculous.

6. Ernst Mayr is a biologist at Harvard who
   (a) agrees with the "Pro" author's position.
   (b) agrees with the "Con" author's position.
   (c) has formed no definite opinion on SETI.
   (d) has spent his life studying UFOs.

ORDER OF EVENTS

7. *a.* Choose the letter that gives the order in which the events happen.
    (1) A radio telescope at Ohio State University begins to search the accessible sky.
    (2) A California-based search program uses multichannel spectrum analyzers.
    (3) Frank Drake searches nearby stars with the Green Bank radio telescope.
    (4) A whole-sky search is begun at the Oak Ridge Harvard-Smithsonian Observatory near Boston.
    (a) 1-2-3-4 **(b)** 2-4-3-1 **(c)** 3-1-4-2 **(d)** 4-3-2-1

    b. What is the BEST strategy for answering part *a*?
    (a) Note the order in which the events are mentioned in the article.
    (b) Look for key words such as *first, second, later,* and *finally.*
    (c) Skim the article, looking for the names of astronomers associated with the events.
    (d) Skim the article, looking for dates associated with the events.

CAUSE AND EFFECT

8. According to the "Pro" author, critics of SETI argue that advanced extraterrestrial civilizations don't exist because
    (a) life has developed only on Earth.
    (b) civilization has developed only on Earth.
    (c) they would have destroyed themselves long ago.
    (d) they would have contacted Earth by now.

9. The "Con" author objects to the use of federal funding for SETI because
    (a) the funding is illegal.
    (b) there are better ways to pay for the program.
    (c) the program could be operated more economically.
    (d) the money would be better spent on Earth's problems.

INFERENCES

10. We can infer that the "Con" article was written at a time of
    (a) cold war tensions.
    (b) economic difficulties.

(c) disillusionment with science.

(d) belief in UFOS.

11. The pronoun "we" in the first three paragraphs of the "Con" article refers to

   (a) the author and Ernst Mayr of Harvard.
   (b) all critics of SETI.
   (c) the author and Senator William Proxmire.
   (d) the author alone.

PREDICTING OUTCOMES

12. Unless the SETI scientists actually contact intelligent life beyond Earth, Congress will probably

   (a) continue its present funding for the next thousand years.
   (b) increase its funding to increase its chances for success.
   (c) decrease its funding or abandon the project completely.
   (d) make a movie based on its findings.

BUILDING YOUR VOCABULARY _____

1. As 1985 ended, scientists were looking back on a quarter century of looking for signs of such advanced civilizations with not a *scintilla* of evidence that any exist.

   Scintilla ("Pro," page 255, line 3, to page 256, line 1) means   **(a)** hope   **(b)** smallest amount   **(c)** solid block   **(d)** major breakthrough.

2. To make a Dyson sphere, you simply *dismantle* all the planets around your star and reassemble the material in a hollow sphere that envelops the star . . . .

   a. The BEST synonym for *dismantle* ("Pro," page 256, lines 27-29) is
      (a) destroy   **(b)** disassemble   **(c)** remove   **(d)** repair.

   b. The BEST clue to the meaning of *dismantle* in part *a* is to be found in

      (a) the preceding sentence.
      (b) the sentence containing the word.
      (c) the following sentence.
      (d) the word itself.

3. We have moved from *speculation* to experiment.

   In this sentence, *speculation* ("Pro," page 258, lines 4-5) means
   (a) wondering   **(b)** arguing   **(c)** gambling   **(d)** looking.

4. Yet this success (which, for all we know, is unique) required an almost incredibly precise blending of the beginnings of life at the *optimum* stage in our planet's development with suitable amounts of heat, light, oxygen, water, and atmospheric protection.

Optimum ("Con," page 260, lines 3-7) means **(a)** earliest **(b)** most optimistic **(c)** most favorable **(d)** corresponding.

5. Yet his "civilization" was utterly *rudimentary.*

Something *rudimentary* ("Con," page 260, lines 26-27) is **(a)** undeveloped **(b)** warlike **(c)** stupid **(d)** complex.

STUDYING THE WRITER'S CRAFT

1. For background information or support for their opinions, writers of *persuasive,* or *argumentative, prose* often refer to the published works of authorities, or experts in a field.

   a. Who are the authorities whose published works are used by the authors of the "Pro" and "Con" articles?

   b. In which paragraphs of each article are the writings of the experts used?

   c. For what purpose does the author of each article use the writings of the expert?

2. Authors seeking to convince us of something may cite numbers to support their arguments.

   a. How does the author of the "Pro" article use numbers in his argument *for* an advanced extraterrestrial intelligence? (*Hint*: See paragraphs 2 and 3.)

   b. How does the author of the "Con" article use numbers to support his argument *against* an advanced extraterrestrial intelligence?

3. Writers of persuasive prose often have strongly held opinions on a subject. If the writers are fair, though, they will allow the opposition to have its say.

   a. In the "Pro" article, where does the author acknowledge the critics of SETI? What is the argument of these critics?

   b. In the "Con" article, where does the author allow the proponents, or supporters, of SETI to have their say? What argument do they make in favor of advanced extraterrestrial civilizations?

ACTIVITIES FOR LISTENING, SPEAKING, WRITING

1. Imagine that searchers in the new SETI program were to discover one of the extraterrestrial artifacts mentioned in the "Pro" article: a "galactic equivalent of the television cameras stores use to keep an eye on us," a Dyson sphere, or "things like space colonies and processing plants mining raw materials in the asteroid belt—right here in our own solar system." Use your imagination to write a brief description of one of these alien artifacts or a newspaper article about it. What does it look like? What does it do? If you are handy at drawing, you might try creating an original illustration to accompany your written description or article.

2. In October 1992, astronomer Jill Tarter turned on the most powerful radio telescope ever built. The controversial one hundred million dollar NASA SETI project was launched. Currently a new and still more technologically advanced radio telescope, the Green Bank Telescope, is being built in West Virginia. What are your feelings about the time, energy, and funding allocated to these projects? Do you think SETI should be a national priority? Prepare a short, persuasive argument expressing your opinion on the issue.

3. As his final argument for SETI, the author of the "Pro" article writes, "The whole point is that we do not know that there is not a message. Intuition may be wrong, but we don't know for sure that nobody is out there." (page 258, lines 1-3) Arguments with double negatives (not . . . not) can be a bit slippery. Might we not argue, using the same reasoning, that we don't know for sure that elves or unicorns do not exist?

   The crucial questions are: (1) How does the absence of proof one way or another affect the *possibility* of the existence of something? (2) How does it affect the *probability*? Get together with a small group of your classmates to discuss these questions. Begin by agreeing on definitions for *possibility* and *probability*.

FUTURE PEOPLE
Theme 5

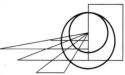

Science and technology change more than the world around us. They also change us. New developments in transportation, communication, and medicine shape and reshape our lives. Doesn't television dramatically affect the way we act and think and feel? Will genetic engineering soon alter our very bodies and minds? As a result of tomorrow's inventions, what kind of people will we become?

In the stories that follow, each writer has chosen to take only a small step into the future. The people in these stories are not alien creatures from some distant world. Instead, they are very much like us.

In "Changelings," medical technology has virtually eliminated all forms of antisocial behavior. Thanks to genetic engineering, parents in "Pursuit of Excellence" can "program" their offspring for physical and mental superiority. In "SQ," new techniques of testing for sanity challenge the entire human race.

These gifts of science and technology come with a price tag. In each story, the characters must decide whether or not they are willing to pay that price. The article that ends this theme discusses an unexpected price of science and technology. In "High-Tech Loneliness," the author explains how our inventions serve to keep us apart and lonely. As we read the stories and article that follow, we are faced with the same question: What kind of future people do we want to be?

Changelings

by Lisa Tuttle

She stared at him in a panic and snatched her hand from his. "What op—I don't remember! What's wrong with me—is this me?" Turning her face away from him, she began to cry.

Pick up today's newspaper. Switch on your radio or TV. If you turn to the news, it's all bad now, or nearly. Drunk driving takes a daily toll of young people's lives. Drugs and guns turn our streets into bloody battle-fields. Violence—against women, against children, against everybody—dominates the news.

Suppose now that future technology could offer a simple cure for criminal behavior. Instead of locking people up in prisons at great expense and then letting them out again only to repeat their crimes, why not cure them once and for all?

In "Changelings," Lisa Tuttle explores this question through the life of an ordinary American family. Being concerned about our future as a people, she extends the original question with grim logic. What if the cure were used first on criminals, later on potential criminals, and eventually on anyone who disagrees? What if people volunteered to be cured? Would you?

Lisa Tuttle

As a columnist, journalist, and teacher of courses in science fiction, Lisa Tuttle has worked in both the United States and England. Her first science-fiction novel, *Windhaven* (1980), was written in collaboration with George R.R. Martin. Since then, she has written other books not only of science fiction (*Familiar Spirit*, 1983), but also of horror (*A Nest of Nightmares*, 1986) and feminism (*Heroines: Women Inspired by Women*, 1988).

Much of Lisa Tuttle's finest work appears in her short stories. They have been published in many science-fiction magazines and anthologies. In 1974, her stories won her the John W. Campbell Memorial Award. Some of her best stories, such as "Changelings," deftly combine human interest and horror.

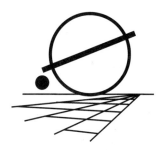

Ryan turned away from the window. The house felt empty; the silence was not right. He knew that he should hear the soft sounds of his wife getting his daughter ready for bed.

Annie walked in naked.

"Annie," Ryan said, gently reproving. He went to kneel beside her. Her hair lay in moist curls around her head, and there were tiny droplets of water all over her body. The damp patch on the carpet where she stood began to spread. She turned her brilliant blue eyes, her mother's eyes, on Ryan and said accusingly, "Mommy didn't come dry me off."

Ryan smoothed her damp hair. Russet, he thought, auburn. The love-liest words for the loveliest color. It reminded him of autumn. He pressed 10 his face against her head, but she smelled of Ivory soap and childhood, not of apples or leaves.

She pulled away, putting her hands on her hips, and made a mouth at him, the way she had seen her mother do. "Daddy. It's my bedtime."

"I'll put you to bed," he said. "You shouldn't run around naked, you know."

"Well, Mommy didn't *come*. I was looking for her."

"A child."

Ryan and Annie looked up together. May stood in the doorway, her hair mussed, her face soft and slightly puffy, as if she had been asleep.

"There's a child, a little girl. Ryan?"

"Annie, sweetheart—"

But she had run to her mother. "I waited and waited but you didn't come."

"Ryan?"

"Annie, sweetheart," Ryan said. "Run to your room and put on your jammies. Mommy and I will be in to kiss you goodnight in a minute." 10

"Mommy, why didn't you come dry me? Mommy? Why? Mommy?" Annie tugged at May's full skirt. Ryan caught the note in her voice that presaged tears. Poor Annie. She knew. She could sense it.

Dawning panic on May's face as she bent to enfold Annie's wet body to her. Her eyes did not leave Ryan's. "Oh, Ryan. This is—oh, Ryan—"

"Annie."

"Annie," May murmured. She stood up, holding Annie, and bent her face into Annie's neck. "Annie, Annie. Oh, Annie."

Annie threw her arms around her mother's neck and buried her face 20 against her. But she said nothing. She was not reassured.

"I'll take her to bed?" May asked.

"At the end of the hall."

"Wait for me."

Ryan sank into the couch and stared at the Van Gogh print on the opposite wall. Crazy old Van Gogh. He had cut off his own ear. Ryan wondered what they had done to him after that.

"Five years, Ryan. At least five years." May came and sat beside him on the couch, taking his hand between hers. "How old is she? Of course we called her Annie, after my sister, right?" 30

Ryan nodded wearily.

"This has happened before, hasn't it, Ryan? It's happened before? Has it?"

"Yes."

"But I don't remember! I don't! We were married, the two of us, together, here—" she touched the couch and looked around. "Here, in this house. But no Annie, no children. Oh, Ryan, what does it mean? How could I lose—five years? Or more? How could it happen? Why? What is it?"

"You just forget things," he said very softly. 40

"But why? Always? Will my memory come back? Why?"

"The operation. It's something to do with that."

She stared at him in a panic and snatched her hand from his. "What op—I don't remember! What's wrong with me—is this me?" Turning her face away from him, she began to cry.

Ryan stood and went to the window, where he stared out at the placid streets. The pools of light beneath each streetlamp were empty. The neighborhood was silent. People didn't go out much after dark anymore, though the streets were safer than they had ever been. He turned back into the room. May had stopped crying. She had never been one for crying.

She said, "When I was little, my sister Annie told me that every seven years each cell in a person's body has been replaced. I guess I was about five then. It really worried me. She told me that every seven years you become a completely new person. A *different* person. I used to be afraid. I thought that when I was seven, I wouldn't remember the old me. I thought that if my brain cells were all replaced then," she turned her palms upward into the air, "poof go my memories."

"But by the time you were seven, you had forgotten about it. Until Annie reminded you."

"I've told you this before?"

Ryan nodded.

"The last time I forgot? Is it like this every time?"

"Not exactly."

"How often? How long has this been going on? Have we been to the doctor?"

"More than one. There's nothing . . . nothing that can be done. It might be just an immediate reaction, and it should stop soon." But her periods of amnesia had been increasing in frequency.

"What operation was this?" May asked.

"Government sponsored for a better future."

She glanced at him sharply. "A volunteer thing?"

"Not in the least. People turned each other in—and then, of course, there were the criminals, and those on file as subversives."

"Of course. I was a subversive in college. A teen-age radical. What did the operation do to me?"

"Made you a better, happier citizen. The object was to remove your destructive tendencies and install something, a tracer device, so that if you should backslide, they could find you."

"Are you . . . ?"

"No. There's a new bill up, though, about 'testing for subversive and criminal potentiality,' and if it passes, which it will . . ."

May stared at the floor. "I don't remember. I could have been in fairyland for the past five years. Or what Annie told me about being made new, or—"

"Or you could be a changeling."

She looked up. "How did you know—"

"That was the story Annie wanted?"

She nodded. "I told her no story tonight."

"But she never goes to sleep without a story."

"She was very good about it. Very quiet. She—I suppose she could feel there was something wrong, that I was different. I didn't even know what drawer her pajamas were in. Oh, Ryan, can't we do something? When will I be all right again?"

Ryan shrugged, caught her look of need. "I'm sorry, but it varies. A few hours or a few days." 10

"Never any longer?"

He shook his head. Last time it had been six days before her memory came back. The duration grew longer, and the time between occurrences lessened. The first time she had been set back only to the time of the operation.

"Can we call a doctor?"

"I told you—"

"Oh, please, darling—just let's call Ben. It will make me feel better to talk to him. He knows about me?"

20

Ryan nodded. "I'll call him."

She leaned across the couch to hug him, and he pulled her to him, holding on tight.

May went back into the bedroom while Ryan called Ben. "I'll just lie down for a while," she said.

Ben would come, of course. He was the family doctor and a long-time family friend. He promised to be by within an hour.

Ryan went into the bedroom. It was dark, but the curtains were open, and there was some light from the street. He saw the gleam of May's eyes.

"I didn't mean to disturb you," he said.

30

"I'm not sleepy. He's coming?"

"In about an hour."

"Oh?"

"I told him it wasn't an emergency. Really, darling, we can't just break up his whole evening."

"I'm sorry."

"Don't be silly."

He went to the dresser, to the box that held the cuff links and tie clips he never wore, relics of a time past.

He took out a folded, brittle newspaper clipping and unfolded it by the window in a shaft of light from the streetlamp, although he knew the picture well enough to look at it in the dark.

40

It had been a front-page photo. May's head was sandwiched between two others, leaning out of the window of an occupied building. A banner proclaiming the building's liberation stretched below them. Three arms thrust forward in jubilant fists. And May's face, smiling, alive, victorious . . . holy.

"For this," he said softly.

"Ryan? What are you—oh. I wish you'd throw that away. I don't like it." He turned and saw that she had raised herself on her elbows. "That's not me. It was a stupid, violent time that we grew up in. You had the sense then . . . I didn't. I'm a different person now, though. I don't know how I could have ever been like that . . . I can't even remember what it felt like."

"Of course you can't." He folded the paper and put it in his back pocket.

"Ryan? Come here." Her voice was shy.

"Not now," he said, as gently as he could, and left the room without touching her.

He didn't like the way the living room felt, and he knew the rest of the house would be no better. He felt like a deserter, but he went outside. He would walk for a few minutes.

Outside was no better. It was quiet and the air felt thick and still. He could taste the smog. He began to walk, hoping he would see someone to speak to, but he saw no one. He headed up toward the highway, toward a diner he had occasionally stopped in for a cup of coffee.

The diner, when he reached it, was empty except for the counterman, its emptiness made the more vivid by the merciless fluorescent lights shining down endlessly on all the hard, clean, bright surfaces.

"Evening," said the counterman cheerily. "What can I do for you?"

Ryan straddled one of the high brown stools. "Just a Coke. Thanks."

"This is a slow time," the counterman said. "Past the regular dinner hour, but not so late that other places are closed. You live nearby, don't you? We don't get many walking in—when I saw you didn't have a car, I knew you must be from nearby. There y'are—anything else?"

"No, thanks."

"Walk for your health?"

"I just wanted some air."

"Nice night for walking, I guess. Real warm for this late in the season."

Ryan wished another customer would come in. The counterman's persistent friendliness made him uncomfortable, and his physical appearance inspired dislike in Ryan: the shining head beneath thinning hair, the watery blue eyes, the horsey teeth beneath the stiff ginger mustache. . . . Ryan turned his attention to the voice from the radio that was playing at the end of the counter. It was a news broadcast, full of hopeful messages about the state of the union. There was less and less coverage given to the rest of the world these days—no one wanted to hear about wars or crime.

The counterman seemed to follow Ryan's attention. "Gives you hope, doesn't it?"

"What?"

"The news. It's all good now, or nearly. Just remember how it was 10 ten years ago—or even five. People didn't go out on the streets—you wouldn't have gone out for fresh air unless you were crazy. You would have been beaten up and robbed. Mugged." He said the word as if it were foreign and he wasn't sure of the pronunciation.

"Thanks to the operation," Ryan said.

"That, and other things. The government finally cracking down on criminals. Democracy is great, but people have to *deserve* it. There were a lot of changes that had to be made."

"Did you have the operation?" Ryan asked.

"Me? No. I've always been a good citizen. I've always done my duty." 20 The way the counterman looked at him made Ryan uneasy, and he had to caution himself against paranoia. The day May was in the hospital he had gone around all day suspecting people of spying on him, of being out to get him, of making accusations disguised as innocuous conversation.

Ryan realized that he was standing, fumbling in his pocket for change.

"I've got to be going," he said. "I didn't tell my wife I was going out—she'll worry—"

"But you didn't drink your Coke."

"I guess I'm not thirsty." He put a quarter on the counter. 30

The counterman pushed it back. "I won't charge you for it, then. Drink it myself." He smiled. "Have a good walk." His "Come back again" was cut off by the closing of the heavy glass door.

Headlights cut across Ryan's face as he turned up his driveway, and he felt the familiar paranoid beating of his heart as he realized the car was turning into his driveway just behind him.

"Ryan? Is anything wrong?"

It was Ben.

"No, no. I just stepped out for some air."

"Well, you stepped into the wrong place for it," Ben said, getting 40 out of his car. "Phew. It stinks tonight. Supposed to clear by tomorrow, though."

Ben was one year away from compulsory retirement. He'd chosen to continue working through the past two optional years. They went into the house together.

"May's in the bedroom, resting."

"Fine." He scrutinized Ryan's face. "You shouldn't let this get to you, you know. I'm sure it's only some preliminary adjustment."

"Why don't you go in and see her?" Ryan knew that Ben would catch the hard edge of dismissal in his voice, knew also that Ben would not be offended by it.

"Sure, sure," Ben said. He put his hand on Ryan's shoulder. "Take it easy." 10

Ryan sank into the couch, ignoring the voices that came quietly from the other room.

"She'll sleep now," Ben said when he came out of the bedroom. "Could I trouble you for a cup of coffee?" He followed Ryan into the kitchen.

"What did you tell her?"

"She just wanted to talk."

"She's sleeping, you said?"

"No, but it shouldn't be long."

"Why didn't you just turn her off?"

"I wouldn't do that, Ryan." 20

"Why not? You're a doctor; you should know all about implants. I turned her off myself, once. Accidentally. I was frantic until I found the place again to turn her back on."

"The little death," said the doctor.

"No. More like turning off and turning on a doll. Ben, they've taken my wife away from me and given me a docile robot-housekeeper. They destroyed her! Now she's losing her past—"

"It's nothing to worry about, Ryan. This whole business of the memory—it will pass, I promise you."

"How do you know? Maybe for some people—but when they're 30 tampering with minds—it could get worse. She'll be nothing but a shell, without memories, and they'll reprogram her into a model citizen—that's what they—"

"Your voice, Ryan—lower your voice."

Ryan took a coffee cup and saucer out of the cupboard, his hands shaking.

"How did we let this happen, Ben? How could we? It won't stop. It was only the criminals at first—but they took my wife, my sweet, beautiful May just because she was on their bloody list."

"She wasn't harmed, Ryan. You're being overly dramatic. You must 40 face up to the fact that May had certain . . . tendencies and beliefs that could be harmful."

"She never did anything! They forced her to have this op—"

"Calm down, Ryan. If May had had an illness you would have wanted it operated on, removed—"

"The analogy doesn't hold, *Doctor*. May used to be interested and aggressive and very alive. She wanted to change things—she was a constructive person, not a destructive one. You've seen the change—you can't say it's for the better. I can't believe this is you, Ben, spouting—" Ryan stopped, comprehension dawning. "You. You've had the operation, too. You have an implant like May, haven't you, Ben?"

"Yes. Yes, I have. But don't you see—" 10

"Why you?" Ryan asked softly. "You've never been a radical."

"I was against the operations at first. I thought that they removed the will. Now I understand—"

"Of course. And now you're a puppet as well."

"You're being paranoid. There is no great 'they' corrupting us—we run our own lives."

"Oh, we let it happen, all right. We wanted to burn out the badness in our criminals. Then in our potential criminals. Then in anyone who disagrees. Change their minds. Indoctrinate our children."

"Ryan, it's all for the good." 20

"It always is. The good of the State. Well, damn the State!"

"As your doctor and your friend I must advise you to stop this foolish talk. Get some sleep. Take a vacation. Don't worry so much."

"That's a great prescription. This country has gone rotten precisely because we've closed our eyes."

Ben turned away. "I'd better leave now."

Ryan saw his own hand go out toward the back of Ben's neck. His fingers found it, pressed, and he caught Ben before he could hit the floor. The implant was in the same place as May's.

"How convenient," he murmured. He looked up from the sleeping 30 Ben to see Annie standing in the doorway in a long blue nightgown, her little bare feet curling on the linoleum as she watched in silence. In a year she would have to go to kindergarten, and they would begin on her, feeding her drugs for docility and propaganda in the name of education.

"Is Doctor Ben sick?"

"Just sleeping, hon. Run back to bed now."

"Can't sleep."

"Sure you can."

"No story," she said, widening her eyes at him. A finger went to her 40 mouth, and she chewed it thoughtfully, staring at him.

"Run back to bed, and Daddy will come tell you a story."

When she had gone, he laid Ben down in some semblance of comfort. He thought about going to Canada. He had thought about it before. Things weren't much better up there, but in Canada and in the northwestern states like Washington and Oregon the underground was supposed to be strong. May had told him that, before the operation. They should have gotten out then, but when you've spent your whole life, as Ryan had, accepting and obeying, it was hard to give up everything and go.

If he went now, he would have to leave May. He couldn't take her—the implant was part tracer, and the police would have them back as soon 10 as they were missed.

He went back into the bedroom.

"Darling? Has Ben gone?"

"Yeah."

"I didn't hear his car. I was listening for it."

"You should be asleep."

"I know. Is Annie still up?"

"Yes, she came out and saw Ben."

"Oh. I heard her—I didn't hear any other voices—I don't know, I thought she was playing with the phone. I must have been dozing." 20

"Of course you were. Go back to sleep. The sooner you do, the sooner it will be morning."

She laughed. "Like Christmas. If I wait for Santa, he'll never come. Ryan . . ."

He went to her, bent over, and kissed her. His hand went behind her neck and pressed, and her lips fell slack and asleep beneath his.

He went into Annie's room and helped her to dress, telling her that they were going for a ride.

"But it's late."

"Not for grown-up people. And you're not asleep, anyway. You like 30 to go for rides."

"Yes," she said doubtfully. "Will Mommy come?"

"No. Mommy's sleeping."

"Like Doctor Ben?"

He looked down at her sharply.

"You turned him off, didn't you?"

"What do you mean?"

"You turned off Doctor Ben."

"What do you know about things like that? Where did you hear it?"

"I just know." Her eyes grew vague. She looked away. "Can I bring 40 Raggedy Ann?" Ryan picked up the doll from the bedside table, where it slumped against the pink Princess telephone.

The streets were eerily empty. Didn't people go out anymore? Ryan turned on the radio in the car and settled into driving.

"The President spoke to the nation this afternoon, expressing his gratitude to the people of the United States for making such a drastic drop in the crime rate possible. Reminding his listeners that 'Eternal vigilance is the price of freedom,' Mr.—"

Ryan punched the key for another station and got some bouncy, innocuous music.

"We learned that in school," Annie said suddenly.

"What?"   10

"Eternal vigilance."

"Annie, you don't go to school."

"Ballet school. I do so."

"You learned that in ballet school?"

"Miss Fontaine tells us lots of things."

"Not always about ballet, I take it." He had convinced May that ballet lessons would be more useful to Annie than nursery school. There were no more safe places.

"You shouldn't have," she said.

"What?" She was as uncanny as her mother about reaching into his 20 thoughts.

"Done what you did to Doctor Ben. That's against the law. And the things you said to him. They were wrong, too."

"How long were you spying on us?" Fat, ugly spiders were crawling up his spine. His sweat made him cold. He looked at her. She was leaning away from him, her face close to the window, fogging it with her breath and tracing lines with one finger. "Answer me!" Her left hand crept to her mouth at the sharpness in his voice.

"It was against the law," she whispered.

"Annie—" With an effort he gentled his voice, returned most of his at- 30 tention to the road. They were on the freeway now, heading out of town, and there was some traffic. "Annie, you know your Daddy wouldn't do anything wrong. Sometimes the laws are wrong, and people must change them."

"People change laws by voting. People who break laws are sick and they must be helped." The words were not hers; her voice was virtuous and intent.

"Does Miss Fontaine tell you that, too?"

"Nuh-uh. That's Sargent Dare."

"Who's Sargent Dare?"

"*You* know. On TV."   40

"The TV doesn't always tell you the truth, punkin. Life isn't that simple. The TV is wrong sometimes, but what your parents tell you—"

"Tell me a story. You said you would. Tell me the one about the changeling."

"I don't know that one."

"Yes you *do*. About how the fairies come and steal away the human baby and put a fairy child in its place—yes you *do* know it. Tell me."

"Not while I'm driving, sweetheart." Glancing down at her, he saw that she was near tears. She should have been asleep long ago, poor kid. "Look, why don't you climb over into the back seat and lie down and go to sleep?"

"Story first."   10

"You'll have to give me time to think of one, then."

"OK."

But all he could think of was May, how she had been before, and the way they had changed her. Annie began to speak then, and he pulled himself out of bitterness to listen.

"On Sargent Dare there was this show where this boy's parents were very bad people." She was speaking to her Raggedy Ann doll, Ryan saw. She used that ploy often, dragging the doll into a room where her parents were occupied, and talking to it, meaning for them to hear as well. "They weren't really bad people, but they were sick. They had bad thoughts, and 20 so they broke the law. They broke the law a whole lot, but nobody knew about it except their little boy. Then he learned in school about the law and so he called the police and told them. He remembered the number.

"But don't worry, Raggedy, they didn't put his parents in jail. The police are our friends. They help us. They took his parents and did a little operation and made them happy. They came home and they smiled and they never broke the law again and they gave the little boy presents. And they all lived happily ever after."

There was a road block up ahead. A routine police check. One of the measures that was ridding the country of crime. Ryan had been through 30 a dozen of them, at least. He slowed the car, his throat tight.

He felt Annie sliding closer to him on the seat. She put her hand on his arm.

"We'll live happily?" she asked. "Happily ever after?"

REVIEWING THE STORY

THE MAIN IDEA

1. The central conflict in the story can be summarized as Ryan against
   (a) his wife (b) nature (c) his society (d) himself.

DETAILS

2. Most of the story takes place in a **(a)** hospital **(b)** home **(c)** diner **(d)** car.

3. The main character is **(a)** Ben **(b)** May **(c)** Annie **(d)** Ryan.

4. The "changelings" in the story are
    (a) characters on Sargent Dare's TV show.
    (b) government agents who control people's minds.
    (c) citizens who have been subjected to mind control.
    (d) members of the underground in Canada, Washington, and Oregon.

5. Two persons who have had the government-sponsored operation are **(a)** Ryan and May **(b)** May and Annie **(c)** Ben and May **(d)** Ryan and Ben.

6. Of all the characters in the story,
    (a) only the counterman is Ryan's true friend.
    (b) only Ryan wants to escape.
    (c) only Annie is on Ryan's side.
    (d) Ben is the only one Ryan can trust.

ORDER OF EVENTS

7. Choose the letter of the event that happens FIRST in the story.
    (a) Ryan goes out to the local diner.
    (b) May undergoes the operation and implant.
    (c) Annie tells her father about Sargent Dare's TV show.
    (d) Ben pays a house call to see May.

CAUSE AND EFFECT

8. All of the following are effects of the government-sponsored operation EXCEPT **(a)** less crime **(b)** memory loss **(c)** disobedience **(d)** obedience.

9. Annie's mind has been influenced by **(a)** an operation **(b)** a teacher and TV **(c)** the underground in Canada **(d)** Ben.

INFERENCES

10. Ryan "turned off" Ben in order to
    (a) prevent Ben from reporting him to the police.
    (b) enable Ben to sleep better that night.

    (c) be able to speak to May in private.

    (d) show Annie that her father obeyed the law.

11. We can infer that Annie used the telephone to

    (a) call Doctor Ben about her mother.

    (b) report her father to the police.

    (c) tell Sargent Dare about changelings.

    (d) tell Miss Fontaine she would be late for ballet class.

PREDICTING OUTCOMES

12. We can predict that Ryan will probably

    (a) escape to join the underground.

    (b) return home to "wake up" Ben and May.

    (c) send his daughter to Canada without him.

    (d) be caught and forced to have the operation.

BUILDING YOUR VOCABULARY _____

1. "Annie," Ryan said, gently *reproving*.

    Reproving (page 270, line 5) most nearly means **(a)** convincing **(b)** praising **(c)** scolding **(d)** demanding.

2. Ryan stood and went to the window, where he stared out at the *placid* streets.

    Streets that are *placid* (page 272, lines 4-5) are **(a)** flat **(b)** peaceful **(c)** busy **(d)** threatening.

3. But her periods of *amnesia* had been increasing in frequency.

    People with *amnesia* (page 272, lines 25-26) suffer from **(a)** dizzy spells **(b)** memory loss **(c)** weakness **(d)** rage.

4. The counterman's *persistent* friendliness made him uncomfortable. . . .

    The BEST synonym for *persistent* (page 274, lines 39-40) is **(a)** false **(b)** hesitant **(c)** peculiar **(d)** continuing.

5. The way the counterman looked at him made Ryan uneasy, and he had to caution himself against *paranoia*.

    a. *Paranoia* (page 275, lines 21-22) is an irrational

        (a) fear of high places.

        (b) suspicion and fear of other people.

(c) distress at feeling closed in.

(d) belief that one is seriously ill.

b. The BEST clue to the meaning of *paranoia* is in the

(a) word itself.

(b) sentence preceding the one containing the word.

(c) sentence containing the word.

(d) sentence following the one containing the word.

STUDYING THE WRITER'S CRAFT

1. In describing Ryan's speech and gestures, the author frequently uses adverbs to *characterize* Ryan and his feelings about his wife. For example: " 'You just forget things,' he said very softly." Here the adverb *softly* tells how Ryan spoke.

   a. Give several other examples of such adverbs in the first part of the story (pages 270-274), before Ryan goes out for a walk.

   b. Taken together, what do these adverbs suggest about Ryan's character?

   c. What do the adverbs reveal about Ryan's feelings about his wife May?

2. To make ideas or feelings clearer and more vivid, the author sometimes uses *metaphors*. Unlike similes, these figures of speech compare two things without using the words *like* or *as*. You can use metaphors to enrich your own writing.

   a. In the line "Of course. And now you're a puppet as well" (page 277, line 14), who is speaking? Who is being compared to a puppet? How does the comparison help us understand what the speaker means?

   b. In the line "Fat, ugly spiders were crawling up his spine" (page 279, lines 24-25), to whom do the words "his spine" refer? What feeling is being compared to "fat, ugly spiders"? How does the comparison make that feeling stronger and more vivid?

3. *Foreshadowing* is a clue, a hint of events or information to come. May, speaking to Ryan about their daughter Annie, says, "Oh. I heard her—I didn't hear any other voices—I don't know, I thought she was playing with the phone. I must have been dozing." (page 278, lines 19-20) By the end of the story, what can we infer was actually happening when May heard Annie playing with the phone?

ACTIVITIES FOR LISTENING, SPEAKING, WRITING

1. Choose one of the following scenarios. Then get together with others in your class who made the same choice and discuss this scenario. At the end of ten minutes, write down what you would do in this situation, and why. Be prepared to read your paper to the whole class.

   What would you do in one of the following situations?

   a. You learn that a close friend has stolen a car for a joyride.

   b. You discover that your best friend is carrying a handgun in school.

   c. You find out that your brother or sister is selling drugs to elementary school children.

   d. You discover that your parent was the driver in a hit-and-run accident that killed a child.

2. In this story, Ryan represents most people in our present society, while May, Annie, and Ben represent one kind of imagined future people. In what ways does Ryan differ from the others? Which kind of person would make a better citizen today? Why? Be prepared to discuss your answers with your classmates.

3. Imagine that Ryan has been caught by the police in the roadblock. The government Committee on Subversives has recommended that Ryan have the implant operation. Write a persuasive letter to the President in which you argue either for or against the operation on Ryan. (If you oppose the operation, perhaps you had better not sign your real name to the letter.)

Pursuit of Excellence

by Rena Yount

Evelyn had come to dislike her own face in the mirror. A crowd of norms on the street looked to her like a rough sketch of humanity, with their splotchy complexions and brownish hair, their bodies lumpy, slouched, unfinished.

Wanting to look like our female or male ideal is nothing new. We spend millions of dollars each year to make ourselves look thinner, fitter, or sexier. We take endless time and pains to create bigger muscles or the hair styles of our favorite movie stars. But these are cosmetic improvements, only partial changes of image.

With new advances in the science of genetics, more profound and permanent changes in human beings might become possible. Genes are the master blueprint for every living organism. These tiny cells dictate how and when each part of the organism develops. As recently as 1990, doctors used gene therapy successfully for the first time. They replaced a defective gene with a healthy one in the body of a little girl who would have died otherwise of a fatal inherited disorder. Since then, scientists have made rapid advances in their ability to manipulate genes in both animals and humans.

Beyond gene therapy lies the possibility of genetic engineering, or bioengineering. Instead of altering a few defective genes in a fully developed organism, scientists would program entire patterns of genes in the organism's earliest stage of life. Gene therapy is already science fact. Genetic engineering is still science fiction.

In "Pursuit of Excellence," Evelyn Barr plans her second child. With the help of genetic engineering, her daughter would enjoy perfect health.

She would begin life with the head start of high intelligence and other gifts. Most important to Evelyn, the child must also look like other bioengineered people—with a body designed and sculpted to order like a work of art.

As you read this story of future people, think about Evelyn's values—the things she thinks are important. Do you agree with them?

Rena Yount

Rena Yount has worked at a variety of jobs: graphic designer, editor, data librarian. She has also written articles and books on subjects as varied as music, health care, and zookeeping.

As a graduate of the famous Clarion Writers Workshop, she submitted her short story "Pursuit of Excellence" to the Clarion Writers Contest. The story won third prize. It also became her first published piece of science fiction.

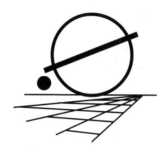

It was a late summer afternoon, and the city of Washington lay quiet in a warm light rain. A minibus hissed over wet pavement, gliding driverless through the traffic loop at Calvert Street, past the towers and multilevel malls, the pedwalks where shoppers rode with their bright umbrellas. Evelyn Barr sat by a bus window: a slender woman in her thirties, with wide cheekbones and a pointed chin.

She was tired. She worked days as a chemist and most evenings as a waitress. She would just have time, today, to stop by home and make sure everything was all right before heading on to her second job. But she watched the rain-blurred mosaic of the passing city with an almost proprietary sense of satisfaction. It was a smoother, cleaner, brighter city than it had been when she moved into it fifteen years before. Make better people, she thought, and they will put the rest of the world in order. 10

My daughter will be one of them, she thought, the familiar tingle of anticipation coming warm and strong. The time was getting close at last.

As she let herself into her apartment, she called, "Randy?"

"In here, Mom," her nine-year-old answered. She went into his room to give him a kiss. His terminal was on and covered with graphs. "Homework?" she asked. 20

"Yeah. I want to get done before Dad gets home so he can help me with my model satellite."

"Good thinking," she said. She ruffled his hair. It was dark, like hers, but curly and unruly, while hers was straight and fine. He had her brown eyes, and her dimples when he smiled.

"Did you lay out your clothes to wash?" she asked.

"Uh-huh. Then I put them in the washer with the other stuff. Then I washed them. It seemed like a good idea. They're in the dryer now."

"Wonderful!" she said. "Now I'll have time for a cup of coffee before I go."

He looked up at her sideways. "Can I have some too?"

"Coffee? Now, you know that's not for children. It'd keep you awake 10 all night."

"Just a little? I did the laundry."

"Well—just a little. With milk."

She hung up her raincoat and went into the kitchen to check the freezer. She and her husband Michael cooked on the weekends and froze portions for dinner during the week. Usually Michael would be home on nights when she worked, but sometimes his own job as production manager for a small publisher kept him late. Randy had had to mature more quickly than a lot of kids; they counted on him to take care of himself when he had to, and to help with work around the 20 apartment.

"What would you like for dinner?" she called to him. "Chicken casserole or nut loaf?"

"Which one did I cut up the mushrooms for?" he asked.

"Nut loaf," she said.

"I want that one."

"Fine," she said, smiling. She began making a salad. The kitchen was small, like all the rooms in their apartment; housing was expensive. But it was neat and well organized, an easy place to work. She moved quickly from sink to counter, rinsing and chopping lettuce and green 30 peppers. Randy called from his room. "Guess what I got for homework."

She set one oven compartment on Thaw/Cook and started the timer. "What?" she asked.

"I get to be president this week."

"Of the class?"

"No, silly. Of Skolania. That's the country our class gets to be, for simulation. Come and look."

"Just a minute." She put Michael's dinner in another compartment and set the controls. As she went into Randy's room she said, "Now, your dinner will be ready in half an hour, so listen for the bell. And don't forget 40 to start Dad's at eight, because he'll be home at eight-thirty and he'll be hungry. It's all set—just push 'Start.' "

"Look at this," Randy said.

"And there's salad in the refrigerator. Are you listening?"

"Sure. Eight o'clock. In the refrigerator. I'll remember. Look here."

He was standing before his terminal. There was a stool for him to sit on, but he rarely used it. He preferred to bounce from foot to foot, jiggling, his slim body full of energy.

"OK," she said, perching on the stool. "I'm looking."

"See, for this project we have five variables. There's population—that's how many people you have. And there's money for agriculture—that's how much you spend for seeds and tractors and stuff. Then there's money for defense, to buy planes and everything, and workers for agriculture, and workers for defense. And if you're president, you have to mess around with all of those so they come out right. Only Kenny Blake was president last week, and boy, did he leave everything in a mess."

Evelyn smiled. Even kids blamed the previous administration.

"See, if you put more money in for agriculture, you get more soybeans." He moved a control, and little rows of green soybean plants ran up one side of the screen. "For a while. But then you don't get any more unless you put more *workers* in too. To use all the tractors and junk. But that means less workers for defense." Sure enough, little blue figures with rifles were disappearing from the DEFENSE graph as he turned a knob. "And Botania, that's the other fourth-grade class, they might start a war. I mean, maybe they won't, but they might. Mary Sue's in that class, and she *loves* to start wars. But, see, if you don't get enough soybeans, then people will starve. Only, you know what?"

"What?" she asked.

He leaned close to the stool and whispered to her. A secret. "I *hate* soybeans."

Suddenly he was bouncing up and down, twirling knobs, yelling, "Yukh! Die, soybeans! Down with soybeans!" Evelyn laughed. Little green plants blipped off the screen by the dozen, the population chart began to glow a warning red, and then a yellow neon flashing began: FAMINE. FAMINE.

Randy giggled, looking at her sideways. "I wouldn't *really* do that," he explained.

"I'm sure you wouldn't."

"I just like to hear what the vice-president's going to say." He flicked a switch, and a voice began. It was deep, grave, adult. "Mr. President, I must direct your attention to a matter of the utmost seriousness. Famine has now reached the following levels—"

Randy cut off the voice, giggling again. "He sounds just like a news announcer."

He punched BREAK and CLS, wiping the screen. Then he pushed RUN and started over, this time in earnest.

Evelyn watched him for a few minutes as he stood, frowning a little, absorbed in the balance he was seeking on the screen. She remembered when school had been like that for her: a challenge and an adventure. She remembered discovering chemistry when she was not much older than Randy. She had loved it even then. How enthralled she had been by the orderly mystery of the world's workings. What a grand kingdom science had seemed to her then; what dreams she had had of the work she would do someday. She had set her heart on being a discoverer, a 10 creator—back when she still thought someone like her could be a real scientist. Watching Randy, her heart ached with pity and loss. Too late, too late, for Randy and for her. A generation ago, she would have been so proud of this boy.

The Augustus, where Evelyn worked evenings, was a small, discreetly inconspicuous restaurant near the Capitol. It was elegantly furnished in dark wood and leather. Evelyn changed into her uniform and began laying out silverware in preparation for the dinner rush. A busboy, passing her, whispered, "Watch out for Jordan; he's in a real mood tonight."
20
Evelyn nodded. Jordan, the owner, was touchy and harsh with the staff. Perhaps he felt their contempt for one of the bioengineered who had not made anything of himself. But it was undoubtedly because of Jordan that the Augustus had developed its particular clientele.

There was not any one thing to set them apart, yet it was impossible to walk into the restaurant and not recognize that almost everyone there was engineered. Their height was part of it, the healthy vigor and perfect proportions, and the ease of those born to prosperity. Each was striking. Some were the slender, flawless blonds so popular when bioengineering began. But it had not taken long for more exotic looks to catch on. The 30 senator at the table nearest Evelyn was massively built, with a regal African face and blue-black skin. She wondered if his parents were black. The woman across from him looked like an Incan princess, gold jangling from her wrists and ears. In the corner sat a young woman, a federal judge, with the perfect oval face and delicate figure of a woman in a seventeenth-century Chinese painting. Her skin, like that of ladies in such paintings, was dead white.

Evelyn had come to dislike her own face in the mirror. A crowd of norms on the street looked to her like a rough sketch of humanity, with their splotchy complexions and brownish hair, their bodies lumpy, 40 slouched, unfinished. The people in the restaurant were as elegant and vivid as portraits in stained glass.

She went to wait on a man with sand-pale skin and a wiry mane of golden hair. She thought of ancient walls carved with winged lions when she saw his face: beaked nose, deep lines curving down around the full lips, fierce upswept brows. He looked up to give his order, and his eyes were blood-red.

She walked back toward the kitchen, disturbed by those eyes. They gave him a mad look. There was more and more experimentation going on with appearance, and probably with other things as well. Not everyone would be stopped by the official limits on bioengineering. The engineered were mostly the children of the powerful, and they gathered 10 more power by their own abilities. Where there was power enough, rules would bend.

Waitresses are invisible people. In her work Evelyn heard bits of talk about corporate dealings and government policy centers, universities, publishing, research—all the places where the engineered naturally concentrated. She knew what it meant when a name was mentioned, and someone said, "A five?" and someone else nodded: one of the five percent, one of us.

She and Michael had argued for a long time about engineering their child's appearance. "All this money to engineer high intelligence, good 20 health—I can see that," Michael said. "It's not that important how she looks." Evelyn said, "She has to be recognized as one of them. It'll make a difference in whether she forms the relationships she'll need, whether she really belongs." He shook his head in disapproval and disbelief. "You make it sound like some kind of exclusive club."

"It is!" she said. "The most exclusive club that's ever existed. Members recognize each other instantly, across a room. They give jobs to each other and marry each other and have kids like themselves, or better. The engineered are different from us, Michael. They know it. The difference gets bigger all the time. We can push our daughter across the line before 30 it's too late. . . ."

Evelyn picked up a drink for the red-eyed man, soup for the senator and the princess. She thought of Michael in his production department, supervising other norms. He rarely had direct contact with the engineered writers and editors. Maybe he really did not understand what was happening. Maybe he was too much of an idealist to want to.

But he had to understand. He must not stand in the way of the child.

When she got back to her apartment after work, Michael was stretched out in a chair in the living room, half asleep. He got up to kiss her, and took her raincoat. 40

"Thanks, dear," she said. "How's Randy?"

"Fast asleep. We almost finished his satellite."

She smiled. "I'm surprised he let you stop at 'almost.'"

She slipped into Randy's room, whispered the light on low, and looked down at him. His dark hair curled over his forehead; his arms were flung above his head in sleep.

When she came back out, Michael told her about the new graphics designer at his office. She watched him across the tiny living room: a lanky man with receding hair and a homely, gentle face. She thought, I really am lucky. The five years of their marriage had been hard, with the extra work and constant saving. But Michael had taken it cheerfully. And he was wonderful with Randy.   10

She reached automatically for the shelf near her chair and got out the chart.

Michael shook his head with a touch of exasperation. "Hey—we won't get any farther on that tonight."

"But there are so many decisions to make."

"After we talk to the geneticist. It's nearly midnight, anyway, and we're getting up early. Do you want to be late for your first appointment?"

She thought with a flash of sympathy, he'll be so glad when this is all over and the baby's really on its way. And he was right; she should   20 go to bed. After all the preliminary steps—the Applications Review Board, the interviews with social workers—they had finally been assigned to the geneticist who would do their engineering. They would be meeting the geneticist for the first time in the morning, and she wanted to be fresh for that interview. Still, she couldn't resist opening the chart and running her fingers down it lovingly.

SEX. Female. She had one son. And Michael considered Randy his own, so there was no quarrel.

SOMA-TYPE. Height, build, pigmentation. Hair, skin, eyes. With so many possibilities, how would they ever choose?   30

INTELLIGENCE. As high as possible, she thought fervently. The highest. So her daughter would never be held back in the work she wanted to do, never meet the helpless, pitying looks of people trying uselessly to explain.

ASSERTIVENESS. There she quarreled with Michael. She wanted high assertiveness—someone who could hold her own. Michael argued for moderation, saying that it made for a happier person. He had teased her gently: "Our daughter doesn't have to be a world shaker." She had frowned and shaken her head.

SPECIAL TALENTS, RESISTANCES, TOLERANCES . . .   40

She sighed, laid the chart aside and smiled at Michael. "All right, I'm coming. But *this weekend* . . ."

He threw up his hands in mock dismay. "I concede! This weekend, we'll have it out. Now come on and get some sleep."

It was forty minutes by tubetrain from Washington to New York, half an hour by bus and pedwalk to the towering building that was the East Coast headquarters of the Federal Population and Genetics Commission. They entered from the elevated walkways on the third level and almost immediately got lost. They asked directions twice, wandering through waiting rooms full of plastic benches, past signs that said "GE-NETICS RATING APPEALS RM 476-A" and "ARTIFICIAL INSEMINATION REGIS-TRANTS APPLY 1:30–5 PM."

Finally they found the elevators that would take them up to the Genetic Surgery Division. As they waited, it seemed to Evelyn that people glanced at them with a mixture of envy and resentment. Some were probably people with genetic defects, who would not be allowed to have their own children at all. And most people could not afford actual gene surgery, even if they qualified. But we've earned it, Evelyn thought. We've worked long and hard for our chance.

On the twenty-second floor, a receptionist directed them to a small carpeted waiting room. Evelyn sat down and tried to calm herself. After a few minutes a woman walked up to the receptionist's desk. She was remarkably tall, with heavy blond hair pulled into a loose knot at the back of her neck. Her face could only have been created by a Greek sculptor or a bioengineer. She had the classic straight line of forehead and nose, the small bowed mouth, the strong graceful curve from cheek to chin. She beckoned them over and smiled down at them. "I'm Dr. Morland, your geneticist. Please come with me." Her eyes were gray. Of course, Evelyn thought. Gray-eyed Athena, divinely tall . . .

They followed her into a roomy office. Evelyn looked around at the tall windows, the bookshelves, the charts of the double-helix DNA molecule on the wall. Here we are, she thought. It's beginning.

Dr. Morland congratulated them on their decision to have an engineered child. "You two have excellent genetic ratings, and I'm sure that this child will be rewarding both for you and for our society as a whole. Now—since this is your first appointment, let me review the options open to you."

What Morland told them was familiar to Evelyn from Commission publications, until she heard with dismay that prices for most alterations were going up again. She was frantically trying to recalculate costs in her head when Morland reached "intelligence."

"You can choose an IQ range up to approximately one hundred fifty on the Hoffman scale," she said. "That's equivalent to two hundred on the old scale." On the old scale two hundred had been the top, the outer limit. The Hoffman scale just kept going. "The cost for IQ will depend on whether—"

"Excuse me." Evelyn sat up very straight. "I thought that engineering could take the IQ up as high as Hoffman one eighty with no trouble."

Dr. Morland paused. "It can be done, although not without trouble. Nothing involving intelligence is simple. The policy of the Commission is not to aim for more than forty points over the higher of the parents' IQs. Larger gaps tend to produce serious problems in adjustment between parents and child."   10

"You mean we have no choice? That's a legal limit?"

"It isn't a matter of law. However, it's a firm Commission policy, growing out of our experience. After all, Hoffman one fifty is quite a high IQ."

"But there are already engineered who are higher—and they're having kids now, and their kids can go up another forty points. I don't want my daughter left behind before she even starts."

"Of course not. But that isn't the case." Morland smiled her serene, Greek-goddess smile. "First of all, not all the engineered *want* children brighter than they are. Also, at this point no one can go much beyond 20 one eighty. No single gene controls intelligence. We have to work with a whole series of genes that influence the formation of brain cells, the keenness of certain types of perception, and so on. Those same genes also affect other characteristics, so in trying to increase intelligence, we could produce bad side effects. We don't know enough yet to go too far. Your child will be near the top of the range. She should have every chance to excel in any field she enters."

She paused a moment. Evelyn was sick with resentment.

Morland went on. "The cost of altering intelligence will depend on whether both of you contribute genes. The alternative is to use one gamete 30 from one of you, and the other from an engineered donor who has some of the qualities you want, such as high intelligence. Then we simply have to assure dominance of those qualities by repressing the appropriate genes on your gamete. That's relatively simple. The amount of actual gene surgery—removing some of your genes and inserting others in the chromosomes—is greatly reduced."

She paused, looking from one to the other. Evelyn, her stomach still tight with anger, said nothing.

"We want it to be our own child," Michael said.

Morland nodded. "Many people feel that way."   40

"It's going to be rough, though," Michael went on. "With these new prices, I'm not sure we can afford all the alterations we had in mind."

She nodded again. "It's too bad, but prices do go up. I see by your preliminary chart that you aren't interested in special tolerances or talents—music and so forth. That's good, since those are quite expensive. As for the rest, you'll have to balance your priorities against what you can afford. I see you have down soma-typing, for instance. That's fairly simple, and not so expensive in itself. Still, you might want to save money there and put it toward intelligence."

Michael nodded. "That's probably what we'll have to do. The intelligence is the most important thing, after all."

"That's true. Now—this is the complete schedule of rates. This chart also shows interrelations between various qualities, so you can see the implications of your choices. You'll need to complete these forms. . . ."

Evelyn was staring from Morland to Michael, her face gone rigid. Were they going to pretend that appearance was not important? Michael had promised! She had worked so hard to convince him! And Morland—did she think, because they were norms, it did not matter if their child got second-class treatment?

Michael was on his feet, shaking hands across the desk. "Thank you for your time."

"Certainly. I'll look forward to seeing you again."

Evelyn forced herself to nod and smile politely. Five years, she thought. Scrimping and driving themselves. Now they were trying to steal her daughter's future.

She was silent while they made their way through the huge building to the sunlit plaza. As they walked out, Michael said, "The price rise is a real shame. But now at least we have a better idea just how much we can do."

"You mean how little," Evelyn said.

Michael looked at her, startled. "Hey, come on—it's not that bad."

"It's not? No soma-typing, and limited intelligence—"

"Wait a minute. I wouldn't call Hoffman one fifty limited."

"Oh, it's not—for a norm." Evelyn turned away and walked blindly into the plaza. She stopped before a fountain that sent a dozen jets of water foaming high into the air. All around her, people went briskly about their business, their footsteps clicking on the pavement. Michael came up beside her and took her arm.

"Hon, listen. I know you have your expectations all set—but I think you're overreacting. The doctor's right. She'll still be near the top."

"When the top is already Hoffman one eighty? Do you think thirty IQ points are a slight margin? And the top will keep going up."

"All right. Maybe it will. But you know, there's something to what the geneticist said about the gap between parents and child. I keep thinking of Anna Holden and her son. Remember when he left?"

Anna Holden had lived in their complex for a while: a dowdy, middle-aged woman, pouring her family trust fund into the child of her dreams. She brooded over him constantly, and raged and cried when he went beyond her. "My own son, not even sixteen, and he won't tell me a thing. All day at school, all night in that lab—I'm sorry I had it fixed up for him. He won't even *talk* to me. My own child, my son." What could he say to her? One night she stood screaming down the hall: "Come 10 back here! Come back, you hear me?" Her son strode away, his back straight, his long hair swinging. He had the face of a young Comanche. "I'm your *mother*," Anna yelled. He paused and turned, giving her a look of measureless contempt. "You?"

Evelyn shook her head, pushing the memory away. "Anna was neurotic—always clinging to him. It's no wonder he wanted to get away." She found herself irrationally angry that Michael had even brought the incident up. She thought, My daughter will never hate me. She calmed herself and went on. "The problem is that you're still thinking in our terms. An IQ of Hoffman one fifty would be outstanding for us. For the 20 engineered, it's only moderate."

"Then moderate may have to do, Evelyn. Do you think we'd be able to fight Commission policy? Do you?"

Evelyn shrugged, not wanting to answer. No, the policy would not yield, not for a couple of norms. She stared at the glittering fountain, and her sense of defeat gradually gave way to a grim determination.

"All right, Michael," she said. "She won't be as smart as some. But she'll be one of the engineered. She'll have a fighting chance to do whatever she wants with her life. We just have to give her what she needs to make the most of her chance. She has to have the soma-typing."   30

Michael came around in front of her and looked into her eyes. His plain face was intent and troubled. "Listen. I know how you feel about this. And I was willing to go along, before the price rise. But it isn't that important, Evelyn—it just isn't."

She tried to interrupt, but he hurried on. "I want the best for my children—you know that. I want them to have every chance I can give them. I want them to be happy. I want them to contribute something to the world, and take pride in themselves. Those are the things that matter. If she isn't so beautiful that she doesn't even look human, that won't be a tragedy. I'd rather she looked like you."   40

There was a note of pleading in his voice. He wanted her to yield gracefully, so they would not have to fight—with each other or with

circumstances. After their long struggle, he did not want this sourness at
the end.

She understood. Sympathy warred with her rising anger, so that her
voice came out rough. "Do you think I've waited all these years to have
a child who'll be *sort of* engineered? Who'll be on the edges, talked past,
ignored? Do you know what it would do to her, to give her engineered
intelligence but not make her really one of them? To be held back, looked
down on, kept from using what's in her—nothing's worse than that.
Nothing could be crueler."

Michael looked away, silenced by her outburst. After a moment he 10
said, "I just don't see how we could do it. With these new prices—I went
over our savings just last night. We'll have to take out a loan even without
soma-typing. If we want that too, we'd have to work another year, maybe
more, and the way the costs keep going up—"

"I'm thirty-six now. We can't afford a host mother. We have to do it
soon."

"Well, there you are."

"Oh, no. We'll get a bigger loan."

"What makes you think we can? Our savings will be gone after this,
and we won't have much in the way of collateral."   20

We'll find a bank that'll give us the money, she thought. Or something. Whatever they had to do. There had to be a way.

After a moment of her grim silence, Michael said, "I'm sorry. I know
how much this child means to you."

She patted his arm. "It's not your fault." But she rankled inside. It
was his child too, wasn't it?

Evelyn was back at the lab by early afternoon. She worked in a
rambling, sunny building whose long halls were permeated by a faint
medicinal smell compounded of many chemicals. No matter what her
mood, entering that building always gave her a secret lift of excitement. 30
The lab was a world leader in biochemical research. That fact still held
magic for Evelyn. She worked under Dr. Lin, an engineered biochemist
who was designing microorganisms to manufacture cheap, high-quality
protein. It was the kind of work Evelyn loved above all others: the merg-
ing of discipline and creativity, the reshaping of life itself. She had
dreamed of doing that kind of work when she was a student. The engineered had already been moving in everywhere; no one had understood
then just what a difference that made.

Evelyn entered Dr. Lin's work area, passed the closed shelves by the
door where various cultures were growing and went to the table at the 40
rear of the room. Wilson, on night shift, had been scheduled to set up a

Kjeldahl analysis to test the amount of protein in several strains. Evelyn glanced at the flasks on the burner and stopped. "Damn," she said under her breath. She checked each flask. There was no crystallization, nothing to measure. She looked them all over again. Wilson must have left out the catalyst. Of all the stupid times to mess up a routine procedure—She went back to her desk and called Dr. Lin.

Lin came in to look, though there was nothing he could do but fume. Evelyn, checking nutrient levels in the cultures near the lab door, could hear his irritated grumbling. "How could anyone be so careless?"

One of the other researchers had followed him in. He shrugged. "It's 10 bound to happen sometimes. People run these tests over and over, and sometimes they'll slip up."

"Did he have to slip on this one? It'll set back my whole schedule. It'll take two weeks to culture enough of some of these strains for another analysis."

"Well, it's your own fault, really. If it was that important, you shouldn't have left it for the night shift, when the regular supervisors aren't around. You can't leave important work to norms."

There was a split second of realization, of stillness, before Evelyn straightened up and walked away. 20

Later that afternoon, she worked out a new schedule for comparative protein tests, to cut the time loss as much as possible. Dr. Lin stopped by as she was hanging up her lab coat and getting ready to leave.

"Thanks for doing the new schedule," he said. "If you'd been here, this mistake never would have happened. I don't know what I'd do without you." Seeing the apology in his eyes, she was torn between gratitude and resentment. "You're the best assistant in the whole section," he said. "You're really a very able chemist. If it weren't for bioengineering—"

"I know."

There was a small silence. She smiled stiffly and left. 30

Evelyn was off work at the restaurant that night, but Michael would be late again. In the living room, after dinner, she called banks. The evening applications clerks regarded her with bland courtesy from the view screen. She had a neat sheet of figures before her in Michael's handwriting; he had done the most recent review of their savings and prospects. She gave the clerks account numbers and balances, income, lists of collateral, credit reference numbers. They punched it all into their terminals, applied their credit equations and politely told her where her upper limit would fall on their standard loan policy charts. Since her loan request was substantially above the limit, they offered her appoint- 40 ments with their loan officers for an individual review of her case. Evelyn set up three appointments. But she knew with a sinking in her stomach that Michael was right. They would not get a loan big enough to cover soma-typing.

She sat with her chin in her hand, thinking. The apartment was quiet, except for tiny clicks from the dining alcove, where Randy was putting together a puzzle. Where else could she turn? She thought of her sister in Arizona. Evelyn had made her some small loans for graduate school, but they hardly even kept in touch anymore.

"Hey, Mom," Randy called.

"What is it?"   10

"You want to see my puzzle? I'm almost done."

"Not right now, Randy."

"But I'm almost done, I got it all figured out."

"Not now. I'll look at it later."

"But Mom—"

"Randy," she said sharply, "leave me alone. I'm busy."

He fell silent. She put a hand over her eyes, thinking, What am I going to do? Then she punched call numbers for Arizona. The screen flickered and cleared, and there was her sister, nervous and vaguely apologetic as always. When Evelyn brought up the question of a loan, 20 she looked distressed and began to run on about troubles at the irrigation project. Her designs had been off because of the water needs of the new hybrids, and her supervisor was furious; her husband Warren was facing a shake-up in his department; when the new design programs were installed she might not have a job at all. She really did not see how they could make a loan right then.

Anyway, she added hesitantly, sometimes she wasn't sure that all this engineering was such a good idea after all.

"Oh, come on," Evelyn said, startled into impatience. "Where would we be without it? Who do you think has pulled off most of the break- 30 throughs of the last twenty years? Industry, transportation, cleaning up the environment, the cities—"

"No more slums in Washington?" her sister asked. Evelyn did not answer. "There are some out here," her sister went on. "And people unemployed—you should see them. What good is an automated factory to the people who used to work there?"

So that's it, Evelyn thought. The human race is remaking itself, and she's worried about losing her job. Aloud, she said, "Things take time. You can't do everything at once."

"No—I know that. It's just that the things that do get done seem to 40 be mostly for the people at the top. And the distance between the top and the bottom just gets bigger. . . ."

Evelyn listened a few minutes longer, then cut the conversation off. She should not have expected her sister to understand, she thought wearily. If she understood, she'd be saving for an engineered child of her own.

Her sister was out and the banks were out. Where else was there, where else . . .

A crash from the kitchen made her jump. "Randy?" she called.

"It's OK, it's not anything," he said. She got up and went to look. Randy was down on his knees, brushing together pieces of the blue-glass serving bowl. He looked up at her, scared.

"Randy! *What* are you doing? You broke our best bowl! You *know* 10 you're not supposed to get into that cupboard."

"I was gonna make something in it. For when Dad gets home—for a surprise." His voice trembled.

"I don't care what you were going to do, you're not allowed—and *stop* that. You'll cut your hands, scraping it up that way. Get me the broom."

He brought the broom and she swept up the pieces. "I'm sorry, Mom," Randy said.

"Well, you ought to be. I don't have time for this kind of thing, Randy. I have things to do."

She knelt and ran her hand over the floor tiles, feeling for any slivers 20 she had missed.

"Are you going to have the new baby soon?" Randy asked in a small voice.

"As soon as we can manage," Evelyn said irritably.

"Cost a lot of money to have an engineered baby, doesn't it?"

"It certainly does."

"Is it really exciting?"

Evelyn looked up. Randy was plucking studiously at a towel that hung by the sink. Children, she thought. The times they pick to need reassurance.

"Come over here, Randy," she said. Still kneeling, she put her arm 30 around his waist as he came up. His eyes were large and brown—so like her own. "Sure, it's exciting. But norm babies are too. Having an engineered baby is a good thing to do, because people like that can help us solve a lot of the world's problems. Raising a baby is a lot of work, though. We'll need you to help us."

"Won't she be smarter than me and everything?"

"Someday she will. For a long time she'll be your little sister, and you'll have to help her. Someday she'll be smarter than all of us. But she'll still be ours."

When she had put Randy to bed, she came back to sit in the living 40 room and think about money. She did not know where to turn. The tiny apartment, the crampedness that had never bothered her before, seemed to close in on her. She felt trapped and alone. Michael was tired, and he did not understand, and he was not going to try anymore. Even if she found someplace to borrow the money, she would have to convince him all over again that soma-typing mattered. She rubbed at her eyes in weary frustration. This child was the most important event in her life, but the decisions were still half his, and he could block her. In a flash of anger she thought, I ought to just leave. Then I could make my own choices.

She was shocked by the thought. Leave Michael? After five years of 10 happy marriage? Besides, added a coolly rational part of her mind, if she left she would lose half the savings. She would never be able to pay for the surgery.

She stood up abruptly. Nonsense, nonsense. Michael was a good, kind man. Somehow they would work this all out.

The next morning was Saturday. Michael, with Randy helping, began cooking chicken and chopping vegetables for the next week's meals. Evelyn could hear them talking in the kitchen while she spread out the family financial records on the desk in the bedroom. She did not doubt that Michael had been thorough, but in her restlessness she had to see for 20 herself. She began going over Michael's figures, checking the price increases against their savings and projected incomes.

Half an hour later, she called Michael. Her voice was strained. He came to the bedroom door, a paring knife in his hand, Randy close behind. "What is it, hon?"

"Michael, we have six thousand dollars more in savings than you put down here."

He stared at her blankly for a few seconds. Then he frowned. "You know what that's for."

"We can replace it later," she said, her voice rising. "We need it now. 30 What are you trying to do?"

Michael touched Randy's shoulder. "You go on and finish peeling the potatoes. Be careful with the knife, like I showed you. Your mother and I have to talk." Randy looked from one to the other. Then he left.

Michael closed the door. He came over to the side of the bed near the desk and slowly sat down. "We're going to have a second child," he said. "But we already have one. No matter what we've done without, we've always put a little something aside for Randy's education, so he would have that much security. That isn't going to 40 change now."

"You're telling *me* that? You've decided what my son needs, and you weren't even going to discuss it with me?"

Michael's face darkened. "He's my son too."

"Oh, I know you love Randy. That's not the point. He won't need the money for years, and by then we can replace it."

"We shouldn't be replacing it. We should be adding to it. It's not going to be much in any event, with costs the way they are. We won't be able to add much after the girl is born, with all the tests and psychologists and special schools—"

"So you just decided, you just decided all by yourself—"   10

Evelyn's voice was rising, but Michael shouted over her. "What do you mean, I decided? It never occurred to me you'd want to use Randy's money."

"It's too late for Randy. Whatever it costs, we have to make this child—"

"Right, right. We have to make her one of the masters of the earth." He waved his hand in dismissal, but she flared back at him.

"You say that and you think it's just an expression. But it's real. They *are* the masters of the earth—the new human beings. Can't you understand that? Whatever's worth running, they run—politics, business, education—" 20

"Is that all that matters to you? Randy's a person too. We can't take everything away from him—"

"Then we'll use a donor. If we use an engineered donor's genes instead of yours, it'll be cheaper, and we can afford everything."

"Instead of *my* genes? When you've already had a child, and I haven't? Oh, no. How about using a donor instead of *your* genes?"

"No. No."

"Why not? The child would still be yours, more than Randy is mine—out of your own body, and with you from birth."

"No." Evelyn shook her head slowly back and forth. "I have to have 30 my daughter."

Michael laughed with a bitterness that shocked her. "Of course. You have to have *your* daughter. The new you that can do all the things you can't. Do you really think you can live through a child?"

Evelyn's face went cold. When she answered, her voice shook. "I don't care what you say. She's going to have the chance I didn't. And she'll be my daughter."

"Mine too, believe me. So—no donors."

"Then we'll have to use Randy's money."

"No."   40

Evelyn closed her hands and eyes tightly for a moment, then tried once more.

"Michael, listen. Randy is my son, my first child. He'll always be special to me, even more just because he *is* a norm, because he's like us. But we can't afford to pretend. He's *only a norm.*"

Michael stared. "So anything this other child needs—pretty hair, anything—is more important than Randy."

"She is! She's more important than any of us."

"My God, Evelyn. What are you saying? A family can't live that way. If that's the way it's going to be, I don't want an engineered child at all!"

"Then don't have one!" She jumped to her feet. "You don't deserve 10 one!" He was just like all the other sheep. What had ever made her think she wanted his genes in a child of hers?

But Michael's anger suddenly dissolved, and he sat shaking his head. "Evelyn, Evelyn, look what's happening. We've waited for this for so long. We can't let it set us against each other."

She watched his homely face, twisted with concern, and felt a flood of contempt. It was the same contempt she felt for her own face in the mirror. Weak, she thought. The engineered are right to look down on people like him.

Michael came toward her, fumbling for her hands. "I don't want to 20 fight with you."

Evelyn did not meet his eyes. A thought had occurred to her, simple and cool as first light. She could get most of the savings from him in exchange for custody of Randy.

Again she recoiled from her own thoughts, shocked and ashamed. To give up Randy, to *sell* him—Still, the small cool thoughts unfolded. She could afford it then—her child, using her genes and sperm from a donor. It would be cheaper. And better.

"We can work it out," Michael was saying. "We're both upset right now, that's all. I didn't mean to deceive you about Randy's money, I really 30 didn't."

"I know," she said. "We're both tired." Never to see Randy again. Oh, the stab of loss at the thought. And yet, underneath, so deep she could almost ignore it, there ran a treacherous current of relief. Never again to be wrenched by pity and regret. No more to see his face, the mirror of her own: her own failure confirmed in the eyes of her son.

Michael's hands were warm and tight around hers. He was her husband; he was a good man. Once more he said, "We'll work it all out." 40

She tried to smile. Still, she did not meet his eyes. "Of course we will," she said. But she knew already that they would not work it out.

REVIEWING THE STORY

THE MAIN IDEA

1. Which of the following questions best expresses the main idea of the story?

   (a) Is bioengineering against the law?
   (b) Is success worth any price or sacrifice?
   (c) Should parents try to have more than one child?
   (d) Will all bioengineered children reject their parents?

DETAILS

2. In this story, a husband and wife are planning their

   (a) son's computer program.
   (b) move to New York City.
   (c) future child.
   (d) new careers.

3. In the bioengineering that Evelyn and Michael investigate, the characteristics of a newborn can be ordered

   (a) only by already bioengineered parents.
   (b) only by parents who are geniuses.
   (c) for a specified price per characteristic.
   (d) for free as a government-sponsored service.

4. Evelyn and Michael disagree about the need for soma-typing, which determines **(a)** intelligence **(b)** sex **(c)** talents **(d)** appearance.

5. Evelyn works as a **(a)** production manager **(b)** teacher and geneticist **(c)** bank officer **(d)** chemist and waitress.

6. At the end of the story, in order to afford the traits she wants for her daughter, Evelyn is willing to

   (a) settle for no soma-typing.
   (b) work a third job.
   (c) give up custody of her son.
   (d) borrow money from her parents.

ORDER OF EVENTS

7. Choose the letter that gives the order in which the events happen.

   (1) Evelyn visits Dr. Morland.
   (2) Evelyn watches her son do his homework.

(3) Evelyn works at the Augustus.

(4) Evelyn asks her sister in Arizona for a loan.

    (a) 4-3-1-2 **(b)** 2-3-1-4 **(c)** 1-2-3-4 **(d)** 2-1-4-3

CAUSE AND EFFECT

8. As a result of her job in the Augustus, Evelyn

   (a) envies bioengineered people.

   (b) admires normal people, or norms.

   (c) accepts herself as she is.

   (d) appreciates her husband.

9. Evelyn cannot have both soma-typing and high intelligence for her future daughter because the combination

   (a) is biologically impossible.

   (b) costs too much.

   (c) is against the law.

   (d) has already been used for her son.

INFERENCES

10. Bioengineering has led to a

    (a) more democratic society.

    (b) new kind of rule by a powerful few.

    (c) rapid increase in the number of people on Earth.

    (d) widespread fear of science.

11. At the end of the story, without directly telling us, the author clearly wants us to regard Evelyn and her values with **(a)** sympathy **(b)** complete surprise **(c)** enthusiastic approval **(d)** disapproval.

PREDICTING OUTCOMES

12. Unless Evelyn changes drastically, we can predict that the conflict over soma-typing is likely to

    (a) end in a compromise—with both Evelyn and Michael giving in a little.

    (b) end by Evelyn's giving up the idea of soma-typing.

    (c) lead to the breakup of Evelyn and Michael's marriage.

    (d) bring Evelyn and Michael closer together.

BUILDING YOUR VOCABULARY _____

1. But she watched the rain-blurred mosaic of the passing city with an almost *proprietary* sense of satisfaction.

   Proprietary (page 287, lines 10-11) has to do with **(a)** polite behavior **(b)** keen observation **(c)** excellence **(d)** ownership.

2. That's the country our class gets to be, for *simulation*.

   A *simulation* (page 288, lines 36-37) is a **(a)** copy of reality **(b)** reward **(c)** source of inspiration **(d)** punishment.

3. But it was undoubtedly because of Jordan that the Augustus had developed its particular *clientele*.

   a. The restaurant's *clientele* (page 290, lines 23-24) refers to its **(a)** reputation **(b)** menu **(c)** customers **(d)** appearance.

   b. The BEST strategy for answering part *a* is to

   (a) look for other appearances of the word *clientele* in the story.
   (b) recognize a more familiar word within *clientele*.
   (c) reread the paragraph before the one with *clientele*.
   (d) skim the paragraph after the one with *clientele*.

4. Then we simply have to assure *dominance* of those qualities by repressing the appropriate genes on your gamete.

   A quality that has *dominance* (page 294, lines 32-34) over another quality is **(a)** stronger **(b)** weaker **(c)** older **(d)** younger.

5. Our savings will be gone after this, and we won't have much in the way of *collateral*.

   Collateral (page 297, lines 19-20) is

   (a) interest charged to a borrower.
   (b) something valuable pledged to guarantee repayment of a loan.
   (c) a special discount offered for paying interest in advance.
   (d) the credit rating of people with no savings.

STUDYING THE WRITER'S CRAFT _____

1. To indicate the future *setting* of the story, the author mentions several details of advanced science and technology. What are some of these details?

2. Evelyn desperately wants her daughter not just to be, but also to look like one of the bioengineered. For this reason, the author pro-

vides several *descriptions* of these men and women. What different physical types are represented by the bioengineered? Despite their differences, what characteristics mark them clearly as belonging to the favored five percent of the population?

3. The author devotes a substantial part of her short story to the *characterization* of nine-year-old Randy.

   a. Randy is clearly an attractive, likeable boy. How does the author engage our sympathy in favor of Randy?

   b. Why is it important for the story that we like Randy?

ACTIVITIES FOR LISTENING, SPEAKING, WRITING

1. Find a partner, and act out the next conversation Evelyn and Michael have about their future daughter after the story ends. Based on the facts in the story, try to reach a peaceful resolution to their conflict. Report the results of your conversation to the whole class.

2. Reread the two paragraphs in the story that reveal Evelyn's feelings about her appearance. (page 290, lines 38-42, and page 303, lines 16-19) Ideal standards of physical appearance can make many people miserable. In almost every society, some people feel too fat or too thin, too dark or too light, too tall or too short. In our own society, what are some of the ideal standards of physical appearance for men and women? How can people—actually most people—who don't conform to these standards still feel good about themselves? Be prepared to discuss these issues with your classmates, either in small groups or with the whole class.

3. Imagine that you write a daily advice column in a Washington, D.C., newspaper. You have just received a letter from Evelyn or Michael Barr, describing her or his problem and asking for your advice. Write a brief reply to E.B. or M.B., telling what you think she or he should do, and why.

SQ

by Ursula K. Le Guin

"Mental health is freedom," he said. "'Eternal vigilance is the price of liberty,' they say, and now we have an eternally vigilant watchdog: the SQ Test. Only the testees can be truly free!"

Science-fiction books and movies often tell stories of monstrous villains who try to take over or even destroy the world. Daring heroes or heroines step in to save humanity from these evil creatures. In real life, however, it's not always that easy to tell the villains from the heroes. People sometimes do terrible things with what they think are the best intentions. This is especially true of *fanatics*—individuals who are so sure they are right that they simply can't allow other people to believe or behave differently from them.

In "SQ," Le Guin depicts a world spinning wildly out of balance in an orgy of psychological testing. You probably know the term *Intelligence Quotient* (IQ), which is the numerical grade a person scores on a standardized test of intelligence. If we can have an Intelligence Quotient, Le Guin slyly suggests, why not also a Sanity Quotient (SQ)? In fact, we are led to wonder, why stop there? Why not a Patriotism Quotient (PQ)? Or a Morality Quotient (MQ)? The possibilities for judging people through tests seem endless.

Is "SQ" simply a humorous story about testing? Or does it touch on much broader issues?

Ursula K. Le Guin

Le Guin has won many awards both for science fiction and works of fantasy. Her novels and short stories reflect her broad interests, ranging from the mysticism of Chinese Taoism to the scientific study of anthropology. (The "K" in her name stands for "Kroeber." Her father, Professor Alfred Kroeber, was a well-known anthropologist.)

Underlying her fiction is a concern with balance. How can humans live in balance with nature? How can we live in peaceful balance with one another? Le Guin explores answers to these questions in her popular science-fiction novels *The Left Hand of Darkness* (1969) and *The Dispossessed* (1974), as well as in the trilogy of fantasy novels titled *Earthsea* (1977).

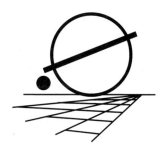

I think what Dr. Speakie has done is wonderful. He is a wonderful man. I believe that. I believe that people need beliefs. If I didn't have my belief, I really don't know what would happen.

And if Dr. Speakie hadn't truly believed in his work, he couldn't possibly have done what he did. Where would he have found the courage? What he did proves his genuine sincerity.

There was a time when a lot of people tried to cast doubts on him. They said he was seeking power. That was never true. From the very beginning all he wanted was to help people and make a better 10 world. The people who called him a power seeker and a dictator were just the same ones who used to say that Hitler was insane and Nixon was insane and all the world leaders were insane and the arms race was insane and our misuse of natural resources was insane and the whole world civilization was insane and suicidal. They were always saying that. And they said it about Dr. Speakie. But he stopped all that insanity, didn't he? So he was right all along, and he was right to believe in his beliefs.

I came to work for him when he was named the Chief of the Psychometric Bureau.[1] I used to work at the UN, and when the World Government took over the New York UN Building, they transferred me up to the thirty-fifth floor to be the head secretary in Dr. Speakie's office. I knew already that it was a position of great responsibility, and I was quite excited the whole week before my new job began. I was so curious to meet Dr. Speakie, because of course he was already famous. I was there right at the dot of nine on Monday morning, and when he came in, it was so wonderful. He looked so kind. You could tell that the weight of his responsibilities was always on his mind, but he looked so healthy and positive, and there was a bounce in his step—I used to think it was as if he had rubber balls in the toes of his shoes. He smiled and shook my hand and said in such a friendly, confident voice, "And you must be Mrs. Smith! I've heard wonderful things about you. We're going to have a wonderful team here, Mrs. Smith!"

Later on he called me by my first name, of course.

That first year we were mostly busy with Information. The World Government Presidium and all the Member States had to be fully informed about the nature and purpose of the SQ Test, before the actual implementation of its application could be eventualized. That was good for me too, because in preparing all that information I learned all about it myself. Often, taking dictation, I learned about it from Dr. Speakie's very lips. By May I was enough of an "expert" that I was able to prepare the Basic SQ Information Pamphlet for publication just from Dr. Speakie's notes. It was such fascinating work. As soon as I began to understand the SQ Test Plan, I began to believe in it. That was true of everybody in the office and in the Bureau. Dr. Speakie's sincerity and scientific enthusiasm were infectious. Right from the beginning we had to take the Test every quarter, of course, and some of the secretaries used to be nervous before they took it, but I never was. It was so obvious that the Test was *right*. If you scored under 50, it was nice to know that you were sane; but even if you scored over 50, that was fine too, because then you could be *helped*. And anyway, it is always best to know the truth about yourself.

As soon as the Information service was functioning smoothly, Dr. Speakie transferred the main thrust of his attention to the implementation of Evaluator training, and planning for the structurization of the Cure Centers, only he changed the name to SQ Achievement Centers. It seemed a very big job even then. We certainly had no idea how big the job would finally turn out to be!

---

1. **psychometrists** (sy-kuh-MET-rists): psychologists trained to use objective tests to measure mental abilities.

As he said at the beginning, we were a very good team. We all worked hard, but there were always rewards.

I remember one wonderful day. I had accompanied Dr. Speakie to the Meeting of the Board of the Psychometric Bureau. The emissary from the State of Brazil announced that his State had adopted the Bureau Recommendations for Universal Testing—we had known that that was going to be announced. But then the delegate from Libya and the delegate from China announced that their States had adopted the Test too! Oh, Dr. Speakie's face was just like the sun for a minute, just *shining*. I wish I could remember exactly what he said, especially to the Chinese delegate, 10 because of course China was a very big State and its decision was very influential. Unfortunately I do not have his exact words because I was changing the tape in the recorder. He said something like, "Gentlemen, this is a historic day for humanity." Then he began to talk at once about the effective implementation of the Application Centers, where people would take the Test, and the Achievement Centers, where they would go if they scored over 50, and how to establish the Test Administrations and Evaluations infrastructure on such a large scale, and so on. He was always modest and practical. He would rather talk about doing the job than talk about what an important job it was. He used to say, "Once you know 20 what you're doing, the only thing you need to think about is how to do it." I believe that that is deeply true.

From then on, we could hand over the Information program to a subdepartment and concentrate on How to Do It. Those were exciting times! So many States joined the Plan, one after another. When I think of all we had to do, I wonder that we didn't all go crazy! Some of the office staff did fail their quarterly Test, in fact. But most of us working in the Executive Office with Dr. Speakie remained quite stable, even when we were on the job all day and half the night. I think his presence was an inspiration. He was always calm and positive, even when we had to 30 arrange things like training 113,000 Chinese Evaluators in three months. "You can always find out 'how' if you just know the 'why'!" he would say. And we always did.

When you think back over it, it really is quite amazing what a big job it was—so much bigger than anybody, even Dr. Speakie, had realized it would be. It just changed everything. You only realize that when you think back to what things used to be like. Can you imagine, when we began planning Universal Testing for the State of China, we only allowed for 1,100 Achievement Centers, with 6,800 Staff? It really seems like a joke! But it is not. I was going through some of the old files yesterday, 40 making sure everything is in order, and I found the first China Implementation Plan, with those figures written down in black and white.

I believe the reason why even Dr. Speakie was slow to realize the magnitude of the operation was that even though he was a great scientist, he was also an optimist. He just kept hoping against hope that the average scores would begin to go down, and this prevented him from seeing that universal application of the SQ Test was eventually going to involve everybody either as Inmates or as Staff.

When most of the Russias and all the African States had adopted the Recommendations and were busy implementing them, the debates in the General Assembly of the World Government got very excited. That was the period when so many bad things were said about the Test and about Dr. Speakie. I used to get quite angry, reading the *World Times* reports of debates. When I went as his secretary with Dr. Speakie to General Assembly meetings, I had to sit and listen in person to people insulting him personally, casting aspersions on his motives, and questioning his scientific integrity and even his sincerity. Many of those people were very disagreeable and obviously unbalanced. But he never lost his temper. He would just stand up and prove to them, again, that the SQ Test did actually, literally, scientifically show whether the testee was sane or insane, and the results could be proved, and all psychometrists accepted them. So the Test Ban people couldn't do anything but shout about freedom and accuse Dr. Speakie and the Psychometric Bureau of trying to "turn the world into a huge insane asylum." He would always answer quietly and firmly, asking them how they thought a person could be "free" if they lacked mental health. What they called freedom might well be a delusional system with no contact with reality. In order to find out, all they had to do was to become testees. "Mental health *is* freedom," he said. "'Eternal vigilance is the price of liberty,' they say, and now we have an eternally vigilant watchdog: the SQ Test. *Only the testees can be truly free!*"

There really was no answer they could make to that. Sooner or later the delegates, even from Member States where the Test Ban movement was strong, would volunteer to take the SQ Test to prove that their mental health was adequate to their responsibilities. Then the ones that passed the test and remained in office would begin working for Universal Application in their home State. The riots and demonstrations, and things like the burning of the Houses of Parliament in London in the State of England (where the Nor-Eurp SQ Center was housed), and the Vatican Rebellion, and the Chilean H-Bomb, were the work of insane fanatics appealing to the most unstable elements of the populace. Such fanatics, as Dr. Speakie and Dr. Waltraute pointed out in their Memorandum to the Presidium, deliberately aroused and used the proven instability of the crowd, "mob psychosis." The only response to mass delusion of that kind was immediate implementation of the Testing Program in the disturbed States, and immediate amplification of the Asylum Program.

That was Dr. Speakie's own decision, by the way, to rename the SQ Achievement Centers "Asylums." He took the word right out of his enemies' mouths. He said: "An asylum means a place of *shelter*, a place of *cure*. Let there be no stigma attached to the word *insane*, to the word *asylum*, to the words *insane asylum*! No! For the asylum is the haven of mental health—the place of cure, where the anxious gain peace, where the weak gain strength, where the prisoners of inadequate reality assessment win their way to freedom! Proudly let us use the word *asylum*. 10 Proudly let us go to the asylum, to work to regain our own God-given mental health, or to work with others less fortunate to help them win back their own inalienable right to mental health. And let one word be written large over the door of every asylum in the world—WELCOME!"

Those words are from his great speech at the General Assembly on the day World Universal Application was decreed by the Presidium. Once or twice a year I listen to my tape of that speech. Although I am too busy ever to get really depressed, now and then I feel the need of a tiny "pick-me-up," and so I play that tape. It never fails to send me back to my duties inspired and refreshed.   20

Considering all the work there was to do, as the Test scores continued to come in always a little higher than the Psychometric Bureau analysts estimated, the World Government Presidium did a wonderful job for the two years that it administered Universal Testing. There was a long period, six months, when the scores seemed to have stabilized, with just about half of the testees scoring over 50 and half under 50. At that time it was thought that if forty percent of the mentally healthy were assigned to Asylum Staff work, the other sixty percent could keep up routine basic world functions such as farming, power supply, transportation, etc. This proportion had to be reversed when they found that over sixty percent 30 of the mentally healthy were volunteering for Staff work, in order to be with their loved ones in the Asylums. There was some trouble then with the routine basic world functions functioning. However, even then contingency plans were being made for the inclusion of farmlands, factories, power plants, etc., in the Asylum Territories, and the assignment of routine basic world functions work as Rehabilitation Therapy, so that the Asylums could become totally self-supporting if it became advisable. This was President Kim's special care, and he worked for it all through his term of office. Events proved the wisdom of his planning. He seemed such a nice, wise, little man. I still remember the day when Dr. Speakie 40 came into the office, and I knew at once that something was wrong. Not that he ever got really depressed or reacted with inopportune emotion, but it was as if the rubber balls in his shoes had gone just a little bit flat. There was the slightest tremor of true sorrow in his voice when he said, "Mary Ann, we've had a bit of bad news, I'm afraid." Then he smiled to reassure me, because he knew what a strain we were all working under, and certainly didn't want to give anybody a shock that might push their score up higher on the next quarterly Test! "It's President Kim," he said, and I knew at once—I knew he didn't mean the President was ill or dead.

"Over 50?" I asked, and he just said quietly and sadly, "55."

Poor little President Kim, working so efficiently all that three months while mental ill health was growing in him! It was very sad and also a useful warning. High-level consultations were begun at once, as soon as President Kim was committed; and the decision was made to administer the Test monthly, instead of quarterly, to anyone in an executive position.

Even before this decision, the Universal scores had begun rising again. Dr. Speakie was not distressed. He had already predicted that this rise was highly probable during the transition period to World Sanity. As the number of the mentally healthy living outside the Asylums grew fewer, the strain on them kept growing greater, and they became more liable to break down under it—just as poor President Kim had done. Later, he predicted, when the Rehabs began coming out of the Asylums in ever-increasing numbers, this stress would decrease. Also the crowding in the Asylums would decrease, so that the Staff would have more time to work on individually orientated therapy, and this would lead to a still more dramatic increase in the number of Rehabs released. Finally, when the therapy process was completely perfected, there would be no Asylums left in the world at all. Everybody would be either mentally healthy or a Rehab, or "neonormal," as Dr. Speakie liked to call it.

It was the trouble in the State of Australia that precipitated the Government crisis. Some Psychometric Bureau officials accused the Australian Evaluators of actually falsifying Test returns, but that is impossible since all the computers are linked to the World Government Central Computer Bank in Keokuk. Dr. Speakie suspected that the Australian Evaluators had been falsifying *the Test itself*, and insisted that they themselves all be tested immediately. Of course he was right. It had been a conspiracy, and the suspiciously low Australian Test scores had resulted from the use of a false Test. Many of the conspirators tested higher than 80 when forced to take the genuine Test! The State Government in Canberra had been unforgivably lax. If they had just admitted it, everything would have been all right. But they got hysterical, and moved the State Government to a sheep station in Queensland, and tried to withdraw from the World Government. (Dr. Speakie said this was a typical mass psychosis: reality evasion, followed by fugue and autistic withdrawal.) Unfortunately the

Presidium seemed to be paralyzed. Australia seceded on the day before the President and Presidium were due to take their monthly Test, and probably they were afraid of overstraining their SQ with agonizing decisions. So the Psychometric Bureau volunteered to handle the episode. Dr. Speakie himself flew on the plane with the H-bombs, and helped to drop the information leaflets. He never lacked personal courage.

When the Australian incident was over, it turned out that most of the Presidium, including President Singh, had scored over 50. So the Psychometric Bureau took over their functions temporarily. Even on a long-term basis this made good sense, since all the problems now facing 10 the World Government had to do with administering and evaluating the Test, training the Staff, and providing full self-sufficiency structuration to all Asylums.

What this meant in personal terms was that Dr. Speakie, as Chief of the Psychometric Bureau, was now Interim President of the United States of the World. As his personal secretary I was, I will admit it, just terribly proud of him. But he never let it go to his head.

He was so modest. Sometimes he used to say to people, when he introduced me, "This is Mary Ann, my secretary," he'd say with a little twinkle, "and if it wasn't for her I'd have been scoring over 50 long ago!" 20

There were times, as the World SQ scores rose and rose, that I would become a little discouraged. Once the week's Test figures came in on the readout, and the *average* score was 71. I said, "Doctor, there are moments I believe the whole world is going insane!"

But he said, "Look at it this way, Mary Ann. Look at those people in the Asylums—3.1 billion inmates now, and 1.8 billion staff—but look at them. What are they doing? They're pursuing their therapy, doing rehabilitation work on the farms and in the factories, and striving all the time, too, to *help* each other toward mental health. The preponderant inverse sanity quotient is certainly very high at the moment; they're mostly insane, 30 yes. But you have to admire them. They are fighting for mental health. They will—they *will* win through!" And then he dropped his voice and said as if to himself, gazing out the window and bouncing just a little on the balls of his feet, "If I didn't believe that, I couldn't go on."

And I knew he was thinking of his wife.

Mrs. Speakie had scored 88 on the very first American Universal Test. She had been in the Greater Los Angeles Territory Asylum for years now.

Anybody who still thinks Dr. Speakie wasn't sincere should think about that for a minute! He gave up everything for his belief. 40

And even when the Asylums were all running quite well, and the epidemics in South Africa and the famines in Texas and the Ukraine were under control, still the workload on Dr. Speakie never got any lighter, because every month the personnel of the Psychometric Bureau got smaller, since some of them always flunked their monthly Test and were committed to Bethesda. I never could keep any of my secretarial staff any more for longer than a month or two. It was harder and harder to find replacements, too, because most sane young people volunteered for Staff work in the Asylums, since life was much easier and more sociable inside the Asylums than outside. Everything so convenient, and lots of friends and acquaintances! I used to positively envy those girls! But I knew where my job was.

At least it was much less hectic here in the UN Building, or the 10 Psychometry Tower as it had been renamed long ago. Often there wouldn't be anybody around the whole building all day long but Dr. Speakie and myself, and maybe Bill the janitor (Bill scored 32 regular as clockwork every quarter). All the restaurants were closed; in fact most of Manhattan was closed, but we had fun picnicking in the old General Assembly Hall. And there was always the odd call from Buenos Aires or Reykjavík, asking Dr. Speakie's advice as Interim President about some problem, to break the silence.

But last November 8, I will never forget the date, when Dr. Speakie was dictating the Referendum for World Economic Growth for the next 20 five-year period, he suddenly interrupted himself. "By the way, Mary Ann," he said, "how was your last score?"

We had taken the Test two days before, on the sixth. We always took the Test every first Monday. Dr. Speakie never would have dreamed of excepting himself from Universal Testing regulations.

"I scored 12," I said, before I thought how strange it was of him to ask. Or, not just to ask, because we often mentioned our scores to each other; but to ask *then*, in the middle of executing important world government business.

"Wonderful," he said, shaking his head. "You're wonderful, Mary 30 Ann! Down two from last month's Test, aren't you?"

"I'm always between 10 and 14," I said. "Nothing new about that, Doctor."

"Some day," he said, and his face took on the expression it had when he gave his great speech about the Asylums, "some day, this world of ours will be governed by men fit to govern it. Men whose SQ score is Zero. Zero, Mary Ann!"

"Well, my goodness, Doctor," I said jokingly—his intensity almost alarmed me a little—"even *you* never scored lower than 3, and you haven't done that for a year or more now!" 40

He stared at me almost as if he didn't see me. It was quite uncanny. "Some day," he said in just the same way, "nobody in the world will have a Quotient higher than 50. Some day, nobody in the world will have a Quotient higher than 30! Higher than 10! The Therapy will be perfected. I was only the diagnostician. But the Therapy will be perfected! The cure will be found! Some day!" And he went on staring at me, and then he said, "Do you know what my score was on Monday?"

"Seven," I guessed promptly. The last time he had told me his score it had been 7.

"Ninety-two," he said.

I laughed, because he seemed to be laughing. He had always had a puckish sense of humor. But I thought we really should get back to the 10 World Economic Growth Plan, so I said laughingly, "That really is a very bad joke, Doctor!"

"Ninety-two," he said, "and you don't believe me, Mary Ann, but that's because of the cantaloupe."

I said, "What cantaloupe, Doctor?" and that was when he jumped across his desk and began to try to bite through my jugular vein.

I used a judo hold and shouted to Bill the janitor, and when he came, I called a robo-ambulance to take Dr. Speakie to Bethesda Asylum.

That was six months ago. I visit Dr. Speakie every Saturday. It is very sad. He is in the McLean Area, which is the Violent Ward, and every 20 time he sees me, he screams and foams. But I do not take it personally. One should never take mental ill health personally. When the Therapy is perfected, he will be completely rehabilitated. Meanwhile, I just hold on here. Bill keeps the floors clean, and I run the World Government. It really isn't as difficult as you might think.

REVIEWING THE STORY

THE MAIN IDEA

1. In this story, psychological testing
   (a) saves the world from mental illness.
   (b) turns the world into a huge insane asylum.
   (c) proves that mental health is freedom.
   (d) helps people find suitable marriage partners.

DETAILS

2. The purpose of Dr. Speakie's work is to distinguish
   (a) the sane from the insane.
   (b) geniuses from everyone else.

    (c) loyal citizens from rebellious citizens.

    (d) artistically talented people from the untalented.

3. This story is told from the first-person point of view with

    (a) Dr. Speakie as narrator.

    (b) President Kim as narrator.

    (c) Mary Ann Smith as narrator.

    (d) an omniscient (all-knowing) author as narrator.

4. Toward the end of the story, the staff of the Psychometric Bureau gets smaller and smaller because staff members

    (a) resign in protest over the Test.

    (b) leave the Bureau for better jobs.

    (c) take long vacations and don't come back.

    (d) fail the Test and are committed to asylums.

5. At the end of the story, the World Government is being run by

    (a) Bill, the janitor.

    (b) Mary Ann, Dr. Speakie's secretary.

    (c) Dr. Speakie.

    (d) no one.

6. To pass the SQ Test, a testee (subject) must score **(a)** over 100 **(b)** under 100 **(c)** over 50 **(d)** under 50.

ORDER OF EVENTS

7. Choose the letter of the event that happens LAST in the story.

    (a) President Kim fails the SQ Test.

    (b) China adopts the SQ Test.

    (c) Dr. Speakie fails the SQ Test.

    (d) Universal World Application of the SQ Test is decreed.

CAUSE AND EFFECT

8. According to the narrator, the steady rise in SQ Test scores never discourages Dr. Speakie because he

    (a) distrusts the accuracy of the scores.

    (b) has seen them rise and fall before.

    (c) is an optimist.

    (d) is unaware of their significance.

9. The chief effect of the Government crisis caused by the trouble in the State of Australia is that

   (a) President Kim is relieved of his duties in the World Government Presidium.

   (b) Dr. Speakie becomes acting Interim President of the United States of the World.

   (c) Mrs. Smith takes over Dr. Speakie's duties at the Psychometric Bureau.

   (d) the number of inmates in the Asylums nearly doubles.

INFERENCES

10. The MOST appropriate word for Dr. Speakie is (a) confident (b) gloomy (c) cautious (d) doubtful.

11. The LEAST appropriate word for the narrator, Mary Ann, is (a) naive (b) skeptical (c) steady (d) loyal.

PREDICTING OUTCOMES

12. If Mary Ann Smith's character and attitudes remain the same, we can safely guess that she will probably

   (a) sooner or later fail the SQ Test.

   (b) volunteer to work on the staff of an Asylum.

   (c) continue to run the World Government indefinitely.

   (d) be replaced by Bill the janitor.

BUILDING YOUR VOCABULARY _____

1. When most of the Russias and all the African States had adopted the Recommendations and were busy *implementing* them, the debates in the General Assembly of the World Government got very excited.

   Implementing (page 312, lines 7-9) means

   (a) putting off to a later date.

   (b) putting into effect.

   (c) examining closely.

   (d) debating excitedly.

2. The only response to mass delusion of that kind was immediate implementation of the Testing Program in the disturbed States, and immediate *amplification* of the Asylum Program.

   a. The BEST synonym for *amplification* (page 312 line 42, and page 313, lines 1-2) is **(a)** restoration **(b)** termination **(c)** reduction **(d)** expansion.

   b. For help in choosing the correct answer in part *a*, you might consider

   (a) the rest of the sentence as a context clue.
   (b) related words such as *ample* and *amplifier*.
   (c) the meaning of the word *implementation* earlier in the sentence.
   (d) the next paragraph, beginning with "That was Dr. Speakie's own decision. . . ."

3. "Let there be no *stigma* attached to the word *insane*, to the word *asylum*, to the words *insane asylum!*"

   A *stigma* (page 313, lines 6-7) is a mark of **(a)** shame **(b)** pride **(c)** authority **(d)** acceptance.

4. The State Government in Canberra had been unforgivably *lax*.

   Lax (page 314, lines 37-38) means **(a)** secretive **(b)** strict **(c)** carelessly easygoing **(d)** excessively burdensome.

5. He stared at me almost as if he didn't see me. It was quite *uncanny*.

   The word that is LEAST similar in meaning to *uncanny* (page 316, line 41) is **(a)** weird **(b)** eerie **(c)** supernatural **(d)** ordinary.

STUDYING THE WRITER'S CRAFT

1. Even before we learn who she is, the narrator reveals her **character** in the first three paragraphs of the story. What qualities does the narrator display as she talks about Dr. Speakie? What kind of person is she?

2. The way characters in a story speak reveals as much about them as do their actions.

   a. Mary Ann Smith, the narrator, likes to use phrases such as: "implementation of Evaluator training," "structurization of the Cure Centers," "amplification of the Asylum Program," and "self-sufficiency structuration." What kind of person talks or writes like this? What does this kind of language suggest about Mrs. Smith?

b. Dr. Speakie keeps changing the name of the places to which people who fail the SQ Test are sent. What was their original name? What was their second name? What was their third name? What seems to be the general purpose of these successive changes of name?

3. By using Mary Ann Smith as the narrator, or *first-person point of view*, Le Guin gives us a peculiar view of people and events. A reader would not see these things as Mary Ann does. What are some of the differences between Mary Ann's view of people and events in the story and the reader's view?

ACTIVITIES FOR LISTENING, SPEAKING, WRITING

1. One definition of *sane* is "being able to foresee and evaluate the effects of one's actions." On the basis of this definition, how sane is Dr. Speakie at the beginning of the story? Write an explanation of your answer.

2. The American poet Emily Dickinson (1830-1886) wrote the following poem:

> Much Madness is divinest Sense—
> To a discerning Eye—
> Much Sense—the starkest Madness—
> 'Tis the Majority
> In this, as All, prevail—
> Assent—and you are sane–
> Demur—you're straightway dangerous—
> And handled with a Chain—

What is Emily Dickinson's view of madness (insanity) in the poem? How does the poet's view of madness compare with that of Dr. Speakie? Would he agree or disagree with Emily Dickinson about the nature of madness? Write one or more paragraphs explaining your answer.

3. While "SQ" is an amusing story, it also touches on serious issues in the real world. Among these issues are the abuse of testing, the threat of a fanatic like Dr. Speakie, the problems caused by devoted dupes like Mary Ann, and the basic issue of making judgments about one's fellow humans. What other issues does the story touch on? Be prepared to discuss one or more of these issues with your classmates.

High-Tech Loneliness: How Our Inventions Keep Us Apart

by Mitchell Gordon

But now, technology is separating us from others.

Science and technology were supposed to shrink our planet. With jet travel and communication satellites bringing people ever closer, we assumed that we would soon be citizens of a global village. We thought that the whole world would become our neighborhood. Instead, Mitchell Gordon argues, we spend more and more time alone, rarely interacting with other people.

   The article that follows appeared in *The Futurist*, a magazine of the World Future Society. As a founding member of the Philadelphia chapter of the Society, Gordon has an abiding interest in the quality of life of future people. What do you think of his account of the "cocooning syndrome"? Does it apply at all to your life?

Mitchell Gordon

It seems that each year we invent new ways to keep human beings from meeting each other.

Home entertainment is fast becoming the leisure of choice, as more and more people take advantage of the wide assortment of electronic entertainment available. Video stores sprout everywhere; videotapes siphon customers from theaters and museums; and now video games attract those who once would have participated in traditional out-of-home sports such as bowling.

We now have all kinds of food establishments racing to *deliver* food. Is this the beginning of the end of the restaurant renaissance? Going to a restaurant involves parking, walking, and sometimes waiting in line—and even some element of risk from street crime. Compare this to the no parking, no walking, no waiting, no standing, no risk, no hassle way of life we have in our own homes when we have our meals delivered. Even preparing our own food is less and less of a hassle with prepackaged meals getting better and better and microwave ovens making cooking quick and efficient.

Futurists call this social phenomenon "cocooning," where families stay close to the homestead and interact very little with their outside surroundings. Home shopping networks, faxed mail, home computers and offices—such things threaten to rip the social fabric by keeping people from interacting with each other. In the long run, this cannot be healthy for our culture.

Already we are seeing the effects of a less-interactive society: People find that it is not as easy as it once was to meet others—especially those of the opposite sex. Traditional meeting places such as fairs, town dances, clubs, etc., are experiencing lower attendance because of the cocooning lifestyle. Society's crackdown on drunk driving has made singles retreat from the bar setting. For many, the way to meet other people has been reduced to reading the "Personals" section in the back pages of magazines.

It used to be that religious and educational parochialism separated the sexes and structured how people should meet. Sunday was filled with "blue laws" that shut down taverns and other social hangouts. And to this day we find the sexes separated in some religious and private schools—even in some universities—throughout the students' growing years. But now, technology is separating us from others. Paradoxically, the advanced technology that brings more of the world to us, making us a global society, also leads us to spend less time interacting with the larger segments of society.

Social interaction might seem to be increasing because people are 10 traveling more, but the cocooning syndrome is spreading to our hotels and resorts as well. Increasingly, everything is done to keep people from leaving the immediate confines of their hotel and exploring its environs. This is why the Atlantic City experiment—allowing legalized gambling in order to attract visitors to the once-popular resort—failed in its goals of revitalizing the community as a whole: The casino operators did everything they could to keep people from leaving the casinos and exploring the rest of the city. Entertainment within the casino was provided, food was plentiful, gift shops for browsing were placed right in the hotels. As a result, comparatively few visitors wandered away from the casinos to 20 the city's central business district, and most of the city saw no economic improvement.

Now, this same phenomenon is happening worldwide, as hotels become travel meccas in and of themselves. The irony is that people now fly to a foreign land for a week and never meet the people who actually live there.

To get people out of their homes and hotels, extraordinary measures must now be taken. Museums are fighting back with high technology, such as large-screen 70-mm film auditoriums and Disney-type movable exhibits. Marketplaces—the former centers of urban life and social interaction—are being refurbished or constructed from scratch (such as Boston's Quincy Market or Baltimore's Harbor Place), as people learn that we need attractions other than those provided by television or the local fast-food store.   10

These sorts of places are the great battlefields in the war against cocooning. Their developers may be remembered as heroes of a new revolution—a revolution against the onslaught of a passive society.

Mingling with other people and exploring our surroundings should not be abandoned because of advanced home entertainment technologies. What we do in our spare time should not be decided in a combat between cocooning technology and the lure of our public places. There should be equal time for both.

REVIEWING THE ARTICLE _____

THE MAIN IDEA

1. Which word best expresses the main idea of the article? (a) association (b) exploration (c) regulation (d) isolation

DETAILS

2. According to the article, prepackaged meals and microwave ovens encourage people to eat meals (a) in restaurants (b) at hotels and resorts (c) at home (d) in gambling casinos.

3. Each of the following is mentioned as a drawback of going to a restaurant EXCEPT (a) parking (b) greater expense (c) waiting in line (d) street crime.

4. Boston's Quincy Market and Baltimore's Harbor Place are cited as places of (a) social interaction (b) high technology (c) cocooning (d) legalized gambling.

5. The author of the article says that guests at hotels and resorts rarely (a) find entertainment there (b) eat meals in them (c) shop there (d) wander away from them.

6. Museums are employing high technology to
   (a) compete with marketplaces for customers.
   (b) get people out of their homes and hotels.
   (c) provide an alternative to casino gambling.
   (d) improve the quality of home entertainment.

ORDER OF EVENTS

7. Choose the letter that gives the order in which topics are discussed in the article.
   (1) refurbishing museums and marketplaces
   (2) enjoying home entertainment
   (3) dining at home
   (4) traveling to foreign lands
        (a) 2-3-1-4 (b) 1-2-3-4 (c) 3-4-1-2 (d) 4-3-2-1

CAUSE AND EFFECT

8. Because of cocooning, people
   (a) go more often to traditional meeting places.
   (b) spend more time in bars.
   (c) have less trouble meeting others.
   (d) have more trouble meeting others.

9. The effect of legalizing gambling in Atlantic City was supposed to be
   (a) spreading the cocooning syndrome.
   (b) keeping people from leaving the casinos.
   (c) revitalizing the community.
   (d) providing funding for museums and marketplaces.

INFERENCES

10. We can infer that "futurists" (page 323, lines 17-19) are
    (a) future people.
    (b) science-fiction writers.
    (c) experts on future trends.
    (d) people who interact very little with their outside surroundings.

11. The author seems to believe that social interaction and exploration of our surroundings

 (a) are not necessary today.
 (b) should be encouraged.
 (c) lead to cocooning.
 (d) are doomed to disappear.

PREDICTING OUTCOMES

12. If the new public museums and marketplaces succeed, we can predict that cocooning will be practiced by (a) nobody (b) fewer people (c) more people (d) everybody.

BUILDING YOUR VOCABULARY _____

1. It used to be that religious and educational *parochialism* separated the sexes and structured how people should meet.

 Parochialism (page 324, lines 1-2) is BEST associated with (a) narrow limitations (b) extreme flexibility (c) revolutionary change (d) popular romance.

2. *Paradoxically*, the advanced technology that brings more of the world to us, making us a global society, also leads us to spend less time interacting with the larger segments of society.

 When a cause leads *paradoxically* (page 324, lines 6-9) to an effect, the effect is (a) expected (b) inevitable (c) unexpected (d) both expected and inevitable.

3. Social interaction might seem to be increasing because people are traveling more, but the cocooning *syndrome* is spreading to our hotels and resorts as well.

 A *syndrome* (page 324, lines 10-12) is a
 (a) contagious disease spread by social interaction.
 (b) set of symptoms defining a disorder or disease.
 (c) travel terminal, such as an airport or train station.
 (d) special discount offered travelers by hotels and resorts.

4. Increasingly, everything is done to keep people from leaving the immediate confines of their hotel and exploring its *environs*.

 a. The BEST synonym for *environs* (page 324, lines 12-13) is
 (a) lobby (b) gambling (c) neighborhood (d) reputation.

b. Two useful clues to the answer for part *a* are the

(a) preceding paragraph and use of the word *environs* elsewhere in the article.

(b) association of *environs* with *andirons* and the fireplaces in hotel lobbies.

(c) analysis of *environs* into *envy* and *irons*.

(d) sentence context and the related word *environment*.

5. Marketplaces—the former centers of urban life and social interaction—are being *refurbished* or constructed from scratch. . . .

Refurbished (page 325, lines 6-7) means (a) torn down (b) fixed up (c) refinanced (d) remade into condominiums.

STUDYING THE WRITER'S CRAFT _____

1. By studying the ways in which professional writers organize their materials, you can learn how to organize your own writing more effectively. In planning his article, the author of "High-Tech Loneliness" had three purposes: (1) to present a problem, (2) to offer one solution, and (3) to persuade readers to agree with this solution.

   a. Which of the eleven paragraphs in the article present the problem?

   b. Which paragraphs in the article deal with the solution?

   c. Which paragraph in the article tries to persuade readers to agree with the solution?

2. Besides identifying and describing cocooning, the author wants his readers to regard this social phenomenon as a problem. Mention at least two or three places in the article that point to cocooning as something undesirable, perhaps even dangerous.

3. In writing his article, the author frequently uses a form of **figurative language** called **metaphor**. You can use metaphors to make your own writing more vivid and interesting.

   a. In the statement "video stores sprout everywhere," which word is used metaphorically? What two things are compared in the metaphor? How does the comparison make the statement more effective?

   b. The key word *cocooning* is also a metaphor. To what are people who practice cocooning compared? How is this comparison valid and useful in helping us to visualize the social phenomenon of cocooning?

c. The second-to-the-last paragraph of the article (paragraph 10) uses an extended metaphor. To what are "these sorts of places" (museums and marketplaces) compared? What other comparison does the author make within the paragraph? How do these comparisons heighten our sense of the conflict between "these sorts of places" and cocooning?

ACTIVITIES FOR LISTENING, SPEAKING, WRITING

1. Thanks to video hookups and computer networks, some students are already able to study at home aided by such electronic technology. In time, home schooling could become available to all future people. What advantages do you think home schooling would have over traditional education? As another form of cocooning, what disadvantages might home schooling have? In short, what would students gain and what would they lose? Be prepared to discuss these questions either in small groups or with your entire class.

2. The article mentions only two public places that serve to lure people out of their private cocoons: museums and marketplaces. What other kinds of public places today enable people to meet one another? Where do you and your friends hang out? Write a brief description of at least one such place. What can people do together in such a place? Also comment on features like travel, parking, convenience, safety, and cost.

3. Do you prefer to watch a movie on TV in your home or in a movie theater? How would you explain your preference? What advantages and drawbacks do you find with each way? Be prepared to discuss your views with your classmates.

FUTURE WORLDS

Theme 6

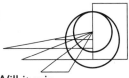

Everybody wonders about the future. You may ask: Will it rain this weekend? Where should I spend next summer? Will I get married some day? Perhaps your concerns about the future are weightier: Could overpopulation or pollution turn the Earth into a wasteland? Would a nuclear war wipe out the human race? Tomorrow, near or far, concerns us all.

Each story of a future world in this theme is based on a serious problem. "There Will Come Soft Rains" tells of the world soon after a nuclear war that has left no survivors. Combat to the death between the captain of a starship from Earth and a monstrous creature from an unknown planet may decide the fate of humanity in "Arena." In "A Pail of Air," the problem is one of survival after a cosmic accident to the Earth.

Why do science-fiction writers, peering into the future, tend to see so many problems and perils? More than most of us, these writers are aware that progress through science and technology often creates as many problems as it solves. Their stories offer us the opportunity to look at future consequences of our present behavior and think about them. As the article "How Easy to See the Future" points out, this opportunity may be the greatest gift of science fiction.

There may be another reason for the trouble that looms so large in the future worlds of science fiction. Without adversity, there would be no conflict, no problem for the hero or heroine to try to overcome. Although a future world without difficulty or danger might be pleasant, it would make a very dull story.

Step into three different worlds of tomorrow. They may challenge or even disturb you, but you certainly won't find them dull.

There Will Come Soft Rains

by Ray Bradbury

It quivered at each sound, the house did. If a sparrow brushed a window, the shade snapped up. The bird, startled, flew off! No, not even a bird must touch the house!

In the following story, you can visit a wonderful house of the future. Take a guided tour through the electronic marvels of this remarkable home. You'll see a house that seems to have everything. Yet something is clearly missing.

Like many science-fiction writers, Ray Bradbury warns that our vaunted technology, used stupidly, could endanger the entire human race. What caused the widespread disaster implied in the following story? Could such a disaster happen in the real world—your world? How might it be prevented?

Ray Bradbury

Since the 1940s, readers all over the world have enjoyed the finely crafted fiction of Ray Bradbury. His short stories have been reprinted in collections such as *The Martian Chronicles* (1950), *The Illustrated Man* (1951), and *The Stories of Ray Bradbury* (1980), which contains 100 stories. Along with his novels, the stories offer a bizarre blend of science fiction, fantasy, and horror. Two of the best movies based on his works are *Fahrenheit 451* (1967) and *Something Wicked This Way Comes* (1983).

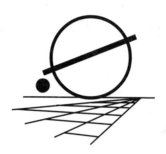

In the living room the voice-clock sang, *Tick-tock, seven o'clock, time to get up, time to get up, seven o'clock!* as if it were afraid that nobody would. The morning house lay empty. The clock ticked on, repeating and repeating its sounds into the emptiness. *Seven-nine, breakfast time, seven-nine!*

In the kitchen the breakfast stove gave a hissing sigh and ejected from its warm interior eight pieces of perfectly browned toast, eight eggs sunnyside up, sixteen slices of bacon, two coffees, and two cool glasses of milk.

"Today is August 4, 2026," said a second voice from the kitchen ceiling, "in the city of Allendale, California." It repeated the date three 10 times for memory's sake. "Today is Mr. Featherstone's birthday. Today is the anniversary of Tilita's marriage. Insurance is payable, as are the water, gas, and light bills."

Somewhere in the walls, relays clicked, memory tapes glided under electric eyes.

Eight-one, tick-tock, eight-one o'clock, off to school, off to work, run, run, eight-one! But no doors slammed, no carpets took the soft tread of rubber heels. It was raining outside. The weather box on the front door sang quietly: "Rain, rain, go away; rubbers, raincoats for today . . ." And the rain tapped on the empty house, echoing.   20

Outside, the garage chimed and lifted its door to reveal the waiting car. After a long wait the door swung down again.

At eight-thirty the eggs were shriveled and the toast was like stone. An aluminum wedge scraped them into the sink, where hot water whirled them down a metal throat which digested and flushed them away to the distant sea. The dirty dishes were dropped into a hot washer and emerged twinkling dry.

Nine-fifteen, sang the clock, *time to clean.*

Out of warrens in the wall, tiny robot mice darted. The rooms were acrawl with the small cleaning animals, all rubber and metal. They thud- 10 ded against chairs, whirling their mustached runners, kneading the rug nap, sucking gently at hidden dust. Then, like mysterious invaders, they popped into their burrows. Their pink electric eyes faded. The house was clean.

Ten o'clock. The sun came out from behind the rain. The house stood alone in a city of rubble and ashes. This was the one house left standing. At night the ruined city gave off a radioactive glow which could be seen for miles.

Ten-fifteen. The garden sprinklers whirled up in golden founts, filling the soft morning air with scatterings of brightness. The water pelted win- 20 dowpanes, running down the charred west side where the house had been burned evenly free of its white paint. The entire west face of the house was black, save for five places. Here the silhouette in paint of a man mowing a lawn. Here, as in a photograph, a woman bent to pick flowers. Still farther over, their images burned on wood in one titanic instant, a small boy, hands flung into the air; higher up, the image of a thrown ball, and opposite him a girl, hands raised to catch a ball which never came down.

The five spots of paint—the man, the woman, the children, the ball— remained. The rest was a thin charcoaled layer.

The gentle sprinkler rain filled the garden with falling light. 30

Until this day, how well the house had kept its peace. How carefully it had inquired, "Who goes there? What's the password?" and, getting no answer from lonely foxes and whining cats, it had shut up its windows and drawn shades in an old-maidenly preoccupation with self-protection which bordered on a mechanical paranoia.

It quivered at each sound, the house did. If a sparrow brushed a window, the shade snapped up. The bird, startled, flew off! No, not even a bird must touch the house!

The house was an altar with ten thousand attendants, big, small, servicing, attending, in choirs. But the gods had gone away, and the ritual 40 of the religion continued senselessly, uselessly.

Twelve noon.

A dog whined, shivering, on the front porch.

The front door recognized the dog voice and opened. The dog, once huge and fleshy, but now gone to bone and covered with sores, moved in and through the house, tracking mud. Behind it whirred angry mice, angry at having to pick up mud, angry at inconvenience.

For not a leaf fragment blew under the door but what the wall panels flipped open and the copper scrap rats flashed swiftly out. The offending dust, hair, or paper, seized in miniature steel jaws, was raced back to the burrows. There, down tubes which fed into the cellar, it was dropped into the sighing vent of an incinerator which sat like evil Baal[1] in a dark corner. 10

The dog ran upstairs, hysterically yelping to each door, at last realizing, as the house realized, that only silence was here.

It sniffed the air and scratched the kitchen door. Behind the door, the stove was making pancakes which filled the house with a rich baked odor and the scent of maple syrup.

The dog frothed at the mouth, lying at the door, sniffing, its eyes turned to fire. It ran wildly in circles, biting at its tail, spun in a frenzy, and died. It lay in the parlor for an hour.

Two o'clock, sang a voice.

Delicately sensing decay at last, the regiments of mice hummed out 20 as softly as blown gray leaves in an electrical wind.

Two-fifteen.

The dog was gone.

In the cellar, the incinerator glowed suddenly, and a whirl of sparks leaped up the chimney.

Two thirty-five.

Bridge tables sprouted from patio walls. Playing cards fluttered onto pads in a shower of pips.[2] Martinis manifested on an oaken bench with egg-salad sandwiches. Music played.

But the tables were silent and the cards untouched. 30

At four o'clock the tables folded like great butterflies back through the paneled walls.

Four-thirty.

The nursery walls glowed.

Animals took shape: yellow giraffes, blue lions, pink antelopes, lilac panthers cavorting in crystal substance. The walls were glass. They looked out upon color and fantasy. Hidden films clocked through well-oiled sprockets, and the walls lived. The nursery floor was woven to resemble a

1. **Baal** (BAY-ul): ancient Middle-Eastern god, depicted as a false god in the Old Testament.
2. **pips:** markings on playing cards.

crisp, cereal meadow. Over this ran aluminum roaches and iron crickets, and in the hot still air butterflies of delicate red tissue wavered among the sharp aromas of animal spoors! There was the sound like a great matted yellow hive of bees within a dark bellows, the lazy bumble of a purring lion. And there was the patter of okapi feet and the murmur of a fresh jungle rain, like other hoofs, falling upon the summer-starched grass. Now the walls dissolved into distances of parched weed, mile on mile, and warm endless sky. The animals drew away into thorn brakes and water holes.

It was the children's hour.

Five o'clock. The bath filled with clear hot water. 10

Six, seven, eight o'clock. The dinner dishes manipulated like magic tricks, and in the study a *click.* In the metal stand opposite the hearth where a fire now blazed up warmly, a cigar popped out, half an inch of soft gray ash on it, smoking, waiting.

Nine o'clock. The beds warmed their hidden circuits, for nights were cool here.

Nine-five. A voice spoke from the study ceiling:

"Mrs. McClellan, which poem would you like this evening?"

The house was silent.

The voice said at last, "Since you express no preference, I shall select 20 a poem at random." Quiet music rose to back the voice. "Sara Teasdale. As I recall, your favorite. . . ."

> *There will come soft rains and the smell of the ground,*
> *And swallows circling with their shimmering sound;*
>
> *And frogs in the pools singing at night,*
> *And wild plum trees in tremulous white;*
>
> *Robins will wear their feathery fire,*
> *Whistling their whims on a low fence-wire;*
>
> *And not one will know of the war, not one*
> *Will care at last when it is done.* 30
>
> *Not one would mind, neither bird nor tree,*
> *If mankind perished utterly;*
>
> *And Spring herself, when she woke at dawn*
> *Would scarcely know that we were gone.*

The fire burned on the stone hearth and the cigar fell away into a mound of quiet ash on its tray. The empty chairs faced each other between the silent walls, and the music played.

At ten o'clock the house began to die.

The wind blew. A falling tree bough crashed through the kitchen window. Cleaning solvent, bottled, shattered over the stove. The room was ablaze in an instant!

"Fire!" screamed a voice. The house lights flashed, water pumps shot water from the ceilings. But the solvent spread on the linoleum, licking, eating, under the kitchen door, while the voices took it up in chorus: "Fire, fire, fire!"

The house tried to save itself. Doors sprang tightly shut, but the windows were broken by the heat and the wind blew and sucked upon 10 the fire.

The house gave ground as the fire in ten billion angry sparks moved with flaming ease from room to room and then up the stairs. While scurrying water rats squeaked from the walls, pistoled their water, and ran for more. And the wall sprays let down showers of mechanical rain.

But too late. Somewhere, sighing, a pump shrugged to a stop. The quenching rain ceased. The reserve water supply, which had filled baths and washed dishes for many quiet days, was gone.

The fire crackled up the stairs. It fed upon Picassos and Matisses[3] in the upper halls, like delicacies, baking off the oily flesh, tenderly crisp- 20 ing the canvases into black shavings.

Now the fire lay in beds, stood in windows, changed the colors of drapes!

And then, reinforcements.

From attic trapdoors, blind robot faces peered down with faucet mouths gushing green chemical.

The fire backed off, as even an elephant must at the sight of a dead snake. Now there were twenty snakes whipping over the floor, killing the fire with a clear cold venom of green froth.

But the fire was clever. It had sent flame outside the house, up 30 through the attic to the pumps there. An explosion! The attic brain which directed the pumps was shattered into bronze shrapnel on the beams.

The fire rushed back into every closet and felt of the clothes hung there.

The house shuddered, oak bone on bone, its bared skeleton cringing from the heat, its wire, its nerves revealed as if a surgeon had torn the skin off to let the red veins and capillaries quiver in the scalded air. Help, help! Fire! Run, run! Heat snapped mirrors like the first brittle winter ice. And the voices wailed, Fire, fire, run, run, like a tragic nursery rhyme, a

---

3. **Picassos and Matisses:** paintings by the Spanish painter Pablo Picasso (1881-1973) and the French painter Henri Matisse (1869-1954).

dozen voices, high, low, like children dying in a forest, alone, alone. And the voices fading as the wires popped their sheathings like hot chestnuts. One, two, three, four, five voices died.

In the nursery the jungle burned. Blue lions roared, purple giraffes bounded off. The panthers ran in circles, changing color, and ten million animals, running before the fire, vanished off toward a distant steaming river. . . .

Ten more voices died. In the last instant under the fire avalanche, other choruses, oblivious, could be heard announcing the time, playing music, cutting the lawn by remote-control mower, or setting an umbrella 10 frantically out and in, the slamming and opening front door, a thousand things happening, like a clock shop when each clock strikes the hour insanely before or after the other, a scene of maniac confusion, yet unity; singing, screaming, a few last cleaning mice darting bravely out to carry the horrid ashes away! And one voice, with sublime disregard for the situation, read poetry aloud in the fiery study, until all the film spools burned, until all the wires withered and the circuits cracked.

The fire burst the house and let it slam flat down, puffing out skirts of spark and smoke.

In the kitchen, an instant before the rain of fire and timber, the stove 20 could be seen making breakfasts at a psychopathic rate, ten dozen eggs, six loaves of toast, twenty dozen bacon strips, which, eaten by fire, started the stove working again, hysterically hissing!

The crash. The attic smashing into kitchen and parlor. The parlor into cellar, cellar into sub-cellar. Deep freeze, armchair, film tapes, circuits, beds, and all like skeletons thrown in a cluttered mound deep under.

Smoke and silence. A great quantity of smoke.

Dawn showed faintly in the east. Among the ruins, one wall stood alone. Within the wall, a last voice said, over and over again and again, even as the sun rose to shine upon the heaped rubble and steam: 30

"Today is August 5, 2026, today is August 5, 2026, today is . . ."

REVIEWING THE STORY

THE MAIN IDEA

1. The title of the story comes from a poem by Sara Teasdale (page 337) about how nature

   (a) is threatened by pollution, ozone depletion, and global warming.

   (b) will continue though humans disappear completely.

(c) threatens to destroy all human beings.

(d) mourns for those who die in wars.

DETAILS

2. Bradbury reveals the story's *setting* (the time and place when the story occurs) by means of

(a) a local daily newspaper.

(b) an automated voice in the kitchen ceiling.

(c) a local television news broadcast.

(d) a conversation between two family members.

3. Events in the story occur during (a) one day (b) an hour (c) a week (d) an unspecified period of time.

4. The mice and rats mentioned in the story are

(a) fire-fighting instruments.

(b) mechanical cleaning devices.

(c) rodents living in the cellar.

(d) creatures in Sara Teasdale's poem.

5. When the story begins, the McClellans

(a) are away on vacation.

(b) are out in the garden.

(c) are all dead.

(d) have gone to the city.

6. At the end of the story, the house

(a) continues to run normally.

(b) is totally destroyed by an earthquake.

(c) is destroyed by a fire.

(d) is being rebuilt by its new owners.

ORDER OF EVENTS

7. Choose the letter that gives the order in which the events happen.

(1) A fire destroys the house.

(2) The empty house goes through its daily routine.

(3) The McClellan boy and girl play catch.

(4) A surprise nuclear attack levels the city.

(a) 3-4-2-1 (b) 1-2-3-4 (c) 4-3-1-2 (d) 2-3-1-4

CAUSE AND EFFECT

8. At the beginning of August 4, the house is running normally because of its

    (a) loyalty to the McClellan family.
    (b) programmed memory tapes and electric eyes.
    (c) neighbors and service companies.
    (d) intelligence and ability to solve new problems.

9. The fire in the house is caused by (a) an accident (b) a dog (c) a man (d) an atomic explosion.

INFERENCES

10. Someone in the McClellan family enjoyed (a) politics (b) music, literature, and art (c) fishing, hunting, and camping (d) big-game hunting.

11. The family dog probably died of (a) rabies (b) gunshot wounds (c) old age (d) radiation poisoning.

PREDICTING OUTCOMES

12. Which of the following is MOST likely to happen?

    (a) The one remaining wall of the house will stand forever.
    (b) In time, nature will cover over the ruins of the house and the entire city.
    (c) It will never rain again in Allendale, California.
    (d) The people of Allendale will rebuild their city.

BUILDING YOUR VOCABULARY _____

1. In the kitchen the breakfast stove gave a hissing sigh and *ejected* from its warm interior eight pieces of perfectly browned toast . . . .

    Ejected (page 334, lines 5-6) means (a) made (b) baked (c) threw out (d) announced.

2. At eight-thirty the eggs were *shriveled* and the toast was like stone.

    Shriveled (page 335, line 3) means (a) brown and burned (b) cold and wet (c) wrinkled and dried out (d) rotten and smelly.

3. Here the *silhouette* in paint of a man mowing a lawn.

   a. A *silhouette* (page 335, lines 23-24) is **(a)** an artist's signature **(b)** an outline drawing **(c)** a humorous cartoon **(d)** a color engraving.

   b. The BEST strategy for figuring out the meaning of *silhouette* would be to

   (a) skim all of page 335.

   (b) read only the sentence containing the word.

   (c) read the paragraph containing the word and the paragraphs before and after.

   (d) divide the word into smaller elements to analyze its meaning.

4. Animals took shape: yellow giraffes, blue lions, pink antelopes, lilac panthers *cavorting* in crystal substance.

   Cavorting (page 336, lines 35-36) means **(a)** fighting angrily **(b)** dancing playfully **(c)** sleeping deeply **(d)** eating hungrily.

5. Now the walls dissolved into distances of *parched* weed, mile on mile, and warm endless sky.

   Parched (page 337, lines 6-8) means **(a)** mowed **(b)** overgrown **(c)** wet **(d)** dry.

STUDYING THE WRITER'S CRAFT

1. A short story writer must pack a lot of information into each paragraph.

   a. In the first paragraph of the story, what words or phrases hint that something may be wrong?

   b. In the second paragraph, what clues enable you to guess how many adults and children make up the McClellan family?

2. Reread the paragraph on page 338, line 35 to page 339, line 3. ("The house shuddered . . . five voices died.") This paragraph comes at the *climax*, the turning point in the battle between the fire and the house. To make this crucial moment intensely vivid, the author uses a great deal of figurative language.

   a. A *simile*, which is a comparison using "like" or "as," helps you see something more vividly. What similes do you find in the paragraph?

b. Once the house is set ablaze, the fire and the house are both *personified*, or described as if they were living persons. What details in the paragraph reinforce the personification of the house? Why do you think Ray Bradbury took the trouble to personify the fire and the house?

3. Look at the passage headed *"Two thirty-five."* (page 336, lines 26-32)

   a. What unusual verbs do you see there?

   b. What examples of **alliteration** (the use of words that begin with the same sound) do you find? How does the first example help you "hear" what is being described?

ACTIVITIES FOR LISTENING, SPEAKING, WRITING

1. Write a letter to someone who lived about eighty years ago. Describe some of the ordinary things in your own home that would seem like futuristic marvels to that person.

2. The United States dropped the first atomic bomb on Hiroshima, Japan, on August 6, 1945 and a second bomb on Nagasaki three days later.

   a. Using an encyclopedia, a history book, or any other reference work, be prepared to present a brief oral report to your class on the effects of the atomic bomb on the people of Hiroshima and Nagasaki.

   b. Consider the following statement: "If people cannot learn from the past, they can read science fiction to learn from the future." How might this statement apply to the story by Ray Bradbury? Discuss your ideas on this topic with your classmates.

3. What future development in science or technology would you most like to see? What benefits to people could it bring? What problems might it cause? Write notes and a brief outline of your ideas, and be prepared to share them with the members of your class.

Arena

adapted by James Blish

The Gorn moved. It was closing in on Kirk. It looked quite capable of killing him with its bare hands. Kirk moved sidewise, warily.

Unlike the other science-fiction stories in this book, "Arena" was not originally written as a short story. It was, in its first version, a screenplay by Gene L. Coon for an episode in the television series *Star Trek*. James Blish rewrote the script as one of twenty-one stories in *The Star Trek Reader*.

Launched in 1966, the *Star Trek* series about intergalactic adventures in a future world became immensely successful. Both the television series and several motion pictures based on it dramatize the adventures of Starship *Enterprise* and its crew: Captain Kirk, Mr. Spock, Doc "Bones" McCoy, and others. Devoted fans, called *Trekkies*, have made the television series the most popular one ever produced. It even spawned two spin-off series: *Star Trek: The Next Generation* and *Star Trek: Deep Space Nine*.

The title of this story refers to the public *arenas* in Ancient Rome. On these flat, sandy battlefields surrounded by cheering spectators, armed warriors called *gladiators* fought each other, usually to the death. As you read the story, ask yourself these questions: In the duel between Captain Kirk and the alien Gorn, who is the winner and who is the loser? And why?

One of the old-timers of science fiction, Blish started out as a member of the informal club called the *Futurians*. This small group of young, enthusiastic science-fiction writers met in New York City from 1938 to 1945. Fellow Futurians who, like Blish, became famous include Isaac Asimov, Damon Knight, and Judith Merril. In later years, Blish helped found the Milford Science Fiction Writers' Conference to aid and encourage young writers.

Blish's own science fiction deals with important philosophical questions on a grand scale. His widely admired novel *A Case of Conscience* (1958) is the first in a series of novels that probe basic human values and behavior. In *Cities in Flight* (1970), a collection of four science-fiction works, he also creates a richly detailed future world out among the stars.

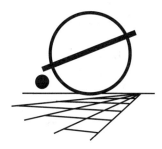

Captain James Kirk of the USS *Enterprise* was the absolute master of the largest and most modern vessel in the Starfleet Service, of all the complex apparatus and weaponry aboard her, and of the manifold talents of 430 highly trained crewmen.

And at the moment, he was stranded on a nearly barren artificial asteroid, location unknown, facing a tyrannosaurlike creature whose survival depended upon its killing Kirk, and equipped with absolutely nothing except a small translator-recorder useless as a weapon.

The situation had developed with bewildering rapidity. Originally, 10 the *Enterprise* had received a call from the Earth outpost on Cestus Three, part of a planetary system on the very edge of an unexplored quadrant of the galaxy. The base commandant, an old soldier named Travers, had asked Kirk to beam down with the tactical staff of the *Enterprise*; and since things were quiet in this sector of space and Travers was famous in the Service for setting a good table, all six men had accepted cheerfully.

But the invitation had been a trap—a prerecorded trap. They had found the settlement in smoking ruins, the personnel dead. Furthermore, within minutes after its arrival the landing party was also under attack—and so was the *Enterprise*.

Evidently, the enemy, whoever he was, did not have the transporter and had no idea of its capabilities; after five minutes' inconclusive exchange of shots, the landing party was whisked away clean. The enemy ship broke off the engagement and fled, at fantastically high acceleration.

Kirk had no intention of letting it get away, however. It seemed obvious that any attempt to ambush the *Enterprise's* tactical staff and captain, and then to destroy the starship itself, could only be a prelude to a full-scale invasion. Furthermore, the unknown enemy was well 10 armed—the damage its ship had suffered thus far had been minor, despite its flight—and peculiarly ruthless, as witness its having wiped out 512 helpless people at an inoffensive scientific outpost simply to bait its trap. As Science Officer Spock had pointed out, that ship could not be allowed to reach its home base; presumably, as long as that unknown world was kept in the dark about Federation strength, it would hold off its next attack—thus buying precious time for a defense buildup.

The enemy seemed equally anxious to avoid leading the *Enterprise* to its home planet. It took complex evasive action, again at incredibly high speed; the *Enterprise* had difficulty in closing with her even at warp 20 eight, two factors above maximum safe speed.

And then, suddenly, everything stopped.

It was absolutely impossible, but it happened. At one moment, both vessels were flashing through subspace at over a hundred times the speed of light—and in the next, both were floating in normal space, motionless relative to a small, nearby solar system, engines inoperative, all weapons dead.

"Report!" Kirk snapped.

But there was no damage, nothing abnormal—except that the *Enterprise* could neither move nor fight, nor, apparently, could the enemy.   30

"We're being scanned, sir," Communications Officer Uhura said.

"From the alien ship?"

"No, sir," she said. "From that solar system ahead. Nothing hostile—no tractors or weapon sensors, just scanners."

"Stopping us like this might be considered hostile," Kirk said drily.

"Getting something else, Captain—a modulation of the main frequency . . ."

Abruptly, the lights dimmed and there was a low hum from the main viewing screen. The starry scene from outside promptly dissolved into a twisting, confused mass of color and lines. At the same time a humanoid 40 voice, strong and yet somehow youthful, shook the air of the bridge. The voice said:

"We are the Metrons."

Kirk and Spock exchanged speculative glances. Then the Science Officer said, quite composedly: "How do you do?"

The voice's owner paid no apparent attention. It continued:

"You are one of two craft that have come into our space on a mission of violence. This is not permissible. Our analysis further shows that your violent tendencies are inherent. Hence we will resolve your conflict in the way most suited to your natures. Captain James Kirk!"

"This is Captain Kirk," Kirk said, after a moment's hesitation.

"We have prepared a planetoid with a suitable atmosphere, tempera- 10 ture, and gravity. You will be taken there, as will the captain of the Gorn ship that you have been pursuing. You and your opponent will be provided with a translator-recorder. You can keep a record, or communicate with each other, should you feel the need. But not with your ships. You will each be totally alone, and will settle your dispute alone."

"Just what makes you think you can interfere . . ." Kirk began angrily.

"It is you who are doing the interfering. We are simply putting a stop to it—within your own violent frame of reference. The place we have prepared for you contains sufficient resources for either of you to con- 20 struct weapons lethal to the other. The winner of the ordeal will be permitted to go on his way unharmed. The loser, along with his ship, will be destroyed in the interests of peace. The contest will be one of ingenuity against ingenuity, brute strength against brute strength. The outcome will be final."

With that, silently, the ship around Kirk vanished.

The first thing he saw was the Gorn. It was a biped, a reptile, a lizard that walked like a man. It stood about six feet four, with tremendous musculature, dully gleaming skin, a ridge of hard plate running down its back, and a strong, thick tail. The tail did not look prehensile; rather, 30 it seemed to be a balancing organ, suggesting that the creature could run very fast indeed if it wished. The head was equipped with two tiny earholes and a wide mouth full of sharp teeth.

This, then, was the enemy, the raider, the destroyer of Cestus Three. It was wearing a garment like a short robe, belted; at the belt hung a small electronic device. It wore no shoes; clawed feet dug deeply into the ground, indicating considerable weight. Shooting a wary glance down at himself, Kirk discovered that his own clothing and equipment were identical.

Kirk and the Gorn stared at each other. All around them was a rocky, 40 barren terrain, with a peculiar gray-green sky and occasional clumps of vegetation, some of it fairly tall, but none of it familiar. The air was cold and dry.

Kirk wondered if the Gorn was as uncomfortable as he was. Probably, but for different reasons. The meddling Metrons would surely have allowed neither of them an advantage in environment; after all, this planetoid was artificial—deliberately constructed to be an arena for a trial of champions, and for nothing else.

The Gorn moved. It was closing in on Kirk. It looked quite capable of killing him with its bare hands. Kirk moved sidewise, warily.

The Gorn did not appear to want to take any chances. As it too circled, it passed close to a gnarled object like a small tree, perhaps eight to ten inches through the trunk, and about ten feet high. With a quick look at Kirk, the Gorn hissed softly, reached out, and broke off a thick branch. The move seemed to cost it very little effort, whereas Kirk doubted that he could have done it at all.

Then, suddenly, holding the branch aloft like a club, the Gorn was charging him.

Kirk sprang aside barely in time. As the Gorn passed, somewhat off-balance, Kirk swung a killing blow into its midriff. The impact nearly broke his hand, but it seemed to have no other effect. The club lashed back, knocking Kirk sprawling against the rocks.

The Gorn wheeled around, clumsily but swiftly, and pounced. Kirk, dazed, tried to counter with a forearm blow to the throat, but it was like hitting an elephant. Then the creature was gripping him like a grizzly. Kirk's arm just managed to keep the teeth away, but that grip was going to break his back.

Freeing his arms with a sudden twist, Kirk boxed the Gorn's earholes with cupped hands. The Gorn screamed and staggered back, shaking its huge head. Springing to his feet, Kirk picked up a boulder as big as his head and hurled it at the Gorn with all his strength.

It struck the Gorn fair on the chest. The creature lurched slightly, but it did not seem to be hurt. Hissing shrilly, it bent to pick up a boulder of its own. The thing must have weighed a thousand pounds, but the Gorn got it aloft in one titanic jerk.

Kirk ran.

The rock hit behind him with an explosive crack, and flying splinters cut into the calf of one leg like shrapnel. Still hobbling as fast as he could, Kirk looked back over his shoulder.

The Gorn was not following. Instead, it was heaving up another rock. Then, as if realizing that Kirk was now out of range, it let the huge mass drop. It seemed to be grinning, although as far as Kirk had been able to see, it never wore any other expression.

Kirk looked around, panting. He seemed to be in a gully, though there was no sign that water had ever run in it—after all, there hadn't even been such a planet many hours ago. There were rocks everywhere, some of them brilliantly colored, and an occasional outcropping of quartzlike crystals. Here and there were patches of scrubby, tough-looking brush, some of it resembling cacti, some mesquite, and even an occasional stand of a large, bamboolike growth. There was nothing that looked as though it could possibly be converted into a weapon, no matter what the Metron had said.

Kirk sat down, rubbing his injured leg but taking great care to watch 10 the now-distant Gorn, and looked over the device at his belt. It looked quite like a tricorder, but both smaller and simpler—though simpler, at least, it doubtless was not. Kirk turned it on with the obvious switch.

"Calling the *Enterprise*. Captain James Kirk calling the *Enterprise*."

For a moment, there was no answer. Then the instrument said, in good but rather stilted English:

"You forget, Captain. We cannot reach our ships. We are alone here, you and I—just one against the other."

He looked back the way he had come. Sure enough, the Gorn seemed to be speaking behind one raised hand. 20

Kirk had not, of course, forgotten that he had been *told* he could not raise the *Enterprise*; he had simply wanted to test the statement. What he had forgotten was that the small instrument had been said to be a translator, as well as a recorder. He would have to be very careful not to mutter to himself after this.

After a moment, he said tentatively, "Look here, Gorn, this is insane. Can't we patch up some kind of truce?"

"Out of the question," the translator said promptly. "That would result only in our staying here until we starved. I cannot speak for you, but I see no water here, nor anything I could eat—with the possible 30 exception of you."

"Neither do I," Kirk admitted.

"Then let us not waste time in sentimental hopes. The rules are what they are: One of us must kill the other."

Kirk hung the device back on his belt. The Gorn was right, and that was most definitely that.

He scrambled over to look at the bamboolike stuff. Each stalk was perhaps three to four inches in diameter—and, as he discovered by trying to break a section loose, it was as hard as iron. Hitting it with a rock even produced a distinctly metallic clank. Perhaps it picked up iron from the 40 soil, as horsetails pick up calcium oxalate, or some prairie grasses pick up selenium. Useless.

He moved on up the gully, which got steadily deeper; he lost sight of the Gorn almost at once. Well, the risk had to be taken; staying where he was had gotten him nowhere.

Earthen banks, rather like bluish clay, reared on both sides of him now. One was steep, but the slope of the other was gentle enough to permit him to clamber up it if he had to.

Sticking out of the clay were the pyramidal points of a number of large crystals. Hopefully, Kirk pried one of them out. It was about the size of a hen's egg, and glittered brilliantly even under this sunless sky. The shape and the brilliancy were unmistakable: It was a diamond, and one that would have made the Kohinoor look like a mail-order zircon. And not only were there more of them imbedded in the clay, but the floor of the gully, he now saw, was a litter of them, in all sizes down to fine sand.

An incredible fortune—and again, utterly useless. None of the gems was sharp enough to be used as a weapon point, and he had no way to cut them. Their only use was to show that this planet was indeed an artificial construction—but Kirk had never doubted that, anyhow. He would have traded the whole wealth of them for a hand phaser, or even a medieval crossbow and a quiver of bolts for it.

The gully turned just ahead. Throwing the diamond away, Kirk went around the bend. The Metron had said that there were the raw materials of weapons here somewhere, if only he—

At the next step, his ankle struck a taut vine, and he went sprawling. At the same moment there was a sharp *crack!* as of wood splitting, and then one whole side of the gully seemed to be roaring down upon him.

He rolled frantically in the other direction, but not fast enough to prevent one rock from slamming into his chest. He felt a rib break. Staggering to his feet, he ran for the nearest cover, a sculptured overhang almost deep enough in back to be called a cave. There he stopped, breathing hard and nursing his rib cage—his whole body seemed to be one enormous bruise—and inspected the snare that had almost killed him through the gradually settling dust.

It was very simple and highly ingenious: a length of stretched vine to serve as a trigger, a broken branch, a heap of carefully stacked boulders that had been freed when the branch had been pulled loose.

Above him, Kirk heard the tick of large claws on rock, and then a sharp hiss of what could only have been disappointment. Kirk grinned mirthlessly. It had been near enough. He peered cautiously out of his hole and upward, just in time to see the Gorn on the lip of the gully on the other side, moving away. The creature was carrying something long and shiny in one hand. Kirk could not tell exactly what it was, but the fact that the Gorn had a torn scrap of his tunic wrapped around that hand was clue enough. It was a daggerlike blade, evidently chipped out of obsidian glass.

Then the creature was gone, but Kirk did not feel the least bit reassured. So far, the Gorn was way ahead, not only on strength, but on ingenuity. First a snare—now a dagger.

Well, then, back to the Stone Age with a vengeance. If Kirk could find a flint point, another length of vine, a sufficiently long stick, he might make a spear. That would give him the advantage of reach against the Gorn's dagger. On the other hand, would a spear penetrate that hide? 10 There was only one way to find out.

A sufficiently large chip of flint, however, obstinately failed to turn up. All that was visible on the floor of the overhang was a wash of brilliant yellow powder.

The stuff looked familiar, and on a hunch, Kirk picked up a small handful of it and breathed on it. It gave out the faint crackle characteristic of flowers of sulfur when moistened.

Kirk grimaced. What a maddening planet. Sand of high-purity sulfur, veritable beaches of diamonds, iron-concentrating bamboos; and at the back of the cave here, outcroppings of rocks covered with a yellowish- 20 white effluvium, like saltpeter. The only way he could make any sort of weapon out of a mélange like that would be with a smelter and a forge—

Wait a minute. Just a minute, now. There was something at the back of his mind—something very ancient . . .

With a gulp of hope, he ran back toward the growth of bamboolike stuff.

With a sharp rock, he managed to break off about a three-foot length of one tube, at one of its joints. The tube was closed at one end, open at the other. Ideal.

Now, the diamonds. He took up only the smallest, the most sandlike, 30 measuring them by handfuls into the tube. He could only hope that his memory of the proportions—seventy-five, fifteen, ten—was correct; in any event, he could only approximate the measures under these conditions. Now, one of the large egg-shaped diamonds; this he put into his mouth, since the tunic did not come equipped with pockets.

Back up the gully, down and around the bend to the overhang. Into the tube went sulfur, saltpeter. Covering the end, he shook the tube until a little of the mixture poured out into his palm showed an even color, though certainly not the color it should have been.

A stone point penetrated the bamboo at the base, though it was hard 40 work. A bit of torn tunic for a patch, and ram it all home with a stick.

Then the egg-shaped diamond; then another patch, and ram again. Finally, a piece of flint; it did not have to be large, not any more.

"Captain," the translator at his belt said. He did not answer.

"Captain, be reasonable," the translator said. "Hiding will do you no good. If it is a matter of competitive starvation, I think my endurance is greater than yours. Why not come out, and die like a warrior?"

Kirk ignored it. Shredding another piece of cloth from the tunic, he began to strike the piece of flint over it, using the translator—at last it had a use!—as the steel. Sparks flew, but the cloth would not catch. If it was noninflammable—   10

"You cannot destroy me," the translator said. "Let us be done with it. I shall be merciful and quick."

"Like you were at Cestus Three?" Kirk said.

"You were intruding," the translator said. "You established an outpost in our space. Naturally we destroyed it."

Kirk did not stop striking sparks, but he was at the same time thoughtful. What the Gorn said was perhaps reasonable, from its point of view. Very little was known about that arm of the galaxy; perhaps the Gorn had a right to regard it as theirs—and to be alarmed at the setting up of a base there, and by the advent of a ship the size of the *Enterprise*. 20 Nevertheless . . .

Smoke rose from the shredded cloth. He raised it to his lips, blowing gently. It was catching.

"All right, Gorn," he told the translator. "Come and get me if you think you can. I'm under the overhang just past where you set your snare."

There was a sharp hiss, and then the clear sound of the Gorn's claws, coming at a run up the gully. Kirk had miscalculated. The creature was closer than he had thought—and faster. Frantically he struggled to align the clumsy bamboo tube.   30

The Gorn leapt into view, its obsidian knife raised. Kirk slapped the burning piece of clothes against the touchhole, and the makeshift cannon went off with a splintering roar. The concussion knocked Kirk down; the semicave was filled with acrid smoke.

He groped to his feet again. As the smoke cleared, he saw the Gorn, slumped against the other wall of the gully. The diamond egg had smashed its right shoulder; but it was bleeding from half a dozen other places too, where diamond chips had flown out of the cannon instead of igniting.

The knife lay between them. Leaping forward, Kirk snatched it up, hurled himself on the downed alien. The knife's point found one of the 40 wounds.

"Now," Kirk said hoarsely, "now let's see how tough your hide is!"

The Gorn did not answer. Though conscious, it seemed to be in shock. It was all over. All Kirk had to do was shove.

He could not do it. He rose, slowly.

"No," he said. "We're in the same pickle. You're trying to save your ship, the same as I am. I won't kill you for that."

Suddenly furious, Kirk looked up at the greenish, overcast sky.

"Do you hear?" he shouted. "I won't kill him! You'll have to get your entertainment someplace else!"

There was a long pause. Kirk stared down at the wounded alien; the Gorn stared back. Its translator had been shattered by the impact; it could not know what Kirk had said. But it did not seem to be afraid.

Then it vanished.

Kirk sat down, dejected and suddenly, utterly weary. Right or wrong, he had lost his opportunity now. The Metron had snatched the Gorn away.

Then there was a humming, much like that he had heard so long ago aboard ship, when the screen had been scrambled. He turned.

A figure was materializing under the overhang. It was not very formidable—certainly nothing so ominous, so awe-inspiring as its voice had suggested. Also, it was very beautiful. It looked like a boy of perhaps eighteen.

"You're a Metron," Kirk said listlessly.

"True," said the figure. "And you have surprised us, Captain."

"How?" Kirk said, not much interested. "By winning?"

"No. We had no preconceptions as to which of you would win. You surprised us by refusing to kill, although you had pursued the Gorn craft into our space with the intention of destroying it."

"That was different," Kirk said. "That was necessary."

"Perhaps it was. It is a new thought. Under the circumstances, it is only fair to tell you that we lied to you."

"In what way?"

"We said that the ship of the loser of this personal combat would be destroyed," said the Metron. "After all, it would be the winner—the stronger, the more resourceful race—who would pose the greatest threat to us. It was the winner we planned to destroy."

Kirk lurched to his feet. "Not my ship," he said dangerously.

"No, Captain. We have changed our minds. By sparing your helpless enemy—who would surely have killed you in like circumstances—you demonstrated the advanced trait of mercy. This we hardly expected—and it leaves us with no clear winner."

"What did you do with the Gorn, then?"

"We sent him back to his ship. And in your case, we misinterpreted your motives. You sincerely believed that you would be destroying the

Gorn ship to keep the peace, not break it. If you like, we shall destroy it for you."

"No!" Kirk said hastily. "That's not necessary. It was a . . . a misunderstanding. Now that we've made contact, we'll be able to talk to the Gorn—reach an agreement."

"Very good," said the Metron. "Perhaps we too shall meet again—in a few thousand years. In any event, there is hope for you."

And abruptly, the *Enterprise* sprang into being around Kirk.

Turmoil broke out on the bridge. Ship's Surgeon McCoy was the first to reach Kirk's side.   10

"Jim! Are you all right?"

"To be quite honest with you," Kirk said dazedly, "I don't know. I just wish the world would stop popping in and out at me."

"I gather you won," Spock said. "How did you do it?"

"Yes . . . I guess so. I'm not quite sure. I thought I did it by reinventing gunpowder—with diamond dust for charcoal. But the Metrons say I won by being a sucker. I don't know which explanation is truer. All the Metrons would tell me is that we're a most promising species—as predators go."

"I could not have put the matter more neatly myself," Spock said. "But, Captain, I would be interested to know what it is you're talking 20 about—when you feel ready, of course."

"Yes, indeed," Kirk said. "In the meantime, posts, everybody. It's time we got back down to business. And, Mr. Spock, about that explanation . . ."

"Yes, sir?"

"I suggest you raise the question again, in, say, a few thousand years."

"Yes, sir."

And the odd thing about Spock, the captain reflected, was that he *would* wait that long too, if only he could figure out a way to live through it—and when the time had all passed, Spock would remember to ask the question again.   30

Kirk hoped he would have an answer.

REVIEWING THE STORY

THE MAIN IDEA

1. Which of the following statements best expresses the *theme* of this story (the idea about life implied by the story)?

   (a) It is foolish to trust what someone tells you.

   (b) Might makes right.

(c) The instinct to be merciful is a good human trait.

(d) Wise travelers carry weapons to defend themselves.

DETAILS

2. At the start of the story, neither Captain Kirk nor the Gorn wants the other to learn the
   (a) extent of damage to his starship.
   (b) location of his home planet.
   (c) capabilities of the transporter.
   (d) secret of the scientific outpost on Cestus Three.

3. The artificial asteroid, or planetoid, prepared by the Metrons contains
   (a) raw materials for constructing a weapon.
   (b) enough food and water for survival.
   (c) a race of giant bipedal lizards.
   (d) the remains of the scientific outpost from Cestus Three.

4. The translator-recorders permit communication between
   (a) Kirk and his crew.
   (b) Kirk and the Metrons.
   (c) the Gorn and its crew.
   (d) Kirk and the Gorn.

5. Kirk uses the metallic bamboo to make a (a) spear (b) club (c) cannon (d) splint.

6. With other natural resources on the planetoid, Kirk makes
   (a) a knife and a spear.
   (b) a transporter and a tricorder.
   (c) gunpowder and bullets.
   (d) poison and bait.

ORDER OF EVENTS

7. Choose the letter that gives the order in which the events happen.
   (1) Kirk and Spock discuss what has happened.
   (2) The entire outpost on Cestus Three is wiped out.
   (3) Kirk uses an improvised weapon to wound the Gorn.
   (4) The Metrons restore Kirk to the *Enterprise*.
      (a) 2-3-1-4 (b) 1-2-3-4 (c) 3-2-1-4 (d) 2-3-4-1

CAUSE AND EFFECT

8. The Gorn has the advantage over Kirk because of its
   - (a) better weapons.
   - (b) greater strength.
   - (c) higher intelligence.
   - (d) familiarity with the terrain.

9. As a result of Kirk's decision about the wounded Gorn, the Metrons offer to destroy
   - (a) both starships.
   - (b) Kirk's starship.
   - (c) the Gorn's starship.
   - (d) neither starship.

INFERENCES

10. We can infer that the Metrons dislike (a) humans (b) space travel (c) violence (d) the Gorns.

11. Kirk was able to wound the Gorn through (a) luck (b) brute strength (c) trickery (d) cleverness.

PREDICTING OUTCOMES

12. If Kirk had not been able to make a weapon, what would you predict as the MOST likely outcome?
    - (a) The Metrons would have destroyed both starships.
    - (b) Kirk would have defeated the Gorn by brute force.
    - (c) The Gorn would have killed Kirk.
    - (d) Neither Kirk nor the Gorn would have been able to defeat the other.

BUILDING YOUR VOCABULARY _____

1. The winner of the *ordeal* will be permitted to go on his way unharmed.

   An *ordeal* (page 347, lines 21-22) is best described as a (a) prize (b) difficult puzzle (c) game (d) severe trial.

2. Shooting a *wary* glance down at himself, Kirk discovered that his own clothing and equipment were identical.

   a. *Wary* (page 347, lines 37-39) means **(a)** tired **(b)** cautious **(c)** sleepy **(d)** slow.

   b. The BEST strategy for choosing the correct answer to part *a* is

   (a) recognizing *wary* as a misspelling of *weary*.
   (b) realizing that *wary* is related to *beware* and *aware*.
   (c) skimming the entire paragraph containing *wary*.
   (d) rereading the sentence containing *wary*.

3. The creature *lurched* slightly, but it did not seem to be hurt.

   Lurched (page 348, lines 31-32) means **(a)** cried **(b)** bled **(c)** staggered **(d)** frowned.

4. A sufficiently large chip of flint, however, *obstinately* failed to turn up.

   The word LEAST like *obstinately* (page 351, lines 12-13) is **(a)** obediently **(b)** stubbornly **(c)** persistently **(d)** firmly.

5. Very little was known about that arm of the galaxy; perhaps the Gorn had a right to regard it as theirs—and to be alarmed at the setting up of a base there, and by the *advent* of a ship the size of the *Enterprise*.

   An *advent* (page 352, lines 18-20) is a(an) **(a)** weapon **(b)** adventure **(c)** report **(d)** arrival.

STUDYING THE WRITER'S CRAFT

1. Irony always involves some kind of unexpected opposite. It may be saying the opposite of what you mean ("Oh, great!" when the ball you hit crashes through a neighbor's window), which is **verbal irony**. Or it may be having something happen that's the opposite of what you expect, which is **irony of situation**. Explain the irony in the situation described in the first two paragraphs of the story.

2. A key element in this story is its **plot**, the series of related actions or events that make up a story. What triggers the plot is a **conflict**, or struggle, between opposing people or forces.

   a. What is the basic conflict in the story? How is it resolved?

   b. Besides the physical conflict, Kirk also has an **internal conflict**, a struggle within himself over a moral question. What is this conflict, and how is it resolved?

c. What question or questions raised by the story create *suspense,* that enjoyable uncertainty over the outcome that makes us read eagerly to find out what happens?

3. *Organization,* or structure, plays an important part in this story. The author uses the structural device of a frame in which to set his story.

a. What are the two parts that form the frame of the story?

b. What purpose or purposes does the frame serve?

ACTIVITIES FOR LISTENING, SPEAKING, WRITING

1. In some respects, "Arena" is a survival story. Both Kirk and the Gorn find themselves marooned with minimal resources on an artificial "desert island." Suppose you had to survive alone on a desert island or in the wilderness. If you could take only three things with you, what would you choose? With two of your classmates, reach an agreement on a basic list of three survival essentials. Each group of students will then present its list to the rest of the class. Be prepared to give reasons for your choices.

2. When Mr. Spock asks Captain Kirk how he won the battle against the Gorn, the Captain replies: "I thought I did it by reinventing gunpowder—with diamond dust for charcoal. But the Metrons say I won by being a sucker. I don't know which explanation is truer." (page 354, lines 15-17) Which explanation seems truer to you? Was Kirk a sucker? How did he really win? Be prepared to discuss these questions with your classmates.

3. In an earlier story in this book titled "The Large Ant" (pages 206-214), the narrator, Mr. Morgan, represents one view of the human race. In "Arena," Captain Kirk represents another view. Read (or reread) "The Large Ant." What is the difference between the views of humanity implied by the two stories? Do you agree with one view more than the other? If so, why? Write a brief answer to these questions.

A Pail of Air

by Fritz Leiber

He told us how the Earth had been swinging around the Sun ever so steady and warm, and the people on it fixing to make money and get power and treat each other right or wrong, when without warning there comes charging out of space this dead star, this burned-out sun, and upsets everything.

Not all disasters in science fiction—or in real life—are caused by people. We have plenty of opportunities to test our resourcefulness, courage, and wisdom against fires, floods, earthquakes, hurricanes, and other natural catastrophes. How humans cope with calamity, whatever the cause, is a popular motif in science fiction.

In the following story about a family of survivors in a frozen future world, Fritz Leiber creates a memorable blend of horror, humor, and hope. As you read the story, ask yourself: What is most important to these people? If I were in their world, what would matter most to me?

Fritz Leiber

Winner of many Hugo and Nebula awards, Leiber has been writing fiction for half a century. With a background in the theater, he has a dramatist's sense of plot and an actor's feeling for character. He combined these talents in his time-travel novel *The Big Time* (1961). His many novels and short stories range widely through heroic fantasy, horror, and traditional science fiction. The award-winning novel *The Wanderer* (1965), like his story "A Pail of Air," tells of the disaster caused when a huge object from outer space threatens the Earth.

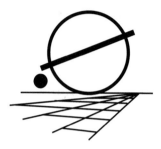

Pa had sent me out to get an extra pail of air. I'd just about scooped it full and most of the warmth had leaked from my fingers when I saw the thing.

You know, at first I thought it was a young lady. Yes, a beautiful young lady's face all glowing in the dark and looking at me from the fifth floor of the opposite apartment, which hereabouts is the floor just above the white blanket of frozen air four storeys thick. I'd never seen a live young lady before, except in the old magazines—Sis is just a kid and Ma is pretty sick and miserable—and it gave me such a start that I dropped the pail. Who wouldn't, knowing everyone on Earth was dead 10 except Pa and Ma and Sis and you?

Even at that, I don't suppose I should have been surprised. We all see things now and then. Ma sees some pretty bad ones, to judge from the way she bugs her eyes at nothing and just screams and screams and huddles back against the blankets hanging around the Nest. Pa says it is natural we should react like that sometimes.

When I'd recovered the pail and could look again at the opposite apartment, I got an idea of what Ma might be feeling at those times, for I saw it wasn't a young lady at all but simply a light—a tiny light that moved stealthily from window to window, just as if one of the cruel little 20 stars had come down out of the airless sky to investigate why the Earth had gone away from the Sun, and maybe to hunt down something to torment or terrify, now that the Earth didn't have the Sun's protection.

I tell you, the thought of it gave me the creeps. I just stood there shaking, and almost froze my feet and did frost my helmet so solid on the inside that I couldn't have seen the light even if it had come out of one of the windows to get me. Then I had the wit to go back inside.

Pretty soon I was feeling my familiar way through the thirty or so blankets and rugs and rubbery sheets Pa has got hung and braced around 10 to slow down the escape of air from the Nest, and I wasn't quite so scared. I began to hear the tick-ticking of the clocks in the Nest and knew I was getting back into air, because there's no sound outside in the vacuum, of course. But my mind was still crawly and uneasy as I pushed through the last blankets—Pa's got them faced with aluminum foil to hold in the heat—and came into the Nest.

Let me tell you about the Nest. It's low and snug, just room for the four of us and our things. The floor is covered with thick woolly rugs. Three of the sides are blankets, and the blankets roofing it touch Pa's head. He tells me it's inside a much bigger room, but I've never seen the 20 real walls or ceiling.

Against one of the blanket-walls is a big set of shelves, with tools and books and other stuff, and on top of it a whole row of clocks. Pa's very fussy about keeping them wound. He says we must never forget time, and without a Sun or Moon, that would be easy to do.

The fourth wall has blankets all over except around the fireplace, in which there is a fire that must never go out. It keeps us from freezing and does a lot more besides. One of us must always watch it. Some of the clocks are alarm and we can use them to remind us. In the early days there was only Ma to take turns with Pa—I think of that when she gets 30 difficult—but now there's me to help, and Sis too.

It's Pa who is the chief guardian of the fire, though. I always think of him that way: a tall man sitting cross-legged, frowning anxiously at the fire, his lined face golden in its light, and every so often carefully placing on it a piece of coal from the big heap beside it. Pa tells me there used to be guardians of the fire sometimes in the very old days—vestals, he calls them—although there was unfrozen air all around then and a Sun too and you didn't really need a fire.

He was sitting just that way now, though he got up quick to take the pail from me and bawl me out for loitering—he'd spotted my frozen 40 helmet right off. That roused Ma and she joined in picking on me. She's always trying to get the load off her feelings, Pa explains. He shut her up pretty fast. Sis let off a couple of silly squeals too.

Pa handled the pail of air in a twist of cloth. Now that it was inside the Nest, you could really feel its coldness. It just seemed to suck the heat out of everything. Even the flames cringed away from it as Pa put it down close by the fire.

Yet it's that glimmery blue-white stuff in the pail that keeps us alive. It slowly melts and vanishes and refreshes the Nest and feeds the fire. The blankets keep it from escaping too fast. Pa'd like to seal the whole place, but he can't—building's too earthquake-twisted, and besides he 10 has to leave the chimney open for smoke. But the chimney has special things Pa calls baffles up inside it, to keep the air from getting out too quick that way. Sometimes Pa, making a joke, says it baffles him they keep on working, or work at all.

Pa says air is tiny molecules that fly away like a flash if there isn't something to stop them. We have to watch sharp not to let the air run low. Pa always keeps a big reserve supply of it in buckets behind the first blankets, along with extra coal and cans of food and bottles of vitamins and other things, such as pails of snow to melt for water. We have to go way down to the bottom floor for that stuff, which is a mean trip, and 20 get it through a door to outside.

You see, when the Earth got cold, all the water in the air froze first and made a blanket ten feet thick or so everywhere, and then down on top of that dropped the crystals of frozen air, making another mostly white blanket sixty or seventy feet thick maybe.

Of course, all the parts of the air didn't freeze and snow down at the same time.

First to drop out was the carbon dioxide—when you're shoveling for water, you have to make sure you don't go too high and get any of that stuff mixed in, for it would put you to sleep, maybe for good, and make the fire 30 go out. Next there's the nitrogen, which doesn't count one way or the other, though it's the biggest part of the blanket. On top of that and easy to get at, which is lucky for us, there's the oxygen that keeps us alive. It's pale blue, which helps you tell it from the nitrogen. It has to be colder for oxygen to freeze solid than nitrogen. That's why the oxygen snowed down last.

Pa says we live better than kings ever did, breathing pure oxygen, but we're used to it and don't notice.

Finally, at the very top, there's a slick of liquid helium, which is funny stuff.

All of these gases are in neat separate layers.   40

I was busting to tell them all about what I'd seen, and so as soon as I'd ducked out of my helmet and while I was still climbing out of my suit, I cut loose. Right away Ma got nervous and began making eyes at the entry-slit in the blankets and wringing her hands together—the hand where she'd lost three fingers from frostbite inside the good one, as usual. I could tell that Pa was annoyed at me scaring her and wanted to explain it all away quickly, yet I knew he knew I wasn't fooling.

"And you watched this light for some time, son?" he asked when I finished.

I hadn't said anything about first thinking it was a young lady's face. Somehow that part embarrassed me.

"Long enough for it to pass five windows and go to the next floor." 10

"And it didn't look like stray electricity or crawling liquid or star-light focused by a growing crystal, or anything like that?"

He wasn't just making up those ideas. Odd things happen in a world that's about as cold as can be, and just when you think matter would be frozen dead, it takes on a strange new life. A slimy stuff comes crawling toward the Nest, just like an animal snuffing for heat—that's liquid helium. And once, when I was little, a bolt of lightning—not even Pa could figure where it came from—hit the nearby steeple and crawled up and down it for weeks, until the glow finally died.

"Not like anything I ever saw," I told him. 20

He stood for a moment frowning. Then, "I'll go out with you, and you show it to me," he said.

Ma raised a howl at the idea of being left alone, and Sis joined in, too, but Pa quieted them. We started climbing into our outside clothes— mine had been warming by the fire. Pa made them. They have triple-pane plastic headpieces that were once big double-duty transparent food cans, but they keep heat and air in and can replace the air for a little while, long enough for our trips for water and coal and food and so on.

Ma started moaning again, "I've always known there was something outside there, waiting to get us. I've felt it for years—something that's 30 part of the cold and hates all warmth and wants to destroy the Nest. It's been watching us all this time, and now it's coming after us. It'll get you and then come for me. Don't go, Harry!"

Pa had everything on but his helmet. He knelt by the fireplace and reached in and shook the long metal rod that goes up the chimney and knocks off the ice that keeps trying to clog it. Once a week he goes up on the roof to check if it's working all right. That's our worst trip and Pa won't let me make it alone.

"Sis," Pa said quietly, "come watch the fire. Keep an eye on the air, too. If it gets low or doesn't seem to be boiling fast enough, fetch another 40 bucket from behind the blanket. But mind your hands. Use the cloth to pick up the bucket."

Sis quit helping Ma be frightened and came over and did as she was told. Ma quieted down pretty suddenly, though her eyes were still kind of wild as she watched Pa fix on his helmet tight and pick up a pail and the two of us go out.

Pa led the way and I took hold of his belt. It's a funny thing, I'm not afraid to go by myself, but when Pa's along I always want to hold on to him. Habit, I guess, and then there's no denying that this time I was a bit scared.

You see, it's this way. We know that everything is dead out there. Pa heard the last radio voices fade away years ago, and had seen some of the last folks die who weren't as lucky or well-protected as us. So we knew that if there was something groping around out there, it couldn't be anything human or friendly.

Besides that, there's a feeling that comes with it always being night, *cold* night. Pa says there used to be some of that feeling even in the old days, but then every morning the Sun would come and chase it away. I have to take his word for that, not ever remembering the Sun as being anything more than a big star. You see, I hadn't been born when the dark star snatched us away from the Sun, and by now it's dragged us out beyond the orbit of the planet Pluto, Pa says, and is taking us farther out all the time.

We can see the dark star as it crosses the sky because it blots out stars, and especially when it's outlined by the Milky Way. It's pretty big, for we're closer to it than the planet Mercury was to the Sun, Pa says, but we don't care to look at it much and Pa won't set his clocks by it.

I found myself wondering whether there mightn't be something on the dark star that wanted us, and if that was why it had captured the Earth. Just then we came to the end of the corridor and I followed Pa out on the balcony.

I don't know what the city looked like in the old days, but now it's beautiful. The starlight lets you see it pretty well—there's quite a bit of light in those steady points speckling the blackness above. (Pa says the stars used to twinkle once, but that was because there was air.) We are on a hill and the shimmery plain drops away from us and then flattens out, cut up into neat squares by the troughs that used to be streets. I sometimes make my mashed potatoes look like it, before I pour on the gravy.

Some taller buildings push up out of the feathery plain, topped by rounded caps of air crystals, like the fur hood Ma wears, only whiter. On those buildings you can see the darker squares of windows, underlined by white dashes of air crystals. Some of them are on a slant, for many of the buildings are pretty badly twisted by the quakes and all the rest that happened when the dark star captured the Earth.

Here and there a few icicles hang, water icicles from the first days of the cold, other icicles of frozen air that melted on the roofs and dropped and froze again. Sometimes one of those icicles will catch the light of a star and send it to you so brightly you think the star has swooped into the city. That was one of the things Pa had been thinking of when I told him about the light, but I had thought of it myself first and known it wasn't so.

He touched his helmet to mine so we could talk easier and he asked me to point out the windows to him. But there wasn't any light moving around inside them now, or anywhere else. To my surprise, Pa didn't bawl 10 me out and tell me I'd been seeing things. He looked all around quite a while after filling his pail, and just as we were going inside he whipped around without warning, as if to take some peeping thing off guard.

I could feel it, too. The old peace was gone. There was something lurking out there, watching, waiting, getting ready.

Inside, he said to me, touching helmets, "If you see something like that again, son, don't tell the others. Your Ma's sort of nervous these days and we owe her all the feeling of safety we can give her. Once—it was when your sister was born—I was ready to give up and die, but your Mother kept me trying. Another time she kept the fire going a whole 20 week all by herself when I was sick. Nursed me and took care of the two of you, too.

"You know that game we sometimes play, sitting in a square in the Nest, tossing a ball around? Courage is like a ball, son. A person can hold it only so long, and then he's got to toss it to someone else. When it's tossed your way, you've got to catch it and hold it tight—and hope there'll be someone else to toss it to when you get tired of being brave."

His talking to me that way made me feel grown-up and good. But it didn't wipe away the thing outside from the back of my mind—or the fact that Pa took it seriously. 30

It's hard to hide your feelings about such a thing. When we got back in the Nest and took off our outside clothes, Pa laughed about it all and told them it was nothing and kidded me for having such an imagination, but his words fell flat. He didn't convince Ma and Sis any more than he did me. It looked for a minute like we were all fumbling the courage-ball. Something had to be done, and almost before I knew what I was going to say, I heard myself asking Pa to tell us about the old days, and how it all happened.

He sometimes doesn't mind telling that story, and Sis and I sure like to listen to it, and he got my idea. So we were all settled around the fire 40 in a wink, and Ma pushed up some cans to thaw for supper, and Pa began. Before he did, though, I noticed him casually get a hammer from the shelf and lay it down beside him.

It was the same old story as always—I think I could recite the main thread of it in my sleep—though Pa always puts in a new detail or two and keeps improving it in spots.

He told us how the Earth had been swinging around the Sun ever so steady and warm, and the people on it fixing to make money and wars and have a good time and get power and treat each other right or wrong, when without warning there comes charging out of space this dead star, this burned out sun, and upsets everything.   10

You know, I find it hard to believe in the way those people felt, any more than I can believe in the swarming number of them. Imagine people getting ready for the horrible sort of war they were cooking up. Wanting it even, or at least wishing it were over so as to end their nervousness. As if all folks didn't have to hang together and pool every bit of warmth just to keep alive. And how can they have hoped to end danger, any more than we can hope to end the cold?

Sometimes I think Pa exaggerates and makes things out too black. He's cross with us once in a while and was probably cross with all those folks. Still, some of the things I read in the old magazines sound pretty 20 wild. He may be right.

The dark star, as Pa went on telling it, rushed in pretty fast and there wasn't much time to get ready. At the beginning they tried to keep it a secret from most people, but then the truth came out, what with the earthquakes and floods—imagine, oceans of *unfrozen* water!—and people seeing stars blotted out by something on a clear night. First off they thought it would hit the Sun, and then they thought it would hit the Earth. There was even the start of a rush to get in a place called China, because people thought the star would hit on the other side. Not that that would have helped them, they were just crazy with fear. But then they found it wasn't 30 going to hit either side, but was going to come very close to the Earth.

Most of the other planets were on the other side of the Sun and didn't get involved. The Sun and the newcomer fought over the Earth for a little while—pulling it this way and that, in a twisty curve, like two dogs growling over a bone, Pa described it this time—and then the newcomer won and carried us off. The Sun got a consolation prize, though. At the last minute he managed to hold on to the Moon.

That was the time of the monster earthquakes and floods, twenty times worse than anything before. It was also the time of the Big Swoop, as Pa calls it, when the Earth speeded up, going into a close orbit around 40 the dark star.

I've asked Pa, wasn't the Earth yanked then, just as he has done to me sometimes, grabbing me by the collar to do it, when I've been sitting too far from the fire. But Pa says no, gravity doesn't work that way. It was like a yank, but nobody felt it. I guess it was like being yanked in a dream.

You see, the dark star was going through space faster than the Sun, and in the opposite direction, and it had to speed up the world a lot in order to take it away.

The Big Swoop didn't last long. It was over as soon as the Earth was settled down in its new orbit around the dark star. But the earthquakes 10 and floods were terrible while it lasted, twenty times worse than anything before. Pa says that all sorts of cliffs and buildings toppled, oceans slopped over, swamps and sandy deserts gave great sliding surges that buried nearby lands. Earth's blanket of air, still up in the sky then, was stretched out and got so thin in spots that people keeled over and fainted—though of course, at the same time, they were getting knocked down by the earthquakes that went with the Big Swoop and maybe their bones broke or skulls cracked.

We've often asked Pa how people acted during that time, whether they were scared or brave or crazy or stunned, or all four, but he's sort 20 of leery of the subject, and he was again tonight. He says he was mostly too busy to notice.

You see, Pa and some scientist friends of his had figured out part of what was going to happen—they'd known we'd get captured and our air would freeze—and they'd been working like mad to fix up a place with airtight walls and doors, and insulation against the cold, and big supplies of food and fuel and water and bottled air. But the place got smashed in the last earthquakes and all Pa's friends were killed then and in the Big Swoop. So he had to start over and throw the Nest together quick without any advantages, just using any stuff he could lay his hands 30 on.

I guess he's telling pretty much the truth when he says he didn't have any time to keep an eye on how other folks behaved, either then or in the Big Freeze that followed—followed very quick, you know, both because the dark star was pulling us away very fast and because Earth's rotation had been slowed by the tug-of-war and the tides, so that the nights were longer.

Still, I've got an idea of some of the things that happened from the frozen folk I've seen, a few of them in other rooms in our building, others clustered around the furnaces in the basements where we go for coal.   40

In one of the rooms, an old man sits stiff in a chair, with an arm and a leg in splints. In another, a man and woman are huddled together in a bed with heaps of covers over them. You can just see their heads peeking out, close together. And in another a beautiful young lady is sitting with a pile of wraps huddled around her, looking hopefully toward the door, as if waiting for someone who never came back with warmth and food. They're all still and stiff as statues, of course, but just like life.

Pa showed them to me once in quick winks of his flashlight, when he still had a fair supply of batteries and could afford to waste a little light. They scared me pretty bad and made my heart pound, especially the young lady.

Now, with Pa telling his story for the umpteenth time to take our 10 minds off another scare, I got to thinking of the frozen folk again. All of a sudden I got an idea that scared me worse than anything yet. You see, I'd just remembered that face I'd thought I'd seen in the window. I'd forgotten about that on account of trying to hide it from the others.

What, I asked myself, if the frozen folk were coming to life? What if they were like the liquid helium that got a new lease on life and started crawling toward the heat just when you thought its molecules ought to freeze solid forever? Or like the electricity that moves endlessly when it's just about as cold as that? What if the ever-growing cold, with the temperature creeping down the last few degrees to the last zero, had myste- 20 riously wakened the frozen folk to life—not warm-blooded life, but something icy and horrible?

That was a worse idea than the one about something coming down from the dark star to get us.

Or maybe, I thought, both ideas might be true. Something coming down from the dark star and making the frozen folk move, using them to do its work. That would fit with both things I'd seen—the beautiful young lady and the moving, starlike light.

The frozen folk with minds from the dark star behind their unwinking eyes, creeping, crawling, snuffing their way, following the heat to the 30 Nest, maybe wanting the heat, but more likely hating it and wanting to chill it forever, snuff out our fire.

I tell you, that thought gave me a very bad turn and I wanted very badly to tell the others my fears, but I remembered what Pa had said and clenched my teeth and didn't speak.

We were all sitting very still. Even the fire was burning silently. There was just the sound of Pa's voice and the clocks.

And then, from beyond the blankets, I thought I heard a tiny noise. My skin tightened all over me.

Pa was telling about the early years in the Nest and had come to 40 the place where he philosophizes.

"So I asked myself then," he said, "what's the use of dragging it out for a few years? Why prolong a doomed existence of hard work and cold and loneliness? The human race is done. The Earth is done. Why not give up, I asked myself—and all of a sudden I got the answer."

Again I heard the noise, louder this time, a kind of uncertain, shuffling tread, coming closer. I couldn't breathe.

"Life's always been a business of working hard and fighting the cold," Pa was saying. "The earth's always been a lonely place, millions of miles from the next planet. And no matter how long the human race might have lived, the end would have come some night. Those things don't matter. 10 What matters is that life is good. It has a lovely texture, like some thick fur or the petals of flowers—you've never seen those, but you know our ice-flowers—or like the texture of flames, never twice the same. It makes everything else worthwhile. And that's as true for the last man as the first."

And still the steps kept shuffling closer. It seemed to me that the inmost blanket trembled and bulged a little. Just as if they were burned into my imagination, I kept seeing those peering, frozen eyes.

"So right then and there," Pa went on, and now I could tell that he heard the steps, too, and was talking loud so we maybe wouldn't hear them, "right then and there I told myself that I was going on as if we 20 had all eternity ahead of us. I'd have children and teach them all I could. I'd get them to read books. I'd plan for the future, try to enlarge and seal the Nest. I'd do what I could to keep everything beautiful and growing. I'd keep alive my feeling of wonder even at the cold and the dark and the distant stars."

But then the blanket actually did move and lift. And there was a bright light somewhere behind it. Pa's voice stopped and his eyes turned to the widening slit and his hand went out until it touched and gripped the handle of the hammer beside him.

In through the blanket stepped the beautiful young lady. She stood 30 there looking at us the strangest way, and she carried something bright and unwinking in her hand. And two other faces peered over her shoulders—men's faces, white and staring.

Well, my heart couldn't have been stopped for more than four or five beats before I realized she was wearing a suit and helmet like Pa's homemade ones, only fancier, and that the men were, too—and that the frozen folk certainly wouldn't be wearing those. Also, I noticed that the bright thing in her hand was just a kind of flashlight.

Sinking down very softly, Ma fainted.

The silence kept on while I swallowed hard a couple of times, and 40 after that there was all sorts of jabbering and commotion.

They were simply people, you see. We hadn't been the only ones to survive; we'd just thought so, for natural enough reasons. These three people had survived, and quite a few others with them. And when we found out *how* they'd survived, Pa let out the biggest whoop of joy.

They were from Los Alamos[1] and they were getting their heat and power from atomic energy. Just using the uranium and plutonium intended for bombs, they had enough to go on for thousands of years. They had a regular little airtight city, with airlocks and all. They even generated electric light and grew plants and animals by it. (At this Pa let out a second whoop, waking Ma from her faint.)   10

But if we were flabbergasted at them, they were double-flabbergasted at us.

One of the men kept saying, "But it's impossible, I tell you. You can't maintain an air supply without hermetic sealing. It's simply impossible."

That was after he had got his helmet off and was using our air. Meanwhile, the young lady kept looking around at us as if we were saints, and telling us we'd done something amazing, and suddenly she broke down and cried.

They'd been scouting around for survivors, but they never ex-   20 pected to find any in a place like this. They had rocket ships at Los Alamos and plenty of chemical fuel. As for liquid oxygen, all you had to do was go out and shovel the air blanket at the top level. So after they'd got things going smoothly at Los Alamos, which had taken years, they'd decided to make some trips to likely places where there might be other survivors. No good trying long-distance radio signals, of course, since there was no atmosphere, no ionosphere, to carry them around the curve of the Earth. That was why all the radio signals had died out.

Well, they'd found other colonies at Argonne and Brookhaven and   30 way around the world at Harwell and Tanna Tuva.[2] And now they'd been giving our city a look, not really expecting to find anything. But they had an instrument that noticed the faintest heat waves and it had told them there was something warm down here, so they'd landed to investigate. Of course we hadn't heard them land, since there was no air to carry the sound, and they'd had to investigate around quite a while before finding us. Their instruments had given them a wrong steer, and they'd wasted some time in the building across the street.

1. **Los Alamos:** town in New Mexico where the first atomic bomb was developed and tested in 1945.
2. **Argonne . . . Tanna Tuva:** locations of atomic-research laboratories in France, the United States, Great Britain, and the former Soviet Union.

By now, all five adults were talking like sixty. Pa was demonstrating to the men how he worked the fire and got rid of the ice in the chimney and all that. Ma had perked up wonderfully and was showing the young lady her cooking and sewing stuff, and even asking about how the women dressed at Los Alamos. The strangers marveled at everything and praised it to the skies. I could tell from the way they wrinkled their noses that they found the Nest a bit smelly, but they never mentioned that at all and just asked bushels of questions.

In fact, there was so much talking and excitement that Pa forgot about things, and it wasn't until they were all getting groggy that he looked and found the air had all boiled away in the pail. He got another bucket of air quick from behind the blankets. Of course that started them all laughing and jabbering again. The newcomers even got a little drunk. They weren't used to so much oxygen.

Funny thing, though—I didn't do much talking at all, and Sis hung on to Ma all the time and hid her face when anybody looked at her. I felt pretty uncomfortable and disturbed myself, even about the young lady. Glimpsing her outside there, I'd had all sorts of mushy thoughts, but now I was just embarrassed and scared of her, even though she tried to be nice as anything to me.

I sort of wished they'd all quit crowding the Nest and let us be alone and get our feelings straightened out.

And when the newcomers began to talk about our all going to Los Alamos, as if that were taken for granted, I could see that something of the same feeling struck Pa and Ma, too. Pa got very silent all of a sudden, and Ma kept telling the young lady, "But I wouldn't know how to act there and I haven't any clothes."

The strangers were puzzled like anything at first, but then they got the idea. As Pa kept saying, "It just doesn't seem right to let this fire go out."

Well, the strangers are gone, but they're coming back. It hasn't been decided yet just what will happen. Maybe the Nest will be kept up as what one of the strangers called a "survival school." Or maybe we will join the pioneers who are going to try to establish a new colony at the uranium mines at Great Slave Lake or in the Congo.

Of course, now that the strangers are gone, I've been thinking a lot about Los Alamos and those other tremendous colonies. I have a hankering to see them for myself.

You ask me, Pa wants to see them, too. He's been getting pretty thoughtful, watching Ma and Sis perk up.

"It's different, now that we know others are alive," he explains to me. "Your mother doesn't feel so hopeless any more. Neither do I, for that matter, not having to carry the whole responsibility for keeping the human race going, so to speak. It scares a person."

I looked around at the blanket walls and the fire and the pails of air boiling away and Ma and Sis sleeping in the warmth and the flickering light.

"It's not going to be easy to leave the Nest," I said, wanting to cry, kind of. "It's so small and there's just the four of us. I get scared at the idea of big places and a lot of strangers."

He nodded and put another piece of coal on the fire. Then he looked at the little pile and grinned suddenly and put a couple of handfuls on, 10 just as if it was one of our birthdays or Christmas.

"You'll quickly get over that feeling, son," he said. "The trouble with the world was that it kept getting smaller and smaller, till it ended with just the Nest. Now it'll be good to start building up to a real huge world again, the way it was in the beginning."

I guess he's right. You think the beautiful young lady will wait for me till I grow up? I asked her that and she smiled to thank me, and then she told me she's got a daughter almost my age and that there are lots of children at the atomic places. Imagine that.

REVIEWING THE STORY

THE MAIN IDEA

1. The main idea of the story is that
   (a) people are helpless in a disaster.
   (b) work makes life meaningful.
   (c) life is worth preserving even under the worst circumstances.
   (d) some day everything on Earth will be destroyed by a natural disaster.

DETAILS

2. The main characters consist of (a) scientists (b) a family (c) the staff of an atomic energy plant (d) a group of strangers.

3. The Nest protects those in it against (a) radioactive fallout (b) loss of heat and oxygen (c) attack by bandits (d) loss of gravity.

4. The narrator is a (a) boy (b) girl (c) man (d) woman.

5. The oxygen in the "pail of air" is used for
   (a) fueling a jet engine.
   (b) eating and drinking.
   (c) keeping strangers away.
   (d) breathing and burning coal.

6. The search party from Los Alamos is looking for (a) bandits (b) survivors (c) atomic energy (d) oxygen.

ORDER OF EVENTS

7. Choose the letter that gives the order in which the events happen.
   (1) Three strangers enter the Nest.
   (2) Pa tells about the old days.
   (3) The narrator sees a moving light in a building.
   (4) The dark star carries off the Earth.
       (a) 4-3-2-1 (b) 1-2-3-4 (c) 2-4-3-1 (d) 4-2-1-3

CAUSE AND EFFECT

8. The narrator is able to collect pure oxygen in a pail because all of the gases in the Earth's atmosphere have
   (a) been preserved exactly as they used to be.
   (b) combined into a single layer of pale blue liquid.
   (c) been packaged and stored in pails.
   (d) frozen in separate layers.

9. As a result of the dark star's passage,
   (a) the Moon was destroyed.
   (b) all plant and animal life perished.
   (c) most of humanity died.
   (d) the other planets no longer orbited the Sun.

INFERENCES

10. Before the global catastrophe, Pa was probably a(an) (a) explorer (b) astronaut (c) businessman (d) scientist.

11. We can infer that the author of the story probably regards science and technology with (a) approval (b) disapproval (c) fear (d) indifference.

PREDICTING OUTCOMES

12. Looking beyond the story, we can predict that the remaining humans will probably
  (a) perish in outer space.
  (b) rebuild civilization.
  (c) colonize the dark star.
  (d) fight one another to survive.

BUILDING YOUR VOCABULARY

1. He was sitting just that way now, though he got up quick to take the pail from me and bawl me out for *loitering*—he'd spotted my frozen helmet right off.

Loitering (page 361, lines 39-41) means **(a)** washing **(b)** hurrying **(c)** delaying **(d)** lying.

2. Even the flames *cringed* away from it as Pa put it down close by the fire.

The BEST definition of *cringed* (page 362, lines 5-6) is **(a)** leaped boldly **(b)** shrank back **(c)** burned merrily **(d)** cried out loudly.

3. But the chimney has special things Pa calls *baffles* up inside it, to keep the air from getting out too quick that way. Sometimes Pa, making a joke, says it *baffles* him they keep on working, or work at all.

  a. In the first sentence, *baffles* (page 362, lines 11-13) are devices to
    (a) warm up cool air.
    (b) cool down hot air.
    (c) make something airtight.
    (d) block or control air flow.

  b. The BEST clue to the meaning of *baffles* in part *a* is to be found in
    (a) the word itself.
    (b) the sentence containing the word.
    (c) the last sentence of the paragraph.
    (d) the sentence before the one containing the word.

  c. The meaning of *baffles* in the second sentence is **(a)** pleases **(b)** pains **(c)** puzzles **(d)** panics.

4. There was something *lurking* out there, watching, waiting, getting ready.

   Lurking (page 365, lines 14-15) means

   (a) lying hidden and waiting to do harm.
   (b) walking to and fro in the open.
   (c) growling and baring sharp teeth.
   (d) gathering troops for an attack.

5. I have a *hankering* to see them for myself.

   The BEST synonym for *hankering* (page 371, lines 36-37) is   (a) desire
   (b) reluctance (c) inability (d) obligation.

STUDYING THE WRITER'S CRAFT

1. Skilled writers often use *suspense* to whet the curiosity of their readers and keep them reading.

   a. In the first paragraph of the story, the narrator refers to a "pail of air." Where in the story is this puzzling reference explained?

   b. The author ends the first paragraph of the story by writing that the narrator "saw a thing." How does the author keep us wondering what this "thing" is? Where in the story do we learn what the "thing" really is? What is it?

2. To make a work of fiction believable, a writer introduces details that give the story *verisimilitude*, or the appearance of truth. What are some of the details that make the survival of the family in "A Pail of Air" believable?

3. Scattered through the story are many expressions like the following: "You know," "I tell you," "Let me tell you," "You see," "Well," "Funny thing, though," "I sort of," "Imagine that." What effect do such expressions have upon the narrative style? Why do you think the author sprinkled his narration with these phrases?

ACTIVITIES FOR LISTENING, SPEAKING, WRITING

1. The authorities at Los Alamos have decided to honor Pa and Ma with a medal. They ask you to write a speech about them to be delivered aloud when they receive the medal. Working alone or with one or more of your classmates, draft a short speech that pays tribute to the characters and accomplishments of this couple.

2. Did you or any of your classmates ever live through a natural disaster such as an earthquake, flood, fire, blizzard, or hurricane? How did the other people behave in this emergency? What were your own feelings and behavior? How do they compare with the feelings and behavior of the characters in the story? Be prepared to discuss with your classmates the ways in which people act in such crises.

3. Listen while your teacher reads aloud a brief article from a newspaper. The article discusses a threat from outer space that could cause as much damage to the Earth as did the dark star in the story. Take notes as you listen, and be prepared to discuss the ideas in the article with your classmates. (The article appears in a separate answer key accompanying this book.)

How Easy to See the Future

by Isaac Asimov

The best way to defeat a catastrophe is to take action to prevent it long before it happens. . . . To do that, one must foresee the catastrophe in time, and science fiction helps one to do so.

Why read science fiction? The first and best reason is that reading science fiction is fun. It takes you to strange new worlds often inhabited by even stranger creatures. It lets you look at your own world from fresh, new perspectives. At its best, science fiction stimulates, delights, and entertains you.

In the following article, Isaac Asimov suggests that science fiction can offer even more than entertainment. Now that you have read most or all of the stories in this book, would you agree with him? Is science fiction just "escape literature"? Or is it something more? As you read the article, think about other answers to the question: Why read science fiction?

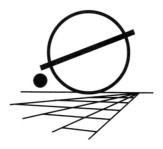

If one were to glance over the thousands of years of history of Homo sapiens, we might make the following generalizations:

1. As time passed, the human way of life continually changed.

2. The change has generally resulted from a technological advance: a new tool, a new technique, a new energy source.

3. As each technological advance broadened the base of human technological capacity, further advances became more frequent and were made in a greater number of directions, so that the rate of change has, in the course of history, continually increased.

Until modern times, the rate of change was so slow as to make the process unnoticeable in the course of any one person's lifetime. It was therefore the illusion of mankind that change did not take place. When, in the face of that illusion, a change had clearly taken place, the response was to view it as something that should not have taken place, as something that represented a degeneration from the "good old days."

The steadily increasing rate of change reached the stage, at about 1800, of becoming clearly visible to many thoughtful individuals. The Industrial Revolution was beginning, and those affected by it could detect change in the course of their own lifetimes.

For the first time, some people grew to understand that not only was change taking place, but that it would continue to take place after their deaths. It meant there would come to be changes still greater than a person had lived to see, changes that he would never see. This gave rise to a new curiosity—perhaps the first really new curiosity developed in historic times—that of wondering what life on Earth would be like after one was no longer alive. The literary response to that new curiosity was what we now call "science fiction."

Science fiction can be defined as that branch of literature which deals with the reaction of human beings to changes in science and technology.

The reference can be to *any* changes, of course, and the science fiction writer chooses those which provide him with a dramatic situation out of which he can weave an exciting plot. There is usually no deliberate attempt to predict what will actually happen, but a science fiction writer is a creature of his times, and in trying to imagine a change in science and technology he is quite likely to base it on those changes he already sees in embryo.

Often this means an extrapolation of the present, an extrapolation that is so clear and obvious as to forecast something that is inevitable. 10 When this happens, the science fiction writer *does* make a successful prediction. Usually, this astonishes almost everyone, for mankind generally, even today, takes it for granted that things do not change.

Here is an example. As the twentieth century opened, oil was coming into use as a source of energy and, thanks to the internal-combustion engine, was beginning to gain on coal.

Now oil, like coal, is a fossil fuel. There is only so much of it in the ground—even if our entire planet were solid coal and oil, there is only so much of it in the ground—and new supplies are being formed at an entirely trivial rate. If oil and coal are being constantly burned, then some- 20 day the natural supply present in the ground will be used up. That is not a matter of argument at all; it is inevitable. The only question is, When?

Mankind, generally, assuming that since there is oil in the ground today, there will be oil in the ground forever (the doctrine of no change), is not concerned with the matter. The science fiction writer, however, avidly seeking out change as a matter of artistic necessity, takes up the possibility of an end of our fossil-fuel supply. It then becomes possible for a science fiction writer to say:

"Coal is the key to metallurgy and oil to transit. When they are done, we shall either have built up such a fabric of apparatus, knowledge, and social organization that we shall be able to manage without them—or we shall have traveled a long way down the slopes of waste towards extinc- 10 tion— Today, in getting, in distribution, in use, we waste enormously— As we sit there all the world is wasting fuel—fantastically."

That certainly sounds familiar these days, but it wasn't said these days. The writer was H. G. Wells, and the book is *Secret Places of the Heart* (not even science fiction, strictly speaking) and the year of publication is 1921.

Imagine Wells foreseeing the energy crunch half a century before it happened! Well, don't waste your admiration. He saw the obvious and foresaw the inevitable. What is really amazing, and frustrating, is mankind's habit of *refusing* to see the obvious and inevitable until it is there, 20 and then muttering about unforeseen catastrophes.

The science fiction writer Laurence Manning wrote a story called "The Man Who Awoke" about a man who invented a potion that would place him in suspended animation for three thousand years. He would then awake and see the world of the future. When he carried this through, he found the world of three thousand years hence was energy-poor. They explained the reason to him as a result of what they called the Age of Waste. They said, "But for what should we thank the humans of three thousand years ago? For exhausting the coal supplies of the world? For leaving us no petroleum for our chemical factories? For destroying the for- 30 ests on whole mountain ranges and letting the soil erode into the valleys?"

The story appeared in the March 1933 issue of *Wonder Stories*, and I read it when it appeared and I had just turned thirteen. Science fiction, everyone said, was "escape literature." Reading it was disgraceful, for it meant turning away from the hard realities of life into a never-never fantasy land of the impossible.

Who lived in a never-never fantasy land? I, who began worrying about our oil and coal in 1933 as a result of Manning's story? Or the rest of mankind who, as always, were convinced that tomorrow would be exactly like today and who waited for the day when the long lines at the gas station came 40 before deciding that there might some day be long lines at the gas station.

Yes, science fiction can have its fantasy aspects. I have written stories about galactic empires, about faster-than-light speeds, about intelligent robots which eventually became God, about time travel. I don't consider that any of these have predictive value; they weren't intended for that. I was just trying to write entertaining stories about the might-be, not at all necessarily about the would-be.

But sometimes—

In the July 1939 issue of *Astounding Science Fiction,* there appeared one of my stories. It was called "Trends" and it dealt with the first flight to the Moon (silly escape literature, of course). I got all the details child- 10 ishly and ludicrously wrong, including having it happen ten years later than it really did happen.

However, even at the age of nineteen, I was aware that all those technological advances in the past that had significantly ruffled the cur- rent of human custom had been attacked by important segments of the population who, for one reason or another, found it difficult to accept change. It occurred to me, then, that this would surely be true of the development of space flight as well. My story "Trends," therefore, dealt primarily with opposition to space flight.

It was, as far as I know, the first description of ideological opposition to mankind's advance into space. Until then, all those who had looked 20 forward to the new development had either ignored the reaction of hu- manity, or had assumed it would be favorable. When there did indeed arise ideological opposition, in the late 1960s, I found myself accepting credit as a seer, when I had merely foreseen the inevitable.

Once uranium fission was discovered, a nuclear bomb was an easy extrapolation, and through the World War II years, the science fiction stories dealing with nuclear bombs nestled as thickly as snowflakes in the pages of the science fiction magazines. One of them, "Deadline" by Cleve Cartmill, which appeared in the March 1944 issue of *Astounding Science Fiction,* came so close to the actual facts that both the author and the editor of the maga- 30 zine were interviewed by suspicious intelligence agents. But when the bomb dropped on Hiroshima, the world was astonished.

More remarkable still was a story "Solution Unsatisfactory" by An- son Macdonald (a pseudonym of Robert A. Heinlein), which appeared in the May 1941 issue of *Astounding Science Fiction.* Written and published before Pearl Harbor, Heinlein described a vast gathering of scientists called together to develop a nuclear weapon. The weapon was invented, used to end World War II, and a nuclear stalemate developed thereafter.

It all made sense, you see, in the light of what was already known in 1940, but who else foresaw it but science fiction writers? 40

Today we face the most predictable of all disasters, that of the conse- quences of overpopulation. The population of Earth is now 4,200,000,000 and that population is increasing at the rate of 1.6 percent a year, which means that each day there are 185,000 more mouths to feed than the day before.

In the course of the last thirty years, when population has risen by 1,500,000,000, the food supply has managed to keep up; thanks to the spreading use of farm machinery and irrigation pumps; of fertilizers and pesticides; and of an extraordinary run of good weather.

But now weather is taking a turn for the worse, and the energy shortage is slowing the machinery and raising the price of fertilizers and pesticides. The food supply will not be increasing anymore; it will prob- 10 ably go down—and with the population going up at a rate of 185,000 per day, isn't it the easiest and surest thing in the world to predict great and spreading famines?

Yet whenever I do, I am greeted with amused disbelief. After all, people look around and see no famine today, so why should there be famine tomorrow?

Now let's consider this: If science fiction writers foresee the problems and catastrophes that will come to face mankind, do they also foresee solutions?

Not necessarily! Science fiction writers foresee the inevitable, and 20 although problems and catastophes may be inevitable, solutions are not. Science fiction writers are all too often forced to pull solutions out of thin and implausible air—or leave the matter with no solution and end the story in dramatic disaster.

The best way to defeat a catastrophe is to take action to prevent it long before it happens. To conserve the oil and work for alternate sources of energy in time. To consider the international effects of the nuclear bomb before ever it is invented. To lower the birthrate before the population grows dangerously high.

To do that, one must foresee the catastrophe in time, and science 30 fiction helps one do so.

REVIEWING THE ARTICLE _____

THE MAIN IDEA

1. Asimov says that unlike most people, science-fiction writers
   (a) are surprised by change.
   (b) cannot imagine new developments in science and technology.
   (c) assume that things will stay as they are.
   (d) can extrapolate from the present to the future.

DETAILS

2. According to the article, most people believe that, compared to the present, the future will be **(a)** similar **(b)** different **(c)** unpredictable **(d)** worse.

3. A new curiosity about the future developed around **(a)** 1700 **(b)** 1800 **(c)** 1900 **(d)** 1950.

4. Asimov defines science fiction as the branch of literature that
   (a) persuades governments to fund scientific research.
   (b) explains new developments in science and technology.
   (c) deals with the past, present, and future.
   (d) deals with human reactions to changes in science and technology.

5. In "Trends," a story Asimov wrote in 1939, he describes the first
   (a) war with atomic weapons.
   (b) flight to the Moon.
   (c) time machine.
   (d) science-fiction anthology.

6. Asimov's prediction of "great and spreading famines" is based on
   (a) his imagination only.
   (b) his experiences as a farmer.
   (c) current facts about the food supply and population trends.
   (d) facts about famines in earlier centuries.

ORDER OF EVENTS

7. Of the following events mentioned by the author, choose the letter of the event that happens LAST.
   (a) The rate of change increases.
   (b) Human life continually changes.
   (c) The rate of change becomes visible.
   (d) Change results from technological advances.

CAUSE AND EFFECT

8. Until about 1800, people did not notice change in their lives because
   (a) it occurred quickly.
   (b) it occurred slowly.
   (c) they were taught to ignore it.
   (d) they preferred the "good old days."

9. As a result of reading Laurence Manning's story "The Man Who Awoke," Isaac Asimov

(a) became a science-fiction writer.

(b) decided to become a scientist.

(c) grew concerned about our waste of oil and coal.

(d) realized that a nuclear bomb could be developed.

INFERENCES

10. The author finds the inability of most people to accept change (a) surprising (b) delightful (c) sensible (d) amusing.

11. We can infer that intelligence agents investigated the science-fiction author Cleve Cartmill because they thought he had

(a) built an atom bomb.

(b) edited a science-fiction magazine.

(c) sold uranium to the enemy.

(d) stolen nuclear secrets.

PREDICTING OUTCOMES

12. Some scientists claim that a global greenhouse effect will cause major climatic changes and coastal flooding. Having read Asimov's article, we may predict that most people would react to this information by

(a) living away from the seacoast.

(b) refusing to believe it.

(c) expecting shortages of food.

(d) taking steps to prevent the problem.

BUILDING YOUR VOCABULARY   _____

1. When, in the face of that illusion, a change had clearly taken place, the response was to view it as something that should not have taken place, as something that represented a *degeneration* from the "good old days."

   a. A *degeneration* (page 378, lines 12-15) makes something or someone (a) better (b) worse (c) older (d) quicker.

   b. The BEST clue to the correct answer for part *a* can be found in

   (a) the rest of the sentence containing the word *degeneration*.

   (b) the sentence before the one containing *degeneration*.

(c) the sentence following the one containing *degeneration*.

(d) an earlier use of *degeneration* in the article.

2. Often this means an *extrapolation* of the present, an extrapolation that is so clear and obvious as to forecast something that is inevitable.

Based on available data, an *extrapolation* (page 379, lines 9-10) is a kind of (a) denial (b) detail (c) invention (d) inference.

3. I got all the details childishly and *ludicrously* wrong, including having it happen ten years later than it really did happen.

The word LEAST like *ludicrously* (page 381, lines 9-11) is (a) laughably (b) luckily (c) absurdly (d) ridiculously.

4. It was, as far as I know, the first description of *ideological* opposition to mankind's advance into space.

Ideological (page 381, lines 19-20) opposition would be based on a person's (a) emotions (b) nationality (c) ideas (d) impulses.

5. The weapon was invented, used to end World War II, and a nuclear *stalemate* developed thereafter.

A *stalemate* (page 381, lines 37-38) is a condition resulting from

(a) a thing kept too long.

(b) the opposition of two equally matched forces.

(c) the fallout from a nuclear explosion.

(d) the end of a major war.

STUDYING THE WRITER'S CRAFT

A skilled writer of expository prose uses both ***abstract concepts*** and ***concrete examples***. The concrete examples help readers visualize and understand the abstract concepts.

ABSTRACT CONCEPT: Violent revolutions against bad rulers all too often lead to equally bad rulers.

CONCRETE EXAMPLE: For example, the Russian Revolution against the corrupt reign of Czar Nicholas II led to the dread dictatorship of Joseph Stalin.

By studying the author's use of abstract concepts and concrete examples in this article, you can learn how to use these tools of the expository writer's craft in your own writing.

1. The article begins with a numbered series of three generalizations and continues with additional abstract concepts for several more paragraphs. Where do these abstract concepts end and the concrete examples begin?

2. The author presents five different concrete examples of successful prediction by science-fiction writers. What are they?

3. Near the end of the article, the author briefly repeats the main points of his article. Which paragraph does this? Which sentence in the paragraph contains the abstract concept? Which sentences contain concrete examples?

ACTIVITIES FOR LISTENING, SPEAKING, WRITING

1. Asimov writes, "As time passed, the human way of life continually changed." Do some things in our lives never change? If so, what are they? How do you feel about them? Write a short essay discussing these general questions and giving concrete examples for your answers.

2. With your classmates, make a list of some of the new things that didn't exist when all of you were born. Which of these new things have changed your lives? How?

3. What new things or ways of living—good or bad—would you predict for the next century? How might they affect your life or your children's lives for better or for worse? Be prepared to discuss these questions with your classmates.

GLOSSARY

(Note: Words often have several meanings. In the following glossary, however, each definition gives only the meaning of a word or phrase as it is used in the story or article.)

Adirondacks: group of mountains in northeastern New York State, noted for their beautiful forests and lakes.

aeronomers (er-ON-uh-merz): scientists who study the upper layers of the atmosphere.

airlock: chamber between two doors, used to maintain oxygen content or air pressure.

alkali (AL-kuh-lie): substance having the chemical properties of a base. Strong bases, like strong acids, can eat away certain metals.

amoeba (uh-ME-buh): one-celled animal.

Andromeda Galaxy (an-DRAH-muh-duh): star system in the constellation Andromeda in the northern sky; the only galaxy in the northern hemisphere that can be seen with the naked eye.

Apollo: series of manned American space missions to the Moon (1968-1975).

Arcturus (ark-TUR-us): brightest star in the constellation Boötes (Boh-OH-tez).

Aristotle (AR-is-TOT-ul) (384-322 B.C.): ancient Greek philosopher and scientist.

Asimov or Asenion: Isaac Asimov, American writer (1920-1992) (see page 142). Asenion is a made-up name.

Astounding: influential American science-fiction magazine edited 1937-1971 by John. W. Campbell.

Athena (uh-THEE-nuh): ancient Greek goddess of wisdom.

atmosphere: layer of gases around a planet, such as the air surrounding the Earth.

autistic withdrawal: psychological disorder marked by extreme self-absorption and apparent indifference to external reality.

BBC: British Broadcasting Corporation.

Bethesda: home of the National Institutes of Health—a government agency—in Washington, D.C.

binary star system: two stars whose gravitational attraction makes them revolve around each other.

bioengineering: changing the genes of unborn children to produce desired qualities.

biped: creature with two legs.

blaggard: Irish term for a scoundrel.

Boyne: river in eastern Ireland, where William III defeated James II in battle (1690). The British King William was hated in Ireland for his harsh rule there.

braille (BRAYL): system of writing for the blind in which letters and numbers are represented by raised dots that can be felt.

bridge: that part of a ship or spaceship used by the captain and other commanding officers.

Buenos Aires (BWAY-nus AHR-eez): capital of Argentina.

bureaucrats: government officials who stick to petty rules, causing delay and frustration.

cacti: plural of *cactus*, a spiny desert plant.

Canberra: capital of Australia.

Cape: Cape Kennedy on the east coast of Florida, where United States space missions are launched.

carrier wave: high-frequency electromagnetic wave that carries the signals received as sounds or pictures in a radio, TV set, telephone, etc.

catalyst: substance that changes the speed of a chemical reaction but is itself unchanged permanently by the reaction.

chromosomes (KROH-muh-sohmz): basic cell structures in living organisms containing the genes that control heredity and development.

Commanche (kuh-MAN-chee): southwestern Native American people.

Concorde: British-French supersonic jet passenger airplane with a characteristic downcurved nose.

Congo: country in central Africa, now called Zaire.

creel: wicker basket for carrying caught fish.

crest: headdress, often of feathers.

crossbow: old type of weapon consisting of a powerful bow mounted on a wooden stock and used to fire short, stout arrows called *bolts*.

crux: important unresolved issue or problem.

curator (KYUR-ayt-er): person in charge of a museum, zoo, or other collection of exhibits.

cut your teeth: begin your learning.

damper rods: device for controlling the rate of a nuclear reaction.

decimal system: mathematical system based on the number ten.

Dillinger, John (1902-1934): notorious American bank robber, murderer, and "public enemy number one," shot and killed by the FBI.

doodling: absentminded scribbling or drawing, often done while talking or listening.

double-helix DNA molecule: complex structure in the nucleus of a living cell, composed of two intertwined strands of *deoxyribonucleic acid*. DNA controls heredity and development in living organisms.

eave: edge of a roof overhanging a wall.

18:10: 6:10 P.M. in 24-hour time (also called *military time*), used in scientific work, the Armed Forces, and often in science fiction.

electrodes: metallic materials that control the flow of electrons in an electric circuit.

electron: negatively charged elementary particle outside the nucleus of an atom.

emissary (EM-uh-sehr-ee): person sent on a mission as an agent.

entomology: scientific study of insects.

"Eternal vigilance is the price of freedom (or liberty)": quotation from a speech made in 1790 by John P. Curran, Irish statesman and orator.

extraterrestrial: not of the Earth; from outer space.

Fermi, Enrico (1901-1954): American physicist who won the Nobel Prize for his experiments with neutrons. He helped develop the first atomic bomb.

flabbergasted: astonished.

flint: hard form of quartz that produces sparks when struck by iron or steel.

forge: workplace for heating and hammering metal into desired shapes.

formaldehyde (for-MAL-duh-hide): strong-smelling solution used as a biological preservative.

For will in us . . .: from the poem *Hero and Leander* (1598) by the Elizabethan poet and playwright Christopher Marlowe (1564-1593). (Shakespeare quotes the second line in his play *As You Like It*.)

Fountain of Youth: legendary fountain whose water could restore youth.

fugue (FYOOG): disordered mental state in which a person performs acts, but, upon recovery, cannot recall those actions.

futurists: people who study future possibilities based on present data and trends.

galactic (guh-LAK-tik): relating to a galaxy.

galaxy: one of billions of huge star systems that make up the universe.

gambit: opening maneuver to gain an advantage. (In chess, a gambit involves the purposeful sacrifice of a pawn or other piece.)

gamete (GAM-eet): mature male or female reproductive cell.

Ganymede: fourth moon of the planet Jupiter.

gas giants: four largest planets in the solar system: Jupiter, Saturn, Uranus, and Neptune. Unlike the other five planets, they are composed of gases rather than solids.

genes . . . chromosomes: chromosomes—structures in the nucleus of a cell, composed of DNA; genes—parts of the DNA molecule that control heredity and development in living organisms.

geneticist: scientist who specializes in the study of genetics, or heredity.

ginger beer: sweet ginger-flavored nonalcoholic carbonated drink.

Go east, young man: allusion to famous advice by the 19th-century American newspaper editor Horace Greeley, who said: "Go West, young man, go West."

Graham Bell: Alexander Graham Bell (1847-1922), American inventor of the telephone (1876).

Great Red Spot of Jupiter: gigantic oval red cloud system that rotates counterclockwise over a specific region of the planet.

Great Slave Lake: lake in northwestern Canada.

greenhouse effect: complex process in which increased carbon dioxide in the air acts like the glass of a greenhouse to trap sunlight and warm the surface of the Earth.

Greenwich mean time (GREN-ich): time in Greenwich, England, used as the basis for standard time around the world.

grizzly: large, powerful brown bear that often fights by tightly hugging its adversary.

gully: deep channel carved by running water.

halogen (HAL-uh-jin): family of elements consisting of fluorine, chlorine, bromine, iodine, and radioactive astatine.

Heinlein, Robert A. (1907-1988): popular and influential American science-fiction writer.

Helen of Troy: ancient Greek queen whose abduction by the Trojan prince Paris led to the Trojan War.

hermetic (her-MET-ik): airtight.

high-tech: short form of *high technology*, the application of advanced or complex devices involving computers and sophisticated electronics.

Hiroshima (hir-uh-SHE-muh): Japanese city on which the United States dropped the first atomic bomb in 1945.

Hitler, Adolf (1889-1945): Nazi dictator of Germany (1933-1945).

Homo sapiens: scientific name for human beings (literally, "wise man").

Hudson: river that flows from upstate New York past New York City.

humanoid: resembling a human or some trait of a human.

hydrofluoric acid: poisonous acid used to etch glass.

hydroxyl radicals: charged group of atoms composed of one hydrogen atom and one oxygen atom (OH), part of many organic compounds in the body.

Incan: one of the Incas, Indian people who ruled an empire in ancient Peru until they were conquered by Spain in the 16th century.

Industrial Revolution: during the 19th century, a period of rapid change in the economy of Western nations, particularly England, caused by the introduction of power-driven machinery and other new technologies.

infrared: invisible light rays with wavelengths longer than those of visible light.

infrastructure: underlying structure, procedures, or things that maintain a system or organization. (For example, highways, tunnels, and bridges form part of the infrastructure of a city.)

inner space: world of the extremely small, such as subatomic particles.

ionosphere (eye-ON-uh-sfihr): upper level of the Earth's atmosphere; possesses electrical properties that permit long-distance transmission of radio waves.

IQ: Intelligence Quotient, a measure of intelligence based on a standardized test.

iridium (ih-RID-ee-um): very hard silver-white metal, especially rich in meteorites.

jugular vein: one of two large veins in the neck through which blood returns from the head to the heart.

Jupiter!: fifth and largest planet; also the supreme god of the ancient Romans. (Used as an exclamation of surprise.)

Keokuk: city in southern Iowa on the Mississippi River.

ketone: organic compound, such as acetone, involved in the metabolism of fats in the body.

Kohinoor: very large and famous diamond from India.

laser beam: intense beam of light (LASER = Light Amplification by Stimulated Emission of Radiation).

Liberty Ship: ship built or rebuilt to carry American troops during World War II.

Life on the Mississippi: autobiographical book by Mark Twain (1883).

lock: (See **airlock**.)

Long Island Sound: body of water between Long Island (New York) and Connecticut to the north.

Mad Hatter . . . Alice: characters in Lewis Carroll's novel *Alice in Wonderland* (1865).

mad Twenties: 1920s in the United States, a period of social and economic excess.

Mariner 9: first unmanned American space mission to orbit and photograph Mars (1971).

martinis: type of mixed alcoholic drink.

mastodon: extinct form of elephant related to the mammoth.

maternal genes: source of traits inherited from the mother.

maw: mouth of a hungry beast (often used figuratively).

Meccas: (from *Mecca* in Saudi Arabia, the birthplace of Mohammed and the holy city of Islam), places that strongly attract people.

medulla (mih-DUL-uh): lowest part of the brain, connecting with the spinal cord.

mélange (may-LANZH): odd mixture.

Mercury: planet in the solar system closest to the Sun.

mesquite (mes-KEET): small desert tree or shrub.

meteor (ME-tee-or): relatively small chunk of flying matter in our solar system. (A meteor that has landed is called a *meteorite*.)

midriff: belly.

Milky Way: galaxy in which our solar system is located. Its stars seen from Earth look like a band of light in the night sky.

motley: many-colored costume of a jester, or court fool.

nanogram: one billionth of a gram (*nano* means one-billionth).

NASA: National Aeronautics and Space Administration.

National Bureau of Standards: United States government agency that establishes the standards for units of measure.

neurons (NOOR-onz): specialized cells that are the basic units of nerve tissue.

neutrons: uncharged elementary particles in the nucleus of an atom.

Niagara: (from *Niagara Falls*), huge torrent or flood of anything.

Nixon, Richard: 37th United States President (1969-1974).

norms: ordinary "normal" people without the advantages of genetic engineering.

nova: exploding star that emits a tremendous burst of light.

obsidian glass: very hard glass, usually black, formed by the heat of a volcano.

okapi: short-necked African animal related to the giraffe.

optical telescopes: telescopes that use mirrors and lenses to receive visual images from distant objects.

ozonosphere (oh-ZOH-nuh-sfihr): layer of ozone ten to thirty miles above the Earth, which blocks radiation of ultraviolet light coming from the Sun.

peripheral vision: sight from the sides of the eyes.

photochemistries: chemical changes caused by light.

photo-electric cell: cell whose electric properties are controlled by light (used in automatic doors).

photons: fundamental units of light energy.

pineal (PIN-ee-ul): small cone-shaped gland in the brain. Its function is unknown.

pituitary: small endocrine gland attached to the base of the brain, sometimes called the *master gland* because of the many bodily functions it controls.

Planetary Society: private, nonprofit organization dedicated to planetary exploration and the search for extraterrestrial intelligence (SETI).

planetoid: body resembling a planet.

platinum: gray-white precious metal related to iridium.

Pluto: ninth and smallest planet in the solar system (named after Pluto, the ancient Roman god of the underworld, where the recent dead waited).

positron: positively charged elementary particle identical to the electron except for its charge.

predators: animals that hunt and kill their prey.

prehensile: capable of grasping objects.

presidium: permanent executive committee that acts for a larger body.

protons: positively charged elementary particles in the nucleus of an atom.

protoplasm: living matter of plant and animal cells; broadly, living matter.

Proxmire, Senator William: former senator from Wisconsin, who opposed the use of taxpayers' money by NASA for projects such as SETI.

puckish: whimsical or impish.

putts: light golf strokes sending the ball a short distance to the hole.

quadrant: one of four parts into which an area has been divided.

Queensland: one of the five continental states of Australia, located in the Northeast.

queue (CUE): line of people.

radio telescopes: astronomical telescopes containing a radio-antenna system that receives electromagnetic radiations of radio frequency from outer space.

rehabs: people who have been rehabilitated, or cured.

Rembrandt van Rijn (1606-1669): Dutch painter and etcher.

resurrection: return of the dead to life.

Reykjavik (RAK-yuh-vik): capital of Iceland.

Rip Van Winkle: hero of a short story by Washington Irving (1783-1859). Just before the American Revolution, Rip falls asleep for twenty years and wakes up a stranger in a strange land.

robotic: done by robots, machines that can function in some ways as humans do.

rotation period: time it takes a spinning body to make one complete turn.

saltpeter: potassium nitrate, used to make gunpowder.

satellite telephone network: telephone system using microwave signals relayed by artificial satellites orbiting the Earth.

serendipity (sehr-un-DIP-uh-tee): knack for accidentally discovering good things.

shale: soft rock easily split into thin layers.

smelter: workplace for melting metallic ores to extract and refine the metals.

smog: mixture of *smoke* and *fog*.

solid-state electronics: a branch of electronics that employs transistors (semiconductors) in place of vacuum tubes.

spectrometer (spek-TROM-uh-ter): instrument for measuring the properties of the components of an emission, such as the wavelengths of the rainbow spectrum formed by a beam of sunlight shining through a prism.

spiral nebula: galaxy from which curved arms of matter extend.

stoneboat: wooden sled for transporting heavy stones.

sufferance: permission.

superconductors: substances that conduct electricity without resistance at very low temperatures.

symposia (sim-POH-zee-uh): formal meetings at which several experts deliver short lectures on a topic to an audience.

tactile: related to the sense of touch.

Teasdale, Sara (1884-1933): American poet.

testee: person being tested.

Third Avenue: once a rundown avenue in New York City, now an important thoroughfare.

thorn brakes: land overgrown with thorn bushes.

titanic: huge; gigantic.

tourmaline: type of gemstone.

trophoblast: outer layer of a fertilized ovum (egg) that has begun to develop into an embryo. Through the trophoblast, the ovum is attached to the wall of the uterus and receives nourishment.

2001 . . . Arthur C. Clarke: allusion to the novel and motion picture *2001: A Space Odyssey* (1968) by Clarke. (See page 165.)

tyrannosaurlike: resembling the tyrannosaur, a very large two-footed meat-eating dinosaur.

UFO: *u*nidentified *f*lying *o*bject; a flying saucer.

ultraviolet light: invisible light rays with wavelengths shorter than those of visible light. (Too much ultraviolet light is harmful to living organisms.)

uranium fission: splitting of the nuclei of uranium atoms resulting in the release of vast amounts of energy.

uranium . . . plutonium: radioactive elements. (Uranium is naturally occurring, whereas plutonium is made in the laboratory.)

uterus: womb; female organ that holds and nourishes offspring until birth.

van Gogh, Vincent (van GO) (1853-1890): Dutch painter who suffered from periods of insanity.

vernier: (VER-nee-er): device for making fine adjustments.

vestals: women who tended the sacred fire kept burning on the altar of the ancient Roman goddess of the hearth, Vesta.

Viking: two unmanned American space missions to Mars (1975).

wax: to become; to grow.

Wonder Stories: science-fiction magazine published by Hugo Gernsback in the mid-1930s.

zircon: mineral heated to form cheap imitation diamonds.